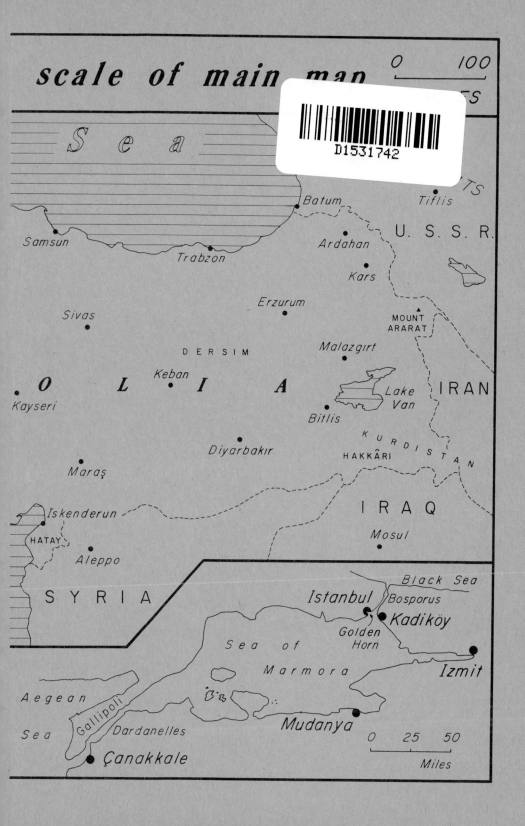

scale of main map

0   100

S e a

Samsun

Trabzon

Batum

Ardahan

Tiflis

U. S. S. R.

Kars

Sivas

Erzurum

▲ MOUNT
ARARAT

D E R S I M

Malazgırt

Keban

O   L   I   A

Kayseri

Lake
Van

IRAN

Bitlis

Diyarbakır

K U R D I S T A N

HAKKÂRI

Maraş

Iskenderun

I R A Q

HATAY

Mosul

Aleppo

S Y R I A

Istanbul *Bosporus*

Black Sea

Kadiköy

Golden
Horn

Sea   of

Marmora

Izmit

Aegean

Mudanya

Sea

Gallipoli

Dardanelles

0   25   50

Çanakkale

Miles

Bridge across the Bosporus

The Foreign Policy of Turkey

Ferenc A. Váli

The Johns Hopkins Press   Baltimore and London

The Johns Hopkins Press, Baltimore, Maryland 21218
The Johns Hopkins Press Ltd., London

Library of Congress Catalog Card Number 79–123197
International Standard Book Number 0–8018–1182–1

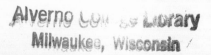

This bridge signifies
Turkey's wish to join Europe.
　　　　　—WILLY BRANDT, in Ankara, May 1969

Contents

CONTENTS

TURKISH SPELLING AND PRONUNCIATION

Turkish spelling and pronunciation is, as a rule, phonetic. Vowels are never diphthongized and their sound values never vary (thus *e* is like the English *e* in "men," *u* like the *u* in "put"). While consonants are generally pronounced as in English some letters have different sound values in Turkish:

c is pronounced as the *j* in "jar"

ç is pronounced as *ch* in "chair"

g has always a hard pronunciation as in "go"

ğ is not pronounced but the preceding vowel is lengthened

ı, the undotted *i*, is an intermediate neutral sound approximately as the *u* in "measure"

j is pronounced as in French (as the *s* in "measure")

ö is pronounced as in German

ş is pronounced as *sh* in "ship"

ü is pronounced as in German

y is always a consonant as in "yard"

The circumflex (∧), as in French, extends the vowel but also softens the preceding consonants (g, k or l).

Preface

THE TRANSFORMATION OF TURKEY FROM A TRADITIONAL ISLAMIC COUNTRY
into a modern nation-state is one of the most impressive developments of
our epoch. From the time when the Ottoman Turks crossed the Dardanelles into Europe and placed the Crescent over St. Sophia in Constantinople, the Ottoman Empire existed as a dividual but still constituent
body of European political life. Although the bulk of Ottoman territorial
possessions were outside geographical Europe, the characterization of
this long-time invalid as the "Sick Man of Europe" implicitly recognized
its role on that continent.

In discussing the reforms of Peter the Great of Russia, Jacob Burckhardt wrote in the 1880's that "the Russian element at least *can* flow into
European civilization because it has no Koran."[1] Remarkable as it seems,
contemporary Turkey seeks to "flow into European civilization" without, however, altogether abandoning the Koran. Her endeavor is not only
to adopt Western technology but also the civilization of the West, while
retaining her own ethno-cultural identity. Turkey, for five centuries a
Hegelian antithesis to the European cultural and political thesis, may be
about to achieve a unique synthesis. Her foreign and domestic policies are
principally dedicated to the attainment of this ambitious goal.

In terms of the size of her population and the volume of her economy,
Turkey is not one of the great powers, though she is the strongest among
the countries of the Middle East. But, as history substantiates, her geopolitical location and the character of her people have assigned her a
potentially higher status than can be expressed in mere statistical figures.
Clausewitz' famous alternative always has conveyed an ominous meaning for Turkey. He taught that when faced with a single enemy one should
march against his capital; when faced with more than one, one should
attack their lines of communication. Until 1922, the location of Turkey's
capital and the historic line of communication between the Black Sea and
the Mediterranean coincided. Even though her capital has been removed
to Ankara, the Turkish straits, Russia's doorway to the Mediterranean
and beyond, remain of global political and strategic significance.

The Turkish state holds the key not only to the Dardanelles but lies

---

[1] Jacob Burckhardt, *On History and Historians* (New York, 1958), p. 213.

along the roads from the Balkans to the Middle East and from the Caucasus to the Persian Gulf. She is regarded as the southeastern redoubt of NATO and as the linchpin between the Atlantic alliance and CENTO. She is a member of most of the European organizations and is an associate member of the European Economic Community. Her political involvement and exposed position confer on her an importance hardly matched by any other medium power.

The objectives, approach, and ways of thinking of Turkey's leaders are accordingly factors which transcend the confines of her own security and condition. Britain paid heavily for her shortsightedness in having forfeited Turkish friendship for two warships at the inception of World War I. No wonder Churchill reminisced of this event: "I can recall no great sphere of policy about which the British Government was less completely informed than the Turkish."[2]

The United States and its European allies have, to a considerable measure, placed their stakes on Turkey. Accordingly, the correct evaluation of that country's policies is of crucial importance. Furthermore, Turkey's aspirations and accomplishments may serve as an example, for she is in many respects a human laboratory: an Islamic nation adopting European civilization, the "bridge" between East and West, a society engaged in a massive development process under democracy. The foreign policy of Republican Turkey has alternated between neutrality and alignment, depending on circumstances. The flexibility which characterized the Atatürk era was, despite Ankara's Atlantic commitments, largely regained by Turkish diplomacy in the 1960's; it is another aspect of foreign policy worthy of scrutiny.

The present study presents this multifaceted picture of Turkey's contemporary international relations. Although she is an "open" country, her real motivations and purpose are not easily discerned. Her image is blurred by visions of the past and illusions of the present. Neither oversimplification of her problems nor the inscrutability of her intentions is acceptable. Her condition and aspirations must be appreciated in the manner in which they appear to her own leaders and not as they may appear to outside observers.

I had the advantage of becoming personally acquainted with the Turkish scenery during World War II while on a confidential wartime diplo-

---

[2] Winston S. Churchill, *The Aftermath* (New York, 1929), p. 380.

matic mission there from 1943 to 1946. I revisited that country in 1965 to study its foreign policy; in 1968 I spent six months in Turkey gathering material for the purposes of this work. During this latter sojourn, I greatly profited from interviews with officials of the Turkish Ministry for Foreign Affairs, leaders of political parties, faculty members of universities, journalists, and members of diplomatic and consular missions in Ankara, Istanbul, and Izmir. Outside Turkey I was able to conduct similar interviews with officials of the United States Department of State, the staff of the Turkish Embassy in Washington, officials of the British Foreign Office, those of the North Atlantic Treaty Organization and of the European Economic Community in Brussels.

The various aspects of Turkish foreign policy, often interrelated, make a comprehensive presentation of the topic a matter of individual selection and render certain duplication unavoidable. As in earlier writings on contemporary political situations, I felt compelled to place my analysis into the proper historical setting. Thus, the first chapter seeks to provide this historic background for the detailed examinations which follow. The next seven chapters discuss the geopolitical and ideological foundations of Turkish foreign policy, the foreign policy attitudes of political parties, Turkey's role in NATO and her relations with the United States and other allies, the relations of that country with Russia and members of the Soviet bloc, Turkish rapport with Greece and the Cyprus problem, and her involvement in the Middle East, as well as an evaluation of Turkey's development policy. The last chapter adds some concluding observations.

An attempt has been made to introduce some consistency in the use of Turkish geographical and other terms. When referring to the period prior to the adoption of the Latin alphabet, I will use terms in the form known to the West. Thus, I shall write *Constantinople* instead of *Istanbul* in reference to events which preceded the Kemalist reform period; however, I shall continue to speak of the Dardanelles and Bosporus because the Turkish version of these names is hardly known outside Turkey. In some cases the contemporary Turkish version or the internationally current version will be indicated in parenthesis. Arabic terms will generally be spelled in the currently used English version except when they are part of the Turkish vocabulary, in which case their present Turkish form will be used.

It would not be permissible to list here the names of all those foreign service officers, American, Turkish, and others, who took the trouble of providing me with information for the purposes of this study. Nor does it seem possible to name those Turkish and Cypriote political leaders who allowed themselves to be interviewed by me. I am grateful to all of them for having given so liberally their valuable time.

For advice and assistance I should like to express thanks to Professors Mahmut R. Belik, Ismet Giritli, Hifzi Timur, Tarik Zafer Tunaya, and Vakur Versan of the University of Istanbul; to Professors Fahir H. Armaoğlu, Suat Bilge, Ahmet Şükrü Esmer, Mehmet Gönlübol, and Şerif Mardin of the University of Ankara; and to Professor Orhan Nasuhioğlu of the Turkish Naval College, as well as to Mr. Orhan Köprülü. I also feel deeply indebted to Professor Bernard Lewis of the University of London. Professors Edward S. Mason and Hollis B. Chenery of Harvard University and Mr. Edwin J. Cohn of the Administration for International Development have been extremely helpful in briefing me on Turkey's development problems.

Without the generous travel grants received from various sources in the course of several years this book could not have been written. Thus I am thankful for the grant given to me by the Asian and African Studies Program of the University of Massachusetts and of its three sister institutions, for the fellowship awarded to me by the North Atlantic Treaty Organization, and for another fellowship granted by the American Research Institute in Turkey.

I feel deeply indebted to Professor Terence Burke for having prepared the map of Turkey which appears as endpapers. I should like to thank Mrs. Katie S. Gilmor and Mr. John F. Kikoski for their research and editorial assistance. I am also grateful to Mrs. Doris Holden who assiduously retyped the manuscript in its final form.

FERENC A. VÁLI

Amherst, Massachusetts

Bridge
across
the
Bosporus

I

From Empire to Nation-State

Allah said to the Prophet: "I have a host which I have called 'Turk' and settled in the East; if any people shall arouse my wrath, I shall give them into the power of this host."—KORANIC APOCRYPHA (Kashgari)

For centuries the Turks have been moving in the same direction. Always from the east to west. There are many countries but one civilization. National progress means participation in this civilization.—ATATÜRK

ACCORDING TO THE TURKISH TRA-dition, the founders of the Ottoman Empire were, originally, nomad tribesmen who settled around Yenişehir in western Asia Minor in the first half of the thirteenth century. This area along the Byzantine border-land was given to them in fief by Ala-ed-Din, the Seljuk sultan of Konya (the ancient Iconium), and in return they were to protect the border against the infidels.

THE TURKS

Central Asian Turks began moving into the domains of the Abbasid caliphs of Baghdad in the tenth century; converted to Islam, they were assigned to extend the *Daru'l-Islam* (the World of the Faithful) and also to fight other enemies of the caliphate. As occurred with the Germanic mercenaries of Rome, however, the Turkish immigrants soon established independent principalities. Seljuk founded the dynasty that bears his name, and in 1071 his grandson, Alp Arslan, defeated the Byzantine Emperor Romanos IV at the famous battle of Manzikert (in Turkish: Malaz-gırt). Thereafter, most of Asia Minor[1] passed under the control of the Seljukides. The Hellenized or partly Hellenized inhabitants of that part of

---

[1] The Greeks called Asia Minor Anatolia. It is now *Anadolu* in Turkish.

the East Roman (Byzantine) Empire became, to a large extent, converted to Islam and were assimilated by the conquerors.[2] Due to the Crusades, the "frontier" between Christendom and Islam oscillated during the next 100 years and eventually froze.

The particular group of "warriors of the faith" (*Ghazi*-s) who settled in the Islamic–Byzantine borderland was small—we are told that they numbered only 400 "tents." This *Ghazi* principality, unlike similar border states, instilled a new ultimately global dynamism into Islam—a dynamism injected this time by a non-Arab people.[3] It became the nucleus of a powerful new state which developed in the course of the next 100 years into a "world" empire.

It is hardly doubtful that the character of this people and the qualities of their leaders were responsible for a "miracle" second only to the Roman Empire's growth from a Tiberian hamlet. The Osmanli or Ottoman Turks were so called after their first outstanding leader, Osman or Othman (1259–1326), the founder of a dynasty which continued to reign for the next 600 years. The military and political organization of this fledgling people was geared to permanent warfare, to conquest, and to domination over alien nations.[4] This system proved to be most durable and served to distinguish the Ottoman Empire from other, more short-lived oriental empires, and from those of Alexander or Napoleon.

During its time of expansion and greatness, the source of Ottoman power was the person of the sultan (who had many titles, among them that of a Padishah). He subsequently assumed the rank of a caliph, the successor of the Prophet and "shadow of God on earth." He was surrounded and assisted by a "slave family" of courtiers, administrators, and soldiers (the famous Janissary corps). The sultan's household was re-

[2] Byzantine misrule, the dynamism of the Islamic advance, and the belief that God is on the side of the victors contributed to the expansion of the Muslim religion and the simultaneous "Turkification" of the Anatolian population.

[3] For the traditional view concerning the foundation of the Ottoman state see Freiherr Joseph von Hammer-Purgstall, *Geschichte des Ottomanischen Reiches* (Pest, 1827), vol. I; Ilhami Masar, *Das wahre Gesicht der Türkei* (Istanbul, 1967), pp. 33–35. For a revised appraisal see Paul Wittek, *The Rise of the Ottoman Empire* (London, 1958), *passim*. See also M. Fuad Köprülü, *Les Origines de l'Empire Ottoman* (Paris, 1935).

[4] Arnold J. Toynbee considers the Ottoman system the result of an adaptation of the nomad Steppe people to more sedentary conditions when they became "shepherds of men" and used slaves (as they formerly had used dogs) to keep order among and acquire more "human cattle." *A Study of History,* abridgment of vols. I–VI (New York, 1956), pp. 173–74.

cruited by force from Christian families[5] whose sons were trained and educated in strict discipline to become fervent Muslims. According to their talent, they could become palace attendants or members of the bureaucracy or of the armed forces; the most successful ones among them rose to become Grand Vezirs, provincial governors, or great military leaders. All they possessed belonged to their master; in fact, they depended entirely on the whim of the sovereign whom they had to serve without murmur. Other contingents of the Ottoman armies consisted of feudal fief-holders serving as cavalrymen (*sipahis*); but the "slave system" essentially prevented the growth of a hereditary nobility or aristocracy. Offices of religious dignitaries (who also were the judges) were reserved, by tradition, to free Muslims.

Settled at the marches of the Islamic world, the state of Osman expanded, first toward the west but later toward the east. Orhan, the son of Osman, captured Bursa (Brussa) and made it the first Osmanli capital. Before his death, in or around 1355, the Turks crossed the Dardanelles and entered the European parts of the decaying Byzantine state. Soon, under the reign of Murad (1359–89), they annexed the major portion of the Balkan peninsula, leaving behind them the city and surroundings of Constantinople, which by then had become encircled by Ottoman territory. Simultaneously, the Ottoman sultanate expanded across Asia Minor, gradually incorporating all Seljuk Turk principalities in that area. The setback which the Osmanlis suffered after the Mongolian invasion of Timur Lenk (Tamerlane) in 1401 halted their advance only temporarily. After the body's truncation, the head of the long-moribund East Roman Empire (the City of Constantinople, or Byzantium) was finally conquered by Sultan Mehmet II in 1453. The city, also known as "the Second Rome," became the seat of his empire.

The stimulus of a political and ideological frontier sparked the expansion of the Osmanli Turks who, within 100 years, had created a colossal military and political power that territorially replaced the Roman Empire of the East. Indeed, the geographical configuration of the Ottoman state, as well as much of its ethnic composition, recalled its territorial predecessor. It covered the area in Europe, in Asia, and in Africa

---

[5] The collection of a levy of boys was known as *devşirme;* it was not completely discontinued until the eighteenth century. See Léon Lamouche, *Histoire de la Turquie depuis les origines jusqu'à nos jours* (Paris, 1934), pp. 24–25; Basilike D. Papoulia, *Ursprung und Wesen der "Knabenlese" im Osmanischen Reich* (Munich, 1963).

that the Byzantine Empire covered in its heyday. But though the political purpose and missionary goal of Byzantium were the service of the Orthodox Christian faith, the universal state of the Ottomans was ostensibly dedicated to the cause of Islam. The Byzantines had superimposed a Graeco-Roman ethos on their numerous non-Hellenic subjects. Similarly, the Osmanlis were themselves impregnated by Arab-Muslim ideology while supplementing their system of government with many institutions adopted from their Byzantine predecessors. Much of the original Turkish substance of their culture was lost. While the Ottoman Empire flourished, a considerable proportion, perhaps more than one-half of its population, consisted of non-Muslim, Christian elements, and among the Muslims the Turks could hardly hold a majority. Thus, the empire was multinational, religiously almost evenly divided, and more Arab-Islamic than Turkish. In its usage as an official language, the original Turkish came under the influence of the more refined Arab and Persian languages. Only foreigners called the empire "Turkish"; inside the Muslim world, it was known as *Memalik-i Osmaniye* or, more recently, *Osmanlı Imperatorluğu* (Ottoman Empire). It was even considered insulting when a subject of the sultan was called "Turk,"[6] for this word connoted a rather boorish Anatolian peasant. When the Romans conquered much of their known world, they exported the name of Rome to all the corners of their empire, but in building their realm, the Turks had, to a great extent, lost their identity within this Islamic Empire. It took many centuries before they were able to recover it.

THE OTTOMAN PAST

The Ottoman Empire was a theocratic state. The sultan, even before he assumed the title of caliph,[7] combined religious and political authority. In fact, the original Islamic concept of state and society did not distinguish between religious and secular, or spiritual and temporal, duties. The sultan was high priest, hereditary ruler, and military leader. His authority was limited only by the precepts and traditional interpretation of the

[6] See Harry Luke, *The Old Turkey and the New* (London, 1955), pp. 9, 195.
[7] Sultan Selim I became guardian of the Holy Cities of Mecca and Medina. The Caliph, "successor" of the Prophet Mohammed, was the chief *Imam* (priestly leader of the people) and "Commander of the Faithful"—that is, defender of Islam, so recognized only by the Sunni Muslims.

4

Koran. He was master of life and death not only over his "slave house-hold" but also over all of his subjects.

Islam was more than a religion: it was a way of life, a philosophy, and a political and legal system. But its tenets could not, by definition, be made applicable to non-Muslims, except for the Koranic precept that sub-mitting "peoples of the Book" (the Bible) should be spared and protected by their Muslim rulers. Thus, the Ottoman state failed to have—nor was it interested in having—legislative tools to regulate the internal life of non-Muslims. Accordingly, the non-Islamic religious communities of the Otto-man Empire were allowed to enjoy self-government in matters of culture, religion, and private legal relations between their members. This was the *millet*[8] system. The leader of a *millet*,[9] responsible to the sultan for the management of the affairs under his direction, was the highest ecclesi-astical office-holder of the respective community. Chief among such lead-ers was the head of the *Millet of Rum*,[10] the Greek Oecumenical Patriarch of Constantinople. All Orthodox Christians were deemed to belong to this group unless special *millet* status had been conferred on them.[11] De-spite this fragmentation, the Ottoman administration was highly central-ized, and the *millet* system was not a source of weakness for centuries. It was not until the late eighteenth and early nineteenth centuries that re-ligious and national minorities began to rebel against Ottoman authority.

Theocratic governments are, by their very nature, rigid; they are able to transform themselves in response to external stimuli only with great difficulty and frequently only by sacrificing theocracy itself. As we shall see, the Ottoman state was beset by major problems in its attempt to adapt to the requirements of modern, national, technological, and demo-cratic statehood. But as long as Ottoman statecraft and military technol-

---

[8] *Millet* is an Arabic-Turkish word meaning "people" but, due to the Islamic association, a people determined by its religious affiliation and not by ethnic or linguistic criteria.

[9] The head of the *millet* was known as *Millet Başı* in Turkish and *Ethnarchos* in Greek.

[10] *Rum* is derived from "Romaios"—that is, Roman, as the Byzantines officially called themselves.

[11] In the course of time, such status was given to the members of the Serbian Orthodox Church, the Vlach (Rumanian) Church, and finally to the adherents of the Bulgarian Exarchat. Other Christian *millets* were formed by the Gregorian Armenians, and also by various Catholic communities within the Empire. As late as 1850, a Protestant *millet* was also recognized mostly for Armenians who joined Protestantism. Jews, under the Grand Rabbi of Turkey, were also considered a separate *millet*.

ogy were equal to the forces of Christian Europe, the "monolithic" structure and dogmatic messianism, which would prove to be sources of weakness in the period of decline, secured for the empire a status of unparalleled excellence. Another source of strength of the Ottoman state was the continued rule of sultans of the House of Osman, a unique phenomenon which precluded the dynastic succession crises that prevailed among European ruling families.

Internationally, the Ottoman Empire expanded and exerted pressure in every direction until the end of the sixteenth century. Under Sultan Selim (1512–20) Syria and Egypt were conquered and the Holy Cities of Mecca and Medina were placed under the protection of the Osmanli ruler. His successor, Suleyman the Magnificent, defeated the Hungarians at the battle of Mohács (1526), annexed the central part of Hungary, and threatened Vienna. During his reign, Baghdad was captured and the Ottomans became a naval power in the Mediterranean, controlling the North African shore to the border of Morocco. Under Suleyman the empire reached its peak of power, although it was still advancing in certain areas: in 1571 Cyprus and in 1664 Crete were taken. In 1683 the Sultan's army besieged Vienna; a few years earlier, Podolia and parts of the Ukraine were seized from Poland. But the failure before Vienna marked the beginning of a constant military and territorial retreat. In the Treaty of Karlowitz,[12] the Ottomans surrendered their Hungarian possessions (including Transylvania) and the newly conquered Polish lands; Morea was awarded to the Republic of Venice.

The Ottoman penetration into central Europe and into the Mediterranean (where even Spain felt its menace) caused fear and dismay in all lands adjacent to these areas. France used the Ottoman presence to balance the overwhelming power of the Hapsburgs in Germany, the Netherlands, and Spain. From the time of Francis I, the French monarchs sought support or even alliance in Constantinople in order to outflank their Hapsburg adversaries. In return, Viennese diplomacy tried to foment wars between the Ottoman Empire and Persia at the eastern flank of the sultan's domains.

In view of the special position that France held at the Sublime Porte (as the Ottoman government was officially known), she was one of the

---

[12] It was the first real peace treaty concluded by the Sublime Porte; up to that time, the *Jihad* (Holy War against the infidels) was interrupted only by limited armistices.

first powers whose citizens were given the rights known as capitulations.[13] The capitulatory system originally stemmed from an Islamic unwillingness and incapability of handling the status and legal affairs of non-Muslims. Not unlike the *millets*, foreign residents (mostly businessmen and tradesmen) were permitted, under agreements concluded with Christian states, to manage their own communal and private affairs. Accordingly, foreign consuls were in charge of the legal and financial matters of their nationals, including criminal and civil jurisdiction. These privileges, originally less a favor than simply the result of the Ottoman system, were subsequently felt to be a derogation of the Ottoman state's sovereignty.

The internal decay of the Ottoman Empire began much earlier than its external decline. Yet, it is extremely difficult to demonstrate a reciprocal relationship between domestic defects and the loss of power in the foreign field.[14] It is perhaps correct to say that the reverse in military fortune and power potential was due equally to two ascendant factors: first, the weakening of the internal Ottoman power; and second, the shifting of power relations between the European states and the Ottoman Empire to the obvious disadvantage of the latter.

DECLINE, REFORM, AND REVOLUTION

It is virtually impossible to determine the exact date of the beginning of the decline of Ottoman power.[15] Even after the disastrous wars against the western coalition of the Holy Roman Empire (Austria) and Venice,

[13] The name is derived from the low Latin word *capitulum*, which meant "chapter." The treaties providing for these extra-territorial rights were divided into chapters and were first drafted in Latin. The Republic of Venice, having had important trading contacts with Byzantium, was the first to conclude such a treaty in 1521. The capitulation treaty with France was signed in 1535; see J. C. Hurewitz, *Diplomacy in the Near and Middle East* (Princeton, 1956), vol. I, pp. 1–5. For the Capitulations see Nasim Sousa, *The Capitulatory Regime of Turkey: Its History, Origin, and Nature* (Baltimore, 1933).

[14] Even after the defeats suffered at the hands of the Holy Roman Empire armies, contemporary Ottoman leaders, though criticizing certain abuses, did not relate the military disasters to domestic defects. See the writings of (Sari) Mehmed Pasha, *Ottoman Statecraft: The Book of Counsel for Vezirs and Governors*, translated by Walter Livingston Wright, Jr. (Princeton, 1935).

[15] Toynbee considered the Russian-Turkish Treaty of Kuchuk-Kaynarja (1774) as the beginning of Ottoman decline. This treaty gave the Tsar the right of protection over Orthodox Christians and ceded the northern littoral of the Black Sea (including the Crimea) to Russia; *A Study of History*, p. 173. On the other hand, Lamouche sets the date for the year 1812, when the Treaty of Bucarest provided for the cession of Bessarabia to Russia and recognized the autonomy of Serbia; *Histoire de la Turquie*, pp. 249–50.

7

which ended with the Treaties of Karlowitz (1699) and Passarowitz (1718), respectively, the Ottoman Empire remained a formidable power. For example, by the Treaty of Belgrade (1739), which concluded the war of 1737–39, the Ottomans regained the territories lost at Passarowitz, including Belgrade; the war of 1788–91 with Austria and Russia ended in a draw.

The emergence of Russia as a great power brought about a major shift in the balance of power, to the detriment of the Ottoman Empire. Peter the Great already had sought to eliminate Ottoman control from the northern shores of the Black Sea.[16] When this plan was successfully completed under his successors, Russia appeared as a naval power in the Black Sea (which previously had been an internal Ottoman lake), the sultan had to abandon his vassal, the Tartar Khan of Crimea, and Russian armies invaded Moldavia and Wallachia, the so-called Danubian principalities. Empress Catherine the Great conceived the first of a number of plans for the partition of the Ottoman Empire among Russia, Austria, and Venice; her son, Constantine, was to take over a restored Byzantine state with Constantinople as its capital, thereby setting an example for subsequent Greek ambitions known as the "Megali Idea" (the grand idea or scheme).[17]

But Austria was not proceeding in accordance with Russian expectations. The Tsars had advanced themselves as protectors of all the Slavic peoples, especially those professing the Eastern Orthodox faith. By the end of the eighteenth century, it was realized that Russian influence over the Balkan peninsula would contravene the vital interests of the Hapsburg Empire. Although France had been backing the Sublime Porte since the early sixteenth century, Britain did not appear on the stage until this point. In order to prevent the take-over of the Bosporus and Dardanelles (the Turkish straits) by Russia and the entry of Russian naval forces into the Mediterranean, Britain joined in the defense of the tottering Ottoman power.

Amid increasing power rivalries and threats to its independent existence, the Sublime Porte soon recognized that its survival depended on the skillful employment of a balancing diplomacy, built upon a central strategy of inhibiting the most dangerous and threatening power by

---

[16] See B. H. Summer, *Peter the Great and the Ottoman Empire* (Oxford, 1949).
[17] See Roderic H. Davison, *Turkey* (Englewood Cliffs, N.J., 1968), pp. 65–66.

invoking the assistance of the others. Generally, but not exclusively, the empire of the tsar was considered the most immediate and formidable danger. The sultan's advisers also realized that their greatest asset was the strategically invaluable possession of the straits (including the City of Constantinople); whereas other territories of the empire were divisible among the contending powers, the straits area was not.

Whereas Austria, after the end of the eighteenth century, regarded the integrity of the Ottoman Empire as an indispensable element of European equilibrium and of essential interest to her security, France and Britain occasionally shifted their policy against the Porte. During the French revolutionary and Napoleonic wars, Bonaparte's Egyptian campaign was considered a hostile act against the integrity of the Ottomans. Later, when Napoleon fought Austria and Russia, he sought an Ottoman alliance against the latter (1805–7). Russia and Britain had previously supported the Sublime Porte against the French; now they both turned against the sultan. The sudden volte-face of Tilsit (similar to the reversal of policies under the Stalin-Hitler pact in 1939) exposed the Ottoman Empire to a danger of partition. In late 1807 and early 1808, secret negotiations took place between Napoleon and Tsar Alexander I about the disposal of the Ottoman state; only their inability to reach an accord concerning the straits and Constantinople prevented an agreement and, eventually, persuaded the French emperor to turn against Russia.[18]

The more enlightened Ottoman leaders wished to parry such external and internal dangers. Although none of the protective measures they took were fully successful, they did prolong the life of the empire until the end of World War I.

The antiquated Ottoman system proved to be the greatest hurdle for any attempt to rejuvenate and invigorate the state. Most of the sultans had ceased to be leaders and lived in the seclusion of the palace, exposed to intrigues and often threatened by their own courtiers and bodyguards. The *millet* system ceased to function reliably because of the nationalist or separatist ambitions of many of the national and religious groups. The capitulations created extraterritorial foreign colonies which monopolized and exploited economic resources.

The power potential of an empire may, in most cases, be equated

18 Vernon J. Puryear, *Napoleon and the Dardanelles* (Berkeley, 1951), *passim*.

with its military power. The erstwhile organizational and technological superiority of Ottoman armies over those of the West had been reversed; now they were distressingly inferior. The suppression of the parasitic Janissary class, after several revolutionary changes involving bloody massacres and the deaths of two sultans, enabled Mahmud II to set up armed forces on the modern pattern in the 1820's.[19] During the *Tanzimat* period, which lasted for about 40 years from 1839,[20] the Ottomans wished to convince the world that the empire had embarked on the road to Westernization and should be accepted as an equal in the European family of nations. Equality under the law for all Ottoman subjects irrespective of creed and nationality, economic modernization (Western institutions of customs, taxation, banks, and public works), modern methods of transportation and communications (railroads, telegraph), and a reformed administrative system (with consultative popular bodies) were the main features of this reorganization. An attempt was even made to provide a new ideological foundation for the empire based on "Ottomanism"—a dynastic national sentiment with a subdued Islamic content that was to embrace the Christian subjects of the sultan.[21] Ottomanism, however, had little appeal to the Christians, for separatist movements continued to threaten the integrity of the state.

Among the Christian nations living under Ottoman rule, the Serbs revolted first (1817) and were followed by the Greeks (1821). The Rumanians in the Danubian principalities had always enjoyed limited self-government, yet they wished to be united and attain independence. Montenegro also constituted herself as a secular state. All of these nations were able to gain recognition as sovereign states during the nineteenth century. Bulgaria, in the center of the Balkan peninsula, also obtained statehood in 1878. Hellenic national feeling spread over the Greek-inhabited islands of the Aegean and eastern Mediterranean, especially Crete. But large areas of Asia Minor (Anatolia) were also populated by

[19] Other reforms included educational measures (attempts to teach French and to secularize teaching), European-type ministries, the fez and frock coat instead of turban and oriental robes.

[20] *Tanzimat*—reorganization—began with the Imperial Edict of Gülhane (1839) and was followed in 1856 by the *Hatt-i Humayun* (illustrious rescript). The latter was to implement the principles announced in 1839 and for the first time contained no reference to the Koran.

[21] For Ottomanism (*Osmanlılık*, in Turkish) see Davison, *Turkey*, pp. 80–81.

Greeks, as well as Turks. Armenians, mainly settled in eastern Anatolia but also scattered over many parts of Asian Turkey and Constantinople, likewise started a long series of clandestine and later overt bids for autonomy or independence.

Secessionist endeavors were not restricted to Christians. Mehmet Ali, Pasha of Egypt, who had modernized his army before the Turks modernized theirs, established a *de facto* independent state, conquered Syria, and even marched into Anatolia (1832). He was supported by the French, whereas the sultan had to rely on the assistance of Britain and Russia.[22] Russian troops landed on the Asian shore of the Bosporus, north of Constantinople, to protect the capital. By the Treaty of Hunkâr-Iskelesi (1833), the sultan signed a defense alliance with the tsar and promised to consult the Russian government on matters of "tranquillity and safety" and to close the Dardanelles to foreign warships.[23] British, French, and Austrian pressures forced the Russians to withdraw, but the precedent of garrisoning the straits attracted the imagination of later Russian and Soviet chancelleries.

Twenty years later, Tsar Nicholas I attempted to solve the "Eastern Question" by placing the Sick Man of Europe under his control. This time both France and Britain, with the diplomatic support of Austria, stepped in to save the Ottoman Empire. Russia suffered defeat in the resulting Crimean campaign, and by the Treaty of Paris (1856), the territorial integrity of the empire was once more secured. In addition, Russia had to demilitarize her Black Sea shores. The treaty also formally admitted the Ottoman Empire into the European community, and her great-power status was thus recognized.[24]

In 1877–78, Russia took her revenge: her troops penetrated deep into the Balkans and reached the outskirts of Constantinople. The Treaty of San Stefano, setting up a Great Bulgaria, did not win Britain's approval; she had already sent her fleet to the defense of the Ottoman capital. The Congress of Berlin (1878), convened under Chancellor Bismarck of Germany, reduced the frontiers of the new Bulgarian state, placed Bosnia-Herzegovina under the occupation and administration of Austria-

---

22 Russia, in 1828–29, intervened in favor of the revolting Greeks and, by the Peace Treaty of Adrianople (Edirne), obtained territorial concessions in Asia.

23 For text see Hurewitz, *Diplomacy*, vol. I, pp. 105–6.

24 For the text of the Paris Peace Treaty, see *ibid.*, pp. 153–56.

Hungary, and confirmed the cession of Batum, Kars, and Ardahan along the Asian border of Turkey to Russia.[25] In return for British protection, the sultan had previously assigned the island of Cyprus "to be occupied and administered by England." Should Russia restore to Turkey Kars and other conquests of this war, it was agreed that "Cyprus will be evacuated by England."[26]

The first Ottoman constitution was enacted under the reformist grand vezir, Midhat Pasha, prior to the war of 1877–78. It was partly inspired by the liberal Belgian constitution and partly by the conservative Prussian one which reserved ultimate authority for the monarch. Perhaps St. Petersburg's fear that the new constitution would strengthen and unify the empire prompted the outbreak of the war. After its frustrating end, Sultan Abdulhamid dissolved the parliament, which was not convoked again until 1908.

It was more or less realized by 1878 that Ottomanism was a failure; the Christians of the empire were unreliable and could never be assimilated. There was also widespread distrust of the Western powers, which at that time were extending their colonial empires in Africa and Asia, including some Ottoman territories. Thus, France annexed Tunisia as her protectorate in 1881, and the British occupied Egypt in 1882. Abdulhamid sought to canvass popular support from among the conservative Muslim population of his empire, which included Arabs, Kurds, and Albanians. He again placed emphasis on his office as caliph and favored Pan-Islamic movements. He found foreign support from Germany, whose emperor posed as the friend of the world's 300 million Muslims.

The sultan's personal rule, however, degenerated into an oriental despotism that raised European doubts about the viability of the Ottoman Empire. Fortunately for Turkey, Russia was involved in her Far Eastern expansion, and Britain and France refrained from outright hostile actions during most of Abdulhamid's reign. Austria–Hungary, on her part, wished to keep the Balkans quiet, while Germany extended diplomatic support to the Sick Man of the Bosporus.

Despotism and cultural stagnation created internal unrest, and Tur-

[25] For the Treaty of Berlin of July 13, 1878, see *ibid.*, pp. 189–91.
[26] The Cyprus Conventions between Great Britain and the Ottoman Empire was concluded on June 4, 1878; *ibid.*, pp. 187–89. Also Martens, *Nouveau Recueil Général de Traités,* VI Série, 3, pp. 272–75.

key became a hotbed of plots and conspiracies. The most powerful group among Abdulhamid's Turkish opponents was the Young Turks (Committee of Union and Progress) who had many followers among officers of the army. Although some groups continued to profess Ottomanism, the Young Turks became convinced that rejuvenation had to be based on Turkish nationalism instead of Islamism, or on the unifying force of the house of Osman. Some of the young Turks cherished Pan-Turkism or Turanism, an aspiration to unify all Turkic peoples that was directed against Russia.

In July 1908, a revolution broke out in Macedonia, where Ottoman forces were stationed. Spreading like a forest fire, the revolutionary fervor overtook Muslims and Christians alike whose energies were directed toward the restoration of the constitution of 1876. The sultan submitted to the demand and a new parliament was convoked. Religious and reactionary groups attempted, however, to overthrow the constitutional government. This sparked a new revolutionary wave which swept the sultan away in 1909; he was exiled and replaced by his brother, Mehmet V.

The Young Turk government first ruled constitutionally, but popular elections did not favor the Turkish element of the empire. Not only were Turks outnumbered but non-Turkish Muslims, Arabs, Kurds, and Albanians began to develop their respective national sentiments. Renewed modernization efforts were thwarted by the rapid succession of events. In 1911 war with Italy over Tripolitania resulted in the loss of that province. In 1912 the four Balkan powers—Bulgaria, Serbia, Greece, and Montenegro—invaded the Ottoman provinces of the Balkans. European Turkey became restricted to the area west of Constantinople. Russia supported her Orthodox brethren while France and Britain remained interested spectators. Only Germany and Austria-Hungary initiated diplomatic activity to save as much of the Ottoman Empire as possible.

After the Treaty of London (May 30, 1913), all that was left of Turkey in Europe was the area east of the Enos-Midya Line. When the Second Balkan War broke out, because the victorious powers could not agree on how to divide the spoils, the Ottomans recovered the city of Adrianople (Edirne) from the Bulgarians. The islands of the Aegean Sea were divided between Greece and Turkey by a decision of the great powers on December 16, 1913: except for Imbros (Imroz) and Tenedos (Bozcaada), at the entrance of the Dardanelles, all islands were ceded to

Greece. The Italians, however, as a result of their war with Turkey over Tripolitania, still held Rhodes and the so-called Dodecanese islands.

The disastrous defeat, this time inflicted on the Ottomans by a coalition of small powers and not by Russia, left the country in a state of complete disorientation. Leaders of the Committee of Union and Progress exercised control over the sultan and the destinies of the empire. The country was economically exhausted and militarily disorganized. Decision-making depended on a few energetic individuals who lacked the experience of seasoned diplomats of the old school and were overly impressed by the one European power that they believed would be their real friend and supporter. This was the state of affairs in the summer of 1914 when, at the outbreak of World War I, Turkey cast her lot with Germany.

WORLD WAR I AND THE RISE OF NEW TURKEY

Whether the Ottoman Empire could have stayed neutral during World War I must remain a matter of speculation. Participation in the hostilities, in view of the exhaustion of Ottoman resources, was certainly not in Turkey's interest. Whether she could have been forced into entering the war by the entente powers appears unlikely. These belligerents were primarily interested in using Turkish waterways to supply Russia; such passage by commercial vessels through the straits would have been possible while Turkey remained outside the conflict. Turkey as an active ally was an asset to the Central Powers for two reasons: she barred the route from the Mediterranean to the Black Sea and kept busy a considerable number of enemy forces which might otherwise have been employed on the western and eastern fronts of Germany and Austria–Hungary. Otherwise, her offensive capabilities against Russia on the transcaucasian front and against the Suez Canal were of little consequence.

The reasons the Ottoman state entered the war on the side of Germany and Austria–Hungary were twofold: (1) German influence had gained ascendancy during the short period following the Balkan wars; the Turkish army was equipped and trained by the Germans, and an all-powerful German military mission resided in the capital; Enver Pasha, the most outstanding leader of the Young Turks and Minister of War, was a convinced Germanophile and cherished Pan-Turanistic dreams which could only be realized to the detriment of Russia; (2) although the majority of the Turkish leaders sympathized with Britain and France, they could not point to any tangible help which could be expected from these powers. Furthermore, the Turkish elite was frustrated by the economic interference of these powers and their nationals in the affairs of the empire. (This was less true for the Germans who were late-comers to the Near and Middle East.) To get rid of the capitulatory system at last seemed to many a worthwhile reason for entering the war.[27]

It should also be remembered that on July 22, 1914, when the conflict was still restricted to Austria–Hungary and Serbia, it was Enver Pasha who suggested the signing of a treaty of alliance with Germany. On August 2, when German forces were already massing to invade Belgium, a secret treaty was signed committing the Ottoman Empire to join Germany should the latter be involved in the war.[28] Nevertheless, the Sublime Porte at first declared its neutrality; but a further event precipitated the decision to fight. The British government had requisitioned two Turkish warships, one nearing completion in one of their shipyards, and another in England for repairs. By a grandiose gesture, the kaiser presented the Ottoman navy with two brand-new German warships which had taken refuge in the straits from the British.[29] These vessels, still manned by their German crew, bombarded Russian targets along the Black Sea coast in late October; Russian, French, and British declarations of war on the empire followed forthwith.

Sultan Mehmed V, in his capacity as caliph, declared a *Jihad* (Holy War against infidels); however, this failed to impress Muslim soldiers fighting in the French and British ranks. Nor did it discourage Arabs from revolting against their Turkish masters.

The Ottoman Empire was immediately engaged in hostilities in eastern Anatolia against the Russians and in Mesopotamia, Arabia, and Palestine against the British and their allies. Furthermore, in March 1915, a formidable armada of British–French combined naval and land forces undertook to capture the Dardanelles in order to open up the shipping route to the Black Sea. The Ottoman army under German command suc-

---

[27] See Lamouche, *Histoire de la Turquie,* pp. 358–60; Davison, *Turkey,* pp. 115–16. To what extent Germany held a position of predominant influence with the Ottoman government is a moot point; more recently this influence was disputed by Ulrich Trumpener, *Germany and the Ottoman Empire, 1914–1918* (Princeton, N.J., 1968), *passim.*
[28] For text see Hurewitz, *Diplomacy,* vol. II, pp. 1–2.
[29] The two ships were the battleship *Goeben* and the heavy cruiser *Breslau.*

cessfully repulsed the attack. It should be noted that a Turkish colonel, Mustafa Kemal, who later became the founder of modern Turkey, distinguished himself in combat on the Gallipoli peninsula.

Turkish resistance was less successful in other theaters of the war: Russians penetrated deep into eastern Anatolia; the British captured Baghdad and, with the help of Arab irregulars, entered Palestine and Syria. Only in Anatolia, and only after the outbreak of the revolution in Russia, were the Turks able to regain their lost territories. This was an area of mixed Armenian and Muslim population, and because the former assisted the Russian advance and committed atrocities against Muslims, the government of Constantinople had ordered in 1915 the deportation of all Armenians, except those in Constantinople. This measure, accompanied by widespread excesses, resulted in the tragic extermination of a considerable part of the Armenians.

With the collapse of the Central Powers, Turkish resistance came to an end, and an armistice was signed at Mudros on October 30, 1918, which, among other stipulations, permitted Allied forces to enter the straits and Constantinople. The armistice line followed roughly the northern borders of Syria and Mesopotamia, but the Allies were, in addition, allowed to occupy "any strategic points in the event of a situation arising which threatens the security of the Allies."[30]

During the war, the Allies had entered into a number of agreements for the partition of the Ottoman Empire. As a result of diplomatic notes exchanged between March 4 and April 10, 1915, Britain and France had reversed their century-old policy and agreed that "the question of Constantinople and the Straits would be definitely solved" by incorporating the area into the Russian empire.[31] France was to receive Syria and Cilicia, and Great Britain was to be compensated by a larger sphere of influence in Persia. Under the so-called Sykes-Picot Agreement, Russia was further to receive most of eastern Anatolia (including the towns of Erzerum, Trabzon, Van, Bitlis, and Kurdistan), while the British were to have Palestine and Mesopotamia. Finally, French control over Syria and Cilicia

---

[30] For the text of the Armistice Treaty at Mudros see Hurewitz, *Diplomacy,* vol. II, pp. 36–37.

[31] The City of Constantinople, the western bank of the Bosporus, of the Sea of Marmara, and the Dardanelles, as well as southern Thrace to the Enos-Midya Line; also the area between the Bosporus and the Sakarya River to a point in the Gulf of Izmit; the islands of the Sea of Marmara, and Imbros and Tenedos, at the entrance of the Dardanelles—were all to be annexed by Russia. *Ibid.,* pp. 7–11.

was once more confirmed.[32] Under the agreement of May 23, 1915, Italy was also to receive a share of the Ottoman Empire: in addition to the Dodecanese Islands, Antalya and its hinterland was to become an Italian sphere of interest.[33] Under the Saint-Jean de Maurienne Agreement between Britain, France, and Italy, the latter was even promised the administration of Smyrna (Izmir) and Mersin.[34] The Constantinople Agreement and other arrangements with Russia had, as a consequence of Russia's withdrawal from the war, lapsed; but Britain, France, and Italy submitted to the Paris Peace Conference their respective demands based on the previous agreements.

After a century and a half of struggle for rejuvenation and survival, the Ottoman Empire lay prostrate; its Arab provinces had seceded; its capital was at the mercy of occupying forces; and even the heartland of Turkism, Anatolia, was threatened with dismemberment. It appeared that the Sick Man of Europe had passed away and that its severed limbs as well as its truncated body would no longer enjoy sovereign existence.[35] The draft peace treaty handed to the representatives of Sultan Mehmed VI Vahideddin confirmed this appearance. It stipulated that Greece was to receive the remaining portion of European Turkey (eastern Thrace), except for a narrow piece of territory west of Constantinople; Izmir (Smyrna) and its hinterland in western Anatolia was to be under Greek administration. In addition to the abandonment by the Turks of all Arab lands (Syria, Mesopotamia, Hejaz), a sovereign Armenian state and a self-governing Kurdistan were to be formed in eastern Anatolia. Furthermore, France and Italy were to be entitled to carve out "spheres of economic influence" from the remaining Anatolian provinces. Capitulations, abolished during the war, were to be restored and the country placed under external financial control. The straits were to be governed

[32] This agreement is based on an exchange of diplomatic notes dated from April 26 to October 23, 1916. The original details had been worked out by the experts of the Foreign Office and of the French Ministry of Foreign Affairs, Sir Mark Sykes and Charles François Georges-Picot. *Ibid.*, pp. 18–22.

[33] This agreement was negotiated at the time of Italy's entry into the war against Austria-Hungary, Germany, and Turkey; *ibid.*, pp. 11-12.

[34] Italy was left out of the advantages foreseen under the Sykes-Picot Agreement. She therefore insisted on her share in the partition of Turkey, in addition to the agreement of May 23, 1915. This second agreement was concluded at Saint-Jean de Maurienne on April 19, 1917. Approval by the Russian government, because of the revolutionary situation in Russia, could not be obtained; *ibid.*, pp. 23–25.

[35] President Wilson's Fourteen Points had, however, stated that the Turkish portions of the Ottoman Empire "should be assured a secure sovereignty."

by an international regime. On August 10, 1920, the dictated Peace Treaty of Sèvres was signed by the subservient government of Constantinople.[36]

The Young Turk ministers had fled after the conclusion of the armistice. One of the few leaders who wished neither to serve the occupying Allies nor to despair at the future of the Turkish nation was Mustafa Kemal Pasha (promoted to the rank of General after his bravery at Gallipoli). Throughout the war, he was a sharp critic of the ruling Young Turk circles: he was opposed to the German alliance and, although serving with outstanding success on various battlefronts, distrusted the strategy of Enver. He had asked for and received a commission as Inspector General over several army units in Anatolia, ostensibly to restore order but with the avowed aim of organizing resistance. He arrived in central Anatolia in May 1919, just a few days after the Greek landing at Smyrna—a maneuver taken as a great insult to Turkish national pride.[37]

During the summer of 1919, Mustafa Kemal, with the assistance of his friends and associates, held several congresses, organized the Union for the Defense of Rights of Anatolia and Rumelia, and encouraged armed resistance, which was at first carried out by irregulars fighting Greeks, French, and Italians in western and southern Anatolia. In eastern Anatolia, a regular Turkish army under the command of Kazim Karabekir Pasha joined the Kemalist movement. Under the pressure of the nationalists, the sultan's government called for parliamentary elections on November 7, 1919. The new parliament, consisting mostly of nationalist deputies, adopted the National Pact on January 28, 1920, a program which foresaw complete independence, the integrity of territory inside the armistice line inhabited by the Ottoman-Muslim majority, and opposition to restrictions of a political, juridical, or financial nature.[38]

In the face of open resistance to the measures they had introduced,

---

[36] After five years, the local parliament of the region of Smyrna (Izmir) might ask for the final incorporation of the area into Greece. Similarly, within one year, autonomous Kurdistan might ask the League of Nations for a confirmation of her status as an independent state. For the text of the Treaty of Sèvres see Hurewitz, *Diplomacy*, vol. II, pp. 81–89.

[37] See Lord Kinross, *Atatürk* (New York, 1965), pp. 174–264. For the life story of Mustafa Kemal see also Irfan and Margaret Orga, *Atatürk* (London, 1962); Şevket Süreyya Aydemir, *Tek Adam* (The Unique Man), 3 vols. (Istanbul, 1963–65).

[38] For text, see Hurewitz, *Diplomacy*, vol. II, pp. 74–75; Elaine D. Smith, *Turkey: Origins of the Kemalist Movement and the Government of the Grand National Assembly* (1919–1923) (Washington, D.C., 1959).

the Allies formally occupied Constantinople and arrested many deputies. The sultan dissolved the parliament. Kemal convoked a Grand National Assembly in Ankara which consisted partly of parliamentary deputies and partly of other representatives who came from all sections of Turkey. On April 23, 1920, the assembly passed a resolution establishing its own government; although the sultan's office was still recognized, he was considered a prisoner of the Allies. The constitutional act of January 20, 1921, declared that "sovereignty belongs without reserve to the nation" and that the Turkish state "is administered by the Grand National Assembly and its Government."[39] The country was no longer called the Ottoman Empire but officially, for the first time, Turkey.[40]

In return, the sultan's government sentenced Mustafa Kemal to death *in absentia,* and its forces, the Army of the Caliphate, unsuccessfully tried to suppress what was considered a rebellion. Actually, the sultan's authority was restricted to Constantinople and its surroundings. The Greek army, however, advanced into the interior of Anatolia and was stopped only at the two battles of Inönü.

In February 1921, the Allies invited both the Constantinople and Ankara governments to participate in a conference in London where a revision of the Sèvres treaty (still unratified) was offered. Nevertheless, the Ankara government refused to accept the proposals which were far from satisfying the requirements of the National Pact. The Greeks resumed their offensive and were repulsed only at the Sakarya River, 50 miles west of Ankara.

Kazim Karabekir's forces had in the meantime moved into Armenia, and the Treaty of Alexandropol (later called Leninakan) of December 3, 1920, restored the Turkish border as it was before 1878 (reincorporating Kars and Ardahan), except for the port of Batum. On March 16, 1921, a Treaty of Friendship was concluded between Ankara and the Russian Socialist Federated Soviet Republic which confirmed the border arrangements.[41] Soviet logistic and diplomatic assistance strengthened the position of the Kemalist government against the Allies. At this point, the Allies began to fall apart. The first to go was France, which concluded a separate Agreement for the Promotion of Peace with Ankara.[42] The

[39] Smith, *Turkey,* pp. 157–58.
[40] See Davison, *Turkey,* p. 123.
[41] Hurewitz, *Diplomacy,* vol. II, pp. 95–97.
[42] *Ibid.,* pp. 97–100.

agreement provided for a withdrawal of French forces behind the Syrian border and for a special administrative regime in the district of Alexandretta (Iskenderun).[43]

In August 1922, the reinforced Turkish army defeated the Greeks and expelled them from Anatolian territory within less than a month. Turkish and British troops thereupon confronted each other at Çanakkale, on the Dardanelles, until the Armistice of Mudanya (October 11, 1922) ended all hostilities. Under this agreement the Turks entered eastern Thrace as it was evacuated by the Greeks.

Kemalist Turkey thus won the war which she led not for the restoration of the Ottoman Empire but for the survival of the Turkish people as an independent nation. Now the leaders of new Turkey were challenged to win the peace. On November 1, 1922, the sultanate was abolished and Mehmet VI fled abroad. The caliphate was, however, to be held by another member of the house of Osman. This measure was intended only to appease Islamic sensitivity, both inside and outside Turkey; in 1924, even the caliphate was abolished and all members of the Osman dynasty were banished. Turkey then became a republic under Mustafa Kemal, its first president.

The Peace Conference of Lausanne was held from November 20, 1922, to February 4, 1923, and again from April 23 to July 24, 1923, when the peace treaty was signed. The Lausanne treaty essentially fulfilled the demands set by the National Pact; it also carried the distinction of being the instrument which gave international recognition to the present status of Turkey. Consequently, it is held in great respect. Except for the area of Alexandretta (Iskenderun), which was added in 1939 to the national territory, the territorial provisions of the treaty have remained valid to the present day. On Turkey's European border, the Lausanne treaty restored to Turkey Edirne's railroad station on the western bank of the Maritsa (Meriç). In the Aegean, Greece kept all of the islands, except Imbros (Imroz) and Tenedos (Bozcaada), although Mytilene, Chios, Samos, and Nikaria were to be demilitarized. The Dodecanese Islands and Rhodes were finally ceded to Italy, together with the small island of Castellorizzo (Meis).

Turkey renounced her rights to all Arab lands and to Cyprus; the

---

[43] Ankara considered that the Sanjak of Alexandretta (Iskenderun) was inhabited by a majority of Turks and thus hoped to recover it.

Mesopotamian border remained undecided until the Mosul area was finally allotted to British-mandated Iraq.[44] The Western powers agreed to the complete abolition of the capitulations.

The status of the large Greek minority in Anatolia had become intolerable because of the murderous war between the two nations, and the atrocities committed by both sides. The Lausanne conference resorted to a drastic remedy: the Greeks (Orthodox Christians) in Turkey were to be exchanged for the Turks (Muslims) in Greece.[45] Only those Greeks who settled in Constantinople and the surrounding area (including the islands of Imbros and Tenedos) before October 30, 1918, and the Turks of western Thrace were expressly exempted from this compulsory exchange. Within the next few years, about one and one-third million Greeks left Anatolia, and more than one-half million Muslims were settled in Turkey.[46]

A Convention on the Regime of the Straits was signed by the participants in the Lausanne conference as well as by the Soviet Union. The principle of free navigation for all ships was confirmed, and detailed regulations were set for the transit of various types of craft. An international commission was to supervise the navigation. Turkey undertook to demilitarize the straits area, and the League of Nations was entrusted with the task of protecting the waterways against aggression.[47]

As soon as the international status of Turkey was settled, President Mustafa Kemal began his far-reaching internal reforms. He proved to be a much more radical Westernizer than any earlier Ottoman statesman. His aim was to turn Turkey into a European state and the Turkish people into a European nation because he believed that there was only one type

[44] The Lausanne treaty referred the Mosul question to the Council of the League of Nations. The Council received the report of a commission which made investigations in the area, asked for an advisory opinion from the Permanent Court of International Justice as to its own competence, and finally passed a resolution in favor of Britain (Iraq). Turkey refused to recognize the competence of the Council to arbitrate, instead of mediate, the question.

[45] The determination of persons to be exchanged was to be on the basis of religion. Thus the Karamanli Greeks, speaking Turkish, had to leave Turkey because they were of the Greek Orthodox faith. On the other hand, many Muslims (Turks) of Crete and Epirus, speaking only Greek, were also subject to the exchange.

[46] See Stephen P. Ladas, *The Exchange of Minorities: Bulgaria, Greece and Turkey* (New York, 1932).

[47] For the text of the Peace Treaty of Lausanne and the straits convention, see Hurewitz, *Diplomacy*, vol. II, pp. 119–27. For further details of the Regime of the Straits, see chapter V below.

of real civilization: the Western one. Never before or since has such a drastic attempt been made to convert an Islamic people—or a people without a tradition anchored in the Roman–Christian culture and belief-system—into a European nation. Despite rumors to the contrary, Kemal had no intention of converting his people to Christianity. But he did want them to adopt Western European principles and attitudes which had become secularized following the Middle Ages. Although he showed little interest in Islam (having earlier paid lip-service to it for opportunistic reasons), he did not wish the Turks to abandon the faith of their fathers. He thought that the religious content of Islam could be divorced from political, social, and cultural institutions.[48]

Accordingly, his reforms were political, social, and cultural. The state was founded on a strictly secular basis. The new constitution, passed by the Grand National Assembly on April 20, 1924, declared that "the Turkish State is a Republic" and "Sovereignty belongs unconditionally to the nation." Although the 1924 version of the constitution still stated that "the religion of the Turkish State is Islam," this provision was repealed in 1928.[49] The religious courts were abolished, and the entire educational system was placed under the supervision of the Ministry of Education. Western legislation was introduced in all matters, including family affairs; thus, the Shariat (sacred Muslim law) no longer remained applicable.

Ankara became the constitutional capital of the new Turkish state. To deprive Constantinople, henceforth officially Istanbul, of its character after 16 centuries as the capital of an empire was motivated by various reasons. The occupation of the city after World War I showed its vulnerability; furthermore, Turkey's government was to be removed from the implications and influence of the city on the Golden Horn where a cosmopolitan atmosphere, the memories of the sultan-caliph, and big business in the hands of foreigners or non-Turks might militate against the new order.

Discriminations against the female sex were to be abandoned: the

[48] During the War of Independence, when Greeks and other non-Muslims fought, religious motivations proved more effective than national sentiment. Also when the Army of the Caliphate, operating under the *fetva* of the *Şeyhülislam* (religious opinion issued by the highest interpreter of the Koran) had to be opposed, Islamic incentives were used by Mustafa Kemal.

[49] For the English text of the Constitution of 1924, see Donald E. Webster, *The Turkey of Atatürk* (Philadelphia, 1939), pp. 297–306.

new civil and criminal codes banned polygamy, and women were to be admitted to all professions and schools.

The wearing of the fez, traditional Turkish headgear since Sultan Mahmut II, was forbidden, and the use of European hats was introduced.[50] The dervish orders were dissolved and priests of all denominations were prohibited from wearing religious vestments unless performing ecclesiastical functions. The Gregorian, instead of the Muslim, calendar was adopted; Sunday, instead of Friday, the Islamic holy day, was declared a weekly day of rest.

The introduction of Western codes of law and the disestablishment of Islam and of other denominations put an automatic end to the remnants of the *millet* system. Thus, the administration of the country became secularized and centralized. Equality before the law, for Muslims and non-Muslims alike, became the rule. Although the cultural and educational rights of national minorities were respected, the elimination of "communities" (*millet*) and the restriction of religious groups to mere brotherhoods of worship rendered members of national religious minorities more vulnerable to public pressures.

The de-Islamization and Europeanization reforms soon extended to script and language. In 1928 the Arabic alphabet was dropped and replaced by Latin characters.[51] A sweeping language reform sought to do away with Arabic and Persian grammatical forms and to substitute ancient or living Turkic for Arabic and Persian words. In addition, new words were artificially constructed from Turkish roots. In 1932 all prayers, including the call from the minaret, were ordered to be made in the Turkish language and not in Arabic, the language of the Koran.

In 1934 a law was passed which required everyone to adopt a surname in place of the occasional adjectives often attached to names.[52] Mustafa Kemal himself gave family names to members of his entourage: his chief lieutenant, Ismet Pasha, twice victor over the Greeks at the village

[50] The Turkish word for European headgear is "şapka," which had a deprecatory meaning. The expression "şapka giymek" (to put on a hat) meant "turning into an infidel, a traitor." With the European hat (having a vizor) one could not touch the ground with the head when performing a prayer; thus, the introduction of the hat contained anti-Islamic connotations.

[51] In fact, Latin characters suited the Turkish language better than the Arabic script which was geared to the Arabic language. Thus, Turkish was to be written phonetically, and this helped fight illiteracy.

[52] Such as the "long Ahmed" or "Mehmet from Bursa." A few Turkish families, mostly those of a higher social standing, used surnames already.

of Inönü, received "Inönü" as a surname. Mustafa Kemal was officially endowed by the National Assembly with the surname Atatürk (Father-Turk), with which he has entered the pages of history.

The radical reforms of the Kemalist regime, especially those which were or could be interpreted as anti-Islamic, provoked widespread opposition and often overt revolts. Attempts were made on Atatürk's life. In the east, where traditional ways of life were more deep seated and where the Kurdish tribal system prevailed, religious tribal leaders (sheyks) fomented rebellions. All of these attempts to impede or retard modernization were ruthlessly suppressed, and prison and death sentences were meted out to the opponents of the regime.

During the Lausanne negotiations, Kemal organized the People's Party, which, after the formal establishment of the republic, became the Republican People's Party. It remained the only political party throughout Atatürk's lifetime and even after, although there were two attempts to set up "loyal" opposition parties.[53] Turkey's supreme leader certainly intended to expose his country to real democracy, but he was not sure whether his countrymen would be willing or able to implement all of the reforms which he considered indispensable. He therefore practiced a kind of "benevolent autocracy" which should not be identified with leftist or rightist dictatorships. He distrusted both communism (he had the Communist Party suppressed)[54] and Fascism–Nazism and wished to save his country from their contagion. Although he often acted as a despot (in the manner in which Turks were accustomed to be handled before his time), there is reason to believe that he considered his one-party or one-man rule transitional until a rejuvenated modern and democratic Turkey could stand on her own feet.[55]

Foreign relations of Atatürk's Turkey were dominated by the concern to assert his country's genuine independence and sovereignty, qualities sorely lacking during the last century of Ottoman administration. Certain mementoes weighed heavily on the foreign policy line of Turkey—

[53] These were the Progressive Republican Party in 1924, which was suppressed due to the Kurdish revolt of 1925, and the Free Republican Party in 1930, which had to be dissolved because it proved to be too popular.

[54] Kemal showed tolerance toward Communists, whereas the Kemalist movement depended on Soviet assistance but never allowed agents of Moscow to take over leadership. Eventually, in 1925 all Communist activity was forbidden. See George S. Harris, *The Origins of Communism in Turkey* (Stanford, Calif., 1967).

[55] See Kinross, *Atatürk,* pp. 494–97.

mementoes of foreign intervention in the affairs of Turkey, of economic dependence (partly the result of the capitulatory system, partly of the chronic bankruptcy of the Ottoman treasury), of a lack of jurisdiction over alien or foreign-protected citizens (also due to the capitulations). Strong memories also remained of the recurrent need for foreign military assistance which culminated in the German overlordship during World War I and of the occupation of Istanbul by the Allies. The peaceful international period following the Lausanne Peace Treaty greatly helped the implementation of a constructive diplomacy.

Turkey, alone among Germany's allies, was not a defeated country, although she did lose much real estate. She was not a territorially dissatisfied state and had no "irredenta," although there were Turks in the Alexandretta district. Thus, Atatürk's foreign policy direction, "Peace at home, peace abroad," could easily be obeyed.

During the war of independence, the Ankara government sought cooperative help from Moscow. After the Turkish disappointment over Mosul, a Treaty of Friendship and Neutrality was ostentatiously concluded with the Soviet government on December 17, 1925.[56] Despite this seemingly anti-British move, Turkey mended her fences with Britain by entering six months later into a treaty with that country which settled the border issue.[57]

Atatürk's advisers urged him to lead Turkey into an alliance with one of the great powers, but the president chose to make friends with all Turkey's neighbors as well as with other powers—to pursue a "neutralist attitude" in the modern sense. For the ten years after 1923, the country was not threatened. The arch-enemy, Russia, still suffered under the convulsion of her own transformation. It was more difficult to establish friendly relations with Greece in view of the life-and-death struggle in which Turkey so recently had been involved. Nevertheless, by 1930 a Treaty of Friendship was concluded with Greece, and four years later the Hellenic kingdom became an ally.

Turkey professed great respect for international law and international treaties; the idea of collective security under the League of Nations also appealed to her.[58] She looked, however, with suspicion upon Mussolini's

[56] Hurewitz, *Diplomacy*, vol. II, pp. 142–43.
[57] Frontier treaty between the United Kingdom and Iraq, and Turkey of June 6, 1926; *ibid.*, pp. 143–46.
[58] In 1932 Turkey became a member of the League of Nations.

Italy, even before the invasion of Ethiopia; the menacing proximity of the Dodecanese islands to the Anatolian mainland was viewed with much distrust in Ankara, especially the heavily fortified island of Leros. Hitler's rise to power gave Turkey the impetus to seek defensive alliances with her western neighbors. On February 9, 1934, the Balkan Entente Pact was concluded by Turkey, Greece, Rumania, and Yugoslavia. A treaty of mutual defense primarily directed against Bulgaria, the pact held that, should a non-Balkan power attack any of the signatories and be assisted by a Balkan power, the other signatories would also be obliged to go to war against the aggressors. Turkey and Greece, however, were exempted from such an obligation should it involve them in hostilities against the Soviet Union or Italy, respectively.[59]

The failure to stop Italy's Ethiopian aggression revealed the ineffectiveness of the League's collective security system. Thereupon, in the spring of 1936 the Turkish government asked for a revision of the regime governing the straits as laid down by the Lausanne Treaty. A conference for this purpose assembled in Montreux, and on July 20, 1936, a Convention on the Regime of the Turkish Straits was signed by Turkey, Britain, France, Japan, the USSR, Australia, Bulgaria, Rumania, and Yugoslavia; after some reluctance, Italy acceded to the convention in 1937. Two most important changes were brought about by the Montreux convention for Turkey: first, the international regime was abolished; second, Turkey was made the "guardian" of these waterways and was authorized to establish fortifications along their course. A compromise was reached between conflicting British and Soviet proposals concerning the use of the straits by warships in time of peace and war.[60]

The contractual revision of the straits regime, at the time of such unilateral actions as the occupation of the Rhineland by Hitler, was a notable triumph of Turkish moderation and diplomacy. Another peaceful change obtained by Turkey concerned the long-coveted Sanjak of Alexandretta (Iskenderun), a region called Hatay by the Turks. This area was already given a special status within the French-mandated Syria under the Franco-Turkish Agreement of October 20, 1921.[61] In 1936 France

[59] See also Altemur Kiliç, *Turkey and the World* (Washington, D.C., 1959), pp. 52–54.

[60] For the text of the Montreux convention, see Hurewitz, *Diplomacy*, vol. II, pp. 197–203. For detailed description, see chapter V below.

[61] *Ibid.*, pp. 97–100.

undertook to grant independence to Syria, whereupon Turkey first broached the question before the council of the League and subsequently opened direct negotiations with France. Early in 1937 an agreement was reached which established Hatay as a separate political entity loosely bound to Syria (which was to handle Hatay's foreign affairs) but where Turkish and Arabic would both serve as official languages. Later, owing to disturbances in the area and following Turkish pressures, France agreed that an election be held in July 1938 in the presence of Turkish troops.

Atatürk, however, did not see the successful end of the Hatay affair. On November 10, 1938, on the eve of World War II, he died. His personal role in creating modern Turkey almost effaces the contribution of those who assisted him and the part played by the people of Turkey. The ideas which guided, and still guide Turkey, are mostly his ideas. Turkish statesmen, politicians, professors, and even common people still quote him and profess, rightly or wrongly, to follow his directions.

In foreign policy, Atatürk displayed the greatest asset of a successful national leader: moderation. He was not carried away by his unprecedented and even unexpected success in the war of independence. Although he refused to compromise on issues which he considered vital for the survival of the Turkish nation, he settled on a status quo policy as soon as these goals were attained. He said, "Turkey does not desire an inch of foreign territory, but will not give up an inch of what she holds."[62] He made friends with the former enemies of his country: with Greece, the erstwhile bitter foe, and with Britain, which stood behind the Byzantine dream of King Constantine. He did not hesitate to accept help from Moscow while consciously retaining his Western orientation.

The basic philosophy of national life and national success which he outlined for his people may have appeared overly ambitious or unrealistic to his contemporaries; it appears much less unrealistic now. Turkey may have survived the ordeal of World War I, but without Atatürk she would not be the Turkey of today. For those who are skeptical about the role individuals play in shaping national destinies, the example of the Father of the Turks, despite all his personal weaknesses, would provide an adequate and positive answer.

[62] Kinross, *Atatürk*, p. 521.

WORLD WAR II AND AFTER

The "gathering storm" found Turkey, just as many other states, unprepared for the struggle that lay ahead, a struggle that might have engulfed the country of Atatürk had it not been for skillful diplomacy and a stroke of luck. Since the late twenties, Ankara had considered Fascist Italy her potential aggressor, and Mussolini's invasion of Albania in April 1939 persuaded the Turkish government to abandon nonalignment in the approaching clash between the Axis powers and Western democracies.

Following the German entry into Prague and Italy's invasion of Albania, Britain sought alliance among East European countries. She extended guarantees to Poland and, subsequently, to Rumania and Greece. Turkey was invited to join in these moves which were intended to forestall World War II and to protect the countries threatened by German and Italian aggressiveness. France already possessed alliances with Yugoslavia and Rumania.

On May 12, 1939, an Anglo-Turkish declaration was issued to ensure security in the Mediterranean area and in the Balkans; the declaration was to be replaced by a formal treaty of alliance in which France also was to participate. A similar declaration with France was delayed because she was reluctant to cede Hatay to Turkey. By June 20, however, the French government was ready to agree to this cession, and a declaration identical to the British declaration was drawn between Paris and Ankara on June 23, 1939.

When contemplating entry into an alliance with the two Western powers, Turkey acted in the belief that the Soviet government also would soon join Britain and France in an agreement for military cooperation to oppose the Axis powers. In fact, during that summer (1939), British and French diplomacy was feverishly engaged in harmonizing their commitments with Soviet participation and, to this end, was simultaneously conducting military talks with Moscow.

The unexpected Hitler–Stalin pact, signed in Moscow on August 23, 1939, created an entirely new situation and took Ankara, as well as other capitals, by surprise. Throughout her negotiations with Britain and France, Turkey had made it clear that (as with the Balkan Entente undertakings) she would assume no obligations which would involve her in hostilities with the Soviet Union. Soviet complicity in the invasion of Poland followed the signing of the Hitler-Stalin pact and created uncertainties as to Moscow's ultimate intentions. Turkish Foreign Minister Saracoğlu journeyed to the Soviet capital on September 26, 1939, before final decisions were made concerning the formal treaty of alliance to be concluded with Britain and France.

Saracoğlu spent three weeks in Moscow in fruitless negotiations with Soviet Foreign Commissar Molotov, who tried to induce Turkey to adopt an attitude of complete neutrality and to close the straits to the "Western imperialists." Turkey, on the other hand, asked for an agreement that would guarantee Soviet assistance should she be attacked. Molotov, however, would only discuss such an agreement if it would exclude aggression by Germany and suggested common defense of the straits. But the Turkish foreign minister refused to be drawn into an agreement that would be incompatible with Turkey's already existing commitments and with the international convention concerning the straits. Eventually he returned empty-handed to Ankara where, on October 19, 1939, a Mutual Assistance Treaty was signed by Britain, France, and Turkey. Under Article 1 of this treaty, the two Western Powers agreed that,

in the event of Turkey being involved in hostilities with a European Power in consequence of aggression by that Power against Turkey, France and the United Kingdom will co-operate effectively with Turkey and will lend her all aid and assistance in their power.

Turkey, on the other hand, promised in Article 2 (1):

In the event of an act of aggression by a European Power leading to war in the Mediterranean area in which France and the United Kingdom are involved, Turkey will collaborate effectively with France and the United Kingdom, and will lend them all aid and assistance in her power.

The Western powers also committed themselves to assist Turkey should she be involved in a war in the Mediterranean area because of her commitments under the Balkan Entente. Protocol No. 2, attached to the treaty, exempted Turkey from any action in the case of an armed conflict between her allies and the Soviet Union. By another agreement signed on the same day, Britain and France granted Turkey financial benefits for the purchase of war material and for the support of her exports, which had suffered under German acts of discrimination.[63]

[63] For the text of the treaty, see Hurewitz, *Diplomacy*, vol. II, pp. 226–28; for the Anglo–French–Turkish negotiations preceding the treaty and *Saracoğlu's* visit to

The Soviet government expressed displeasure over the treaty and prophesied that Turkey would regret it; Germany and Italy threatened Turkey with all kinds of economic and other reprisals. At that time Ankara was even under the impression that Germany had expressed disinterest in the territories of southern Europe, even as far as Constantinople and the straits. It should be recalled that Hitler, in like manner, abandoned interest in the Baltic countries which were first occupied by and then incorporated into the Soviet Union; this was also true of Finland, attacked in November, 1939, and Bessarabia, seized from Rumania in 1940.

Until Italy's entry into World War II in June 1940, the Mediterranean area remained peaceful. During that period, Turkish diplomacy tried to transform the Balkan Entente into a more effective instrument. At the annual conference of Balkan states in February 1940, Saracoğlu submitted a plan for collective self-defense against the aggression of any non-Balkan country, with the exclusion of the Soviet Union. But the more exposed members, Yugoslavia and Rumania, were unwilling to join. Bulgaria continued to press for a revision of the frontiers.

In late spring of 1940, Hitler's forces invaded the Low Countries and France, expelled the British Expeditionary Army from the continent, and entered Paris; Italy declared war on Britain and France on June 10, 1940, thus making the alliance with Turkey operative. Nevertheless, Ismet Inönü, who had succeeded Atatürk in 1938 as president, refused, with the approval of the British foreign secretary, to enter the war by invoking Protocol No. 2 of the alliance treaty (that such action could involve her in hostilities with the Soviet Union). Many observers may have considered this a weak excuse, but the armistice soon concluded by a defeated France provided an even stronger argument for Turkey to stay out of the war at that time. It was, however, never alleged by Ankara that the treaty had lapsed, only that action under it had been withheld.[64]

Indeed, the greatest danger to Turkey's independent existence, after

---

Moscow, see Kiliç, *Turkey and the World,* pp. 75–80; Türkkaya Ataöv, *Turkish Foreign Policy, 1939–1945* (Ankara, 1965), pp. 11–65; Metin Tamkoç, "Turkey's Quest for Security Through Defensive Alliances," *The Turkish Yearbook of International Relations* (1961): pp. 9–14.

[64] For the argument whether Turkey violated her treaty obligation, see Kiliç, *Turkey and the World,* pp. 82–83; Ataöv, *Turkish Foreign Policy,* pp. 73–75; Franz von Papen, *Memoirs* (London, 1952), pp. 460–61; Sir Hughe Knatchbull-Hugessen, *Diplomat in Peace and War* (London, 1949), pp. 165–70.

the fall of France and during Britain's struggle for survival, was an agreement between Berlin and Moscow directed at partitioning the region of the Near East between themselves. The situation was reminiscent of the short-lived cooperation between Napoleon and Tsar Alexander I in 1807 and 1808, when they discussed the dismemberment of the Ottoman Empire. At this juncture, however, Hitler was unwilling (as Napoleon had been before him) to abandon the straits to the Moscovite power.[65] After the campaign against France, Hitler had already made up his mind to solve the "Eastern Question" by attacking and defeating Russia.

Soviet proposals for spheres of influence in the Near and Middle East coincided with the Italian attack on Greece in October 1940. Under the Balkan Entente Treaty, Turkey was not obliged to intervene as long as Bulgaria remained neutral. Facing only the Italians, the Greeks resisted successfully until April 1941, when the Germans, penetrating across the Balkans into Bulgaria, invaded both Yugoslavia and Greece. The defeat of Greece brought German armies to the Turkish border in Thrace and on the Greek islands of Mytilene, Chios, and Samos. At the same time, German success in North Africa threatened to cut off Turkey's vital supply lines across the Mediterranean and possibly even the Suez Canal. To compound these calamities, a pro-Axis revolt in Iraq became a menace to Turkey's eastern flank.[66]

Hitler's decision to march against the Soviet Union instead of Turkey (as was feared in Ankara) saved the latter from the devastations of the war. The gigantic battles in the vastnesses of Russia reduced the Near East for the time being to an area of secondary interest. On June 18, 1941, four days before Germany's invasion of Russia, the Turkish government signed a Treaty of Territorial Integrity and Friendship with Berlin.[67] London was fully informed of this move and showed understanding.

[65] Under a Soviet memorandum submitted in November 1940 to Germany, Moscow claimed that "the security of the Soviet Union in the Straits is assured by a conclusion of a mutual assistance pact between the Soviet Union and Bulgaria, which geographically is situated inside the security zone of the Black Sea boundaries of the Soviet Union, and by establishment of *a base for land and naval forces of the USSR within the range of the Bosporus and the Dardanelles* by means of a long-term lease." Moscow also asked for a *retrocession of Kars and Ardahan* and that "the area south of Batum and Baku in the general direction of the Persian Gulf be recognized as the center of the aspirations of the Soviet Union." Hurewitz, *Diplomacy*, vol. II, pp. 228–30. Italics are added.

[66] For details of the coup led by Rashid Ali al-Gaylani, see Majid Khadduri, *Independent Iraq, 1932–1958* (2d ed.; London, 1960), pp. 210–43.

[67] Hurewitz, *Diplomacy*, vol. II, p. 231; Papen, *Memoirs*, pp. 478–79.

The murderous struggle between Germans and Russians temporarily gave Ankara a sense of security. During this fighting, Soviet attitudes toward Turkey oscillated according to the fortunes of war. First, while German armies penetrated deep into the plains of Russia, Stalin praised Ankara for its steadfast and scrupulous neutrality. However, after the victory of Stalingrad and once Soviet armies began to roll back the Germans, Moscow gradually changed its mood toward Turkey.

From mid-1941 until mid-1943, all belligerents felt that the neutrality of Turkey was in their interest. Only after Italy was knocked out of the war and the Mediterranean was cleared of the enemy did the leaders of the Grand Alliance question Turkey's neutrality. Churchill's various plans to strike at the "soft belly" of the Axis included the participation of Turkey. While the Turkish government was, in principle, ready to comply with her commitment as an ally of Britain, she viewed Russia with alarm and did not wish to jeopardize her strength. As President Inönü told Churchill, Turkey did not wish to be occupied by Germany and then "liberated" by the Soviet Union.[68]

Talks to persuade the Turkish government to reconsider its neutral position opened with Churchill's visit to Adana in January 1943, and culminated with the visit of the Turkish president to Cairo, where conversations were held with President Roosevelt and Churchill after the Teheran summit conference in November-December 1943. The Turkish view was that, should Turkey declare war or the Allied forces enter Turkey, only an adequately equipped Turkish army and air force could successfully risk the expected onslaught of the still-powerful German armies in the Balkans.[69] It was believed that without sufficient air cover no operations should be undertaken against the German-held islands in the Aegean Sea; it was feared that Istanbul, Ankara, and Izmir might share the fate of Coventry or Rotterdam should a poorly armed Turkey join the Allies.[70]

Turkish reluctance to enter the war with the Allies created some ani-

[68] See Necmedin Sadak, "Turkey Faces the Soviets," *Foreign Affairs* (April 1949): pp. 449–61.
[69] The British wished to impress Ankara by occupying, shortly after the Italian surrender, the islands of Kos and Leros of the Dodecanese Archipelago, just off the coast of Turkey. These British forces were, however, soon evicted by the Germans. See Winston S. Churchill, *The Second World War: Closing the Ring* (Boston, 1951), pp. 203–25.
[70] See Knatchbull-Hugessen, *Diplomat in Peace and War*, pp. 191–204.

mosity among Anglo-American political circles and gave rise to renewed sharp propagandistic attacks from Moscow. Turkey's every step was closely watched; for instance, the passage of twelve German vessels through the straits was strongly condemned by Britain and later exploited by the Soviets. The ships were formerly used as auxiliary war vessels, and the question was whether they should have been refused passage under the convention of Montreux.[71]

As Germany's military posture deteriorated, Turkey slowly shifted her attitude from complete neutrality to sympathetic nonbelligerence favoring the Allies.[72] Although in Teheran Stalin had supported the Anglo-American demand that Turkey should be induced to enter the war, by late 1944 Moscow preferred that Ankara stay out of hostilities; in the postwar period, they planned to exploit Turkish aloofness during the war. Pressed by the United States and Britain, however, the Turkish government broke off diplomatic relations with Germany on August 2, 1944, and interned German citizens.

At Yalta in February 1945, Roosevelt, Churchill, and Stalin discussed the revision of the Montreux convention, and the Soviet view gained support. It was agreed that the question would be taken up by the three foreign ministers at a later meeting.[73] The Yalta conference also resolved that only those powers which had fought the Axis or had declared war on Germany by March 1, 1945, should be invited to the forthcoming San Francisco conference to set up the United Nations. Thereupon, on February 23, the Grand National Assembly of Turkey passed a resolution declaring a state of war with Germany. At that time German forces were far away from the borders of Turkey. Eleven weeks later, World War II ended in Europe. The Turkish government was invited to San Francisco and became a founding member of the United Nations.

A comparison of Turkey's position during World War II with that of the Ottoman Empire in World War I is informative. In 1914 the Young Turk government allowed their country, exhausted from the Balkan wars, to be dragged into the conflict, although it had not been attacked nor was otherwise vitally involved. The position of Ankara during the critical years of 1939–44 was most delicate. For reasons of self-preserva-

[71] See chapter V below.
[72] For instance, in February, 1944, chromium exports to Germany, vital for their war industry, were suspended; Ataöv, *Turkish Foreign Policy*, pp. 120–22.
[73] See chapter V below.

33

tion, the Anglo-French Alliance had to be concluded; however, France's collapse, the danger of Soviet-German collaboration against Turkey, and Germany's advance into the Balkans and the Aegean required an ability to adapt to the shifting power positions of the belligerents. Turkish diplomacy succeeded in preserving confidence in the country without provoking either Hitler or the Soviet Union and, ultimately, in staying out of hostilities. But Turkey's caution in respecting Soviet susceptibilities proved of no avail once Moscow thought the time ripe to turn against Ankara.

The Soviet campaign against Turkey gathered full steam after Yalta, while Soviet forces were occupying Bulgaria. Moscow refused to extend the Turkish-Soviet Treaty of Neutrality and Non-Aggression signed in 1925. According to a Soviet note submitted on March 19, 1945, this treaty was no longer in accord with the new situation and needed serious improvement. Turkey was ready to discuss the details of a new treaty, but in June Soviet Foreign Minister Molotov set two conditions: a revision of the Turco-Soviet border (that is, return of the Kars-Ardahan districts handed back to Turkey in 1921) and an agreement to establish Soviet bases in the straits. The Turkish point of view, throughout these diplomatic exchanges, was that the straits convention could be revised only in agreement with other signatory powers and that Turkish territory was inviolable. Not for a moment did Ankara let itself be seduced by Moscow's offer of a strip of northern Syria, including the city of Aleppo, in return for the areas she coveted.

At the Potsdam summit conference during the summer of 1945, the question of the Turkish straits was once more discussed. It was agreed that the problem of how to revise the Montreux convention was to be treated first between the three Potsdam powers and Turkey. Consequently, both the United States and Britain submitted proposals to Ankara; these were accepted by Turkey as a basis for discussion at an upcoming conference of the signatories.[74]

By 1946 Soviet pressures and threats had increased. Now claims were raised which included an even larger slice of eastern Anatolia.[75] Commu-

---

[74] For a detailed discussion of these changes, see chapter V below.

[75] On December 20, 1945, an article was published in the *Pravda, Izvestia,* and the *Red Star* by two members of the Academy of the Georgian Soviet Republic claiming "historic rights" to areas beyond Kars and Ardahan including a considerable portion of the Turkish Black Sea coast; Kiliç, *Turkey and the World,* pp. 125–26.

nist insurgents threatened to take over Greece, and along Turkey's eastern borders, Kurdish and Azerbaijani puppet governments were established on Iranian territory under the protection of Soviet forces. On August 7, 1946, Moscow sent notes to Turkey and to the Anglo-Saxon powers containing its formal proposals concerning the replacement of the Montreux regime by one more pleasing to the Soviets. The draft provided for only "Black Sea Powers" to pass warships through the straits and suggested that Turkey and the Soviet Union should "organize joint means of defense of the Straits." It was not so much these proposals as their obvious implications which were alarming to Turkey, but her reply remained adamantly negative. At this point, the government of Ankara received diplomatic support from the United States, British, and French governments.[76]

The attitude of the West and especially of the United States had changed; the Cold War was already a fact of life. Washington realized that Soviet designs were clearly directed toward subverting Turkish resistance and that their ulterior aim was to extend Communist control over the Near and Middle East. On March 12, 1947, at a joint session of Congress, President Truman asked for and obtained assistance for Greece and Turkey on the basis of the so-called Truman Doctrine. Under this doctrine, the United States pledged to provide military and economic aid to these two countries and others in the area when threatened by communism.[77]

After Turkey's diplomatic rope-dancing during World War II, she could have reverted (even by upholding the Franco-British Alliance of 1939) to the neutralist attitude practiced under Atatürk. It was the Soviet threat, more menacing in its modern Stalinist form than the Tsarist pressures experienced in the past, that compelled Ankara to seek close political and military ties with the West. How to avoid the embrace of the Moscovite giant, whose victims in Eastern and Central Europe provided tragic precedents, was rightly conceived as a question of life and death. The threatening shadow of Moscow determined Turkey's basic policy lines during the decade following 1946 and, with a reduced emphasis, still determines it at present.

After Atatürk's rise to power and his victory in the War of Indepen-

---

[76] For the Soviet note, see Hurewitz, *Diplomacy*, vol. II, pp. 268–71.
[77] *Ibid.,* pp. 273–75.

dence, the ideological orientation of his Turkey was clearly directed toward the European West. The foreign policy of Ankara, however, was designed to establish friendly relations in every direction, including Moscow. The postwar development, nevertheless, induced Turkey to seek exclusive orientation toward the West, not only ideologically but also in foreign and military policies. In the next years, Ankara's diplomatic efforts would be devoted to attaining full participation in the complicated political, military, and economic system of Atlantic and European integration. Her ambition was not only to safeguard her national security but also to develop her socioeconomic status to match that of Western European nations.

In 1950 Turkey succeeded in obtaining admission to the Council of Europe (although her geographical location may have raised doubts about her being a "European state," as required by the statute of that organization). Earlier, as a member of the Organization for European Economic Cooperation, she had profited from Marshall Plan aid. She joined the Organization for Economic Cooperation and Development when it replaced the Marshall Plan system in 1960. Turkey experienced many difficulties, however, and had to exert herself to obtain admission to the most important of all alliances: the North Atlantic Treaty Organization.

When the NATO treaty was concluded on April 4, 1948, Turkey (and also Greece) was denied membership. The reasons for this negative attitude varied according to the powers concerned: the United States was reluctant to enter into commitments stretching into the Middle East, a region which it refused to consider "Atlantic"; Britain and France, already members of a dormant alliance with Turkey, considered another treaty superfluous; the Scandinavian members of NATO feared to get involved in a conflict in the remote areas of Asia Minor over which they had no control. But Turkey, with a clear vision of what she desired, refused to accept any substitute, such as associate membership in NATO or membership in a future Middle Eastern Defense Alliance. She wished to have direct-assistance agreements with the giant of the Western world, the United States. Other devices to obtain that much-cherished relationship, either a bilateral defense treaty with Washington or America's entry into the Franco–British–Turkish Treaty of Mutual Assistance, were unacceptable to the United States.[78]

[78] See Kiliç, *Turkey and the World*, pp. 140–59.

The Korean War gave Turkey an excellent opportunity to demonstrate her solidarity with the forces of collective security. On June 27,
1950, the Security Council invited members of the United Nations to repel the armed attack against the Republic of Korea by North Korea, aided
and abetted by the Soviet Union. The United Nations command was
established under the leadership of the United States, and Turkey offered
to send a mixed brigade (4,500 men). This was the third largest contingent, after the American and South Korean forces, to participate in the
struggle. The Turkish contingent particularly distinguished itself in combat and earned much praise.[79] In September 1951, both the United States
and Britain were ready to sponsor the accession of Turkey and Greece to
NATO. The protocol of accession entered into force on February 18,
1952,[80] and thus Turkey achieved its prime objective.

During the 1950's, Turkey entered into two more defensive alliances,
in addition to NATO, all of which will be discussed in the later chapters
of this study. The Balkan Defense Treaty was concluded with Yugoslavia
and Greece in 1953; in 1955, a Pact of Mutual Cooperation was signed
with Iraq, the so-called Baghdad Pact, which was joined in the same year
by Britain, Pakistan, and Iran. With Iraq's defection in 1958, the alliance
was renamed the Central Treaty Organization (CENTO).

Turkey wished to impress the world not only with her prudent foreign
policy but also with her allegiance to the West and Western political institutions. The attestative means used to achieve this was a voluntary
process of democratization. In 1946 the government under President Ismet
Inönü, leader of the Republican People's Party, decided to abandon the
one-party system and to replace it by genuine methods of popular democracy. The Democratic Party, formed in early 1946, participated in the
general elections of June 1946 and, despite pressures and abuses, managed to obtain 62 of 458 assembly seats.

In the face of the difficult international situation and violent internal

[79] To send a Turkish contingent (transportation and logistics were a U.S. responsibility) to the Far East may be compared with the politically motivated gesture of the
Kingdom of Sardinia to participate in the Crimean War alongside Britain and France;
this move secured for Sardinia a seat at the Paris Peace Conference of 1856 and prepared the unification of Italy under her leadership.
[80] Accession of Turkey to NATO required an amendment of the original Article 6
of the treaty which provided a definition of the territories guaranteed under the alliance.
Since the original text mentioned only the "territory of any of the Parties in Europe or
North America," "the territory of Turkey" had to be added. With Greece no such
problem arose.

criticism, President İnönü and the moderate leaders of his party sought to placate the opposition. The president himself gave up his chairmanship of the Republican People's Party to become the nonpartisan leader of the nation. A new electoral law was to secure order and legality. The next general elections were held in May 1950.

The first really free elections in Turkey gave 434 seats to the Democratic Party and 51 seats to the Republican People's Party. A peaceful transfer of power, almost unprecedented under an authoritarian regime, was carried out as a result of the popular ballot. Celâl Bayar became the new president of the republic and Adnan Menderes, the new Prime Minister.[81]

As one writer put it, the first five years of the Menderes administration made up the "honeymoon" period of the United States-Turkish relationship.[82] It was this administration that resolved to participate in the Korean War, and it was due to the endeavors of this regime that Turkey was finally admitted into NATO. Until the revolution of 1960, a web of agreements gradually tied Turkey, militarily, politically, economically, and culturally, to the United States and the countries of Western Europe. The foreign policy line pursued under İnönü was essentially continued. The ties binding Turkey to the West became stronger and relations with the United States were intensified beyond the proportions of rapport with other countries. Because of American preponderance in NATO and due to the economic assistance Turkey received from America, the influence of the United States became strongly felt in almost every field of state activity, outdistancing earlier French, British, and German influences.

Relations with the Greek neighbor were excellent until the Cyprus question introduced recurrent spells of estrangement and even of open hostility between Turkey and her partner in NATO. After the death of Stalin, the Turco-Soviet confrontation lost some of its acrimony, but a rapprochement did not occur before the 1960's.[83]

Turkey's domestic, political, and economic situation underwent drastic changes from 1950 to 1960. The general elections of 1954 yielded more seats in the Grand National Assembly to the Democratic Party. But after

[81] The Democratic victory is well described by Ahmed Emin Yalman, *Turkey in My Time* (Norman, Okla., 1956), pp. 239–51.

[82] Kiliç, *Turkey and the World*, pp. 143–47.

[83] Turco-Greek relations and the Cyprus problem, and contacts with the Soviet Union, will be discussed in chapters V and VI, respectively.

an initial spurt, the economy began to flounder. The new establishment began to display authoritarian tendencies while it was open to the violent criticism of the opposition parties. In turn, this criticism infuriated the government and persuaded it to resort to methods of repression.

The Menderes government leaned heavily on the rural population representing about 70 percent of Turkey's population—a stratum less affected by the secularization of public and private life under Atatürk and his successor. The Republican People's Party and intellectual leaders claimed that the government wished to revert to theocracy and that Atatürk's reforms were being endangered by the regime.

In the 1957 elections, despite alleged malpractices, the ruling party failed to receive a popular majority of votes, although it still retained an impressive majority of assembly seats. The political battle between the government and the opposition became even more acrimonious, and the regime used even more drastic measures to silence its opponents. Police action against demonstrators and opposition leaders, including the venerated Ismet İnönü, created utmost indignation, especially among the students, the intellectuals, and the military.

The bloodless military coup of May 27, 1960, overthrew the government, including President Celâl Bayar, and effected the dissolution of the Democratic Party. A Committee of National Union, composed of officers, took over the government. Ministers of the Menderes cabinet and President Bayar were arrested together with other leading members of the Democratic Party. Many were tried by special courts; Menderes and two of his colleagues were executed, although President Bayar's death sentence was commuted and he was later released.

The Turkish revolution of 1960 did not, however, follow the usual pattern of military dictatorships: the ruling junta not only promised to return the administration of the country to democratic rule but managed to fulfill this promise within 17 months. By January 1961, a freely elected constituent assembly was convoked to draft a new constitution, which was approved by popular referendum on July 9, 1961. On October 15, 1961, elections were held and the Committee of National Unity gave way to a government supported by a majority in the Grand National Assembly.[84]

[84] For the story of the 1960 Revolution, see Walter F. Weiker, *The Turkish Revolution, 1960–1961* (Washington, D.C., 1963), *passim;* Ali Fuad Başgil, *La révolution militaire de 1960 en Turquie* (Geneva, 1963), *passim;* Davison, *Turkey,* pp. 152–59.

Officially, the foreign policy line of Turkey throughout the revolution-ary period and thereafter remained unchanged. The message issued by the revolutionary military leaders on May 27, 1960, contained the follow-ing sentences:

We are addressing ourselves to our Allies, friends, neighbors and the entire world: Our aim is to remain completely loyal to the United Nations Charter and to the principles of human rights; the principle of peace at home and in the world set by the great Atatürk is our flag.
We are loyal to all our alliances and undertakings. We believe in NATO and CENTO and we are faithful to them.
We repeat: our ideal is peace at home, peace in the world.[85]

Nevertheless, as the 1960 revolution inaugurated a new phase in Turk-ish domestic politics, it also opened a new chapter in the foreign policies of Turkey. The character of the Turkish nation-state underwent further transformations under the impact of these events. The political upheavals on the domestic Turkish scene, the new democracy, and new political par-ties which were formed in the wake of the revolution did not fail to affect the handling of foreign relations.

Foreign politics under Atatürk and Ismet Inönü were determined by a leader and a small circle of advisers; even under Menderes, the opposition had little opportunity to express views on these subjects. Besides, the im-minence of Soviet threat in the postwar period gave no room for options other than those chosen by the government. It could thus be said that the official policy represented the unanimous will of the nation. But the easing of the pressure from the north and the exposure of Turkey to new inter-national problems as well as to new patterns of political alignment re-quired a more flexible, pluralistic approach to foreign policy to replace the "monorail" approach practiced hitherto.

After 1960, principles of national ideology became liable to conflicting interpretations and doubts. This occurred not only with the Kemalist principles of domestic politics but also with other fundamentals of na-tional policy. There was an attendant impact on foreign-policy attitudes, and the foreign policy of the government became subject to questioning, criticism, and attacks by political parties in parliament and by publicists and journalists in the press. Foreign affairs thus became a topic of public debate—an event unimaginable earlier—and this discussion could not fail

[85] Weiker, *The Turkish Revolution,* p. 21.

to influence policy-making. The end result was a movement of these concerns to the forefront of public attention.

The Turkish state and nation, although heir to many problems that burdened the Ottoman Empire, is a new member of the family of nations and, due to the peculiarities of its location and of its national substance and character, is still engaged in a search to establish its real identity. In this grand national debate, the interaction of domestic and foreign politics continues unabated.

II
Foundations of Turkey's Foreign Policy

Every state must have two kinds of policy. One is the permanent policy, which is taken as a foundation of all its actions and activities; the other is a temporary policy, followed for a period, in accordance with the requirements of the time and circumstances. The permanent policy of the Empire is to prevent any increase in the strength of Russia and Austria, which by virtue of their position are its natural enemies, and to be allied with those states which might be able to break their power and are thus the natural friends of the Empire—From a Memorandum by Ahmed Atif, the Reis Efendi, presented to the divan, 1798, quoted in BERNARD LEWIS, *The Middle East in International Affairs* (Bloomington, Ind., 1964), p. 118.

D
URING THE EXPANSIVE EPOCH OF the Ottoman Empire, its foreign policy (essentially but not exclusively military) was ideologically motivated. Its Islamic universalist ideology determined its expansionist character, the main thrust of which was directed against the infidel West. Subsequently, when missionary zeal eroded and stagnation set in, the main foreign policy objective was the preservation of the status quo by both diplomatic and military means. When, finally, the Turkish nation-state was born out of the chrysalis of the Ottoman Empire, new vistas of foreign policy unfolded—vistas prompted partly by territorial shrinkage, partly because of novel and imposed ideological ambitions. Nonetheless, the Turkish nation-state could not totally dissociate itself, in both internal and external respects, from the Ottoman heritage. After all, new Turkey, the core of the former empire, possessed a geopolitical setting reminiscent of her territorial predecessor.

The international environment in which the new Turkish state was born was no longer identical with that which existed prior to World War I. After World War II, the environment changed again. Although the looming shadow of the Russian colossus was less threatening in its Soviet reincarnation, it regained the momentum it had lost in the interwar period. In the meantime, Western Europe had suffered a loss of military and economic potentials; German and Italian power disappeared, at least temporarily. The ensuing power vacuum was filled by the American super-state when—like a *deus ex machina*—it extended its arm of assistance into the Mediterranean and the Near and Middle East.

Changes occurred within Turkey as well. Under the presidencies of Atatürk and İnönü, foreign policy-making had remained the almost exclusive privilege of a narrow leadership; the post-revolutionary period saw external politics turned into a topic for free discussion and criticism. Elite opinion scrutinized this domain, while democratization and the multiparty system exposed it to the influences of party rivalry. Although undertaken in a planned and systematic manner, the economic modernization and development of the nation also became an important subject of foreign policy considerations. Long-term foreign policy goals notwithstanding, more transient policy goals were by no means neglected; this was demonstrated by the series of Cypriote crises. Among the constant factors of external politics, however, those imposed by Turkey's geopolitical setting remained outstanding.

GEOPOLITICAL FOUNDATIONS

The features of Turkey's topography most relevant to foreign policy are the straits connecting the Black Sea with the Aegean and the mountain-ringed Anatolian high plateau. These are routes from the Russian plains to the Mediterranean and to the Persian Gulf, as well as routes in the opposite direction. Although post-World War I Turkey was stripped of the peripheral burdens of the Ottoman Empire, she inherited the essentials of its geopolitical status.

The Republic of Turkey forms the central chunk of the *ci-devant* empire. Anatolia (Asia Minor), which makes up the major part of Turkey, reaches eastward to the mountains of Kurdistan and westward to the narrow waters dividing Europe and Asia. In the west is the nodal area of Istanbul which with the straits makes up a region extremely sensitive to external political stimuli. It should be noted here that the straits are composed of the Bosporus and the Dardanelles, connected by the oblong Sea of Marmara. On the European side of the straits is eastern Thrace, the southeastern corner of the Balkan peninsula. With this territorial heritage, contemporary Turkey succeeded to many of the advantages and disadvantages of possession a highly strategical area, the defense of which coincides with her survival.

It has been said again and again that Turkey's historical role and relative political importance rest, in large measure, on her incomparable geographical location. This importance can, in fact, be explained by the geographical realities, the character of the polity exercising control over the area, and the international influences on that area.[1] The history of the Ottoman Empire and Atatürk's Turkey demonstrates the delicate interplay of political variables and geographical constants.

By taking possession of the center of a former empire, the Ottomans assumed a dominating stance from which they were able to exercise control in all directions, in the Balkans and Central Europe, the Black Sea region, the Aegean and Mediterranean, Mesopotamia and Arabia, Syria and North Africa. The Anatolian plateau looms over the critical straits area like a mountain stronghold over a rich riverside town. Whenever the straits region and the Anatolian heartland were under different political controls, the owner of the Anatolian hinterland eventually conquered the lowlands along the straits and the Sea of Marmara, including the city named after Constantine.[2] All of this may have been just coincidence. Nevertheless, it appears that an Anatolian state that did not control the "bridge toward Europe" would only be another "country of the Middle East"; united with this historic region, however, it is bound to play a more eminent role, either offensively or defensively.

During the prolonged valetudinarian period of the Ottoman Empire, possessing the straits area saved the Sublime Porte from annihilation; the Dardanelles were to be denied to any country other than the Sick Man of Europe. As we have seen (chapter I), neither Napoleon and Alexander I nor Hitler and Stalin could agree on how to divide this area between themselves, and none of them would relinquish this *pièce unique* to the other. Britain, and later Austria and Germany, intent on preserving the balance of power in the Balkans and the Near East, wished to prevent the Muscovite empire from opening the door to the Aegean and Mediterranean. Occasionally, however, moralistic considerations and less real-

---

[1] "The essence of geopolitical analysis is the relation of international political power to the geographical setting." Saul B. Cohen, *Geography and Politics in a World Divided* (New York, 1963), p. 24.

[2] After the capture of Constantinople by the Latins in 1204, the ruler of the splinter state of Nicaea recaptured the city in 1261. The Ottomans, threatening Constantinople first from the east, then again from the west, conquered it. As well, the forces of the Ankara government under Mustafa Kemal were able to regain possession of the city after the defeat of the Greeks and the Armistice of Mudanya in 1923.

istic voices urged Britain to eject the Turks "one and all, bag and baggage" from Europe.[3] The balancing posture of the tottering empire was well exploited by Ottoman diplomacy and contributed meaningfully to its preservation and nominal great power status. It was only under the lethal pressures of the German advance that Anglo-French diplomacy consented to the surrender of the invaluable treasure of the Turkish straits to Russia in 1915—an act which London and Paris were only too happy to see invalidated by the Bolsheviki Revolution.

While Constantinople was the apple of discord among the great powers, the city and the straits were considered the heart and nerve-center of the Ottoman Empire.

Mustafa Kemal's decision to transfer the capital of Turkey to Ankara, where his government was originally formed, was (as already noted in chapter I) both ideologically and geopolitically motivated. He wished to remove governmental power from a city still overshadowed by the memories of the sultanate and in many respects un-Turkish and cosmopolitan —a city where national minorities (predominantly Greeks, Armenians, and Jews) and nondescript Levantines, many of them alien subjects, dominated trade, industry, and the intellectual life. He also wanted to place the new capital in a genuine Turkish environment. Ankara is on the Anatolian plateau some 220 miles from the Bosporus and is thus strategically better protected than Istanbul. The former capital lies only 16 miles from the Black Sea and 80 to 100 miles from the Bulgarian border; its occupation by the Allies after World War I was well remembered.[4]

The dethronement of Constantinople in no way diminished its geopolitical significance for Turkey; it remained the largest city, the most important harbor, and the economic and cultural center of the country. Even with Ankara as the capital, Turkey would not be what she is without Istanbul and the adjoining European corner. She has just as much vital interest in the straits region as before; the strategical value of the site of Byzantium, guarding the sea route between the Black Sea and the Aegean, cannot be overlooked except by "blind ones."[5]

[3] From a speech by William E. Gladstone, then leader of the Opposition (later British prime minister) in the House of Commons on May 7, 1877.
[4] A Department of State Memorandum placed before President Wilson for the Paris Peace Conference in 1919 suggested that Turkey, deprived of Constantinople and the straits, should choose the town of Konya as her new capital. See Hurewitz, *Diplomacy*, vol. II, p. 41.
[5] According to Greek mythology, Byzas, the eponymous founder of Byzantium,

The old strategic axiom that points of strength are simultaneously points of weakness applies to the straits region. As guardian of the straits, Turkey can deny passage through these waterways and would do so if this were required for her safety in time of war, or by her status as a neutral. She would be ill-advised, of course, to do so in time of peace, for such an action would violate the international convention concerning the navigation of the straits. Rival powers, especially Russia, have in the past been interested in denying Turkey exclusive control over the straits and may be again in the future.[6]

European Turkey cannot be defended easily against superior land forces, even if only conventional weapons are used. Istanbul and the straits are also very vulnerable to air attack. Accordingly, possession of this strategic area conveys political and military advantages, while it simultaneously invites potential aggressors. The Anatolian part of Turkey, however, is a highly "strategical region" from the point of view of defense, and the capture of the straits would only be the beginning and not the end of a struggle.

In fact, Asian Turkey has natural boundaries and a fortress-like interior. From three sides it is surrounded by the sea: in the north by the Black Sea, in the west by the Aegean, and in the south by the Mediterranean. Eastern Turkey, protruding into the land mass of the Middle East, is protected by the mountains of Kurdistan and the Armenian highlands. The Soviet border, especially sensitive since the return of the Kars and Ardahan districts to Turkey, runs along the foot of high mountain ranges now inside Turkey. Only Hatay and the frontier along Syria are more open; the strategic Taurus and Anti-Taurus mountain walls are somewhat remote from Turkey's political boundary.

Turkey has an advantage over many other European and Asian states: her sea frontier is relatively long and much of her land boundaries run along sparsely inhabited and rugged mountainous terrain.[7] Nevertheless, not all parts of the sea frontier are equally favorable for defense: the off-

---

was told by the oracle to set up his new city "across the water, opposite to the blind ones," meaning the citizens of Chalcedon (now: Kadiköy), who failed to recognize the advantages of establishing their town on the top of the hill overlooking the natural harbor of the Golden Horn.

[6] For more detailed discussion of the straits question, see chapter V below.

[7] For Turkey's frontiers, see Lewis V. Thomas and Richard N. Fry, *The United States and Turkey and Iran* (Cambridge, Mass., 1951), pp. 11–18. For further strategical-political considerations concerning Turkey's defense, see chapter IV below.

shore islands of the Aegean Sea are mostly Greek controlled. The Greek archipelagoes in that sea, if under the domination of an enemy power, could easily prevent access to the straits and to Turkey's two principal harbors, Istanbul and Izmir. In such a case, maritime traffic to Turkey would have to be directed to her harbors at the far eastern corner of the Mediterranean, Iskenderun and Mersin. Navigation to that region would be safe, however, only if the island of Cyprus, which blocks the eastern end of the Mediterranean, were controlled by a friendly government.[8]

The maritime borders of Turkey extend over 2,590 miles (Black Sea, 955 miles; Aegean and Mediterranean, 1,230 miles; and the coastline of European Turkey, 405 miles). Her land frontiers extend over 1,910 miles (Bulgaria, 125 miles; Greece, 125 miles; Syria, 835 miles; Iraq, 235 miles; Iran, 290 miles; and the USSR, 300 miles). Thus, the ratio between coastline and land border is approximately three to two, a ratio enjoyed only by a few continental countries. At the same time, the most potentially threatening frontiers—those with Bulgaria and the Soviet Union—are only 125 and 300 miles long, respectively.

In the past, Turkey was caught between the conflicting interests of the great powers. The Ottoman Empire, at the time of its decline, was really a huge buffer state or crush zone.[9] In the interwar period, new Turkey held a balancing position which became more difficult to maintain as the power structure shifted around her borders. The balancing operation came to an abrupt end when Soviet pressures pushed Turkey into the Western alliance system. It so developed that postwar Turkey became the exposed bastion of the southeastern end of the North Atlantic Treaty Organization. A more tenuous shutterbelt[10] protects Turkey's eastern corner which protrudes between Soviet Transcaucasia and the Persian Gulf area. Here Turkey's partners in the Northern Tier are Iran and Pakistan.

Turkey's guardianship of the straits and the provisions of the Montreux convention did not prevent, however, a concentration of Soviet maritime forces in the Mediterranean; nor could Turkey's membership in NATO forestall the leapfrogging of Soviet influence into the Arab countries. In such relative isolation, her defensibility and native power potentials must be assessed in terms of her role as a member of the Western alliance system and—should Turkey one day decide to return to the

---

[8] The Cyprus problem is discussed in chapter VI below.
[9] See James Fairgrieve, *Geography and World Power* (London, 1915), pp. 329–30.
[10] Cohen, *Geography and Politics*, pp. 83–87.

stance of a neutral—as a balancer between the Western and Soviet power blocs.

The geophysical element is not the only significant factor in Turkish foreign policy. The quality of the population is a correlated agent in the shaping of such policy.

ETHNIC FOUNDATIONS

The descent of the Turks into Asia Minor divided the members of the Indo-European language family, peoples who stretch from India across Iran into the Graeco-Slavic Balkan peninsula and further into Central and Western Europe.[11] However, linguistically the Turks of Anatolia are not completely isolated. There is a sprinkling of Turkish-speaking people in the Balkans (in Bulgaria, Yugoslavia, and Rumania, and in Greek western Thrace), on the northern shore of the Black Sea, on both sides of the Caspian Sea, in Iran and Afghanistan; furthermore, in Soviet central Asia, in western China, and in parts of Siberia, compact areas are inhabited by Turkic nations or tribes.[12]

From the cultural-religious point of view, the Ottoman Turks formed the outstretched arm of Islam into Europe. As long as the Turks were inspired by a militant Islamic spirit, they could draw strength from their coreligionaries in the east, even though their linguistic-ethnic body, especially in the Balkans, was surrounded by ethnically and culturally different groups. Islamic Ottoman Turks fought their way into Europe; present-day Turkey has cut off many of her cultural ties with the Islamic east and wishes to lean on European-Western civilization. There is no other Turkish or Turkic independent nation.[13]

[11] This separation coincides with the *satem* or eastern, and the *centum* or western, divisions of the Indo-European linguistic family (with the exception of the Balto-Slavic group, which belongs to the former).

[12] A traveler, driving from southern Bulgaria eastward into central China, would be able to speak and be understood in Turkish; C. L. Sulzberger, *New York Times*, August 11, 1968.

[13] Turkish is only one of the Turkic languages. These languages belong to the Uralo-Altaic language family (together with Finno-Ugrian, Mongolian, and other linguistic groups) or, after a more recent theory, to a linguistic chain ranging from Indo-European, Uralic, to Turkic, and beyond to Mongolian and others. Linguistically, the Turkish spoken in present-day Turkey is part of the Oghuz sub-group, which includes the Azerbaijani and Turkoman dialects, as well as other dialects spoken by Turkic tribes in Iran. See the Introduction to J. Németh's *Turkish Grammar* (The Hague, 1962), pp. 13–14.

Unlike the Ottoman Empire, Turkey is a fairly homogeneous nation-state, with a fast-growing population of over 34 million (1969). It is expected that the population will reach 38 million by 1972,[14] or 45 million by 1979,[15] provided, of course, that there should be no war or other major event to prevent such an increase. It is, therefore, highly probable that by the end of the eighth decade of the current century Turkey will have a population equal to or even exceeding the current population of major West European nations such as France, Britain, or Italy.

The national and linguistic homogeneity of Turkey's population is not, however, complete. The minorities within and around Istanbul are no longer of political significance,[16] and there are Arabs in Hatay and in other parts along the Turkish-Syrian and Turkish-Iraq border.[17] But the most numerous and potentially dangerous minority by far is the Kurds in eastern Turkey.[18]

The Kurdish people are divided among four countries: Turkey, Iran, Iraq, and Syria, with sprinklings in the Trans-caucasian provinces of the Soviet Union. The exact number of Kurds living in Turkey is difficult to ascertain. According to the 1960 census, 1,848,000 declared their mother tongue to be Kurdish, and 712,000 registered Kurdish as their secondary language.[19] If the second group (the bilinguals) is added to the first, the total number of Kurdish-speaking inhabitants of Turkey could be set at 2,560,000—that is, about 9 percent of her population.[20] Other estimates

[14] According to the statement by Turgut Özal, Under Secretary of the State Planning Office; *Yeni Gazette,* October 3, 1967.

[15] Statement by Prime Minister Demirel on December 31, 1967, in Mersin; *Istanbul Bayram,* January 1, 1968.

[16] According to the 1960 census, 65,000 persons in Turkey declared their mother tongue as Greek, and 58,000 as their secondary language; 53,000 declared Armenian as their monther tongue, and 45,000 as their secondary language.

[17] According to the 1960 census, Arabic was the mother tongue of 347,000 persons, and 137,000 considered Arabic as their secondary language.

[18] For recent information on Kurds and the Kurdish question, see: Derk Kinnane, *The Kurds and Kurdistan* (London, 1964); Abdul Rahman Ghassemlou, *Kurdistan and the Kurds* (Prague, 1965); Hassan Arfa, *The Kurds: An Historical and Political Study* (London, 1966); Thomas Bois, *The Kurds* (Beirut, 1966); René Mauriès, *Le Kurdistan ou la mort* (Paris, 1967); C. J. Edmonds, "The Kurds in the Middle Eastern Scene," in Benjamin Rivlin and Joseph S. Szyliowicz (eds.), *The Contemporary Middle East: Tradition and Innovation* (New York, 1965), pp. 283–94.

[19] See *1963 Türkiye Istatistik Yıllığı* (Turkish Statistical Yearbook; Ankara, 1963), p. 63.

[20] There being no public schooling in the Kurdish language, it is assumed that many Kurds have become bilingual and, for various reasons, have found it expedient to declare Turkish as their principal language. It is less likely that Turks would acquire the use of the Kurdish language, except in mixed urban areas.

vary between 2 and 4 million; Kurdish nationalists claim even higher numbers.[21]

The Kurdish language belongs to the Iranian branch of the Indo-European linguistic family and is thus related to the Persian. No uniform Kurdish literary language exists; among the Kurds in Turkey, one of the chief dialects, the *Kirmanji*, is mostly spoken; a smaller group speaks the more refined *Zaza* (also known as *Macho-Macho*).[22]

Kurds have never been politically united and have always lived divided among different tribes. The tribal chiefs (feudal lords) bore the title *derebey* but more lately have been called *aǧa-s*; when they are also religious leaders (heads of former dervish orders), they are called *sheiks*.[23] The Ottoman sultans exercised control over the Kurds through their tribal leaders. Centralized state administration, secularization, and European attire, forcibly introduced by the Kemalist government, were even more incompatible with the accustomed life of the Kurds (who were mostly nomads or semi-nomads) than with that of other inhabitants of Turkey. Three revolts marked the Kurdish armed resistance to these measures, which were seen as threats not only to their tribal regime and traditional religious allegiances but to their social habits as well.

In 1925 Sheik Said of Palu, the hereditary head of the Nakhshbandi dervish sect, led a revolt against the republican government of Ankara in order to re-establish the traditional Islamic order. The uprising, which extended over a large area from the Dersim region to Lake Van, was suppressed within two months with the help of several Turkish divisions and was capped by the hanging of the ringleaders. In 1930 the Jelali tribe revolted on both sides of the Turkish-Iranian border; this uprising had more a nationalistic than religious character. Strategically, the Jelali wished to establish themselves on the slopes and heights of the Ararat Mountains; perhaps they hoped for assistance from Iran and from other Kurds. This rebellion was also suppressed. The last uprising occurred in 1937 in the Dersim region, in the west of the Kurdish-inhabited territory, under the

---

[21] Kinnane's estimate is 2.5 million (*Kurds and Kurdistan,* p. 2); the Soviet Encyclopaedia (1952) mentions 2 to 3 million; Ghassemlou suggests 4.6 million (*Kurdistan and the Kurds,* pp. 22–23); Bois speaks of "at least six millions" (*The Kurds*). A Kurdish nationalist leader, interviewed by this writer, set the number of Kurds in Turkey at 10 million.

[22] The other principal Kurdish dialect is the *Kurdi* (or *Sorani*), spoken in the southern Kurdistan, both in Iran and in Iraq.

[23] Those sheiks who can claim descent from the Prophet use the name *Sayyid* (or *Said*).

leadership of Sheik Sayyid Reza. The revolt was directed against Turkish administrative measures such as the establishment of gendarmerie posts and the construction of roads and schools. The rebels were again defeated and their leaders executed. All of these rebellions were followed by attempts at detribalizing and resettling of unreliable elements in the western parts of Anatolia.[24]

Although the opening of eastern Turkey to technical progress has been much slower than in the central and western parts of the country, railroads and roads have now penetrated deep into the mountainous Kurd regions, urban centers have developed, and a system of state administration and schooling has been established. Nevertheless, these means of basic modernization have not yet reached into the remote villages and hamlets, into the high valleys and pastures where many of the Kurds still live, devoted to their nomadic habitat. Nor has their attachment to their religious traditions or their loyalty to their patriarchal-feudal lords, the *ağa-s*, completely eroded. The influence of the latter is still great in many areas. After the military coup of 1960, the revolutionary government found it necessary to deport more than 50 *ağa-s* and many of their retainers to western Anatolia. This unpopular move was followed by a flare-up of violence in the east: armed assaults and brigandage became widespread. It took the government time and energy to restore a relative safety in the more outlying Kurdish areas.

No doubt the restlessness of the Kurdish minority could affect Turkey's power potentials; the overlap of the Kurdish-inhabited areas with three or four states creates special foreign policy questions.[25] Kurdish nationalism, so much strengthened by the suggestion of the Treaty of Sèvres that an independent Kurdistan be created, remains a problem which Turkish policy-makers cannot ignore.

Yet, in Turkey, the Kurdish language, tribal sentiment, and other Kurdish values are gradually losing ground against the simultaneous pressures of modernization and Turkification. The undeveloped, archaic status of the average Kurds makes them particularly vulnerable; economic and technological development, compulsory military service, and education serve the purposes of both modernizing and merging them into the Turkish ethnic stream. This assimilation is particularly favored by the

---

[24] Arfa, *The Kurds,* pp. 33–44; Kinnane, *Kurds and Kurdistan,* pp. 30–34; Kinross, *Atatürk,* pp. 451–59.

[25] See chapter VII below.

lack of religious barrier between Kurds and Turks; intermarriage is, therefore, easy and does not raise the insurmountable obstacle it does for Greeks, Armenians, and other non-Muslims in Turkey.[26] As soon as a Kurd is linguistically and educationally adapted to be a Turk, he will be accepted as such, even if he harbors a clandestine attachment to "Kurdism." Even in school he will be told that he is a Turk, a "Mountain Turk"; no discrimination is likely to take place if he shows no resistance to being assimilated. Since 1960, however, the campaigns of some political parties in districts of mixed Turkish-Kurdish population have not refrained from exploiting ethnic differences in their favor.[27]

Latent Kurdish separatism certainly impairs the otherwise well-nigh ethnic homogeneity of Turkey's population. Ethnic Turks are Muslims (if we exclude the few Gagauz immigrants—Orthodox-Christian Turks from the northern Black Sea region); even those who are religiously indifferent would not deny this identification. But not all Turkish Muslims are Sunnites. An estimated two to three million Turks in central and eastern Anatolia belong to the *Alevi* sect of Islam—that is, they are Shiites, like most of the Iranians.[28] Among the Kurds, the *Zaza*-speaking are mostly *Alevi-s;* otherwise, Kurds are also Sunnites.[29]

More than 90 percent of Turkey's population live in the Asian (Anatolian) part of the country. Anthropologically, they are of mixed descent: only a small proportion of them stem from the original Seljuks or subsequent Turkic invaders of Anatolia. Basically, they descend from those peoples who have inhabited Asia Minor since prehistoric times: the Hittites and their contemporaries, and those who are known in the Graeco-Roman period as Bithynians, Lydians, Phrygians, Galatians, Cap-

[26] Kurds have Muslim first names, as do the Turks; the surname which they had to adopt after 1934 is also Turkish. Only the language remains as an obvious criterion of differentiation between a Turk and a Kurd; as soon as they become bilingual, even this test fades away. Thus, often in the Turkish west people may be unaware whether their friends are of Kurdish descent. Hassan Arfa described in his book that Sharif Pasha, the former Ottoman minister at Stockholm, declared himself, after the end of World War I, to be a Kurd, a fact of which the family of the author was unaware, although Arfa senior was Iranian minister in Sweden and the two families were great friends; Arfa, *The Kurds,* p. 31.

[27] See chapter III, pp. 92–93, 98–99.

[28] *Alevi* Turks are also, half-contemptuously, referred to as *Kızılbaşı* (red-heads).

[29] It should be mentioned that Sunnite Kurds belong to the *Shafai* rite, whereas Turks belong to the *Hanafi* rite of Muslim theology. Ziya Gökalp wished to differentiate Turks from Kurds in Diyarbakır, his place of birth, not so much by the language they spoke as by whether they belonged to the *Shafai* or *Hanafi* followers; Ziya Gökalp, *Turkish Nationalism and Western Civilization* (New York, 1959), p. 44.

padocians, and others. The present Turkish population, no doubt, includes many assimilated Greeks and Armenians as well as descendants of deported, enslaved, or fugitive persons who were settled there during the heyday of Ottoman expansion. During the period of shrinkage of the empire, there was a considerable influx of refugees and resettlers from the Balkans, from Russian Black Sea regions, and from Mediterranean islands. Finally, the exchange of population after World War I caused half-a-million Muslims (many of them unable to speak Turkish) to settle in Turkey. Immigration from Bulgaria and Rumania also continued after World War II. All of these Muslim immigrants appear to have been easily absorbed.

Only a few Turks have central Asian or Mongolian features; physically, they are Caucasians and may claim to be Europeans, even though their language is not Indo-European but Ural-Altaic. It should not be forgotten that language is no test for differentiation between "Europeans" and "Asians." Finns, Hungarians, and Estonians also speak a Ural-Altaic language, but nobody would deny their being Europeans. On the other hand, Iranians and most of the Indians speak Indo-European languages.

Nor can the Turkish ambition to be recognized as European be negated by referring to Turkey's geographical location. The intercontinental boundary between Europe and Asia is artificial. One may rightly pose the question why the Ural Mountains or the Caucasus should be the dividing line between two continents? Toynbee points out that

the historian cannot lay his finger on any period at all in which there was any significant cultural diversity between the "Asiatic" and "European" occupants of the all but contiguous opposite banks of a Bosporus and a Hellespont that are no broader than the Hudson and not nearly so broad as the Amazon.[30]

The division of Europe and Asia along the Bosporus and the Dardanelles is the fruit of ancient Greek political and geographical imagination. Anatolia was known to the Romans as *Asia Minor,* that is, Little Asia. But the Roman geographer Strabo placed the boundary between the two continents at the Taurus Mountains near the present southeastern border of Turkey.[31] Evidently, being European is neither a geographical nor a linguistic question; it relates rather to way of life, mores, philosophy of life—in other words, to ideology.

[30] Toynbee, *A Study of History,* abridgment of vols. XVII–XX, p. 239.
[31] Cohen, *Geography and Politics,* p. 31.

IDEOLOGICAL FOUNDATIONS

The Turkish national state established by Atatürk was placed on very definite ideological foundations which were opposed to the defunct but still latently operative ideas inherited from Ottoman times.[32] The new nation-state was to be guided by principles whose acceptance and implementation were to prevent any relapse into the "old, sick, and senile"[33] world of the past.

Kemalism, as the state philosophy of the new Turkish Republic can rightly be called, wished to shake off the spirit and policies of the Ottoman past. It wanted to turn over a totally "clean leaf" of Turkish history, one unfettered by the memories and encumbrances of bygone centuries. Atatürk's ambition was also to present the international world with a Turkey that would distinctly differ from the political structure of the empire:

The Ottoman Empire, whose heirs we were, had no value, no merit, no authority in the eyes of the world. It was regarded as being beyond the pale of international right and was, as it were, under the tutelage and protection of somebody else.

We were not guilty of the neglect and errors of the past and, in reality, it was not ourselves from whom they ought to have demanded the settlement of accounts that had accumulated during past centuries. . . . I had no doubt that the whole world would finally recognize the principles which the Turkish nation had to adopt and realize at all cost for their existence, their independence and their sovereignty; because the foundations had actually and in reality already been laid by strength and merit.[34]

Islam, in the past, had instilled a "religious arrogance" in the peoples converted to it and persuaded them to be ashamed of their past;[35] Kemalist Turkey was told by her leaders to deplore the sacrifices made in pursuit of "fictitious aims" under the Ottoman rulers, who had endeavored to form "a gigantic empire by seizing Germany and West-Rome" and also by subjecting the Islamic world to their authority:

It is a generally accepted fact that among the peoples of the Orient the Turks were the element who bore the brunt and who gave evidence of the greatest

[32] For a recent general survey, see Kemal H. Karpat (ed.), *Political and Social Thought in the Contemporary Middle East* (London, 1968), pp. 297–371, especially pp. 297–305, written by the editor; Suna Kili, *Kemalism* (Istanbul, 1969), *passim*.

[33] Gökalp, *Turkish Nationalism*, p. 268.

[34] *A Speech Delivered by Ghazi Mustapha Kemal, President of the Turkish Republic*, October 1927 (Leipzig, 1929), pp. 586–87.

[35] See Burkhardt, *On History and Historians*, p. 52.

strength. . . . But in every offensive we must always be prepared for a counter-attack. . . . The continuous counterattacks from the West, the discontent and insurrections in the Mohammedan world, as well as dissensions between the various elements which this policy had artificially brought together within certain limits, had the ultimate result of burying the Ottoman Empire, in the same way as many others, under the pall of history.[36]

From the ruins of the empire, the "oppressed nation of the Orient, the innocent Turkish nation," emerged to demonstrate by deeds its worthiness to occupy its position among nations. Accordingly, the establishment of the republic "meant the creation of a new State standing on new foundations."

The primordial tenets of Kemalist foreign policy were simple: "Friendship with every nation"; "Peace at home, peace abroad"; "Turkey has no perpetual enemies"; and

the State should pursue an *exclusively national policy* and . . . this policy should be in perfect agreement with our internal organization and based on it. When I speak of national policy, I mean it in this sense: To work *within our national boundaries* for the real happiness and welfare of our nation and the country by, above all, *relying on our own strength* in order to retain our existence. (Italics added.)

This was to be a policy based on national interest, a status quo policy, with "no lust of conquest." At the same time, it was not to be an internationalist foreign policy, wishing to "embrace all mankind in perfect equality and brotherhood," for "no greater mistake could be made than that of being utopian."

Atatürk clearly envisioned the relationship that was to govern the internal organization and external foreign policy of the new republic. He said: "What particularly interests foreign policy and upon which it is founded is the internal organization of the State. Thus it is necessary that the foreign policy should agree with the internal organization." He also realized that, over and above the change in the system of government, a change was required in the mental disposition of the Turkish people.

Ideological guidance was to be derived from the principles embodied in the "Six Arrows." These principles, adopted by the Republican People's Party in 1931 and endorsed in 1937 by the constitution, were: nationalism, secularism, republicanism, populism, statism, and revolu-

[36] This and the following statements are from *A Speech Delivered by Ghazi Mustapha Kemal*, pp. 377, 378–79, and 657.

tionism (reformism).[37] Many of these principles also had foreign policy implications.

Nationalism was synonymous with Turkism and stood for a Turkish nation-state in place of Ottomanist and pan-Turkist or pan-Turanist ambitions. *Secularism* was the antithesis to Islam and suggested Western orientations. *Republicanism* was directed against the re-establishment of the sultanate and caliphate. *Populism* referred to the equality of citizens, irrespective of race, creed, language, or class origin. It was also suggestive of the democratic form of government—another step toward Westernization. *Statism* meant the concentration of the economy in the hands of the government (without, necessarily, nationalizing domestic or foreign property); it also suggested development—that is, economic and technological assimilation with the West.[38] *Revolutionism* or *reformism*[39] stood for the dynamic process of the transformation of the Turkish state and society; since this transformation was directed toward the modernization of Turkey after the Western ideal, it also implicitly carried a Western political orientation.

The underlying motivation for these principles and for the policy of Westernization was the goal of assimilating the Turkish people into the nations of developed Europe. In the eyes of Atatürk and his followers, there was only one civilization, the Western one, and they would join it "in spite of the West."[40] This doctrine distinguished between "civilization" and "culture"; the latter was to be the revived culture of the Turks, much subdued or perverted by Islamic-Arab influences.[41]

---

[37] Kinross, *Atatürk*, p. 518.

[38] "The new Turkish State will not be a world conquering state. The new Turkish State will be an economic state," said Kemal; Richard D. Robinson, *The First Turkish Republic* (Cambridge, Mass., 1963), p. 104.

[39] The original Turkish term *inkilapçilik* has the meaning of both revolutionism and reformism. Subsequently, the word was substituted by the non-Arab term *Devrimcilik,* which indicates "transformation," violent or peaceful.

[40] Niyazi Berkes, *The Development of Secularism in Turkey* (Montreal, 1964), pp. 463–65.

[41] This differentiation stemmed from Ziya Gökalp who wrote: "Culture is composed of the integrated system of religious, moral, legal, intellectual, aesthetic, linguistic, economic, and technological spheres of life of a certain nation. Civilization, on the other hand, is the sum total of social institutions shared in common by several nations that have attained the same level of development. Western civilization, for example, is a civilization shared by the European nations living on the continents of Europe and America. Within this civilization, however, there are English, German, French, etc., cultures, which are different and independent of each other." Gökalp, *Turkish Nationalism,* p. 104. See also Kemal H. Karpat, *Turkey's Politics: The Transition to a Multi-*

The original Kemalist principles underwent various new interpretations, especially under the multiparty system of the post-World War II period. While Atatürk's dicta continued to be considered indisputable dogma, conflicting interpretations were often attributed to them. Some, however, preferred to ignore these dicta and even to challenge their validity under the changed circumstances of the Second Turkish Republic.

Indeed, the constitution of 1961 presented a modified version of the six Kemalist principles by declaring in Article 2: "The Turkish Republic is a nationalistic, democratic, secular, and social State governed by the rule of law based on human rights and the fundamental tenets set forth in the Preamble."[42] The Preamble gave renewed credit to the Kemalist achievements and ideology by expressing "full dedication to the principle of 'peace at home, peace in the world' and . . . to the spirit of national independence, and sovereignty and to the reforms of Atatürk."

Accordingly, the rather vague principle of *populism* was replaced by the qualification of the republic as "democratic." It denoted a departure from the one-party system practiced during the presidential terms of Atatürk and İnönü, as well as a condemnation of the abuse of power committed in the Menderes era—abuses which finally sparked the revolution of May 27, 1960.

The principle of *republicanism* was maintained by the constitutional provision which forbade any amendment that would challenge the republican form of government (Article 9). Although the principle of *Statism* was dropped, Article 129 of the constitution set up the State Planning Organization to prepare plans for economic, social, and cultural development. The principle of *reformism (revolutionism)* was recognized in Article 153, which endorsed the "Reform Laws which aim at raising the Turkish society to the level of contemporary civilization and at safeguarding the secular character of the Republic."

The period subsequent to the revolution of 1960 was marked both by a genuine democratic multi-party system and by a freedom of expression which allowed an unprecedented range of discussion and criticism con-

---

Party System (Princeton, N.J., 1959), pp. 25–27. Because Ziya Gökalp considered Islamic beliefs (though not the Islamic political or social system) part of Turkish culture, he became in his later years estranged from Atatürk. Nevertheless, Kemalism has been greatly inspired by his writings; Uriel Heyd, *Foundations of Turkish Nationalism* (London, 1950), *passim.*

[42] The translation relies on the text of the constitution of 1961, published in the *Middle East Journal* (Spring 1962): pp. 215–38.

cerning the ideological foundations of Turkey's national, social, political, and cultural identity. We must restrict ourselves, however, to an examination of those basic concepts which have a direct or implicit bearing on the foreign relations of the Turkish state.

Ideological questions, with foreign policy overtones, centered on the following main areas: (1) the nature of Turkish nationalism and its relation to Ottoman-Islamic traditions; (2) the secular character of the Turkish state; (3) the meaning of democracy; and (4) "social" or "socialist" concepts in politics. It should be remembered that many of the arguments exchanged in the Second Turkish Republic were rooted in conceptual controversies dating back even to Ottoman times or to the period of the First Republic. The drive toward Europeanization was generally not challenged except by a few Islamic fanatics. But the meaning of Europeanization or modernization was given different interpretations by the promoters of the "Western Ideal" than by those who were more inclined to favor the "Eastern Ideal."[43]

Nationalism

The nature of Turkish nationalism, or Turkism, had been moot even before the evolution of the Turkish national state. Nationalism in Western Europe mostly developed indigenously and spontaneously and was, in a way, discovered after its birth. By contrast, Turkish nationalism was a topic of discussion in Ottoman times before a broad Turkish national consciousness developed.[44] Ottoman political innovators experienced difficulties even when trying to find a proper word to express the concept of "nation" or "nationalism" in Turkish.[45]

---

[43] Garp Mefkuresi (Western Ideal) and Şark Mefkuresi (Eastern Ideal) were originally opposed under the early Kemalist regime when some advisers believed that the Soviet form of government should be adopted; Smith, Turkey, p. 45.

[44] Ziya Gökalp thus described the search for Turkish nationalism: "The ideal of nationalism appeared [in the Ottoman Empire] first among the non-Muslims, then among the Albanians and Arabs, and finally among the Turks. The fact that it appeared last among the Turks was not accidental: the Ottoman state was formed by the Turks themselves. The state is a nation already established (nation de fait), whereas the nation of nationalism meant the nucleus of a nationality based on will (nation de volonté). With intuitive cautiousness, the Turks were reluctant, in the beginning, to endanger a reality for the sake of an ideal." Gökalp, Turkish Nationalism, pp. 73–74. The article, quoted above, was first published in 1913.

[45] Millet (see chapter I) originally had the meaning of "religious community" or "community based on religion." The Muslims (whether Turks, Arabs, Albanians, or

A common heritage of past experiences and shared traditions is one element in the forming of a nation. But for the Kemalists, who wanted to speed the development of Turkish national sentiment, eliminating the Ottoman past, or rather degrading it in the minds of the Turkish people, was the primary endeavor. Turkish youth were to be divorced from the Ottoman historic and cultural heritage. Their interest was to be focused on pre-Islamic Turkish precedents and on a language cleansed of non-Turkic grammatical forms, as evidence of Turkish national identity. School children learned of the legendary Turkish kingdom along the Orkhon River in central Asia but very little about the conquests of Otto-man sultans in three continents. For them, Turkish history began with the arrival of Mustafa Kemal to Samsun in 1919. To ignore, however, long historical heritage proved in the long run to be inconsistent with the idea of genuine nationalism.

Since 1946 the possible traditional-historical contributions to na-tional consciousness have become more acceptable, although the evalua-tion of the Ottoman past remains a controversial question between the strict Kemalist positivists and the conservative traditionalists.[46] After the revolution of 1960, the controversy became even more exacerbated when linked with a foreign policy orientation.

The "Atatürkists" cultivated a self-centered nationalism based on the solidarity of Turks living within the confines of the Turkish state.[47] Mem-bers of the Turkish nation were to be those who spoke Turkish and con-sidered themselves Turks, irrespective of origin, religion, or race. They refused affiliations with other peoples—Islamic or Turkic—and thought of themselves as members of the European community of civilized nations.

The traditionalist view of nationalism covered a broad spectrum of opinions, and its followers entered into heated polemics with their adversaries. Traditionalists extolled the glories of the Ottoman past and stressed the historical link between present-day Turkey and the empire

---

Kurds) did not form any *millet;* they were all members of the *ümmet,* the religious community of Muslims. Subsequently, the meaning of *millet* was transformed into that of "nation" and was also applied to the Turkish nation. See Berkes, *Development of Secularism,* pp. 317–19.

[46] See Bernard Lewis, "History-Writing and National Revival in Turkey," *Middle Eastern Affairs* (April 1955): pp. 101–8.

[47] Kemal H. Karpat, "Ideology in Turkey After the Revolution of 1960: National-ism and Socialism," *Turkish Yearbook of International Relations, 1965,* pp. 68–118, especially pp. 79–93. See also Ilhan Arsel, "Türklük—Islamçilik," *Cumhuriyet,* March 27, 1968.

of the sultans. Moderates among them were followers of Ziya Gökalp and accepted secular Turkish nationalism together with religious allegiance to Islam and membership in Western civilization.[48] Others, like Ali Fuad Başgil, wished to implement positivist nationalism with the transcendental religious thought of Islam.[49] There were also representatives among this group of militant Turkism or pan-Turanism with racial overtones.[50] The ideological differences between Anatolians and Rumelians were also emphasized by some writers.[51] Traditional nationalists were all strongly anti-Communist and, therefore, to a greater or lesser degree, pro-American. But some of them sought to promote greater or almost exclusive orientations toward other Islamic countries.[52]

The protagonists of the revolution of 1960 thought in terms of positivist nationalism; the constitution of 1961 was couched in a language which carefully avoided any reference to traditional nationalist sentiment.[53] This may also be considered a response to the reactionary tendencies of the Democratic Party under Menderes. In the Second Republic, the Republican People's Party together with the Turkish Labor Party operated on the ideological basis of positivist nationalism; the Justice Party inclined toward traditionalist views, moderate or more pronounced. The splinter parties also represented more or less traditional ideologies.[54]

Secularism

Secularist or antisecularist spokesmen mostly, but not exclusively, coincide with positivist or traditionalist supporters of nationalism. Their

[48] It was stated that a faction of the Justice Party claimed to be Ziya Gökalp's follower: *Cumhuriyet*, October 13, 1967.
[49] Ali Fuad Başgil, professor of law at the University of Istanbul, expanded his ideas relative to national sentiment in his book, *Din ve Lâiklik* (Religion and Secularism) (Istanbul, 1953).
[50] Most prominent among them is retired Colonel Alparslan Türkeş, leader of the Nationalist Action Party; he is an ardent Kemalist but combines his admiration for Atatürk with traditionalism and Pan-Turanist leanings. See Weiker, *The Turkish Revolution*, pp. 127–28.
[51] Rumelians are those whose birthplaces were, like Atatürk's, in European Turkey (Rumelia); Anatolian "supremacists" occasionally deny the ethnic Turkish origin of Rumelians; see Karpat, "Ideology in Turkey," p. 88.
[52] Traditionalists are more tolerant toward Kurdism (Kurdish nationalism or separatism).
[53] See Preamble (with a positivist definition of Turkish nationalism).
[54] For attitudes of political parties concerning foreign policy, see chapter III, pp. 80–99.

purpose, however, is not identical. The protagonists of secularism in Kemalist Turkey intended to free the Turkish state and society from the pervasive influences of Islam insofar as they interfered with or even prevented the formation of Turkish nationhood and the modernization of the country. While fighting the political and social grip of Islam, Kemalism developed anticlerical, rationalist, and antitraditionalist characteristics but not necessarily atheistic ideas. It contributed, nevertheless, to widespread indifference to religion in the urban centers but left Muslim devotions essentially unchanged in smaller towns and rural areas. Religious indifference, however, never went to the extent of dissuading even highly educated Turks from the observance of some Muslim rituals. In fact, despite the official secularist creed, only the progeny of a Muslim family were socially accepted as genuine Turks.[55]

With the post-1950 Democratic Party, religious devotion lost much, though not all, of its stigma as being backward or old-fashioned. The revolution of 1960 was definitely secularist, but with the Justice Party in power, the rivalry between secularist and religious forces continued to attract attention. However, the original chasm between the two national sectors considerably narrowed; it now appears that the majority of the politically conscious elite exhibit moderate or synthetizing attitudes.[56]

The constitution of the Second Republic endorsed freedom of conscience and of religion; it further stated that "no person shall be reproached for his religious faith and belief." But it forbade the exploitation or abuse of religion in order to affect the social, economic, political, or legal foundations of the state, or to secure personal or political advantages (Article 19). The contemporary debate seems to concentrate on the issue of what can be considered "exploitation" or "abuse" of religion.

The polemics concerning the role and scope of religion affect the homogeneity of Turkey's population and raise questions of international concern and interest. For instance, the open manifestations of Islamic de-

[55] While the Turkish government welcomed Muslim immigrants from the Balkans (even if they failed to speak Turkish), there was reluctance to accept the *Gagauz,* Orthodox Christian Turks, speaking Turkish, who live along the Black Sea Coast (Bessarabia and Dobrudja); Karpat, *Turkey's Politics,* pp. 62–63.

[56] Since 1949, the teaching of religion has been introduced in elementary and secondary schools, and a Faculty of Divinity created within the University of Ankara. Private schools continued and new ones have been opened for the training of *imam-s* ("men-of-religion"; that is, persons who are qualified to lead the community in prayer). After 1950 it was again permitted to read the *ezan* (call to prayer) in Arabic. All these changes were strongly opposed by secularist intellectuals. See *ibid.,* pp. 271–92.

votion revived animosities between the *Sunni* and *Alevi* believers in parts of eastern Turkey.[57] Leftist leaders were accused by the Justice Party of fomenting the *Sunni-Alevi* struggle in the interest of their party; the Republican People's Party adduced that one reason for this renewed rift has been the alleged governmental toleration of exploiting religion for political purposes.[58]

The visit of Pope Paul VI to Istanbul and Ephesus in July 1967 evoked different reactions among secularists, believers, and Islamic fanatics. His prayer in the St. Sophia (Aya Sofya) Cathedral in particular evoked contradictory, but highly characteristic, comments.[59]

The government has imposed strict controls on extremist movements like that of the *Nur*-ists[60] and, especially, on the secret *Hizb-üt Tahrir* Society,[61] which apparently attracted only the lunatic fringe of society.

The struggle continues between the two more extreme attitudes toward Islamic faith. The extreme secularists still regard Islam as an obstacle to Europeanization and economic development; the Muslim fanatics consider the secular state an enemy of Islam and incompatible

[57] During the Ottoman period, *Alevis* were frequently persecuted and discriminated against. Apparently, after several decades of tolerance during the First Republic, riots between *Sunnis* and *Alevis* have occasionally broken out in a disquieting manner. Concerning fights in the towns of Maraş and Elbistan, see *Cumhuriyet*, June 30, 1967.

[58] Ismet Inönü, chairman of the Republican People's Party, berated the revival of the artificial rift between Sunni and Alevi; *Ulus,* June 30, 1968.

[59] "The prayers pronounced aloud by the Pope in Aya Sofya caused a reaction within the Turkish people who are 99 percent Muslims. . . . He has made a great mistake and put the Demirel Government in a difficult position. It was an attitude inconsistent with our secularism." *Akşam,* July 27, 1967.

"Greetings and gratitude to you, Your Holiness," writes an editorialist in *Tercüman* (July 28, 1967). "By praying in the Aya Sofya you have saved this shrine from being a heap of stones used as a museum and returned it to its sacred nature. By so doing you have not only pleased Christ and the Holy Spirit, but the Muslims of Turkey who have been unable to obtain what you did for years." Life Senator Suphi Karaman strongly criticized those who made it possible for the Pope to pray in the Aya Sofya. Nor did he approve of the prayers performed there in protest by a group of students because this also was an act opposed to Atatürk's reforms; *Milliyet,* July 29, 1967.

[60] The *Nur*-ists (*Nurcular,* in Turkish) are the disciples of Said-i Nursi Bediüzzaman, who died in Urfa on March 23, 1960. He advocated Islamic asceticism. His followers are also militant nationalists.

[61] The *Hizb-üt Tahrir* (freely translated: Partisans of Freedom) Society aimed at setting up a theocratic state in Turkey and demanded that all relations with the "infidels" be severed. The activities of the group were allegedly directed from Beirut. Its members have been threatened with arrest and imprisonment. The president of the Ankara Court of Appeal, Imran Oktem, characterized the *Hizb-üt Tahrir* as "a handful of the mentally sick who want to set up an Islamic state in Turkey." *Milliyet,* September 7, 1968. See also *Cumhuriyet,* September 8, 1967; *Ulus,* August 22, 1967.

with its tenets. The official acceptance of either of these two postulates would reverse the present national objectives and radically alter the international status of Turkey. Radical secularization, aiming at the complete eradication of Islamic traditions, would sever all ties between Turkey and the Islamic Middle East and would, ideologically, place Turkish society in a spiritual vacuum. A victory for the religious extremist would turn Turkey into an Islamic state, an essentially non-European country, and cut short the present modernizing trends. It is highly unlikely that any of these extremist tendencies will gain the upper hand; the government, supported by the majority of the ruling and opposition parties, attempts to pursue a middle-of-the-road policy.

This policy strives to produce a working synthesis between the demand for a secular state and the spiritual needs of the people. The aim of this policy is to demonstrate that Islam as a creed is not incompatible with modernization and Europeanization. Prime Minister Süleyman Demirel expressed this moderate view when he said:

The Turkish citizen has full freedom in his religious faith and convictions. . . . Along with this principle which requires noninterference by the State in religious faith and conviction, it is also prohibited to place religion above the State, and to exploit religious feelings. Thus the principle of secularism means a *balance* between respect for freedom of conscience and the freedom of the State from all sorts of religious interferences and exploitation. It is wrong to consider secularism as a kind of atheism.[62]

To achieve the hoped-for synthesis between the requirements of Westernization and the tenets of Islam is a challenge which has not been met successfully in any Muslim country. The Turkish experiment is, therefore, of an importance which surpasses the borders of Turkey. To reconcile secularization with the Islamic faith is a task Turks can accomplish easier than Arabs, whose culture and ethos are almost inseparably welded to the creed of the Prophet.

Under the present democratic form of government in Turkey, the transformation of Islam into a spiritual dispensation severed from political, social, and economic implications is, one would hope, being achieved by the people themselves and not by the dicta of an autocratic ruler. If a synthesis is attained under such circumstances, it will be culturally absorbed and likely to last.

[62] *Cumhuriyet,* January 17, 1968. (Italics added.)

Democracy

The decision to transform Turkey into a democracy was prompted partly by foreign policy motivations. The timing was exclusively due to the international scene following World War II. There also existed general discontent in Turkey against the high-handed authoritarian rule of the Republican People's Party during the war, but as it appears, the immediate resolution was taken simultaneously with Ankara's entry into the United Nations in 1945.[63] In the past the Ottoman Empire had to endure numerous interventions by foreign powers which forced it to introduce liberal reforms; this time, the decision to liberalize was taken spontaneously.

It should be remembered that Turkey's vacillating wartime policy created misgivings among the Allies and was exploited by the Soviet Union.[64] Ankara had a feeling of isolation, of being regarded as undemocratic or "fascist" in a world which, under the Charter of the United Nations, paid lip service to democracy and human rights. At the same time, Turkey was threatened by Moscow, which then enjoyed popularity as the foremost warrior against Hitlerism, a claim which made many forget its totalitarian and terroristic methods of government.

For all of these reasons, Ankara considered it vitally important to "join the Democratic Club." The foreign policy reasons for becoming democratic were, however compelling, only one of many motivations. Did not Atatürk himself endeavor to align his country, in every respect, with the West? And did not only the hostility of the Turkish masses to his reform prevent his ruling in a democratic manner? Under the existing constitution of 1924, did not sovereignty belong to the people? It was now timely to implement "constitutional reality."

American diplomatic, military, and economic assistance, proffered from 1947 onward, was a further impetus to liberalization. In 1950, under the new electoral law, the Democratic Party won a sweeping victory that ended the ruling monopoly of the Republican People's Party. During the next ten years, however, power corrupted the new ruling

---

[63] See Karpat, *Turkey's Politics*, pp. 137–43. See also the declaration by President Inönü on May 19, 1945, during the San Francisco conference, promising to develop Turkey "in the direction of democracy." Gotthard Jäschke, *Die Türkei in den Jahre 1942–1951* (Wiesbaden, 1955), p. 45.

[64] See chapter I above.

group: they used highly undemocratic methods, stifled freedom of expression, and appeared to jeopardize Kemalist reforms. The military coup of May 27, 1960, created an interregnum lasting 18 months.

The National Unity Committee (the junta) pledged to restore democracy by arranging "just and free elections as soon as possible under the supervision and arbitration of nonpartisan and impartial administration" and to hand over the administration to whichever party won the elections.[65] Committees of university professors worked for many months until a draft could be submitted to a constituent assembly which convened on January 6, 1961. The constitution of the Second Turkish Republic was adopted by the assembly on May 27, the anniversary of the revolution, and approved by 62 percent of the voters on July 9 in a national referendum. The new constitutional-parliamentary period opened with the elections of October 15, 1961. After that event, the National Unity Committee handed over the government to a coalition of the two major parties: the Republican People's Party (whose chairman, Ismet Inönü, became the prime minister) and the Justice Party. The chairman of the military junta, General Cemal Gürsel, was elected president of the republic.[66]

The return to normalcy and democracy in Turkey was received with much satisfaction by her Western Allies who had at first feared that the military regime would remain in power indefinitely, according to the pattern experienced elsewhere. Throughout the process of redemocratization, the Turkish leaders had one eye on their Western friends, for one of the reasons why most, if not all, members of the military junta were reluctant to stay in power was their concern for Turkey's prestige and international status.[67] It was also recognized abroad that the revolution was achieved without bloodshed and that its aftermath was relatively immune to severe oppression or cruel vengeance.[68]

---

[65] Weiker, *The Turkish Revolution*, pp. 20–21.

[66] For the data see Jäschke, *Die Türkei in den Jahren 1952–61*, pp. 107–30.

[67] For the internal debates and confrontations within the National Unity Committee, see Weiker, *The Turkish Revolution*, pp. 116–53; Ergun Özbudun, *The Role of the Military in Recent Turkish Politics* (Cambridge, Mass., 1966), pp. 30–39.

[68] As recalled in chapter I, the leaders of the Democratic Party were tried on the island of Yassiada. Former Prime Minister Adnan Menderes and two other former ministers were sentenced to death and executed; other death sentences were commuted to prison terms. Many other prison sentences were passed. In the years following the Yassiada trial, the prisoners were pardoned but their rehabilitation was delayed. The condemnation of Menderes to death (he was considered a martyr by large segments of

There were two attempted military coups following the surrender of power to the civilians: the first on February 22, 1962; the second on May 20–21, 1963. The first was averted by the intervention of reliable army units; the second was easily defeated and the ringleader, Colonel Talat Aydemir, was sentenced to death and shot. The insurgents evidently wished to re-establish a military dictatorship.[69]

The parliamentary democracy operated after 1961 according to constitutional rules and usages. The uncertain coalition of the Republican People's Party and the Justice Party (considered to be the heir to the outlawed Democratic Party) did not last long; in 1962, Prime Minister Inönü had to renew his cabinet and form a new coalition with some of the smaller parties. Even so, the government was overthrown by a vote of no-confidence in the Grand National Assembly, and early in 1965, the Justice Party combined its parliamentary strength with minor political parties. The prime minister of this new coalition was Suat Hayrı Ürgüplü, the nonpartisan president of the Senate, while Süleyman Demirel, the leader of the Justice Party, accepted the post of vice prime minister.

In October 1965, general elections were held, and the Justice Party was returned with an absolute majority in the assembly. Demirel now formed his cabinet from among the members of his party. In March 1966, Cemal Gürsel was succeeded as president of the republic by another military man, the former chief of the general staff, Cevdet Sunay.

After the expiration of the constitutional term of the national assembly, general elections were again held on October 12, 1969. Once more, the Justice Party obtained a majority, and Süleyman Demirel continued to function as prime minister.

Social Justice

The Kemalist principle of statism was a kind of state capitalism. Because its purpose was to strengthen the economic power of the state, its aims were only indirectly social.

---

the people) remained a controversial issue. For details of the Yassiada proceedings, see Weiker, *The Turkish Revolution*, pp. 25–47.

[69] Özbudun, *Role of the Military*, pp. 34–35.

In the post-World War II period, the idea of democratization prevailed over all other domestic concerns; foreign aid was required, first of all, to enable Turkey to withstand Soviet aggression. Like all Western ideas, however, the concepts of social progress and social justice have taken root among the leading intellectuals, and the protagonists of the revolution of 1960 were inspired by them.

Within the National Unity Committee, members of the younger element (the "colonels") were in favor of drastic legislation to promote welfare and economic equality among the people; they particularly demanded measures to raise the standard of living of the peasantry. The constitution adopted provisions which can be considered as having placed Turkey in the category of a "welfare state."[70]

The conservative hostility to anything "social" stems from the opposition to socialism, largely identified with communism. It has been recalled how Mustafa Kemal used Machiavellian tactics against Communist infiltration at a time when friendship with Soviet Russia was of vital importance for nascent nationalist Turkey.[71] Even during the halcyon years of Turkish-Soviet relations, Communist or Socialist parties and movements remained strictly banned in Turkey.

The Soviet menace, particularly after 1945, elicited anew the traditional Turkish Russophobia, which was now combined with anticommunism. The understandable but often near-pathological suspicion and fear of Russian communism made it difficult for an average Turk to distinguish between Socialist and Communist, especially because the Soviets used both adjectives to characterize their regime.

The animosity was motivated not only by the fear of Russia; this movement was also identified with atheism, anathema to any Muslim believer. On the other hand, the idea of "social justice" is deeply anchored in Islam, and attempts have been made in Turkey to connect Socialist thought with its Islamic pattern.[72] Before the 1961 revolution and after, writers, periodicals, and institutions began to popularize social and So-

---

[70] In addition to declaring Turkey a "social" state (Art 2), chapter three of the constitution is devoted to "Social and Economic Rights and Duties." This chapter provides for the protection of the family, agricultural reform, for fair labor conditions, collective contracts and strikes, social security, compulsory education, measures to assure nourishment of the people, etc.

[71] See chapter I, p. 19.

[72] See Karpat, "Ideology in Turkey," pp. 95–99.

cialist ideas and doctrines and to support economic development and social change.[73]

The foreign policy implications of Turkey's ideological attitudes were obvious: the protagonists of Socialist thought were, to a greater or lesser extent, anti-American or anti-NATO, whereas their adversaries were more or less committed to the official Western orientation. Simultaneously, the pro-Socialist group was more lenient or directly sympathetic toward the Soviet Union and what it stood for, whereas their opponents were either vehemently anti-Soviet and anti-Communist or at least highly suspicious of the Soviets. These ideological attitudes greatly influenced the postures of political parties but did not very significantly affect the basic foreign policy line of the government either before or after the revolution of 1960.

GOVERNMENTAL FOREIGN POLICY

The official foreign policy of the Turkish republic is frequently regarded as essentially unchanging, consistent, resolute, and popularly supported.[74] For a correct understanding of the matter, it is important to distinguish between the fundamental goals of Turkish national policy and long- or short-range foreign policy objectives.

The fundamental goals of national policy, as determined under Atatürk, have not changed, although they have become better defined and updated to meet the more exacting requirements of the world today. Policies for the promotion of these goals have been modified, and from this narrower point of view, it may be rightly stated that the foreign policy of Turkey has undergone considerable change since the death of the founder of new Turkey. All of her foreign policy moves must be appraised in terms of the national interest; but the evaluation of what is in the interest of the nation is often controversial and so beset with nuances that decision-making is rendered highly individual.

---

[73] Among the periodicals which deal with problems of economic development or social and socialist ideas, the most prominent ones were *Forum, Yön, Devrim, Türk Solu, Ant;* none of them was affiliated with any of the political parties.

[74] See Kiliç, *Turkey and the World,* pp. 205–6; Nuri Eren, *Turkey Today—and Tomorrow* (New York, 1963), pp. 244–50; and "The Foreign Policy of Turkey," in *Foreign Policies in a World of Change,* eds. Joseph E. Black and Kenneth W. Thompson (New York, 1963), p. 310.

To attain national goals, in general, both domestic and foreign policies have to be employed. In the case of Turkey, in view of her far-reaching national goal, greater reliance was placed on foreign policy devices than in the case of many other nations. The fundamental national goals of modern Turkey may thus be summarized.

1. Turkey shares with all independent nations the security aim of preserving national territory, national wealth, and sovereign independence. Because of her exposed geographical location, past historical experiences, and cultural "isolation," she is more conscious of independence than most other nations—that is, more sensitive to any real or implied encroachment on her sovereignty. Atatürk believed that an uncommitted posture would best suit Turkey's security needs, but the Soviet threat, which arose in the post-World War II period, persuaded Ankara to seek politico-military alliances.

2. The republic of Turkey, unlike her Ottoman predecessor, is neither expansionist nor otherwise an imperialist power. Nor is she a static, complacent, self-satisfied country. She seeks internal power: economic-industrial, scientific, and intellectual strength, as well as military impregnability. In other words, she seeks to acquire the technological-economic strength of Western great powers such as France, Britain, or, at least, Italy. Accordingly, her economic development is not only a social need; it is primarily a source to strengthen the power of the nation as such. In this respect her paragon is Japan, and she may rightly recall the motto of the Meiji era: "Rich country for a strong army."

3. There is, however, a basic difference between the successful Japanese venture toward technological equality with the West and the Turkish ambition to modernize. The Turks, in addition to technological equality, wish to be recognized as Europeans, to be assimilated into European civilization. The superiority of the West not only in its technology but also in the form of its civilization had been acknowledged by Atatürk. It even has been alleged that merger into the European West had been sought much earlier.[75] This aspiration is now to be accomplished, as expressed by President Sunay:

[75] Turkish writers maintain that the Ottoman sultans sought close association with the West at the time of Mehmet II, the conquerer of Constantinople and of Suleyman the Magnificent, in the 15th and 16th centuries. "The fallacies are so well established that it would perhaps be difficult to convince the average Westerner that to become a part of the West has always been the driving force in Turkish history." Kiliç, Turkey and the World, p. 200.

The Turkish nation has acquired the *quality of becoming a western community of its own will and option.* . . . The Turkish community will attain the *contemporary civilization level* which it desires and deserves only through the path of wisdom and science. The Turkish nation will perpetuate Kemalism, its own ideology, with full confidence and enthusiasm and will definitely realize its aims. To think or do otherwise is to deny Turkdom and the history of reforms.[76]

Accordingly, the national policy goal of Turkey is to be, or to become, a member of the European community of nations and an equal in status, civilization, and prestige.[77] Europe, in this respect, means the Europe west of the Baltic-Adriatic line; thus, Turkey will remain separated geographically from what she considers Europe. But she will have to overcome hurdles other than those imposed by geography; historic, economic, and social-civilizational differences may, in fact, prove more problematic than geographical isolation. The goal is ambitious, perhaps over-ambitious, but Turkish commentators like to point to Russia, which has grown from semi-feudal status into a technological superpower. Furthermore, official Turkey, unlike Russia, recognized that she would be unable to achieve this grandiose purpose without Western assistance. Hence, her diplomacy is directed toward realizing these fundamental policy goals without, however, neglecting the fundamental goal of preserving national security and independence.[78]

The overextended Ottoman Empire, at the time of its decline, had to meet commitments beyond its available domestic resources. Today, it is being realized that Turkey's commitments again are overextended.[79] To comply with the commitments she has imposed upon herself, she is compelled to pursue a prudent, expedient foreign policy in which long- and short-range objectives must be subordinated to the fundamental national purpose. Hence, the primacy of foreign affairs in Turkey's politics.

The same fundamental goals of national policy were supported by

[76] *Son Havadis,* August 31, 1968. (Italics added.)

[77] "Our target is to raise our nation to the level of contemporary civilization. *This target includes everything.*" Demirel before the General Executive Board of the Justice Party on November 28, 1968; *Milliyet,* November 29, 1968. (Italics added.)

[78] Foreign Minister Çağlayangil expressed this idea before the Mixed Budget Committee of parliament on January 6, 1969, in the following manner: "Turkish foreign policy has three major principles: to serve world peace; to secure national security; to assist her economic development efforts with external aid." *Cumhuriyet,* January 7, 1969.

[79] See Lynton K. Caldwell, "Turkish Administration and the Politics of Expediency," in *The Turkish Administrator: A Cultural Survey,* eds. Jerry R. Hopper and Richard I. Levin (Ankara, 1967), pp. 30–31; mimeographed report.

the policy decision-makers throughout the history of the First and Second Turkish Republics; it was only that the range of foreign policy-makers widened considerably in the period of democratization. During World War II, the paramount concern for security overshadowed other objectives, for it was only through skillful balancing diplomacy that Turkey avoided entering a war which involved considerable risk. Because of the Soviet menace after the war, she had to throw in her lot with the West. A community of interest among the United States, the other NATO powers, and Turkey demanded the creation of a strong Turkey. Ties with the Western powers, principally the United States, also served the purpose of speeding Turkey's modernization and European acculturation.

The integral alignment with the United States and NATO, prompted by the fear of Soviet aggression and by the immense advantages of the partnership, created a somewhat shortsighted and unrealistic identification of Turkey's national interests with those of her partners; it also created an illusory belief that America would support *any* Turkish policy objective.

The traumatic effect of the revolution of 1960 induced the Turkish leadership to look more closely into the various questions of Turkish foreign policy in the light of the country's Western involvement. This disillusionment sparked by the lack of Western support in the Cyprus crisis served as another inducement to emancipate Turkey's international relations from the previous one-way policies. A partial return to the Kemalist foreign policy which recommended friendship with all neighbors was effected; this included resumption of more normal relations with the Soviet Union and closer ties with a number of Middle Eastern nations.

In the post-revolutionary coalition period after 1960, the former taboo concerning debate on foreign affairs was lifted. There followed a heated discussion between leftist and rightist groups, including publicists and academies, which concentrated on the usefulness or harmfulness of NATO membership and the special relationship with the United States. The official policy line continuously pursued by the governments of İnönü and Ürgüplü did not deviate essentially from the earlier course. Supported by almost all political parties, it remained basically pro-Western. But apart from the rapprochement with Moscow, it refused to follow the advice freely given by the Turkish Labor Party and some intellectuals who wished to promote a return to neutralism.

After the 1965 elections, the government of the Justice Party under

71

Prime Minister Süleyman Demirel did not allow Turkish ties with the West to suffer. It barred, however, any dogmatic approach and vowed to examine foreign policy issues empirically in the light of Turkey's national interest.

On the whole, it may be said that foreign affairs were conducted in Ankara in a spirit of realism and with no ideological bias;[80] the government tried to avoid giving the impression either of chauvinistic narrowmindedness or egotistic shortsightedness. This more flexible foreign policy was acclaimed by the critics of the government. They pointed out that it was wrong to adjust every step to the American line, a policy which led to the isolation of Turkey demonstrated during the Cyprus debates in the United Nations. Of course, the government spokesmen were anxious to deny that Turkey is, or ever was, an American satellite.[81]

The official foreign policy continued to be carefully scrutinized by the parliamentary opposition and by the foreign policy elite outside parliament. An often heated discussion appeared to create a split between the opposition and the government. The Turkish public-at-large should yet learn to distinguish between an exchange of opinions and a hostile break between opposing debaters. A prolonged discussion carried on within the Grand National Assembly and in the press over whether Turkey should stay in NATO resulted in a consensus that she should (only extreme leftists continued to oppose this view). Similarly, the almost permanent debate over Cyprus produced much acrimonious criticism but never a clear condemnation of governmental policy.

Once the coalition regimes came to an end, it became customary for the prime minister or minister of foreign affairs to inform and consult opposition party leaders on essential national questions (except for the leader of the Turkish Labor Party, suspected of doubtful loyalty). The

---

[80] "We will be always aware of our national interests and remember that we can never sacrifice them to our sentiments. We will be guided by our conscience and by the national interests based on reality and a rationalism and not by sentimental ideas." President Sunay's message dated August 30, 1968; Son Havadis, August 31, 1968.

[81] For instance, Abdi Ipekçi, writing in Milliyet, observed that Turkey pursued a mistaken foreign policy after World War II by abandoning a "policy of personality"; she fell into the status of a satellite and consequently lost her prestige in international politics; Milliyet, April 3, 1968. On the other hand, Demirel pointed out earlier: "In her foreign policy Turkey has traditionally acted with dignity and pride. Turkey's foreign policy is not mortgaged. It is out of the question to mortgage Turkey's foreign policy." Milliyet, September 30, 1967.

advice of Ismet Inönü, the experienced elder statesman, was often sought and highly valued by Prime Minister Demirel and his foreign minister. When Inönü declared himself in favor of Turkey's continued participation in NATO, it appeared to everybody that the case was decided: *Roma locuta, causa finita*.[82] It is, therefore, possible to consider Turkey's foreign policy as a bipartisan and, in many respects, a multi-party policy. This, however, did not exclude major debates and heated attacks on governmental actions or attitudes in international affairs. Since the electoral campaign of 1969, because of the ensuing embitterment of the domestic political climate, foreign policy bipartisanship has also suffered.

Turkey was earnestly endeavoring to improve her image in the international community; in other words, she cared for "international public opinion," whatever this expression may signify. Being extremely realistic and power-conscious, however, she placed little faith in the United Nations; she considered the United Nations' role in Cyprus constructive, though not decisive, and she often felt frustrated by the Security Council's inaction when she regarded herself in the right.[83]

Turkey is also intent on scrupulously carrying out her international commitments. In fact, her foreign policy attitude toward international questions is often too legalistic, perhaps the heritage of Ottoman times when reliance on international agreements was—for lack of physical or economic force—the defensive weapon of its diplomacy.

In Turkey, as in other parliamentary regimes, the Council of Ministers, headed by the prime minister and advised by the minister of foreign affairs, is the chief decision-making organ in foreign affairs. Under prevailing practice, whenever a question of major national interest is discussed, the president of the republic participates and presides. In such cases, the chief of the general staff also attends the meeting. Naturally, the cabinet must enjoy the confidence of the two chambers of the Grand National Assembly—the National Assembly and the Senate—for votes of confidence are required. The parliamentary debate on the annual bud-

[82] Metin Toker (son-in-law of Inönü) wrote in *Milliyet:* "It is impossible not to see that the foreign policy today is Inönü's policy in all respects. This is the best proof that the policy is a *national policy*." *Milliyet,* September 20, 1967. (Italics added.)

[83] "Although the United Nations Organization has not yet attained its objectives and has met with difficulties, this should not discourage us." Foreign Minister Çağlayangil on the twenty-second anniversary of the United Nations: *Milliyet,* October 25, 1967.

get of the Ministry of Foreign Affairs always provides an opportunity to raise questions of international concern.[84]

International agreements must be submitted to the legislature; agreements on economic, commercial, or technical subjects with a duration of less than one calendar year must be reported to the assembly, although they do not require legislative approval. "Executive agreements" may also be concluded by the executive power.[85]

Although basic policy formulations are made in the cabinet, the minister of foreign affairs and his ministry are responsible for day-to-day operational functions. These are not, however, mere routine exercises; they also involve decision-making, analysis, and faithful reporting. In fact, the Ministry of Foreign Affairs and its minister are in the position of exercising independent authority in matters of political detail and are able to influence the higher level decision-making process.

The office of the minister of foreign affairs is a political appointment, although the incumbents often are former diplomats. Thus, Selim Sarper, the foreign minister of the revolutionary junta, had served as Turkey's permanent representative to the United Nations, as ambassador to NATO, and as secretary general of the foreign ministry. His successor, Feridun Cemal Erkin, had been ambassador in Madrid and later in Paris. Prime Minister Ürgüplü chose Hasan Işık, the Turkish ambassador to the Soviet Union, as his foreign minister. When Süleyman Demirel formed his cabinet on October 27, 1965, he departed from custom by entrusting the portfolio of foreign affairs to Ihsan Sabri Çağlayangil, formerly a provincial governor and member of the Democratic Party who had been arrested at the time of the 1960 revolution.[86]

Çağlayangil's background was first considered inadequate for the post of foreign minister; the career personnel of his ministry looked upon him with suspicion, and the opposition raised a hue and cry. The new foreign minister, however, who has a good command of French, developed the best qualities of a cautious and astute statesman and diplomat. He is an indefatigable worker and the staff of his ministry has "adopted" him. He has placed emphasis on personal contacts with foreign diplomats accredited to the Turkish government, as well as with national leaders all over the world. He either received foreign visitors in Ankara—mostly his

[84] See Eren, "Foreign Policy of Turkey," pp. 312–13.
[85] Article 65 of the constitution.
[86] New York Times, October 29, 1965.

colleague foreign ministers from other countries—or traveled himself to foreign capitals. He called himself another "Evliya Çelebi," the famous medieval Turkish traveller who is known as the Turkish Marco Polo.[87]

The career officers of the Turkish Ministry of Foreign Affairs alternate between assignments abroad and service in Ankara. The continuity of Turkish diplomacy was hardly interrupted by the rise of the republic; scions of families, many of whose male members served under the Ottoman regime, continued their service for the new Turkey. The traditions of intelligence, loyalty, education, proficiency in French and English, and bureaucratic efficiency remained the hallmark of Turkish foreign service personnel. They constituted the highest level of Turkish civil service and possessed an international outlook and Western acculturation. The Turkish foreign service has not produced stars like Nicolas Politis of Greece, Paul Henri Spaak of Belgium, Charles Malik of Lebanon, or Dag Hammarskjöld of Sweden, but its ministers are trusted collaborators, keen observers, and well-informed, patient listeners. In the past they were generalists; nowadays, the Foreign Relations Academy provides a more novel, specialized training and offers languages other than English and French in the curricula.

The career personnel of the Turkish foreign ministry feel more than anyone else the compelling urge to proceed toward the fundamental goals of national policy; they are fully dedicated to this ideal, but they experience, perhaps more than those who have less contact with the outside world, the enormous difficulties facing their nation in the achievement of such a Herculean task. They are essentially Western oriented but advocate a flexible foreign policy that would keep open the avenues of rapprochement in every direction. They are fully aware of the usefulness of NATO membership and of American friendship but wish to reserve for their country a freedom of action within the limits of existing treaty obligations. They do not share the view that Western ties have turned Turkey into a satellite. They understand fully the basic differences between the character of the Atlantic alliance and the ties of bondage established between Moscow and its so-called allies. Since many of them had served at one time or another in Communist capitals, they appreciate better than some of their countrymen the advantages of a free society.

The foreign service officers of Turkey, having had experience abroad,

---

[87] *Cumhuriyet*, August 8, 1967.

are less afraid than the staff of other ministries of criticism on policy issues by opposition parties or of the interest of the general public in such affairs. They consider this a healthy development, one inevitable in the course of democratization, and wish to be adaptable in every respect to the changes inside their country and to the evolution of the international scene. They recognize, for instance, the particular importance of Cyprus for Turkey because it is an issue which, in addition to foreign policy and strategical considerations, has attracted emotional interest among the public at large.

The foreign ministry was originally organized after the model of the Quai d'Orsay and partly reorganized after World War II under the impact of international requirements and American influences. The minister is advised by the secretary general who, in turn, is aided by four assistant secretary generals for political, commercial, NATO, and administrative affairs. Political affairs are mainly handled by the five diplomatic affairs departments which represent both a geographical and functional distribution (relations with Europe and the United States; with Asia, Africa, and CENTO; with the United Nations and other international bodies; cultural relations; and protection of Turkish minorities and Turkish citizens abroad). Other departments deal with economic and trade affairs, with press and information services, and with personnel and administrative questions. There is also a Protocol Department, a Political Planning Board, and the Office of the Legal Adviser.[88]

Turkey extended diplomatic representation to countries on all the five continents. She maintains between 60 and 70 embassies or permanent delegations and over 37 consulates or consulates general. Lately, a number of new embassies were opened in Africa and consulates in many parts of the world.[89] The relative importance of the neutralist Third World has now been fully recognized, and Turkish presence in every area is considered useful. Turkey maintained diplomatic relations only with those parts of divided countries (Germany, China, Korea, Vietnam) which the United States recognized and did not follow the British and French initiatives in establishing direct diplomatic contacts with Peking.

To decide on basic questions of national security, Turkey, like the

[88] See Institute of Public Administration for Turkey and the Middle East, *Organization and Functions of the Central Government of Turkey* (Ankara, 1965), pp. 150–62.

[89] *Cumhuriyet*, December 27, 1967; report to the Mixed Budget Committee on the budget of the Ministry of Foreign Affairs.

United States, maintains a National Security Council which is presided over by the president of the republic and includes, among others, the prime minister and the minister of foreign affairs, the chief of the general staff, and the commanders of the land, naval, and air forces.[90]

Lately, Turkey also has undertaken a reorganization of her Central Intelligence Organization, the *Merkezî Istihbarat Teşkilâtı* (MIT), which operates both within and outside the country. It acts under the supervision of the prime minister's office but maintains ties with the foreign ministry and with the Turkish missions abroad.[91]

The Turkish foreign service has managed to stay outside domestic political squabbles. In view of the cleavage between opposing views on foreign policy, this has not always been an easy task. It has been made possible by recruitment and promotion systems based on the official's ability and specialization and not on the pressures of party politics.

Turkish foreign policy ultimately depends, as does her domestic policy, upon the will of the electorate. It is being realized that "national policy" is what the popularly supported government is following. As Çağlayangil told the Labor Party deputy, Behice Boran, during the budget debate:

Behice Boran called for a national policy. What is meant by a national policy? If it means a policy in keeping with national interests we are already following such a policy. If it is a question of a policy on which all political parties agree it is impossible, because the views of Behice Boran are common knowledge.[92]

Behind the façade of a quasi-consensus on national policy aims (something not necessarily endorsed by the Turkish Labor Party), there exists, however, a pluralism officially represented by the various political parties and relevant to the understanding of Turkey's relations with the outside world.

[90] Institute of Public Administration for Turkey and the Middle East, *Turkish Government Organization Manual* (Ankara, 1966), p. 85.

[91] The traditions of the Turkish intelligence service date back into Ottoman times. During and after World War II, Naci Perkel, who retired in 1953, headed the intelligence activities in a brilliant manner. Turkey allowed British and French intelligence agents to work in Turkey but under the constant surveillance of the Turkish services and in such a manner that the Soviets could never raise justified complaints. See Perkel's statement in *Milliyet*, April 8, 1968. For the MIT, see *Cumhuriyet*, August 13, 1968; *Son Havadis*, January 4, 1969.

[92] *Milliyet*, January 8, 1969.

III

Political Parties, Public Opinion, and Foreign Policy

Having enjoyed freedom, and fought for her rights and liberties throughout her history, and having achieved the Revolution of May 27, 1960 . . . the Turkish Nation, prompted and inspired by the spirit of Turkish nationalism, which united all individuals, be it in fate, pride, or distress, in a common bond as an indivisible whole around national consciousness and aspirations, and which has as its aim always to exalt our Nation in a spirit of national unity as a respected member of the community of the World of Nations enjoying equal rights and privileges . . . hereby enacts and proclaims this Constitution.—From the Preamble to the constitution of 1961.

BEFORE 1960, PARTY SPOKESMEN seldom criticized government foreign policy; it was considered unpatriotic to speak openly on such delicate questions. Since the reconstruction of the constitutional government, however, Turkey's external relations have entered inter-party discussions. The newly established Turkish Labor Party first focused public attention on such issues by expressing violent disapproval of the government's pro-NATO and pro-American foreign policy. In view of this criticism, other opposition parties could not remain silent if they were not to lose face before the electorate; the parties supporting the government were also compelled to pick up the gauntlet. The intensification of the Cyprus controversy—a genuine national issue—also contributed to turning Turkish foreign policy into a topic of contention among political parties.

Although there is a clear polarization of opinion between the extreme left and other parties regarding the basic foreign policy line, the differences in the views of the other parties are much less pronounced. It is therefore still possible to speak of a quasi-national foreign policy—that is, one supported in its main outlines by most members of the political spectrum, except for the Labor Party. It should also be remembered that there are divergent views on some issues within the political parties themselves; factions of different parties may hold opinions more similar to those held by groups in other parties.

The parliamentary-democratic process compels the government to listen to critics in the Grand National Assembly, on domestic and foreign policy. The ruling party also has to defend its stand on the foreign relations of Turkey before the electorate. Foreign issues are known to impress the urban voter more than the citizens in smaller towns and villages, except with respect to such questions as the Cyprus conflict which affect the national sentiment or religious feeling.

Political parties in Turkey demand consultation on questions of national importance in foreign affairs. "Foreign policy is not the unconditional monopoly of the ruling power," according to an opposition leader.[1] It also has been the policy of the Demirel government to seek opinions outside the leadership of the Justice Party whenever critical decisions have to be made. The views of former President Ismet Inönü, for example, were always considered most valuable, and his approval of important foreign policy decisions lent them a greater air of legitimacy.

Indeed, despite the dramatic changes in the political parties which characterized Turkish governments before and after the revolution of 1960, the continuity of foreign policy lines has remained uninterrupted.[2] This policy was never challenged, however, by any politically influential group, whether military or civilian, until the last few years. Although the probability of any significant deviation from the present position was unlikely, the government found itself under constant pressure from its own and from other parties. As a result, policy already has been modified in more than nuances. Even if the Justice Party succeeds in preserving its majority in future elections, the parliamentary strength and variety of opinion in the various political parties cannot fail to influence government policies in foreign affairs. If the present policies prove inadequate in the pursuance of Turkey's national objectives, party pressures will be instrumental in bringing about changes. The Justice Party may also be influenced by its own supporters' changing attitudes.

The potential and actual impact of the various political parties on

---

[1] Hifzi Oğuz Bekata, Republican People's Party parliamentary deputy group chairman; *Cumhuriyet*, October 1, 1968.

[2] "It is remarkable . . . that these [violent political] changes have had little discernible effect on Turkish foreign policy, which continues to be determined by the basic facts of Turkey's international position and predicament, rather than by the changing moods of internal politics." Bernard Lewis, *The Middle East and the West* (Bloomington, Ind., 1964), pp. 124–25.

foreign policy attitudes of the second republic requires that their views be examined with some care.

THE JUSTICE PARTY

The Justice Party (*Adalet Partisi*) has been generally considered the heir of the dissolved Democratic Party of Adnan Menderes; but it would be more correct to describe it as *one* of the successors to the pre-revolutionary ruling party. Only one, though important, section of the Justice Party designated itself successor to the Democrats.

The strength of the Justice Party can be assessed when we consider that, shortly after its foundation, in the 1961 elections it obtained 35 percent of the national vote. The Republican People's Party, the traditional party of Atatürk, received 37 percent. In the 1965 elections, the Justice Party won 240 of 450 seats in the assembly—the absolute majority—while the Republican People's Party took only 134 assembly seats. In the 1969 elections, the Justice Party won 256 assembly seats, and the People's Republican Party increased its share, mostly at the expense of smaller parties, to 143 seats.

The Justice Party's main stronghold is the rural and small-town area of western Turkey, including the region around the Sea of Marmara and the Aegean sector. In the cities, it enjoyed much support in Izmir and Bursa; but it also had considerable, though not overwhelming, support in all parts of the country, mostly in rural areas. Accordingly, it essentially represented the more conservative and more religious countryside in a nation where, in 1965, 74.8 percent of the population lived in communities of less than 20,000.[3]

Süleyman Demirel, the present leader of the Justice Party and prime minister of Turkey, is representative of the majority of deputies of his party: he is of peasant stock, relatively young (born in 1924), and a brilliant student who graduated in 1948 as a construction engineer. He also studied in the United States; he was director of the state hydraulic works under Menderes, lost his job after the revolution in 1960, and was returned as a deputy in the 1961 elections.[4] In 1964 he became the leader of his party.

[3] United States Agency for International Development, *Economic and Social Indicators: Turkey*, Ankara, July, 1969 (mimeographed), p. 1.
[4] In 1961 Süleyman Demirel worked as consultant with the American firm Mor-

Demirel is a pragmatic politician who declines to take doctrinaire approaches to domestic and foreign politics. He is pro-Western and in favor of private enterprise. He prefers not to express detailed views on foreign policy issues, except on such national issues as Cyprus or alignment with the West.[5] His lodestar, both domestically and externally, was moderation and peaceful settlement of conflicts, all for the sake of Turkey's greatness.[6] This sense of useful compromise helped him until 1970 to overcome differences within his party which, like every large party organization, was divided on many issues.

One leading faction within the Justice Party is known as the "sworn ones." These deputies are said to have taken an oath in early 1966 to stand by Demirel "to the end," thereby preventing either the extreme rightists or former Democrats from dragging the party into the kind of catastrophe that overtook the Democratic Party under Menderes. This group represented the intellectual elite of the Justice Party; its prominent members included Orhan Eren, Sabrı Keskim, and Aydın Yalçın, a professor of economics. The "sworn ones" (*yeminliler*) are liberal, pro-Western, and rather impatient with religious fanatics and leftists.[7]

Another faction, considered right wing or *ulema*-oriented (although they refused to be so called), was led by former minister Sadettin Bilgiç; their members were definitely conservative, vehemently anti-Communist, and skeptical of radical modernization. They were pro-NATO and pro-American, mostly because they feared socialism and communism; otherwise, they favored collaboration with other Islamic countries. This group, dominant in many local party organizations, has made the party

---

rison-Knudsen; his opponents nicknamed him "Süleyman Morrison Demirel" or "the American Stooge." See *New York Times*, November 25, 1965.

[5] He said, for instance: "Turkey joined NATO under equal conditions with 14 countries because of her *geopolitical situation*. At the base of this alliance there is the idea of perpetuating western civilization just as defending peace and independence. . . . Turkey has made her calculations according to her *national interest*." And about Cyprus: "There is no change in our view about the validity of the agreements [on Cyprus] and the Constitution. The local talks are but seeking the conditions under which the two [Greek and Turkish] communities can coexist in an *independent Republic of Cyprus*." *Milliyet*, December 2, 1968. (Italics added.)

[6] The well-known journalist Nadir Naci wrote of Demirel that his "round" policy resembles his physical build and that his "mild and improvising manner" had prevented explosions in the country; *Cumhuriyet*, November 28, 1968.

[7] See *Hürriyet*, December 3, 1968; see also the article by Aydın Yalçın, "Turkey: Emerging Democracy," *Foreign Affairs* (July 1967): 706–14.

vulnerable to charges of being reactionary or antisecularist.[8] The fact is that large masses of the party's supporters are devout Muslims who would place their confidence only in "Muslim brothers."

After the elections of 1969, some of the right-wing ministers were dropped from the cabinet, among them Sadettin Bilgiç and Faruk Sukan, the minister of the interior. On the other hand, some of the "sworn ones" were included and others became floor-leaders in the National Assembly. On February 11, 1970, 41 deputies of the Justice Party (mostly members of the Bilgiç faction) voted against the budget. The government was defeated by 224 votes to 214 and Demirel submitted his resignation; he was again, however, entrusted by President Sunay to form his third cabinet. On March 15, the new cabinet obtained a vote of confidence by a vote of 232 to 172. In June 1970, 26 dissident deputies were expelled from the party, thereby greatly reducing the majority held by the Justice Party in the assembly.

Despite this incident, party leader Demirel, Foreign Minister Çaglayangil, and many other deputies avoided siding with any one faction to maintain party unity. Except for some details, the foreign policy of the government could be considered to be that of the ruling party. In order to preserve the party's collective hold over the country's bureaucracy, the rural masses, and the military, the Justice Party's top leadership had to follow the narrow path between religious extremism and socialistic statism and, in the field of foreign affairs, between uncritical pro-Western and irresponsible anti-American attitudes. In this latter respect, their position was not too distant from that held by the top leadership of the main opposition party.

THE REPUBLICAN PEOPLE'S PARTY

Whereas the Justice Party involuntarily benefited by inheriting "the mantle of Menderes," the Republican People's Party (*Cumhuriyet Halk*

---

[8] The official emblem of the Justice Party used to be a book under the letters "A" and "P" (for *Adalet Partisi*); according to widespread rumor these letters were to stand for *Allah* (God) and *Peygamber* (Prophet) and the book for the Koran. The emblem was later changed to the symbolic white horse of Turkic mythology. The conservative faction of the party had tried in late 1961 to have one of their leaders, Professor Ali Fuad Başgıl, elected president of the republic. This move almost sparked another military intervention. See Frank Tachau and A. Halûk Ülman, "Dilemmas of Turkish Politics," *Turkish Yearbook of International Relations, 1962,* pp. 1–34.

Partisi) claims to be the only depositary of Atatürk's ideas and to be his old party. Doubtless, this party may pride itself on being *the* party of Atatürk, although all other political parties also assert their reliance on principles first announced by the founder of the Turkish republic. The prestige of the People's Party was, furthermore, greatly enhanced by its leader, the grand old statesman of Turkey and former comrade-in-arms of Atatürk, Ismet Inönü.

Inönü, still widely referred to in Turkey as "Ismet Pasha," was born in 1884 and has become, perhaps, a unique phenomenon. He once, quite correctly, remarked: "I have been a general, a diplomat, a Prime Minister, and the President of the Republic. The only thing left is to be the leader of the opposition."[9] Since that time, he has again been prime minister and again leader of the main opposition party. His position as national leader for such a long period has endowed him with an unparalleled experience in the field of foreign affairs. He possessed neither the broad national vision nor the brilliant statesmanship of an Atatürk; nevertheless, he was a man of strong convictions, though still open to changes of opinion. Extremely cautious and reserved, he was considered a man of many faces and had numerous admirers and enemies, both in his own camp and in his opponents'.[10]

As mentioned earlier, Inönü's stand in favor of NATO practically ended the nation-wide debate about the necessity and usefulness of Turkey's membership. Inönü derived the essentials of his foreign policy philosophy from his World II experiences. What he feared most for Turkey was a violent confrontation between the Soviet Union and the West. Consequently, he favored a course similar to Turkey's policy during World War II: official alliance with the West (now the United States) and a *de facto* friendship with both sides—in essence, a balancing position, which in case of danger from Moscow might engender active support from the West. After the invasion of Czechoslovakia in 1968, he declared: "We have examined the NATO agreement and announced our stand. The recent Czech events have shown how correct this stand was."[11]

[9] *Ibid.,* p. 3.

[10] Inönü was mostly criticized because of his domestic political views: the leftists reproached him for being conservative while preaching "left-of-center" principles. Others berated his "softness" on leftist influences: "The leader of the Republican People's Party did not remain faithful to any idea. Very often he has destroyed what he built up during his life": Turhan Feyzioğlu in *Yeni Tanin,* May 3, 1968.

[11] *Cumhuriyet,* October 15, 1968.

Inönü was the prototype of an empirical and pragmatic politician:

In foreign policy, the nearest dangers should be seen and warded off. We should refrain from making enemies as much as possible in our foreign policy. We cannot have a policy based on animosity. . . . We should take care not to take any hasty step that might lead to incurring the enmity of any great state.[12]

He supported the Demirel government during the Cyprus crisis of November, 1967: "There is no contradiction in my speeches. I said during the Cyprus crisis concerning this problem that the ruling power was on the right path. I have no *idée-fixe*. I support the Government where it should be supported."[13]

During the governmental crisis of March 1970, Inönü complained that he had not been consulted on foreign policy questions for over a year. In his speech before the National Assembly, he detailed his disagreement with the governmental foreign policy under three points: he objected to NATO's "flexible response strategy," as allegedly accepted by the government; he reproached Çağlayangil for not being "impartial" in the Arab-Israeli conflict; and he expressed apprehension that the government would accept a unitary state solution for Cyprus.[14]

With regard to the domestic policy platform adopted by his party in 1966, Inönü accepted the left-of-center program promoted by the agile secretary general of the party, Bülent Ecevit. It was as a result of this policy that in April 1967, 48 deputies and senators resigned from the People's Party and founded the Reliance Party, leaving their former party with only 102 deputies in the 450-member National Assembly and 32 senators in the 185-member Senate. The dissidents accused the People's Party of falling into a "dangerous leftist adventure."[15]

But Inönü's approval of the leftist philosophy is extremely cautious, and he was particularly anxious to show the differences between his party and the Turkish Labor Party by pointing to foreign policy, especially the attitude toward NATO. In fact, an editorialist wrote,

he was expressing in a skillful way, camouflaged with criticisms, that he was in agreement with the Government on important issues such as NATO, nonhostility toward the United States or the USSR and the prevention of unleashed dem-

[12] *Milliyet*, September 4, 1968.
[13] *Cumhuriyet*, January 25, 1968.
[14] *Ulus*, March 13, 1970.
[15] *New York Times*, May 1, 1967.

onstrations with "the forces of the State." When the paint is scratched further, the left-of-center is really dropped although defended superficially. He is more or less saying: "Left of center is not leftism."[16]

Bülent Ecevit intended to pour new blood into the hardened arteries of his party by introducing this new left-of-center policy. He realized that it was impossible to compete with the Justice Party in obtaining the conservative rural vote, but a program to achieve development and modernization through statism and to eliminate social injustice was likely to attract the urban masses as well as the impoverished stratum of the villages. Originally, the left-of-center concept had no foreign policy implications; there was already a "public sector" in Turkey's economy and giving preference to the widening of this sector at the expense of private enterprise could not be interpreted either as anti-Western or anti-American. The problem for Ecevit and his supporters in the party was, first, to persuade the more moderate party leaders and, second, to attract leftist intellectuals without creating an image of extreme leftism.[17]

Although Bülent Ecevit succeeded in winning over Ismet Inönü, other party leaders followed only with reluctance. Some not only refused to go along, they left the party. Ecevit was the heir presumptive to the party leadership, and it was being said that the secession of Turhan Feyzioğlu was due primarily to personal rivalry rather than principle.

The main reason for stressing the left-of-center policy was that only a "change of order" could secure Turkey's development program and save her from economic and social collapse. The advocacy of partial nationalization of foreign trade, expansion of the state ownership over industry, and other measures of a planned economy sounded, in the ears of many, similar to those ideas propounded by the Socialists. Also, the condemnation of "religious fanaticism" and talk of another war of independence smacked of the atheism and anti-Americanism so objectionable to moderates and conservatives alike. It appeared also that the leftist

[16] *Akşam*, August 9, 1968. When Inönü visited Konya and made one of his non-committal speeches, the audience shouted: "A little more to the left, Pasha, a little more to the left!" *Akşam*, March 7, 1968.

[17] Metin Toker, writing in the *Milliyet*, said: "Wise men in Turkey expected two things of Ecevit . . . : to reject the attacks on the USA together with the 'NATO No!' campaign, and to denounce the reactionary movements in Konya. . . . The Ecevit team did the second, but did not do the first. . . . As Demirel is treating the extreme right to gain votes, the Ecevit team is treating the extreme left with the same motive." *Milliyet*, August 7, 1968.

faction of the people's party clearly wished to follow the path of socialism.[18]

There seems to have been a constant tug-of-war in the party between the more extreme leftists and the moderates, the latter often referred to as the "navel-of-center."[19] Inönü evidently stood nearer to the moderates; Ecevit, who was pressured from both sides, was more indulgent with the leftists because he feared losing the support of the vocal leftist intellectuals and other dissatisfied elements. He wanted them to side with and vote for the People's Party, instead of going along with the Labor Party. He was therefore very much reserved with regard to foreign policy, even though the extreme left was vociferously anti-NATO and anti-American. As long as Inönü was active and the party leader, however, he was able to hold the party together and guide its attitude on foreign policy.

After Inönü, the most influential and nationally recognized foreign policy spokesman for the party was Professor Nihat Erim. His position, though sometimes critical of the government, did not essentially differ from the official policy. During the foreign ministry budget debate in February 1968, he said:

Turkey will follow a western-oriented policy as Atatürk showed. Turkey's legislation and state organization are proof of western civilization. *Turkey is a country which is striving to be western and taking her place in the front ranks of western civilization.*

Today there are countries which appear at first glance to be outside the blocs. But, in reality, there is no such country as a neutralist one. Here we have Egypt. . . . Today she is under the control of Russian technicians, Russian experts, Russian money. This shows that the Third World countries have to choose one of the blocs in the first serious clash.[20]

---

[18] It was, for instance, reported that Deputy Murat Önder had said that with the left of center policy his party had become a Socialist party. Muammer Aksoy and Turan Güneş (two other prominent members of the party) supported this view and announced that the party had no longer anything to do with the Six Arrows (the six principles of Atatürk) and demanded a new name for them, a demand against which Inönü very strongly reacted. *Son Havadis,* August 21, 1968.

[19] See *Milliyet,* February 8, 1968. According to *Tercüman* (August 15, 1968) there are three factions in the Republican People's Party: the navel-of-center with Nihat Erim, Kemal Satir, and others; a group which wishes to pull Turkey further left than the left-of-center; and a third group around Ecevit which is the target of the other two factions.

[20] For Nihat Erim's speech in the National Assembly, see *Millet Meclisi Tutanak Dergisi* (National Assembly Reports), February 20, 1968, pp. 441–49; *Ulus,* February 24, 1968. (Italics added.)

According to the official view held by the foreign policy experts of the people's party, Turkey should continue to participate in European organizations, including the European Economic Community. Otherwise, as long as Turkey were not threatened, neutrality would suit her interests better. The secret military agreements which accompanied NATO ties should, however, be rescinded because they were concluded without the approval of the National Assembly under Menderes and even later. Although still useful, NATO should not be used aggressively against the Soviet Union. Moscow, and also Ankara, wanted an independent Cyprus; this was the reason why Greece appeared to have abandoned attempts at unification.

Although the leaders of the Republican People's Party occasionally have said that their party was always leftist (even under Atatürk), it remains to be seen whether the left-of-center venture will attract sufficient support to provide the majority necessary to implement its ambitious program. A cabinet under the chairmanship of Bülent Ecevit is likely to follow not only a different domestic policy, but also a modified, perhaps neutralist, foreign policy. Should the more pronounced leftist orientation not produce the expected results, a more moderate party leadership might step into the place occupied so long by Ismet Inönü. In that case, even a merger with the secessionist group, the Reliance Party, cannot be excluded.

THE RELIANCE PARTY

The Reliance Party (*Güven Partisi*) was founded in April 1967 by a secessionist group of parliamentarians of the Republican People's Party under the leadership of Professor Turhan Feyzioğlu. At the time of its founding, the party had a strength of 33 deputies in the National Assembly and 15 senators in the upper chamber; its numbers were far behind those of the Justice and Republican People's Party but considerably ahead of the other splinter parties. In the 1969 October elections, the Reliance Party won 15 seats in the National Assembly and, in spite of its reduced numbers, remained the third largest political organization in the country.

The group of parliamentarians that established the new party was composed of competent politicians of the People's Party, and their average calibre stood above all other parties. Qualification did not necessarily imply popularity; the question, therefore, was whether such an intellectual group of policy-makers could attract the masses of voters.

The Reliance Party's *raison d'être* compelled it to confront both the People's Party and the ruling Justice Party to fight the leftist "adventure" of the former and to denounce the "incompetence" of the latter.[21] The heat of its struggle was directed against its mother party and socialism-communism in general. The party considered itself the only true standardbearer of Atatürkism and the only representative of the Turkish virtues of courage, freedom, and discipline.[22]

Their broadside was leveled against the People's Party, whose policy they identified with the Turkish Labor Party, as well as with socialism and communism. They enjoyed poking fun at the alleged split in the mother party and spoke irreverently of its leader, Ismet İnönü. They denied that the Turkish nation had to choose, as some leftists maintained, "between freedom and development." The party wished to promote "development in freedom."[23]

With certain reservations, the Reliance Party was pro-NATO but "put the independence of Turkey above everything." As Chairman Feyzioğlu stated,

We entered NATO to safeguard our national interests. Our staying in NATO depends on this. It is certainly impossible for Turkey to allow the Atlantic Alliance to be interpreted in a way to prevent her from defending her vital national interests. This point is also of great importance for the solution of the Cyprus problem in accordance with the vital interests of Turkey and the Turkish community.[24]

Accordingly, the official foreign policy line of the Reliance Party was in line with governmental policy, except on the Cyprus issue where it favored partition. The spokesmen for the party were generally articulate

---

[21] *Daily News* (Ankara), May 27, 1968.

[22] The symbol of the Reliance Party was the ram, associated with courage and gallantry in the Turkish folklore ("koç yiğit," ram, the hero). Among the party's slogans one finds such phrases as: "Stability, freedom, prosperity"; "To fight Communism is a national duty"; "We are tied to democracy and respectful of religious belief"; "We will defeat both poverty and Communism."

[23] *Vatan*, August 23, 1967.

[24] *Yeni Gazete*, November 15, 1968. Coşkun Kırca, another foreign affairs expert of the party, expressed the view that Turkey should seek to possess her own nuclear tactical missiles (the present stock can be used only with American approval). He referred to the rumor that Israel had developed such weaponry which might endanger Turkish cities in the east; *Milliyet*, May 2, 1968.

and appeared to be better informed on international affairs than the average representatives of other parties. This was particularly evident in the case of the four small parties whose interest in matters of international politics seemed rather limited.

SPLINTER PARTIES

The Nation Party (Millet Partisi)

This party was dominated by the personality of one individual: its chairman, Osman Bölükbaşı. A former teacher of mathematics and a graduate of Nancy University in France, he led a secessionist group from the Democratic Party in 1948 to found with others the Nation Party. Before the 1954 elections, he fell out with other leaders, and the government dissolved the party. Bölükbaşı then founded the Republican Nation Party, which later merged with the Peasants Party to become the Republican Nation Peasants Party. In the general elections of 1961, this party obtained 54 seats in the National Assembly; but Bölükbaşı, deprived of sole leadership, resigned from the party and founded yet another party under the former name of Nation Party, which he then dominated. In the 1965 elections, the party won 29 seats in the National Assembly; however, in the 1969 elections, this number was reduced to 6.

Bölükbaşı is a witty popular speaker who appeals to rustic audiences. He is considered eccentric and wayward in his ideas. His party was definitely Islamic-oriented; its vice president, Faruk Önder, was a descendant of the Mevlevi dervish chiefs of Konya. The party managed to include among its members Ibrahim Elmalı, a former Chairman of the Directorate of Religious Affairs.

In the field of foreign affairs, the Nation Party focused its attention on questions around which popular, religious emotions could be raised: Cyprus, the status of Turkish workers abroad, and the American bases in Turkey. Bölükbaşı berated the government for its handling of the Cyprus issue and for its delay in solving the question of bilateral agreements with the United States. He opposed a withdrawal from NATO, attacked the Soviet Union because of Czechoslovakia, and supported the reunification of Germany. He and his associates stressed the Muslim character of the Turkish nation and highly nationalistic sentiment.[25]

[25] Bölükbaşı for German reunification: *Milliyet,* July 28, 1967; on Cyprus: *Milliyet,*

The Nationalist Action Party (Milliyetçi Hareket Partisi)

This party stemmed from the Republican Peasants Nation Party which, in the 1961 elections, received 54 assembly seats, although in 1965 only 11 of its deputies were returned.

During 1965, control of the Republican Peasants Nation Party was seized by the "Fourteen Radicals," the junior officer-members of the National Unity Committee who had been summarily dismissed from the committee in November 1960.[26] Their leader, the one-time leading spirit of the military junta, Colonel Alparslan Türkeş, became the quasi-dictatorial chairman of the party, thereby changing its entire original character.

Although Türkeş was born in Cyprus in 1917, his family later moved to Turkey, where he embarked on his military career, part of which he served in the office of the Turkish military attaché in Washington in 1957–58. It was his voice which at 4 A.M. on May 27, 1960, announced the military take-over on the radio. Until his dismissal from the National Unity Committee, he acted as a chief adviser to General Gürsel, the chairman of the National Unity Committee and later president of the republic.[27]

The main characteristics of Türkeş' philosophy (developed in a brochure entitled "Nine Lights") is his strong national feeling,[28] which even overshadows his allegiance to Islam.[29] His opponents liked to call him Fascist or characterize his party as "national-socialist," and he certainly exercised his role as chairman in an authoritarian manner (most of his

---

November 20, 1967; on NATO: *Vatan*, April 17, 1968; on Czechoslovakia: *Ulus*, August 23, 1958; on treatment of Turkish workers abroad: *Milliyet*, September 12, 1968. See also on the program of the Nation Party speeches of Bölükbaşı: *Osman Bölükbaşı'nın Radyo Konuşmaları* (Osman Bölükbaşı's Radio Speeches) (Ankara, 1966); *Millet Partisi'nin Kıbrıs Mes'elesi ve Adalet Partisi Hükûmeti Programı Hakkındaki Görüşü* (Views of the Nation Party Concerning the Cyprus Problem and the Program of the Justice Party Government) (Ankara, 1966); *Millet Partisi Genel Başkanı Osman Bölükbaşı'nın Avrupadaki Türk İşçileri ve Kıbrıs konularında sayın Başbakana Sundukları Muhtiralar* (Memoranda submitted to the Honorable Prime Minister by the Chairman of the Nation Party, Osman Bölükbaşı, on the subject of Turkish workers in Europe and of Cyprus) (Ankara, 1967).

[26] See Weiker, *The Turkish Revolution*, pp. 131–36; Özbudun, *Role of the Military*, pp. 33–34.

[27] Weiker, *The Turkish Revolution*, pp. 125–30.

[28] Türkeş, at one time (1944), was officially arraigned for propagating Pan-Turanist ideas but was acquitted.

[29] Official announcements of the Republican Peasants Nation Party invariably ended with the phrase: *Tanrı Türkü korusun* (God save the Turk) but instead of *Allah* they use the old Turkic word *Tanrı* for God. See *C.K.M.P.nin Radyo Konuşmaları* (Radio Addresses of the R.P.N.P.) (Ankara, 1966).

former colleagues from the National Unity Committee have left the party). He was also reproached for having established a militant youth organization, the "Lions of Ergenekon," to oppose leftist student movements.[30]

The party's principal concern in the field of foreign affairs was Cyprus (where Türkeş was born) and anti-communism. In the latter area, Türkeş believed that Turkey must rely on NATO and the United States but that the alliance should be employed in conformity with Turkish national interests. He holds very strong views about Greece, which he believes has not abandoned the *Megali Idea* of establishing a Byzantine Empire on Turkish soil. He pleaded for the partition of Cyprus into two almost equal parts. The government, in his opinion, had been unable to explain the Turkish point of view to the United States; hence, many misunderstandings have arisen, such as occurred with the Johnson letter of 1964. Russia remained the archenemy, although the present Soviet empire, it is believed, will eventually disintegrate and peoples subjugated by it will regain their independence. Türkeş favored cooperation against Nasser with some Arab countries such as Saudi Arabia, Jordan, Libya, Sudan, Tunisia, and Morocco. He also blamed the government for its leniency toward leftist (Communist) students and professors. The party favored nationalization of basic industries and mining, although it felt that light industry should remain in the hands of the private sector.[31]

In the fall of 1968, Türkeş reorganized his party and renamed it the Nationalist Action Party, hoping that his violent nationalism would attract elements of other parties. In the elections of 1969, however, he suffered, together with other splinter parties, a decisive defeat. Only he was elected into the new assembly.

New Turkey Party (Yeni Türkiye Partisi)

This party is another example of a political organization which, since its foundation, has changed its leadership and departed from its original purpose and program.

The New Turkey Party was founded in February 1961 by leaders of the former Freedom Party *(Hürriyet Partisi)* to counterbalance the mo-

---

[30] *Hürriyet,* January 10, 1969. Ergenekon is the legendary Turkish homeland in central Asia.

[31] *Milliyet,* August 30, 1967; *Cumhuriyet,* January 23, 1968; *Milliyet,* April 24, 1968; *Daily News* (Ankara), May 25, 1968.

nopolistic power of the Republican People's Party (the Justice Party was also established in 1961). Founders included such prominent figures as Ekrem Alican, Aydın Yalçın, and Hikmet Belbez. Alican, the first chairman of the party, proved to be a better economist than party leader; Yalçın and others left the party (the former joining the Justice Party), and finally the leadership slipped out of the hands of Alican himself.

The New Turkey Party obtained 64 seats in the 1961 elections but managed to win only 19 in 1965, a number later reduced to 15. In the general elections of 1969, the party obtained only 6 seats in the National Assembly.

The party originally stood for liberalism and secularism; later it turned rather conservative, religiously oriented, and centered in the more backward southeast. Yusuf Azizoğlu, deputy of Diyarbakır, had become its leader. The New Turkey Party was suspected of canvassing for Kurdish votes; some of the ex-Democrats also supported it.

Understandably, the rank-and-file of the party was disintrested in foreign politics except when Turkish national or Islamic interests were at stake. They strongly supported the cause of the Cypriote Turks and the Arabs against the Israelis. Otherwise, the party basically approved the foreign policy of the government: they believed that membership in NATO was necessary for Turkey's security and that friendship with the United States was of utmost value. Relations with the USSR were to be kept on the basis of peaceful coexistence. The party strongly opposed the Turkish Labor Party and other leftists for their foreign policy views and other opinions.[32] In March 1970 Yusuf Azizoglu resigned the chairmanship of the party, officially on the grounds of ill-health, and was succeeded by Tahsin Banguoğlu, the vice-chairman.

Unity Party (Birlik Partisi)

The party was founded in 1967 by some dissatisfied elements of the Republican People's Party. Its principal protagonist was Sıtkı Ulay, former General and Commander of the Military College, a member of the junta, and minister of state in the cabinet of Cemal Gürsel. Subsequently, Sıtkı

---

[32] See *Yeni Türkiye Partisi, Seçim Beyannamesi* (New Turkey Party, Election Manifesto, 1965); *Yeni Türkiye Partisi, Tuzügü ve Programı* (New Turkey Party, Statutes and Program), 1967; *Son Baskı,* September 26, 1967; *Cumhuriyet,* March 5, 1968; *Cumhuriyet,* October 7, 1968.

Ulay fell out with the party chairman Hüsevin Balan, and it lost its intended momentum to set up a nation-wide organization.

The Unity Party was represented by only one deputy before the elections of 1969; however, in 1969 the party obtained 8 seats in the National Assembly. Its base, like that of the New Turkey Party, was in the east and southeast of Turkey. The party was openly accused of exploiting religion for political ends; allegations also have been made that it was supported by the Alevi sect or even by Kurdish nationalists. Locally, it competed with both the Justice Party and the Republican People's Party by attacking their respective political line: leftism, on the one hand, and neglect of the eastern provinces, on the other.

From the foreign policy point of view, the only interest which this party offered was its advocacy of Alevi, instead of Sunni, interests and the aid it hoped to obtain from other quarters in the Turkish frontier area— the unruly and undeveloped east where many parties tried to compete for the support of voters still unacquainted with the democratization process.[33]

National Order Party (Millî Istikamet Partisi)

The dwindling, after the 1969 elections, of all splinter parties and the election of a number of independent candidates, mostly former members of the Justice Party, gave rise to the formation of a new right-wing political party which was to rally most of the independents, discontented members of the Justice Party, and the frustrated members of splinter parties.

Necmettin Erbakan, former chairman of the national Chamber of Commerce, and a person devoted to the cause of Islam, had been elected in 1969 independent deputy of Konya. In January 1970, he and his adherents founded the National Order Party (Millî Istikamet Partisi) on a definitely rightist and ulema-oriented program.[34] Whether this new party will be more successful in future elections than other similar political groups and whether it will be able to attract more than a handful of deputies in the National Assembly, seems, in view of the continued support of the country for the Justice Party, rather unlikely. Further, the foundation of another outspoken anti-Communist and antileftist organ-

[33] Cumhuriyet, January 16, 1968; Milliyet, May 30, 1968; Vatan, September 11, 1968; Cumhuriyet, October 17, 1968.
[34] Milliyet, January 26 and 27, 1970.

ization will add to the polarization which has been already created by the activities of the only avowed political party of the Socialist left.

THE TURKISH LABOR PARTY

The Turkish Labor Party *(Türkiye Işçi Partisi)*, founded in the post-revolutionary period, did not run in the elections of 1961. It claimed to be the party of the "workers," but, in fact, the industrial workers failed to support it. Nor could it establish formal collaboration with the trade unions, though some union leaders joined as members and some even served on the executive board of the party.[35]

At the outset, the party refrained from calling itself "Socialist."[36] Marxist–Leninist programs, besides endangering the existence of the party by rendering it suspect of communism, had little appeal to Turkish workers and peasants. The party therefore attempted to present itself as one aiming to end exploitation, to promote welfare, and to protect national interests. Indeed, its platform appeared to be more nationalistic than that of any other political party. Before the 1965 elections, the main emphasis of its campaign was placed on issues of foreign politics: NATO, Cyprus, and friendship with the Soviet Union and the Communist countries of the Balkans. In domestic politics, the Labor Party wished to promote the nationalization of industry, land reform, and the elimination of foreign capital (especially in the oil industry.)[37]

In the 1965 elections, the Labor Party received about 3 percent of the national vote and won 15 seats in the National Assembly. The party has gained votes in the big cities and a few smaller towns, but its supporters have been mostly intellectuals. Only three of its deputies were members of the working class; the others were members of the intelligentsia (students, teachers, lower-level civil servants).[38]

The chairman of the party was Mehmet Ali Aybar, a former professor of law at the University of Istanbul and grandson of a pasha in the days of the Ottoman Empire. Aybar refused to permit his party to be con-

---

[35] See Kemal H. Karpat, "Socialism and the Labor Party of Turkey," *Middle East Journal* (Spring, 1967): 157–72.

[36] A new charter accepted by the party congress in December 1968 declared the Labor Party to be "Socialist." *Cumhuriyet*, December 31, 1968.

[37] The party program is explained in *Türkiye Işçi Partisi Programı* (Program of the Labor Party of Turkey) (Istanbul, 1964).

[38] *New York Times*, November 16, 1965.

sidered "Communist"; his policy was "democratic socialism," and Turkish socialism. He was affiliated neither with the Second International nor officially with the Communist camp led by Moscow. The opponents of the party, however, asserted that the Turkish Labor Party was not invited to the Zurich meeting of the Social-Democratic parties because of its Communist leanings.[39]

Although the party was engaged in a pitched battle with practically all of the other political parties, its main antagonists were the Republican People's Party and the Justice Party. The former, with its left wing and official left-of-center policy, presented the major competition for the Labor Party's endeavors to gain the sympathies of the slum dwellers and other low-income voters. The Justice Party was under fire because it happened to be the ruling party, the symbol of "bourgeois" power, and thus a tool in the hands of the "compradors" (Turkish stooges of foreign capitalists). It was also criticized for having sold out the country to the "American imperialists."[40] Aybar predicted that all of the political parties would disappear in time except for the Labor Party, the party of the laboring masses, and the Justice Party, the representative of the capitalists.

The Republican People's Party retaliated in a rather low key; it did not wish to antagonize intellectuals who were sympathetic to both the left-of-center policy of Ecevit and the program of the Labor Party. On the other hand, the Justice Party, as well as all other parties, refused to recognize the Labor Party as a Socialist party and impeached it as Communist and therefore a stooge of Moscow. Dissolution of the party by the Constitutional Court has often been proposed, but the government thus far has refrained from such action.[41]

The Turkish Labor Party suffered from the illness of all early Marxist parties—extreme factionalism. The party was split, doctrinally and tacti-

[39] Metin Toker wrote in *Milliyet* (October 26, 1967) that the Turkish Labor Party did not participate in the Socialist International in Zurich because they represented "neo-socialism, the socialism of the USA." The writer asked: "If this is not 'socialism,' then there is only one other socialism—that of the Soviet Union, to which the Turkish Labor Party must belong."

[40] *Cumhuriyet*, October 17 and 27, 1967.

[41] A Justice Party Senator denounced the Labor Party in the Senate as being a Communist Party "under a socialist mask." *Hürriyet*, January 26, 1968. On February 20, 1968, Faruk Sukan, Minister of the Interior, explained that the Labor Party was "under the instructions of Moscow." Çetin Altan shouted: "You cannot talk like this!" The Minister replied: "Have you denounced Nazım Hikmet or not?" Altan answered: "He is the greatest poet in the world." *Adalet*, February 21, 1968. (Nazım Hikmet was a Communist poet who sought refuge in the Soviet Union.)

cally, into two main factions "like a melon fallen off a donkey."[42] The extreme left was represented by Deputy Çetin Altan, who preached class war against the bourgeoisie and (though he did not admit it directly) was in favor of the dictatorship of the proletariat. Ilhan Selçuk appeared to advocate an alliance with the noncomprador bourgeoisie against imperialism. All of this sounded like the distinction between the Bolshevik and Menshevik factions, the first desirous of achieving the goal at the first stage, the second in a two-stage operation.[43]

Party chairman Mehmet Ali Aybar appeared to be intent on obtaining power by democratic processes: "Certainly we will come to power with the votes of the people. We will lose power when the majority of the people's votes are lost."[44] Aybar's definition of "free socialism" was disliked by the party's extremists, who looked upon him as an "opportunist" and "revisionist." Aybar said that some Socialist countries had achieved an infrastructure change in 50 years but had failed to change their superstructure (meaning, evidently, the Soviet Union which, since the Bolsheviki take-over, has developed a massive industrial base but failed to "democratize" its regime).

In November 1968, Aybar was able to withstand the onslaught of those party critics who joined to unseat him for his concept of a "cheerful socialism" *(güleryüzlü sosyalizm),* which was approved by the party congress in place of a "revolutionary socialism." The final declaration of the party congress announced that

the National Congress has recognized the existence of a *sui generis* socialism for Turkey and that this is derived from the fact that suprastructural institutions bear local and national character in Turkey similarly to the nature of the labor-capital confrontation. Accordingly, the National Congress embraced and endorsed the thesis launched by the Party Chairman in this ideological strife.[45]

Whereas there was disagreement in the Labor Party on domestic issues and on ideology, their foreign policy program seemed clearly set. They advocated the denunciation of the NATO convention, the departure of all American and other foreign troops, and a status of neutrality. They supported the independence of a neutralized and disarmed Cyprus; they were

[42] Ilhan Soysal's characterization of the split in the Turkish Labor Party; *Akşam,* November 25, 1968.
[43] *Akis,* October 17, 1967.
[44] *Cumhuriyet,* November 13, 1968.
[45] *Cumhuriyet,* November 22, 1968.

violently pro-Arab and anti-Israel, but evidently for reasons that differed from those of Muslim rightists. Political leaders of Turkey generally believed that the advocacy of neutralism by the Labor Party was only tactical; at present, it would be inconceivable for the Turkish masses to accept a pro-Soviet stance.

Against the United States, the Turkish Labor Party and its intellectual associates use vituperative language unusual even in the strife-torn party politics of that country. Thus Aybar said:

The second war for independence has started. The enemy is the United States of America. The USA will go out the way it came in. The passive resistence movement will be intensified. We will surround every American on duty in Turkey with a circle of hatred and vengeance. This circle will be closed in like a circle of fire around a scorpion.[46]

Or, on an earlier occasion:

The Vietnam war is not an ordinary war that concerns only the Vietnamese. It is a war against all underdeveloped nations. It will not be possible to kick the Americans out of Turkey before the United States is defeated in Vietnam.[47]

Mehmet Ali Aybar participated in the proceedings of Bertrand Russell's so-called War Crimes Trial on Vietnam that "condemned" the United States; he headed the inquiry committee and travelled to Hanoi to investigate alleged American atrocities against civilians.

The Turkish Labor Party also was violently critical of the government's development policy. It opposed Turkey's association with the European Economic Community (Common Market); Sadun Aren, a foreign policy expert of the party, predicted that "Turkey will become the Hakkâri of the Common Market."[48]

The party had on occasion opposed Soviet actions: it deplored Soviet economic aid granted to Turkey to "help the Justice Party." Aybar was also critical of Soviet intervention in Czechoslovakia: "The Soviet Union must give up the habit of acting with the superiority of a great power in her relations with other socialist countries."[49] These and other attitudes displayed by some members of the party gave rise to the suspicion that

[46] *Akşam*, November 13, 1967.
[47] *Cumhuriyet*, September 1, 1967.
[48] *Akşam*, October 7, 1968. Hakkâri is the extreme southeastern province of Turkey, considered most backward.
[49] *Akşam*, July 22, 1968.

the Turkish Labor Party sided with Peking against Moscow. As one observer expressed it: "After all, if the conservatives yell 'To Peking,' it won't hurt the Labor Party half as much as when they are told to go 'to Moscow.' Turkey hasn't been fighting China for five centuries."[50]

Generally, however, it apears clear that the Turkish Labor Party is toeing the Soviet policy line. For instance, when attending the Mediterranean Countries' Progressive Forces Conference in Rome (April 1968), its delegates signed a declaration condemning the presence of the American Sixth Fleet in the Mediterranean, a declaration which the Yugoslav Delegation refused to sign because it did not simultaneously condemn the presence of Soviet naval forces in that area. It was pointed out that such an attitude revealed that the Labor Party really does not adhere to a policy of neutralism; otherwise, it would have acted as the Yugoslav Communist Party did.[51] The penetration in force of the Soviet navy into the sensitive Mediterranean Sea "behind" Turkey raised such delicate questions that it made the position of the Labor Party even more difficult.

The Turkish Labor Party is widely considered to be a tarnished Communist organization in a traditionally Russophobic country. As such, its stand is neither facilitated by the activities of clandestine Communist groups operating in Turkey nor assisted by the existence of a Turkish Communist organization abroad, probably located in East Berlin.[52]

While the Labor Party was spreading venomous anti-American propaganda among receptive intellectuals in the main urban centers, the nation-wide anti-Communist campaign hampered its attempts to increase its membership and to enlist prospective voters. Under the former electoral law in 1965, the party had obtained only two deputy seats by direct vote; the remaining 13 seats were gained under the "remainder system" which favored small parties with adherents scattered in many regions of the country. Under the new election law, the Labor Party could not hope to achieve similar gains. It therefore tried to establish in some vilayets (provinces) a territorial base. Like other smaller political parties, it looked

---

[50] See *International Herald Tribune,* July 12, 1968.
[51] Coşkun Kırca in *Yeni Tanin,* April 19, 1968.
[52] The suspected leader of the clandestine Communist Party in Turkey was Mihri Belli. He is a graduate of Robert College in Istanbul and of the University of Missouri. He has been sent to prison several times and was thought to have turned pro-Maoist. His predecessor, Reşat Fuat Baraner, who died in early 1968, was known to be pro-Moscow; *Tercüman,* August 17, 1968.

to eastern and southeastern Turkey—an area which it considered "receptive to the left."[53]

Unlike other parties operating in those areas, the Labor Party did not refrain from exploiting "regional separatism"—in other words, Kurdish sentiment. Tarik Ziya Ekinci, the son-in-law of Sheik Sait, who led the Kurdish rebellion of 1930, was a Labor Party deputy.[54] How Turkish socialism with Marxist undertones could be inculcated into a population devoted to traditional Islam and hereditary institutions is as yet difficult to foresee.

The 1969 elections did not produce the expected results; on the contrary, they reduced the membership of the Turkish Labor Party in the National Assembly to two. The party received only 2.65 percent of the valid votes. After the electoral failure, Mehmet Ali Aybar and 13 members of the central administrative board of the party resigned in November 1969, and the Aren-faction of "scientific Socialists" gained control. Saban Yıldız, a rather colorless member, was eventually elected party chairman, and Behice Boran, a militant deputy, became secretary-general.[55] The more moderate trade-union faction, however, opposed the new leadership, and new upheavals in the party were to be expected.[56]

The activities of the Turkish Labor Party, as well as leftism generally, are ostentatious but find relatively little acceptance among wider circles; it attracted considerable notice because a relatively large segment of the press was at its disposal and because it published and spoke more than its opponents. The party's attitude is, accordingly, of some relevance even in the field of foreign politics.

PUBLIC OPINION AND FOREIGN POLICY

The elusive concept of public opinion deserves a narrower definition and more cautious evaluation in Turkey than in the countries of the West. The incongruities in education, world outlook, and scope of interests are

[53] *Akis,* December 12, 1967; *Son Havadis* (September 4, 1967) accused the Labor Party of organizing "cells" of 5 to 10 people in the east which split and proliferated "like cancer."

[54] According to *Adalet* (April 11, 1968), the Labor Party was trying "to infiltrate the tribes" of which there are several hundred.

[55] *Cumhuriyet,* November 17, 1969; *Milliyet,* December 23, 1969.

[56] At the party congress held in Çankaya (Ankara) in January 1970, an attempt was made to expel from the party both Sadun Aren and Behice Boran; *Yeni Gazete,* January 6, 1970.

much greater between segments of the population and between various regions than in the many developed nations of the world. Not only is there the usual gap between the educated and noneducated classes, there is also a cleavage between the big cities and smaller towns, and between both of these and the villages is terms of civilizational and cultural outlook and development. Finally, there is the significant and graduated difference in economic, civilizational, and cultural standards as one moves from the west of Turkey into the less developed east. These divergencies and limitations must be taken into account if one is to consider the relative quality and value of views on political matters.[57]

In Turkey, speaking generally, foreign affairs is still a stepchild of public opinion on politics. Although the end of paternalism or cabinet decision-making on such matters heralded the beginning of widespread discussion and critical evaluation in the press, in public meetings, and in the institutes of learning, the interest of the average Turkish citizen remained skin-deep. It is much deeper, though, in the big cities than in smaller towns and is hardly noticeable in the villages. The focus of interest also varies according to the level of sophistication and the topics in question. As already has been pointed out, questions affecting national feeling or religious sentiment are more likely to arouse deeper interest.

When examining public opinion on issues of foreign policy, one has to give attention to those in positions to influence ultimate or immediate decision-making. Contemporary Turkey, as other countries, has an official as well as an unofficial elite whose voice has real bearing on the conduct of external affairs.[58]

Opinions of members of the Turkish foreign policy elite may thus be summarized:[59] there is no agreement among those who in general ap-

[57] The role and scope of public opinion in Turkey is discussed by Annamaria Sternberg Montaldi, *Le rôle de l'opinion publique dans la Communauté Atlantique* (Leyden, 1963), pp. 191–210.

[58] The term official elite includes political and governmental leaders (party leaders, top officials, and higher bureaucracy); the unofficial elite comprises "opinion leaders," who are more important than others in the transmission of influence. See Elihu Katz, "The Two-Step Flow of Communication: An Up-to-Date Report on an Hypothesis," in *Human Behavior and International Politics,* ed. David Singer (Chicago, 1965), p. 295.

[59] This evaluation is based mainly on personal impressions gained by this writer from interviews conducted in 1965 and 1968 with members of the official and unofficial elite in Turkey whose anonymity has to be safeguarded. It is, of course, realized that such a presentation does not amount to a detailed public-opinion analysis which could not have been achieved. It is, nevertheless, believed that, despite its inevitable shortcomings, the analysis as submitted will contribute to the elucidation of elite opinion.

proved pro-Western orientation and modernization about whether Turkish foreign policy has changed since 1960. More conservative spokesmen think that nothing really has changed, except that the government now has to be more considerate of the wishes and proposals of the political parties. As to the policy of rapprochement toward the Soviet Union, they remark that the Soviets first approached Turkey, not vice versa.

The prevailing view, however, is that Turkish foreign policy has changed since 1960. Members of the elite who rely on this opinion submit that the revolution of 1960 was more a revolution of the mind than of the political body. Since then the social aspect of politics has been emphasized; the new constitution, in fact, describes Turkey as a social (welfare) state. Economic development has become perhaps the most important aspect of Turkish politics, and its achievement is, to a great measure, a foreign policy question. Development renders Turkey dependent on the outside world and raises the Western and Eastern alignment options. Some respondents pointed out that peasants do not understand foreign policy, except in such occurrences as the killing of Turks in Cyprus. For an even smaller number of interviewees, the cardinal question was how to implement development without infringing on democracy. Education is felt to be the answer—but "we cannot wait a thousand years!"

Highly divergent views were expressed on individual foreign policy issues. Although these views represented a broad spectrum of elite opinion, certain definite patterns could be discerned:

1. The liberal, pro-Western spokesmen were more or less in agreement with the main line of governmental policy, although critical on certain specific issues. On the grand debate concerning participation in NATO, a debate which ceaselessly continues, they asserted that the alliance was a necessity for Turkey. Many agreed that a greater flexibility was needed in the handling of Turkey's relations with foreign powers—yet a flexibility not incompatible with the Western alliance. Also, NATO ties needed to be revised, as did the many secret, so-called bilateral, agreements concluded with the United States.

After 1960 Turkey discovered that she was the last country still to be engaged fully in the Cold War when other members of NATO had, to a greater or lesser extent, normalized their relations with the Soviet camp. It was necessary, she felt, to broaden good relations by seeking better contacts with uncommitted countries and by accepting Soviet offers for a mutual relaxation of tensions. There were a number of areas where friction developed with the United States: disillusionment over American attitudes concerning Cyprus and resentment over the exclusive jurisdiction exercised by the American forces within their bases. Nor should we forget the differences between the Turkish and American temperament and psychology which were not always conducive to cooperation. Yet, these altercations were of a secondary order and could be eliminated.

The liberal, pro-NATO elite, however, was split to a certain extent on the Cyprus and Arab-Israeli conflicts. Some felt that Turkey should have insisted from the beginning on a partition of the island as the only satisfactory way to settle the question and re-establish good relations with Greece. With regard to the Arab–Israeli confrontation, they agreed that Turkey should show sympathies toward the Arabs, but otherwise remain neutral.

A rather tiny minority expressed a dissident opinion about Cyprus. Turkish contentions about the island were either unfounded or highly exaggerated. The 20 percent Turkish population should not try to impose its will on the minority of Greeks. Would, for example, the 20 percent Greek, Armenian, and Jewish population in Istanbul be allowed to consider themselves a community and attempt to claim a status of equality with the Turkish majority? With regard to the Middle Eastern conflict, a somewhat larger number of respondents maintained that "Turkish hearts are with Israel; we have common interests with Israel." But it was neither possible nor wise to declare such a view openly because Arab sensitivities were not to be hurt.

2. A reformist, slightly leftist segment of opinion was much more reserved about NATO and the American partnership. It was felt that Turkey should reduce her participation in NATO and disengage herself from the United States. At present, she has completely delivered herself to America; the 50 secret agreements have given the United States too many rights that impinge on Turkish sovereignty. Turkey should ease her involvement as France did and should not tolerate an alliance which operates against her national interest, as was demonstrated by the American opposition to her Cyprus policy. Some added that American friendship was destroyed because of Cyprus (citing the Johnson letter of 1964). The United States did not trust Turkey but did trust Greece; Turkey for Americans was a *quantité négligeable:* every schoolboy in the United States knew something about Plato but nothing of Turkey.

Turkey's national interest required friendship with the Arab countries.

Annexation of Cyprus by Greece would tilt the status quo in favor of Greece. Turkey was not the Ottoman Empire and Cyprus was not the Crete which was separated piecemeal from the empire and finally incorporated into Greece. Complete autonomy on a federal basis must be secured for the Cypriote Turks.

Turkey must be developed and assistance must be sought from every source, including Moscow. In order to speed development, more *dirigisme* and planning were required and the public sector was to be developed; the private sector was selfish, subservient to American interests, as was the government, which had no proper understanding of how to modernize in an efficient manner. These interviewees sometimes hinted that Soviet methods of industrialization should be studied.

3. According to the leftist (Socialist) and extreme leftist views, it was either questioned or else denied outright that Turkey needed NATO or CENTO. By the time Truman enunciated his doctrine in 1947, the worst threat to Turkey was over. When Turkey really needed defending, at Yalta and Potsdam, she was abandoned. NATO isolated her from her neighbors in the Balkans and in Asia. Turkey had failed to re-establish friendly ties with the Soviet Union when other NATO countries already had come to terms with Moscow. Turkish national interest did not coincide with American interest. Turkey's international interests were limited in scope and by geography and, therefore, were incongruent with the world-wide interests which the United States had to safeguard. To link Turkey with the American defense system could involve Turkey in hostilities in which her interests were not at stake; in view of her proximity to the Soviet Union and the presence of American bases on her territory, she could suffer annihilation within a few minutes. Therefore, these bases must be dismantled and the NATO alliance denounced.

United States and other Western aid was directed to the support of the private sector. For Turkey the government-to-government economic assistance provided by the Soviet Union was preferable. The United States could not grant such assistance because Washington does not carry on trade as Moscow does. Furthermore, the Soviet Union will be repaid by the delivery of Turkish products from the plants set up by its assistance and not on a monetary basis.

The extreme leftist argument declared that the United States had put an end to Turkey's independence, just as Germany did in World War I. The end product of both the moderate and extreme leftist arguments was the same: Turkey must become a neutralist, uncommitted country; all alliances with the West have to be abandoned.

With regard to Cyprus, the extreme leftists opposed what they called the "NATO solution" for the island. They demanded a fully neutralized, demilitarized Cyprus under the guarantee of the great powers, including the Soviet Union. They also were vehemently anti-Israeli. They sided with the Arabs, not for religious reasons, but because the Israelis were, in their opinion, American stooges.

4. The rightist and extreme rightist (Islam-oriented) opinions were xenophobic. They did favor NATO and American support but for reasons of Turkish self-interest and fear of communism. They were, however, less interested in, or indifferent to, economic development; they were more eager to achieve an internal spiritual rejuvenation of the people, a return to the time-honored Turkish and Islamic virtues. They wished to expand Turkish political and economic ties with the Muslim world and favored close friendship with the more conservative Islamic countries, such as Saudi Arabia, Jordan, Tunisia, and Morocco. In their view, Turkey should take up the leadership of Muslim countries and replace the "Communist" regimes of Nasser and his associates in the Middle East.

Cyprus should wholly or largely be incorporated into Turkey. They regarded the Soviet Union with utter suspicion and advocated vigilance against any country or movement identified as Communist. The number of proponents of extreme rightist views among the foreign policy elite was found, however, to be very small.

These opinions often crossed party affiliations and, as mentioned earlier, presented great variations on the particular issues, often being influenced by day-to-day developments.

The principal motive behind Turkish political opinion is national sentiment. Among the political elite and intellectuals in general, ideological motivation, other than nationalistic, is rare. Both leftist and rightist attitudes stem mostly from conflicting conclusions arrived at on the basis of "what is best for Turkey." Convinced Marxist–Leninists or Maoists who would give ideological cultivation priority over their national feeling are few. Islamic fanatics lacking Turkish patriotism likewise are scarce.

It is instructive to relate different lessons drawn from the invasion of Czechoslovakia by Soviet and Soviet-allied forces in August 1968. For the pro-American side, it was evident proof that the NATO shield was indispensable for countries under the shadow of Soviet power. The leftists' interpretation was that "small nations which accepted protection from the Great Powers faced the greatest danger when they wanted to reform and change their system."[60] The pro-government publicists retaliated by telling their readers that the left-wingers have only sided with Mao's China in condemning Moscow and invoked the spectre of Soviet attack against Turkey:

The propaganda made by the Soviets at the expense of millions of rubles fell to dust in a night. Oh, masqueraders of independence who pretend it to be a violation of our honor and dignity when the sailors of the Sixth Fleet stroll with prostitutes, look well with your eyes! Where the Soviets move in, the place of the prostitutes will be taken by your mothers, wives, and sisters![61]

The two biggest urban centers, Istanbul and Ankara, betrayed a dichotomous political picture: left-wing students battled rightist ones; the left-wing teachers' association denounced the United States, while the Nationalist Teachers Confederation berated Communist stooges; the Federation of Trade Unions expressed concern about any sort of extremism; and a dissident trade union organization impeached the "imperialist exploiters." The Reformist Youth Organization spoke against NATO, and the National Youth Organization accused Communists of being behind aggressive incidents.[62] An anti-NATO declaration was issued by 308 university teaching faculty; the opponents of this move pointed out that most of the 308 were young assistants led by 35 professors. Since Turkish universities included teaching faculty of 3,500, the signatories of the declaration represented a mere 10 percent of the total.[63]

In these two cities, no doubt, the extreme left conducted its stridently anti-American campaign and was supported by popular daily papers in a

[60] Ilhan Selçuk in Cumhuriyet (August 27, 1968). He compared the Czechoslovak invasion with the American intervention in the Dominican Republic when the latter "wanted to change its system for the left."

[61] Bedii Faik in Adalet, August 26, 1968.

[62] The two opposing trade union organizations were the Türk-Iş (moderate to rightist) and the DISK (left-wing).

[63] Adalet, April 10, 1968. The press reported that Prime Minister Demirel told "the famous American editor of the New York Times, C. L. Sulzberger: 'The people are not anti-American in Turkey. . . . Because we have greater freedom today left-wing troublemakers can act more easily.' " The report added that "Sulzberger noted that the pro-American Government of Turkey was underestimating anti-Americanism. An elite minority dominating the press and the universities was fostering anti-American sentiment since President Johnson's letter during the Cyprus crisis." Tercüman, August 12, 1968. Concerning the disruption in Turkish universities caused by the violence of radical students, see the New York Times, June 15, 1970.

way that appeared to drown conflicting or more moderate voices. Sometimes opportunistic elements, fearing to be called "reactionary," "unpatriotic," or "American stooges," joined in the ballyhoo while privately deploring its unreasonableness.

In Izmir and Bursa, former Democratic and now Justice Party strongholds, pro-Western sympathies seemed to predominate; here Moslem traditions and some conservatism also prevailed. Nevertheless, undercurrents of anti-Americanism and opposition to NATO ties were also to be found. Both the elite and the people-at-large proved equally patriotic.[64]

In Konya, which is a religious center, left-wingers complained of being harassed and persecuted.[65] In other smaller towns of western and central Anatolia, whispering campaigns, even appeals for a *Jihad* (Holy War against infidels), against Communists, were being reported. In the villages, only a few were not subject to the conservative, religious, and locality-centered attitudes.

Election results could generally be considered the most reliable barometer of Turkish public opinion. It is known, however, that the rural voters cast their votes for persons rather than for the ideas they represent or for the parties to which they belong.[66] As it was sarcastically put to this writer by a member of the Republican People's Party: "They vote for the improvement of roads and the building of mosques."

In the east and southwest, the peculiar ethnic and social conditions and the relative backwardness of the population render any assessment of public opinion hopelessly difficult. That both Islamic-oriented and leftist parties compete for the votes of that region indicates that existing social and separatist unrest may find an outlet in extremist political platforms.[67]

---

[64] In Izmir, in August 1968, a bomb was planted in the Hisar Mosque and the same night a Molotov cocktail was thrown into the office of the United States Information Service. Twenty local organizations denounced these acts as those of Communists; the opposition accused the government of having made use of *agents provocateurs; Cumhuriyet* and *Milliyet,* August 14, 1968.

[65] Konya was the site of Muslim demonstrations, which resulted in the beating of members of the leftist Teachers' Union and in the destruction of the offices of a leftist paper in July 1968; *Akşam,* July 25, 1968; *Ulus,* July 26, 1968.

[66] This "localism" in Turkish politics is analyzed by Frederick W. Frey, *The Turkish Political Elite* (Cambridge, Mass., 1965), pp. 89–98, 196–97.

[67] Several so-called "Eastern Meetings" have been convened in the past few years to discuss the particular problems of that region. The organizers were mostly, but not exclusively, members of leftist parties. Participants at these meetings were accused of "fostering regionalism" or even of "Kurdism"; *Milliyet,* September 17, 1967; *Ulus,* October 24, 1967.

The apparent polarization of political public opinion is, however, misleading. Moderates are most likely to be in the overwhelming majority; yet they are usually silent. Voices of moderation, however, can also be heard:

I was frightened by the reactionary sermon I listened to in a mosque in Kadiköy, in the heart of Istanbul. On my return home, I read the Turkish Bolsheviks' anti-American declaration written not so much in the Russian style, but in the Peking language. . . . We should save Turkdom from both the reactionaries and the Bolsheviks and put an end to this revolutionary atmosphere. We have to look to the West as we have always done since the 17th century whenever we wanted to save the country. The red revolutionary is arm in arm with the reactionary fanatic. Put an end to it.[68]

The opinions of the members of the elite or the occasional expressions of mass opinion are only illustrative. They cannot be taken as a quantitative guide. On the other hand, available opinion polls are restricted to the areas of Istanbul and Ankara and, as such, are not representative of the country as a whole. Furthermore, replies to questionnaires must be accepted with utmost caution: these answers are conditioned by the formulation of the questions, and they may not necessarily reflect the real sentiment of the respondent.[69]

On the question "Which are the problems that interest Turks most?" the following replies were received:

	Percent
Economic problems	62
Disagreements with neighboring countries	12
Need for more schools	20
Other	5
Don't know	1

The question "What country is our best friend?" was answered as follows:

	Percent
USA	18
West German	24
Pakistan	23
Iran	4
We have none	25
Others	6

[68] Falih Rıfkı Atay in *Dünya,* October 10, 1967.

[69] The public opinion poll to be quoted is the *Omnibus Study, Turkey,* performed for the PEVA (Market Studies & Research) Company of Istanbul (mimeographed), Ankara, 1965. The poll was taken from 500 samples in Istanbul and 400 samples in Ankara.

The next question was "Which one is our greatest enemy?"

	Percent
Greece	42
Russia	34
USA	8
We have more than one	4
Others	10
Don't know	2

It was further asked, "Should Turkey, in the world's present situation, taking into consideration Turkey's safety, have any ties with other countries in the form of agreements or should we avoid them?"

	Percent
Yes, we should have such agreements	79
No, should avoid them	13
Don't know	8

"If yes, with which country or countries?"

	Percent
USA (only)	6
USA and others	18
Germany	25
Russia	11
Western bloc	8
With our friends	2
Muslim countries	6
Pakistan	6
Others	17
No answer	1

"If Turkey should have such agreements with the United States and other countries, which other countries?"

	Percent
Germany	41
Russia	18
Great Britain	10
Pakistan	8
Iran	7
France	4
Israel	3
Greece	3
Muslim countries	2
China	2
European countries	1
Arab countries	1

"If you had to list your impressions about various countries, how would you put them in order?"

	Absolutely positive	Positive	Undetermined	Negative	Absolutely negative	Don't know
			(in percent)			
USA	8	43	24	21	1	3
USSR	.25	9	29	48	8	6
Red China	.25	4	8	39	30	19
India	1	40	39	6	1	13
United Arab Republic	1	24	36	24	5	10
East Germany	—	4	10	70	8	8
West Germany	38	56	2	1	—	3

"In your opinion, are the basic interests of Turkey and the United States, the USSR and Red China, the same, somewhat the same, somewhat different, or completely different?"

	The same	Somewhat the same	Somewhat different	Completely different	Don't know
			(in percent)		
USA	12	52	19	6	11
USSR	—	14	35	29	22
Red China	—	2	14	49	35

The respondents were next asked to answer the following question: "What sort of impression did the recent attitude of the United States in international affairs make on you (positive or negative)?"

	Percent
Positive	3
Somewhat positive	23
Somewhat negative	52
Negative	14
Don't know	8

"What are the things which make (good) (bad) impressions on you in the recent attitude of the United States?"

Good impressions:	Percent
Aid to Turkey	17
Aid to underdeveloped countries	14
Cuban policy	1
Vietnam policy	1
Prevention of communism	2
Efforts for world peace	3
Works for humanity	1
Timely and sure actions	1

Good impressions:	Percent
Moderate policies	5
Don't know	5
Others	7
Unanswered	43
Bad impressions:	
Vietnam policy	12
Cyprus policy	31
Petroleum problem	3
Behavior toward Turkey	3
Interference in internal affairs	8
Selfishness	4
Imperialist attitude	2
Insincerity	1
Not neutral	3
Does not protect peace	2
Others	13
Unanswered	18

"Did the activities of the United States in regard to the Cyprus dispute make any difference in your feelings toward that country or no difference at all?"

	Percent
More in favor of the USA	2
Less in favor of the USA	84
No difference	13
Don't know	1

The public opinion inquiry then proceeded to ask this question: "Taking into consideration all the factors, what country do you think holds the world power in its hands?"

	Percent
USA	75
Russia	13
Don't know	3
None	3
Communist China	1
Others	5

Further, it was asked: "In your opinion what country will be the strongest power 25 years from now (insist on only one answer)?"

	Percent
Communist China	16
Russia	14
Don't know	17
USA	15
West Germany	28
Others	10

Another question was: "In general, to what extent do you think that a successful job is being done by the United Nations?"

	Percent
Very good	1
Good	34
Poor	21
Very poor	4
Don't know	1
Unanswered	39

The questions then concentrated on Turkey's participation in NATO and CENTO: "Do you approve of Turkey's membership in NATO?"

	Percent
Approve	78
Disapprove	7
Don't know	4
Unanswered	11

Those who disapproved were further asked: "If 'disapprove,' why are you against NATO?"

	Percent
No use for us	2
Departs from its goal	2
Financial burden	1
It protects the interests of the USA only	1
Other reasons	2

About CENTO: "Do you approve of Turkey's membership in CENTO?"

	Percent
Approve	57
Disapprove	4
Don't know	4
Unanswered	35

"What should be the major aim of CENTO?"

	Percent
Protection against Communist countries	15
General protection against other countries	9
Economic cooperation among member countries	38
Others	1
Don't know	2
Unanswered	35

The last questions concerned the position of foreign companies in Turkey. Thus, the question was posed: "In your opinion is it good or bad for Turkey to have foreign companies operating in the country?"

	Percent
Good	54
Bad	41
Don't know	5

"What are the reasons for being 'good'?"

	Percent
Business is activated	16
Provides capital	12
From the technical point	8
Others	18

"Reasons for being 'bad'?"

	Percent
Let's do it by ourselves	8
They exploit us	9
National wealth is being shared	4
They are after their own interest	6
Others	11
Unanswered	3

The above opinion poll allows us to obtain some measure of information on views held by persons of a certain level of education in the cities of Istanbul and Ankara. The high rating of the Federal Republic of Germany is the most remarkable response; it can be explained partly by the historical prestige that Germany enjoys and also by the fact that so many Turks know West Germany, having worked there in the past ten years.

Another opinion poll held in the spring of 1968 by the Faculty of Political Science at the University of Ankara on specific questions of foreign policy produced the following results:[70]

On the question whether Turkey should withdraw from NATO, only

---

[70] See Coşkun Kırca, "Foreign Policy in Our Public Opinion," *Outlook* (Ankara), May 29, 1968, pp. 6–7. The author, a leading member of the Reliance Party, also pointed out that the organizer of the opinion poll, a professor on the Faculty of Political Science at the University of Ankara, was a deputy in the National Assembly belonging to the Republican People's Party who had signed a declaration calling for the withdrawal of Turkey from NATO.

13.4 percent of the respondents replied positively. Of those questioned, 56 percent wished Turkey to remain in NATO, though with certain changes in the alliance. Among those who voted in favor of participation in NATO, 29.6 percent demanded these changes.

Among those who voted for a withdrawal from NATO, the following reasons were given:

Turkey should withdraw in order to attain her political and economic goals (46 percent of those who voted against NATO); Turkey should withdraw to save her international prestige (3 percent); because NATO failed to provide assistance to Turkey (24 percent); because NATO prevented Turkish intervention in Cyprus (9 percent).

The survey also touched upon the American presence in Vietnam. Of the respondents, 18 percent believed that the United States should immediately withdraw its forces from Vietnam; 28 percent thought that America should continue to fulfill her obligations in Vietnam; 29 percent believed that the United States should increase her attacks against North Vietnam; and other replies varied in content or left the question unanswered. It may be noted that the percentage of those suggesting the continuation of the American presence and an increase in attacks against North Vietnam (altogether 57 percent) approximated the percentage of those who declared for Turkey's continued membership in NATO.

In conclusion, one feels justified in stating that only a relatively tiny minority of Turkey's adult population is clearly opposed to the country's basic foreign policy, including her participation in the Western alliance. Nevertheless, this small nation-wide minority certainly forms a weighty portion of the vocal foreign policy elite. Opinions of members of the Faculty of Political Science at the University of Ankara, many of whom are either politically active or frequent editorialists in popular newspapers, carry some weight in the formation of foreign policy; many of them are violently, others mildly, critical of governmental policies, and a considerable proportion are anti-NATO and anti-American. On the other hand, the higher bureaucracy with foreign policy experience, the majority of outside advisers to governmental agencies, as well as the foreign policy experts and top leaders of the major political parties, agree with the government on the major foreign policy issues.

As long as Turkey is democratically governed, no decisive change can be expected in her course in international politics. The only force that could topple the present system of government is, as in 1960, the military.

Ever since the fall of the Menderes regime, all observers of Turkey's politics watch anxiously for possible rumblings within the ranks of the military. In this respect, it seems to be well substantiated that the younger elements of the Turkish officers' corps have not remained immune to the influence of leftist forces and that ideas promoted by either the extreme left, or the left-of-center, have found willing listeners among their ranks.[71] Up to now, however, competent observers agree that the senior commanders of Turkey's armed forces are committed to democracy.[72]

Accordingly, barring an intervention by the military, the government of Turkey, whether supported by the present majority party or, depending on the results of future elections, by a coalition of the middle-of-the-road political forces, will continue the present basic foreign policy line, notwithstanding vociferous cries by the leftist opposition. As this writer was told by a supporter of the government who voiced a Turkish proverb, "The dog barks but the caravan proceeds."

[71] It has, for instance, been reported that the Annual Report of the Air Force School contained "anti-NATO ideas, provocation for revolution and Communist ideas." The editorialist continued: "Marshal Çakmak [long-time Chief-of-Staff] ended the Communist nest of Nazım Hikmet followers in the War School with one coup. We heartily believe that General Cemal Tural [Chief-of-Staff], a nationalist, who restored the hierarchy in the Army after the Revolution, also will act energetically on this subject." *Adalet,* November 5, 1968.

[72] See *New York Times,* March 31, 1966.

Turkey, the United States, and NATO

Timeo Danaos and dona ferentes.
(I fear the Danaans, though their
hands proffer gifts.)—VIRGIL,
Aeneid, i.48.

No alliance founded on fear has lasted
or will last because, as soon as fear
decreases in intensity, the cement of
the alliance begins to crumble.
—FIELD MARSHAL MONTGOMERY

THE SOVIET UNION'S THREATENING
posture at the end of World War II—as described in chapter I—impelled
Turkey to seek her ties of friendship almost exclusively with the countries
of Western Europe and the United States. It may be asked, however,
whether this readjustment was prompted only by the military menace
from the north or if it was inspired by motives other than security.

In the late 1940's, it appeared to all observers that as a consequence
of the Cold War the globe was being split into Communist and anti-
Communist spheres. At that time, the Third World of neutralist or uncommitted nations had hardly emerged, much less assumed significance.
The ideological approach of both Stalinist Russia and the United States,
as developed under John Foster Dulles, seemed to be based on the "who
is not with me is against me" axiom. In such a dichotomous world, Turkey
could not hesitate about where to place her destiny. Furthermore, it had
become evident that technological assistance and development were
indispensable for any nation that wished to ensure its survival as an
independent state. Finally, we must understand that Turkey's nearly
unique urge to become a member of the European family of nations and
to be recognized as such provided an additional impulse to her desire to
be tied, by every available device, to the West. Identification with that
part of the world and with the civilization represented by it was to
guarantee security, development, and acculturation.

To the realistic Turk of 1945–46, the West no longer meant what it had before the war—namely, Britain, France, and also Germany. The West had become identified primarily with the transatlantic giant, the United States, the source of apparently unlimited strength and wealth. The opportunity to gain at one stroke military security, prosperity, and national fulfillment induced the otherwise suspicious and calculating Turk to throw himself unreservedly into the arms of his newly discovered, generous, and ingenuous ally and friend.

The basic assumptions of this cooperative venture were not the same for Turkey and her Western partners; the United States did not see it as a "love match" in which everything good and bad was to be shared. As one might expect, the honeymoon was not long lasting, and, inevitably, the benefits and disadvantages of the partnership were more closely scrutinized by Turkey than by her allies.

TURKEY AND NATO

The North Atlantic Treaty Organization was called into being to thwart potential aggression by the Soviet Union or its allies. The NATO treaty was signed on April 4, 1948, in Washington by only 12 countries: Canada, Belgium, Denmark, France, Iceland, Italy, Luxembourg, the Netherlands, Norway, Portugal, the United Kingdom, and the United States. Among the strictly Mediterranean countries, only Italy was an original signatory; Turkey and Greece were not admitted to the alliance until February 18, 1952.[1] Consultations in the NATO council and directly among the member governments extended two years before a positive decision was reached. Although many felt that it was essential to protect the southern flank of the alliance, there was considerable reluctance on the part of others to extend the guarantee offered by the treaty to the Caucasian border of the USSR. There were also strategical and ideological objections: Greece and Turkey, although connected by a narrow frontier in Thrace, were isolated from the rest of the NATO community. They could be supported only with the help of sea and air power. Turkey's

[1] See chapter 1, pp. 36–37. Turkey formally applied for admission on August 1, 1950; the protocol on the accession of Greece and Turkey was signed in London on October 22, 1951, and entered into force on February 18, 1952. Before her formal acceptance, Turkey and Greece were invited in October 1950 by the NATO council to cooperate with the agencies of the organization in Mediterranean defense planning. See NATO, *Facts About the North Atlantic Treaty Organization* (Paris, 1965), pp. 189–91.

exposed location in the Middle East was particularly questioned. Nor could Greece or Turkey in any way be deemed "Atlantic"—a restriction already overlooked when Italy was admitted. Greece, if admitted, was to be the only country in the alliance with a population adhering to the Eastern Orthodox religion. In addition, as was pointed out earlier, Turkey was not only a Muslim but also an Asian country; her admission required a change in the wording of the original treaty which specifically referred to Europe.[2]

On the other hand, one could not ignore the fact that these two countries bordered the eastern and northeastern coastline of the Mediterranean and that Turkey was the guardian of the straits, which, in the case of hostilities, could block the entry of the Soviet forces into that sea and the oil-rich Middle East. In the end, it was concluded that the advantages of admitting these two states outweighed the disadvantages. The contribution which Turkey could render by adding, on short notice, an army of 500,000 to 750,000 to the alliance was also considered a gain, even though this army required modernization.

Under the NATO treaty, the signatory states agreed that

an armed attack against one or more of them in Europe or North America shall be considered an attack against them all; and consequently they agree that, if such an armed attack occurs, each of them, in exercise of the right of individual or collective self-defense recognized by Article 51 of the Charter of the United Nations, *will assist* the Party or Parties so attacked by taking forthwith, individually and in concert with the other Parties, such action *as it deems necessary, including the use of armed force*, to restore and maintain the security of the North Atlantic area.[3]

The extension of the treaty to Turkey necessitated a modification of Article 6 which, in its original form, defined the territorial limits of the "North Atlantic area" to be defended by the alliance. Under the Protocol of Accession of Greece and Turkey, Article 6 came to read as follows:

For the purpose of Article 5, an armed attack on one or more of the Parties is deemed to include an armed attack:
(i) on the territory of the Parties in Europe or North America, on the Algerian Departments of France,[4] on the *territory of Turkey*, or on the islands

[2] *Survey of International Affairs, 1951*, pp. 33–34.
[3] NATO, *Facts*, p. 211; Ruth C. Lawson, *International Regional Organizations* (New York, 1962), p. 6. (Italics added.)
[4] The reference to Algeria was dropped upon the request of France when Algeria became independent.

under the jurisdiction of any of the Parties in the North Atlantic area north of the Tropic of Cancer;

(ii) on the forces, vessels, or aircraft of any of the Parties, when in or over these territories or any other area in Europe in which occupation forces of any of the Parties were stationed on the date when the Treaty entered into force or the *Mediterranean Sea* or the North Atlantic area north of the Tropic of Cancer.[5]

With Turkey and Greece in NATO, the command structure of the organization had to be extended into the eastern Mediterranean and to the eastern border of Turkey. When the Federal Republic of Germany joined NATO in 1955, the alliance was felt to be further strengthened. During the following years, the NATO powers endeavored to increase and improve their military power, create greater cohesion, and elaborate common strategical concepts. Turkey's role in all of these developments was not inconsiderable.

Turkey, with other member powers, maintained a permanent delegation at NATO headquarters in Paris and, after 1967, in Brussels. The head of the delegation, who held the rank of ambassador, represented Turkey in NATO's highest authority, the North Atlantic Council, between ministerial meetings. There also were Turkish nationals among the members of the international staff of NATO. Turkish foreign ministers, often joined by other members of the cabinet, represented their country when the council's session was held on a ministerial level. Due to a rotational system, the Turkish foreign ministers (Selim Sarper and Feridun Cemal Erkin) presided over the council in 1961–62. At times, when the meeting was held at the level of heads of government, the Turkish prime minister participated.

On the military side, the chief-of-staff of Turkey's armed forces regularly attended the meetings of the Military Committee of NATO; he was otherwise represented in the committee by a permanent military representative. A Turkish officer became a member of the International Planning Staff and later of the Nuclear Defense Affairs Committee. When a seven-member Nuclear Planning Group was set up in December 1966, Turkey held one of the rotating seats.

Turkey's territory was protected by the European command of NATO, headed by the Supreme Allied Commander Europe (SACEUR). The headquarters for this group was known as the Supreme Headquarters Allied Powers Europe (SHAPE) and has been located in Belgium since

[5] NATO, *Facts*, p. 213. (Italics added.)

1967. The land, air, and sea area of Turkey was divided between two commands: the Commander-in-Chief Allied Forces Southern Europe (CINCSOUTH) in Naples, Italy, with a subcommand (Commander Allied Forces Southeastern Europe) in Izmir, Turkey; and the Commander-in-Chief Allied Forces Mediterranean (CINCAFMED) in Malta, with a subcommand (Commander Eastern Mediterranean) in Ankara.

All members of NATO (except Iceland, which has no armed forces) maintain a National Military Representative at SHAPE, the ordinary channel of communication between NATO headquarters and the national commander in the respective countries. In Turkey the national commander was the chief-of-staff of the Turkish armed forces.

It was, of course, understood that the various NATO commands would exercise operational authority only in time of war. Integration in NATO, as far as Turkey is concerned, extended to the highest command level but not to the troop level. Under the existing agreements, Turkey has "assigned" 15 of her divisions to NATO, but these forces remain under the direct command of her national military authorities. During the two Cyprus crises, for example, when Turkey threatened to invade the island, it became clear that Ankara had not relinquished supreme command over its forces, save in the emergencies foreseen under the NATO agreements.[6]

In principle, Turkey was not opposed to military integration within NATO as was France; she wished only that NATO should take into account the conditions peculiar to Turkey. Some examples would include the isolated location of that country in the southeast protruding corner of the alliance, the need for armed forces for special "national purposes," and the proximity of Soviet territory, as well as some other geographical or national questions.

Since the adoption of the new constitution in 1961, it has been found that inconsistencies exist between NATO commitments and provisions of the constitution. The supreme commander of the Turkish armed forces, under Article 110, is the president of the republic, who exercises the sovereign powers of the Grand National Assembly. The chief of the general staff is, for practical purposes, the commander; however, in the event

[6] In answer to questions, Foreign Minister Çağlayangil said that "integration" is only a series of measures "to ensure a joint and coordinated command of the allied forces in case of war." He emphasized that all Turkish forces are under national command in time of peace. To be in NATO does not prevent Turkey from using these forces "for the maintenance of her national interests"; *Istanbul Bayram,* March 12, 1968.

of aggression of the type foreseen by the various NATO agreements, the Supreme Allied Commander Europe and his subordinate commanders are to take over the command of Turkish and other allied armed forces. Notwithstanding the existing NATO arrangements, it was felt in Turkey that, in case of war, the Turkish army should be led by its chief-of-staff.[7]

Harmonizing Turkey's strategical needs with the all out strategy to be pursued by NATO has also caused considerable difficulty. With the abandonment of the "massive retaliation" principle and adoption of the "flexible response" strategy, growing anxiety has been felt in Turkey that Turkish territory might be traded against time in the event of Soviet aggression. According to press reports, under NATO planning large areas of eastern Anatolia would be abandoned and the main defense line established along the Zagros and Taurus mountain chains. The official denial by the minister of defense simply stated that the defense line starts at the frontiers.[8]

Turkish strategical thinking was not just concerned with the employment of conventional forces; the application of nuclear planning and the use of nuclear forces have disturbed the official and the nonofficial foreign policy elite. In agreement with the NATO command, Turkey consented to the establishment of Intermediate Range Ballistic Missile (IRBM) sites, equipped with United States Jupiter missiles, on Turkish soil. At the NATO council meeting in December 1956, Turkey also asked for tactical nuclear weapons. These nuclear devices were delivered by the United States and were to be controlled by the so-called double key system of activation used in Germany. These nuclear weapons were in the custody of United States forces but, in case of war, would be launched by Turkish crews. The consent of both the American and the Turkish governments is a precondition for their use.

Since 1954, the NATO command has been empowered to use ground-to-ground missiles equipped with tactical nuclear warheads, even against a conventional attack. Much criticism had been levelled against the use of these weapons in the densely populated central European defense line of NATO. On the other hand, it has been pointed out that tactical nuclear

---

[7] The formal conflict between NATO obligations and the wording of the Turkish constitution so far has not been officially raised by Turkey. It seems possible that an interpretation could be given to the texts and a solution agreed upon which would reconcile the apparent inconsistency.

[8] See the speech of Defense Minister Ahmet Topaloğlu during the defense budget debate in the Senate; *Cumhuriyet,* February 2, 1969.

devices could be usefully deployed in the sparsely inhabited mountin areas of eastern Turkey.[9]

While it is unquestionable that the space-time equation, which relied on the graduated response idea, suited the Turkish geographical conditions better than, for instance, the narrow and industrially valuable area between the Elbe and the Rhine Rivers in Germany, it is understandable that even the strategical surrender of territory was viewed with apprehension in Turkey. Thus, Turkey has found it more difficult to reconcile herself to this alteration of NATO nuclear strategy; even the concept of a "residual" or "ultimate deterrent," which would leave the enemy in doubt about the possible consequences of its aggressive action, was looked at askance. There is an impression in Turkey, difficult to refute, that NATO in case of an attack would differentiate between its center and its wings (north and south). Whereas the center would be defended at its perimeter (forward strategy), the southeast wing (Turkey) would be defended either "in depth"—that is, by sacrificing Turkish real estate—or not at all.[10]

In the councils of NATO, there is a realization that natural difficulties would interfere with assisting Turkey should she be attacked; therefore, various plans have been considered which would allay Turkish anxieties. In 1967 the "Mobile Force" idea was submitted providing for a naval and army task unit which could be employed for any emergency involving Turkey or Greece.

At first, Turkey endorsed the plan to establish the Multilateral Force (Polaris missile-equipped submarines with crews of mixed nationalities) suggested by the United States and supported by a few NATO powers, including West Germany. In early 1965, however, before the plan was implemented, Turkey withdrew her support, presumably because of Soviet objections.[11]

Another measure suggested to calm Turkish anxieties and to protect Turkey against a sudden conventional attack was that atomic mines, officially called Atomic Demolition Munitions (ADM), be planted along

---

[9] See Alastair Buchan, *NATO in the 1960's* (New York, 1960), p. 88.

[10] *New York Times,* May 12, 1967. See also the article by the Turkish Rear Admiral (retired) Sezai Orkunt, in *Cumhuriyet,* October 30, 1967. He wrote: "In the event of an aggression against the wings, NATO will do nothing except to take some diplomatic moves . . . or send a small force to show its solidarity."

[11] Officially, financial reasons persuaded Turkey to withdraw from the MLF (Turkey was to bear one percent of the costs, or about $50,000). It has, however, been hinted that possible support by the Soviet Union in the Cyprus conflict was the real reason; *New York Times,* January 15, 1965; *Süddeutsche Zeitung,* January 15, 1965.

her Caucasian or Thracian border. A somewhat similar plan was advanced in the early 1960's by the military command of the Federal Republic of Germany; the mines were conceived as nonprovocative and purely defensive devices to oppose a Soviet invasion that could be placed in a forward position where they might forestall the surrender of territory. The areas in question, however, had sizable populations and were flat, so that all access routes could not be protected. It was pointed out on the other hand that the Eastern Turkish border region was extremely mountainous and sparsely populated.[12]

The plan raised considerable interest. It was emphasized that the explosion of these atomic mines would not release nuclear fallout because the detonations were to be effected underground. Custody of the ADM would remain primarily in the hands of American personnel and the double key method would be applied to their use. Nevertheless, the nuclear-mines plan was dropped when a closer scrutiny revealed that the use of these weapons would necessitate an evacuation of 3 to 3.5 million persons and 10 to 15 million domestic animals. Furthermore, the detonation of these mines in forward border positions would have to be carried out swiftly. The decision to detonate could not be reached within the required time because, under United States law, authority to do so could not be permanently delegated to local Turkish commanders. It was also feared that the use of even such defensive nuclear weapons might elicit a nuclear response from the Soviets which could result in an all out escalation on a global scale.

Lately, the expansion of Soviet activity in the Mediterranean has elicited some response by NATO, a response which closely involved Turkey. The North Atlantic Council resolved to create a new, integrated command with naval units from the United States, Britain, and Italy; Greece and Turkey were also asked to assign vessels from time to time. Cooperation on a larger scale could not be expected from these two countries without increased financial assistance or the transfer of Allied naval vessels to them.[13]

[12] *New York Times*, April 6, 1967; *Milliyet*, September 26, 1967; *Tercüman*, September 29, 1967; *Cumhuriyet*, December 12, 1967.

[13] *New York Times*, December 7, 1968; January 17, 1969. The naval force in question might be much stronger than the Standing Naval Force, Atlantic, composed of a small destroyer fleet. For the Mediterranean, a force including four or five aircraft carriers, five or six cruisers, and 30 to 40 destroyers would be formed. Whether the U.S. Sixth Fleet will have to yield some of its units to the mixed NATO fleet seems

Turkey is the connecting link between NATO and the CENTO alliances. This circumstance has enhanced Turkey's relative importance as a southern bastion of NATO. Through her, land connection can be maintained with Iran and Pakistan. In the Balkans, Turkey is expected to cooperate with Greece against Bulgaria should the latter resort to aggression. Furthermore, Turkey faces the Soviet Union along her long maritime frontier on the Black Sea and along the land bordering the Transcaucasian Soviet provinces; she is also expected to defend the entrances to the straits against air and amphibious attack.

These manifold commitments have compelled Turkey's military leadership to maintain, with the hearty approval of NATO, the third largest military force in terms of numbers in the alliance. Only the United States and, with a small margin, France, surpass her. In 1968 Turkish armed forces included 480,000 men,[14] a number which can be tripled by calling in reserves.

In time of peace, the Turkish land forces are divided into three armies: the First Army in Thrace, which is the largest and is called to watch the Bulgarians as well as the First Hellenic Army, with which it is expected to cooperate; the Third Army, which covers the Soviet Transcaucasian border; and the smallest, the Second Army, which operates along the Syrian and Iraqi borders. The land forces also include a training corps; west, central, and east communications commands; and a number of base commands. The land forces are organized into 17 divisions. The air forces contain 27 squadrons. The Turkish navy is composed of the north and south area commands, and several training commands. It consists of 10 destroyers, 10 submarines, and 90 smaller vessels.[15]

In 1968, 18.4 percent of the budget was spent on military expenditures; it was admitted that half of Turkey's total military expenses are

uncertain. Turkey at first declined, then expressed readiness to participate; *Milliyet*, November 19, 1968; *Hürriyet*, March 26, 1969.

[14] *Cumhuriyet*, December 11, 1967. At the same time, U.S. Armed Forces consisted of 2.8 million men and France had 514,000 under arms. Other NATO members maintained the following forces: Britain, 420,000; West Germany, 402,000; Italy, 400,000; Greece, 162,000; Portugal, 148,000; the Netherlands, 143,000; Canada, 112,000; Belgium, 100,000; Denmark, 52,000; Norway, 32,000; Luxembourg, 1,800; and Iceland, none.

[15] *Milliyet*, July 3, 1967. Although the ground and naval forces of Turkey remained below the NATO standards in equipment, the Turkish Air Force, 53,000 strong, was considered up-to-date. The six-battery Nike-Hercules and Nike-Ajax anti-aircraft missile units defending Istanbul are also attached to the Air Force; see Mehmet Ali Kişlali's account in *Tercüman*, December 12, 1967.

covered by assistance provided in various forms under the alliance. Thus, American military aid between 1946 and 1968 totaled 2,520 million dollars.[16] Since 1964 the Federal Republic of Germany has contributed an average of $15 to 25 million yearly. American military aid was, however, gradually reduced; for 1971 only $75 million were allotted.

Under the NATO agreements, so-called common installations were set up in the various member states. These installations, also referred to as "infrastructures" (air-fields, military headquarters, port installations, missile sites, signals and telecommunications installations, radar warning and navigational aid stations) can be used by the forces of the territorial power. But the individual countries are not expected to bear the total costs. It has been recognized that certain countries, due to their geographical location, configuration, and other circumstances, require more or different types of installations. The cost-sharing is calculated according to the economic capacity of the respective states. Turkey's quota is 1.1 percent (the United States, 30.85 percent; West Germany, 20 percent; Britain, 10.50 percent); the benefit derived for her from this cost-sharing is far superior to the value of her own contribution.[17] Since 1952 the NATO infrastructural aid given to Turkey has amounted to over $400 million.[18]

It is thus beyond doubt that Turkey has greatly benefited from her participation in NATO from the financial point of view. She would not otherwise have been able to modernize her armed forces, although, according to observers, this modernization is by no means complete. Nevertheless, she can now oppose modern land armies without suffering from the inferiority she possessed during and immediately after World War II.[19]

The advantages of Turkey's membership in NATO cannot be assessed merely in terms of military strategy or ancillary financial aid. Through her membership, Turkey was introduced to the circle of the American–West

[16] See statement by Foreign Minister Çağlayangil, *Cumhuriyet,* February 2, 1969. In 1968 Turkey allotted 4.3 percent of her $280-per-capita national income to her armed forces—that is, $12 per year for every citizen. The same figure was $364 in the United States, $129 in the Soviet Union, and among developing nations $16 in the United Arab Republic, $20 in Syria, and $22 in Iraq.

[17] NATO, *Facts,* pp. 135–38.

[18] *Milliyet,* February 2, 1969.

[19] According to press reports, it was the opinion of German military experts that the Turkish Army was well-trained and disciplined but not yet equipped to fulfill NATO standards; *Milliyet* and *Adalet,* October 19, 1968.

European political and diplomatic partnership. Consultation and discussion on a multilateral basis is generally more advantageous to a small power than bilateral contacts with a highly superior power. NATO membership allowed for a continuous and spontaneous exchange of views between Turkey and her collective allies. The value of such diplomatic contacts in political, economic, and cultural relations is inestimable; more than anything else, it has enabled Turkey to establish herself as a "European" power.[20]

For the average Turk, however, NATO appears to be merely a cloak for the presence of the United States. Because of the United States leadership role in the alliance, the stationing of American forces on Turkish soil and the ensuing manifold contacts, both official and unofficial, between Americans and Turks, NATO came to be largely identified, in Turkish eyes, with the USA—for better or worse.

THE UNITED STATES AND TURKEY

The "special relationship" between the United States and Turkey originated simultaneously with the inception of the Cold War and the adoption of a global American foreign policy. At the time Soviet pressure on Turkey appeared to be most alarming, Washington demonstratively sent the U.S. battleship *Missouri* to Istanbul; the ship and her crew received an unprecedented welcome by the people and official circles. Less than a year later, the Truman Doctrine committed the United States "to support free peoples who are resisting attempted subjugation by armed minorities or by outside pressure."[21] On July 12, 1947, four-and-a-half years before Turkey's admission to NATO, the United States and Turkey signed a military assistance agreement.[22] Weaponry and other military equipment were supplied by Washington, together with the personnel for instruction. Programs of road and harbor construction and the establishment of stra-

---

[20] "The desire to reinforce our security within a collective framework led us to join the NATO Alliance. We consider our alliance with NATO a *manifestation of the identity of fate* among the countries embracing freedom and democratic ideals. . . . Besides the security aspects of the NATO Alliance I should like to stress the *additional uses* of NATO, the contribution it makes to our defense power and economy." Prime Minister Demirel in the National Assembly, *Cumhuriyet*, January 27, 1968. (Italics added.)

[21] See chapter I, pp. 35–36.

[22] World Peace Foundation, *Documents on American Foreign Relations, 1947*, vol. IX (Princeton, 1949), pp. 730–32.

tegic installations of various sorts were prepared with American advice and implemented through the financial aid offered by the United States. Besides military assistance, economic assistance was also provided under the Marshall Plan; Turkey's participation in the Korean War deepened her friendship with the comrade-in-arms.

After Turkey's entry into NATO, further indirect American financial and logistical support was made available through infrastructural aid. Turkey had become one of the cornerstones of the Atlantic alliance and "in exchange for each dollar spent in Turkey, America saved three dollars' worth of security."[23] Ambassador George C. McGhee could proudly announce that "Turkey is our most reliable ally."[24]

During the ten years of the Menderes administration, while open criticism of governmental foreign policy was discouraged, Washington and Ankara appeared to live in a state of perfect harmony. The invitation to join NATO was approved by the Grand National Assembly by a vote of 404 to 0, with one abstention. Turkey synchronized her foreign policy with the policies of the major NATO powers but primarily with United States policy. Her voting habits in the General Assembly of the United Nations and, when a member, in the Security Council followed Washington. In her attitude toward the countries of the Middle East, she offered a willing ear to American (and also British) advice. If there was any mild opposition in her stand at the meetings of the Atlantic alliance, it was to urge a more determined and more cautious policy, both toward the Soviet Union and against the "uncertain" Arab and other neutralist states of the Middle East.[25]

In the weeks during and following the Suez conflict of 1956, Turkey generally supported the American stand. In 1957 and 1958, also years of upheaval in the Middle East, Turkey stood firm; she welcomed the Eisenhower Doctrine, which promised to protect the general area against aggression by international communism. She even offered her services in the implementation of the Eisenhower program,[26] an action which brought her into a confrontation with the anti-Western Arab states, especially with her neighbor Syria. When Turkey was again threatened by Moscow,

---

[23] U.S. General W. H. Arnold's statement in *La République*, May 5, 1952.
[24] *New York Times*, November 21, 1952. See also George C. McGhee, "Turkey Joins the West," *Foreign Affairs* (July 1954): 617–30.
[25] For Turkey's participation in the Baghdad Pact, see chapter VII, below.
[26] Kiliç, *Turkey and the World*, pp. 195–97.

Secretary of State John Foster Dulles assured Ankara that, in case of an attack by the Soviet Union, the United States would not limit itself to a "purely defensive operation."[27]

The Middle Eastern crisis reached its climax after the overthrow of the royal regime in Iraq in July 1958; United States forces, partly using bases in Turkey, landed in Lebanon upon the request of Lebanese President Chamoun. The Turkish army was placed on a state-of-alert, not only in response to the situation in the Arab states to her south but also to counter Soviet troop movements along the Caucasian border.[28] At the same time, Ankara was deeply involved in the Cyprus conflict: Greek attempts at unification had to be opposed while delicate negotiations were being conducted with Britain in order to reach a compromise satisfactory to both Greece and Turkey.[29] Washington wished to abstain from any stand on the Cyprus problem but strongly supported Turkey in its opposition to the "Soviet volunteers" which Moscow threatened to dispatch to the island.

In the eyes of most Americans, Turkey had become the ideal ally, and previous negative prejudices toward Turkey were forgotten. They had been principally motivated by the Turkish policies against Greeks and Armenians during and after World War I, as well as by Turkey's ambiguous posture during World War II. At this time, however, these memories were being replaced by enthusiasm for Turkish heroism in Korea and for Turkey's impressive steadfastness against Russia. By the late fifties, however, much criticism was being leveled against mismanagement of economic assistance by the Menderes government and its irresponsible spending. U.S. anxiety mounted when the government resorted to violent measures to suppress opposition.

The revolution of 1960, American leaders were pleased to learn, was directed against neither NATO nor the United States. A copy of the armed forces manifesto, which was first read on the radio at 4 A.M. on May 27, 1960, was slipped under the main entrance of the American embassy in Ankara; in this document, the revolutionary junta promised to remain loyal to all of Turkey's alliances. The United States noted with satisfaction that the military government, unlike those of many other countries, was

[27] See *Survey of International Affairs, 1956–1958* (London, 1962), pp. 361–62.
[28] Gotthard Jäschke, *Die Türkei in den Jahren 1952–1961* (Wiesbaden, 1965), p. 86.
[29] For the Turkish attitude in the Cyprus conflict, see chapter VI below.

soon replaced in fact by a constitutional and democratic civilian administration.

Although the once rather subdued anti-American voices began to appear in the press and in the pronouncements of political leaders of the left, collaboration based on mutual trust continued in the post-revolutionary period. The Cuban missile crisis of October 1962 gave clear evidence of the unswerving (many in Turkey now would say "blind") loyalty of the Turkish leaders to American leadership.

President John F. Kennedy informed all of the allied countries of the Soviet placement, despite claims to the contrary, of intermediate-range ballistic missiles with nuclear warheads on Cuba and of the American counter-measures. Prime Minister Inönü was informed by a letter from the American ambassador in Ankara. It asked for Turkish cooperation and once more confirmed American commitments to Turkey. The Turkish government expressed a pledge of support, and Inönü announced in the National Assembly: "Just as we will ask our allies to fulfill their duties of solidarity when we face a danger, we shall certainly fulfill our own duty when our allies ask us to do so."[30]

During the evening of October 26 and early morning of October 27, two letters were received by the White House from Soviet Premier Khrushchev, both dated October 26, 1962. The first, long and emotional, admitted the existence of missiles in Cuba and offered their withdrawal in return for an American agreement to lift the quarantine and a pledge not to invade the island. The second letter, couched in official language, sought to establish a parallel between Cuba and Turkey: missiles in Cuba would be withdrawn in return for the withdrawal of American missiles in Turkey; furthermore, the Soviet Union would pledge not to invade Turkey if the United States would make a similar pledge about Cuba.[31]

The withdrawal of the Jupiter missiles placed in Turkey had been suggested by the United States since the spring of 1961, but no agreement had been reached with Turkey; Turkish military leaders considered them important for the defense of their country. At the meeting of the NATO council in the spring of 1962, Secretary of State Dean Rusk again raised

[30] Metin Toker, "Four Eventful Years with Ismet Paşa," a series of articles in *Milliyet*. The above quotation is from the issue of February 4, 1969.
[31] A firsthand account of the events is to be found in Robert F. Kennedy, *Thirteen Days: A Memoir of the Cuban Missile Crisis* (New York, 1969), especially pp. 93–99. The text of Khrushchev's second letter, dealing with Turkey, is printed in the same volume, pp. 196–201.

the question with the representative of Turkey, but upon Turkish objection, the matter was dropped.[32] The president of the United States was thus faced with the dilemma of removing these missiles under Soviet threat (without, for lack of time, consulting NATO or Turkey) or destroying the Soviet missiles in Cuba from the air, in which case the Soviets would attack Turkey. All NATO—actually all mankind—would be involved. In Ankara the Soviet Ambassador Ryzhov told members of the government that a nuclear war was on Turkey's doorsteps.[33]

President Kennedy eventually refused to trade Turkey for Cuba; in his reply to Khrushchev, dated October 27, he simply ignored the second message of the Soviet premier (which was presumably the result of some confusion or dissension in Moscow) and accepted the offer contained in the first letter, which did not refer to Turkey. The Cuban missile problem was solved in such a manner; later, in early 1963, the Jupiter missiles were removed from Turkish soil.

The Cuban crisis revealed the interdependence of American security with that of her NATO allies; but it also made Turkey realize that a decision by Washington might jeopardize her safety and even her existence. While the successful resolution of this crisis somewhat allayed world tensions and, at least for the time being, stalled other Soviet expansionist moves (the pressure on Berlin, for example, was lifted), the danger which it created for Turkey kindled criticism against the American influence which so much monopolized the foreign policy of Turkey. The already simmering discontent erupted into violent fault-finding; the missile crisis has since been highly dramatized by the press and leaders of Turkey.

Although the Cyprus crisis of 1964 rightly may be considered as the catalyst for the decline of Turco–American relations, the specific event which triggered the reaction was President Lyndon B. Johnson's letter of June 5, 1964.

Since late 1963, when President Makarios of Cyprus repudiated the constitution adopted under the Zurich–London Agreements, the fate of the Turkish Cypriots had caused deep concern in Turkey. Several times during the spring of 1964 the government of Ankara considered military intervention in this island—a step which it felt the existing agreements authorized. During the first days of June 1964, preparations were in prog-

[32] The Jupiter missiles were considered obsolete and unnecessary because of the Polaris missile-manned submarines in the Mediterranean.
[33] Metin Toker in *Milliyet*, February 5, 1969.

ress to invade Cyprus because the presence of United Nations forces seemed insufficient to quell disturbances.[34] The American ambassador was given warning of the impending military operation, and this elicited the letter by President Johnson.[35]

The president expressed "grave concern" over the contemplated invasion and did not find it "appropriate" to be presented with a "unilateral decision." He called the attention of the Turkish prime minister to the NATO obligations which do not allow member countries to wage war on each other, and to the possibility of a direct involvement by the Soviet Union. Here the president significantly added: "I hope you will understand that your NATO Allies have not had a chance to consider whether they have an obligation to protect Turkey against the Soviet Union if Turkey takes a step which results in Soviet intervention without the full consent and understanding of its NATO Allies."

President Johnson also recalled Turkey's obligations as a member of the United Nations and under the direct American-Turkish agreements:

I wish also, Mr. Prime Minister, to call your attention to the bilateral agreement between the United States and Turkey in the field of military assistance. Under Article IV of the Agreement with Turkey of July 1947, your government is required to obtain United States consent for the use of military assistance for purposes other than those for which such assistance was furnished. Your government has on several occasions acknowledged to the United States that you fully understand this condition. I must tell you in all candor that the United States cannot agree to the use of any United States supplied military equipment for a Turkish intervention in Cyprus under present circumstances.

While admitting that what he said was "much too severe," the president wished to assure the Turkish prime minister that the United States has not been in the past, and will not be in the future, unaware of Turkish interests in Cyprus. But, once more warning the Turkish government that its contemplated action could involve the "gravest issues of war and peace," he wrote:

You have your responsibilities as Chief of the Government of Turkey; I also have mine as President of the United States. I must, therefore, inform you in the deepest friendship that unless I can have your assurance that you will not take such action without further and fullest consultation I cannot accept your injunc-

[34] For the events in Cyprus, see chapter VI below.

[35] President Johnson's letter of June 5, 1964, was first made public in the Turkish press in January 1966. The original English text, together with Prime Minister Inönü's reply, was published in the *Middle East Journal* (Summer 1966): 386–93.

tion to Ambassador Hare of secrecy and must immediately ask for emergency meetings of the NATO Council and of the United Nations Security Council.

The plan to intervene militarily in Cyprus was abandoned, and we may assume that the principal reason for this inaction was the American attitude, expressed in the president's letter. Prime Minister Ismet Inönü replied on June 14, 1964, in a letter where he stated: "We have, upon your request, postponed our decision to exercise our right of unilateral action in Cyprus conferred to us by the Treaty of Guarantee."

The prime minister explained further that since the renewed outbreak of violence in Cyprus his government had consulted the United States several times. He listed the various occasions when such consultations had taken place and said that he had received no answer when requesting support for a military action. He dwelt at length on the breach of international agreements committed by the president of Cyprus, Archbishop Makarios, and by the Greek government. He then wrote:

I put it to you, Mr. President, whether the United States Government which has felt the need to draw the attention of Turkey to her obligation of consultation, yet earnestly and faithfully fulfilled by the latter, should not have reminded Greece, who repudiates Treaties signed by herself, of the necessity to abide by the precept "Pacta sunt servanda" which is the fundamental rule of international law.

The prime minister of Turkey strongly objected to the American intimation that no assistance would be available against a Soviet aggression:

The part of your message expressing doubts as to the obligation of NATO Allies to protect Turkey in case she becomes directly involved with the USSR as a result of an action initiated in Cyprus, gives me the impression that there exists between us a wide divergence of views as to the nature and basic principles of the North Atlantic Alliance. I must confess that this has been to us the source of great sorrow and grave concern. Any aggression against a member of NATO will naturally call from the aggressor an effort of justification. If NATO's structure is so weak as to give credit to the aggressor's allegations then it means that this defect of NATO needs really to be remedied.

Our understanding is that the North Atlantic Treaty imposes upon all member states the obligation to come forthwith to the assistance of any member victim of an aggression. The only point left to the discretion of the member states is the nature and the scale of this assistance. If NATO members should start discussing the right or wrong of the situation of their fellow-member victim of a Soviet aggression, whether this aggression was provoked or not and if the decision on whether they have an obligation to assist this member should be made to depend on the issue of such a discussion, the very foundations of the Alliance would be shaken and it would lose its meaning.

The Johnson letter has left a lasting imprint on Turkish-American relations. It was not only interpreted as a support of the Greek thesis but as
an abandonment of Turkey. Prime Minister Inönü was reported to have
announced to his cabinet: "Our friends and our enemies have joined hands
against us."[36] Subsequent press comments repeatedly refer to the letter as
a "betrayal" of Turkey, as a "blow to national dignity,"[37] or as having
"broken the Turkish nation's heart."[38]

The letter was probably a step in the right direction to dissuade Turkey from using force in Cyprus, but, phrased as it was, the missive was
not the appropriate tool to promote the desired goal. Long before the
Turks were ready to strike—and there is evidence that Washington was
kept informed of this action under advisement—the United States should
have maintained close contact with Ankara in order to avoid a sudden
and abrupt exchange of messages on this vital subject. Even so, instead of
sending an ultimatum-like letter, the dispatch of a high-ranking State
Department official who could have conveyed the president's message in
a more diplomatic tone would have been preferable. The letter itself
avoided a discussion of the legal issue to which the Turkish government
attached greatest importance. The remainder that NATO weapons could
not be used without the approval of the alliance or the United States certainly lacked tact because it exposed the dependent character of the Turkish ally. The threat that no assistance could be expected against a Soviet
aggression toward Turkey, following an action against Cyprus, was likely
to shake confidence in American commitments.

The inadequacy of the Johnson letter was, furthermore, brought into
evidence three years later when Turkey again, in November 1967, prepared to land military forces on Cyprus. This time, the White House sent
an emissary, the former Under-Secretary of Defense Cyrus Vance, who
accomplished his task of preventing the outbreak of Turkish-Greek hostilities and negotiated a settlement of the dispute to the satisfaction of the
Turkish government without creating false impressions and resentment.[39]

The conflicting views on Cyprus and on the nature of the Atlantic

---

36 *The Times* (London), August 27, 1964.
37 *Cumhuriyet,* November 25, 1968.
38 *Akşam,* September 21, 1967.
39 Former Prime Minister Ismet Inönü, now leader of an opposition party, paid
tribute to Cyrus Vance: "He worked hard for peace and the solution of the crisis.
He achieved this to a certain extent. . . . We owe him gratitude." *Vatan,* December 8,
1967.

alliance were demonstrated in the Johnson letter and in Inönü's reply. This experience induced the Turkish leaders to re-evaluate their relationship with the United States and their role in NATO. As to their rapport with Washington, it was really not a *re*-evaluation: up to that time, the Turkish leaders had never seriously analyzed the context of American interests relating to Turkey or the Turkish national interest as it related to the United States' role in the affairs of Turkey. That Turkey ceased to follow the American initiatives automatically, but acted only after due consideration with regard to national interest, amounted to a change. It was, for instance, realized that all major countries of the Atlantic alliance had, to some extent, mended their fences with the Soviet Union, whereas Turkey had stayed behind as the last inflexible "Cold Warrior." Similarly, Turkey had completely neglected her relations with the Third World. Consequently, she had found herself voted down on the Cyprus dispute in the United Nations by her official opponents (the Soviet bloc countries), by the neutralists, and also by some of her official allies. Thus, the search for new orientations began.

Within a few years, Turkish diplomacy was able to bring the country from an uncomfortable isolation to a new complex of relationships which included the establishment of more friendly relations with the Soviet Union and its allies, the transformation of previously cool into cordial contacts with the Arab states, and the concurrent maintenance of her status within NATO and close contacts with the United States. She did not follow de Gaulle's France in undoing her military participation in NATO; rather she revised her orientation, established contacts where there had been none, or introduced cordiality where there had been frigidity.

A Turkish commentator expressed this change in the following terms:

Our foreign policy has been changing because of the events affecting it directly or indirectly for the last three or four years. The American stand in the Cyprus problem caused this change to a certain extent. After Johnson's letter and Inönü's answer, *Turkey's policy swung from one-sidedness to many-sidedness.* . . . The Arab–Israeli clash was the last development to have a big influence on our foreign policy although it did not directly concern us. . . . Those who infer passivity from the principle "Peace at home, peace in the world" may question the wisdom of supporting the Arabs, that is, the Eastern Bloc and the non-aligned countries. But even they should admit that our *foreign policy needed a shake-up.* Turkey had to save herself from the "satellite" complex which was felt in the public. . . .
  Looking at all these signs we may conclude that the *Turkish foreign policy is on the path to being more realistic.* The real problem now is to be able to resist

the external pressures which will be exerted and increased in order to change this course.[40]

Another observer remarked:

Turkey did not improve her relations with the Soviet Union just because of Cyprus (those improved relations were necessitated by changing world conditions), but the fact is that the Turkish public now weighs a nation's friendship or animosity by its stand over Cyprus. Perhaps this is primitive but this is the truth.[41]

And Ahmet Şükrü Esmer, professor of diplomatic history at the Ankara University, wrote:

Turkey has shown with her behavior over the Middle East crisis that her foreign policy has reached a new phase. Since 1950, and especially after joining NATO in 1952, Turkey had always followed in the wake of the United States. The first awakening began with Cyprus. Johnson's letter, written in bad form to Inönü, and his threatening Turkey with Russia, led to this *revision of policy*. . . . It is understood that the Americans who were used to seeing Turkey as a satellite are not pleased with this development.[42]

It is now generally acknowledged in Turkey, in the ministry of foreign affairs as well as by the leaders of the ruling Justice Party, and the moderate or rightist opposition parties, that the total dependence of Turkey on the United States, the uncritical acceptance of American requests or suggestions, and the blind imitation of everything American did not benefit Turkey. Or, if correct in the past, such conduct is no longer useful or prudent under the changed conditions of the sixties and seventies. However, the accusation that Turkey is or has been an American "satellite" is strongly denied in official circles and by those who disagree with the rampant anti-American sentiment.

A variety of accusations have been levelled against the United States. A sampling might include the following: American military presence and the so-called bilateral treaties with Washington have impaired

[40] Ecvet Güresin in *Cumhuriyet,* July 17, 1967. (Italics added.)
[41] Metin Toker in *Milliyet,* December 11, 1967.
[42] *Ulus,* July 27, 1967. (Italics added.) Nadir Nadi, editor of *Cumhuriyet* and well-known foreign policy commentator, wrote: "In 1946–47 the only country which welcomed the American sailors was Turkey. . . . Today the situation has changed and the 'Go home' demonstrations against the Sixth Fleet exceed the limits of oral expression. . . . The wrong and humiliating behavior of the USA over the Cyprus crisis caused this change." *Cumhuriyet,* February 11, 1969.

the sovereign rights of Turkey; the United States is interfering in the domestic affairs of that country; America views Turkey as nothing more than a frontier outpost which can be turned into a battleground at will, like Korea or Vietnam, when American interests so demand; the United States was secretly given the right to occupy Turkish territory in the event of a domestic uprising in Turkey; and, finally, the Americans use Turkish territory to carry out their espionage or for the launching of spy aircraft, such as the U-2 in 1960.[43]

These and other attacks against the American ally and NATO were refuted one by one by official pronouncements and also denounced by moderate press organs. Thus the ministry of foreign affairs denied the allegation by *Akşam* that the United States forces are authorized to occupy Turkey for security reasons when necessary.[44] Foreign Minister Çağlay-angil let himself be interviewed in order to clarify misrepresentations about NATO's aims and powers. He denied the accusation that the new NATO strategy only serves American interests and that the "integration" of forces exists against Turkey's interests:

In the First and Second World Wars an allied chain of command could only be secured a long time after the outbreak of war. According to the view of military strategists, if this had been secured at the beginning, these wars could have been greatly shortened and immense savings could have been made in manpower and material casualties. So it is necessary to prepare plans in time of peace and establish the chain of command during peace time.[45]

The foreign minister denied that NATO could drag Turkey into a war against her will:

It is impossible for NATO to drag Turkey into a war against her wishes. Because, as it is known, to decide on an armed confrontation NATO requires a political decision by its Ministerial Council. Such a decision can only be taken by a unanimous resolution of all NATO members. In other words for such a decision, Turkey's positive vote is needed.[46]

[43] These accusations are repeated again and again in the press, as for instance: *Cumhuriyet*, October 26, 1967; *Akşam*, November 10, 1967; *Yeni Gazete*, November 27, 1967; *Akşam*, March 8, 1968, April 5, 1968, May 7, 1968. Turkish sources also complained that Washington wished "to punish" Turkey because the government failed to control the production of opium which, in the form of heroin, is being smuggled into the United States; *New York Times*, June 14, 1970; *Washington Post*, July 24, 1970; *Milliyet*, July 22 and August 29, 1970.
[44] *Cumhuriyet*, November 6, 1968.
[45] *Istanbul Bayram*, March 12, 1968.
[46] *Ibid.*

In his final statement the Minister emphasized that "NATO is not a hindrance to Turkey's following an individual foreign policy in keeping with her national interests; on the contrary, it enables her to follow a more active policy within NATO."[47]

Similarly, President Sunay was anxious to refute the view which held that Turkey had become a "satellite" through her alliance with the United States:

To consider these commitments incompatible with national sovereignty, national dignity and interests, and to regard them as having caused Turkey to fall into the satelliteship of other states is a mistaken view. The latest developments in the international situation have proved once again the necessity for and usefulness of our alliances.[48]

Press reports occasionally emphasized that Turkey was acting "very independently" within the NATO frame. Thus, in October 1968, she refused to allow the "Orient Express" maneuvers to be held along the Syrian border because of the unrest in the Middle East. [49] Publicists also pointed out that in our present atomic age it would be futile to speak of "independence" in the sense of complete freedom of action.[50] In the foreign ministry, responsible officials often insisted that Turkey was being consulted on actions and policies of the Alliance. They admitted that there is a "hegemony of fact" on the part of the United States because of her superior power, but pointed out that this is not a "binding hegemony." Rather it is a "leadership by persuasion" which, in case of disagreement, one could easily oppose.

The Cyprus controversy also encouraged an undercurrent in Turkish opinion that attributed a pro-Greek bias to the Americans. It was said that the Department of State is infiltrated with "Hellene-born" officials, that President Johnson's private secretary was a Greek, that Vice-President

---

47 *Ibid.*

48 *Son Havadis,* August 31, 1968. President Sunay was referring in his above statement to the invasion of Czechoslovakia by Soviet and other forces.

49 *Cumhuriyet,* November 26, 1968.

50 "The fools say 'independence.' In this atomic age there is no independence. If Turkey collapses, Russians will stretch as far as Dakar. The Turkish Bolsheviks have been working for this since 1920. Never! We will stay in the forefront of the fight for freedom with the United States. This is the guarantee of Turkey's independence under the existing conditions. We will be neither Tito's tail, nor Moscow's stooge." Falih Rıfkı Atay in *Dünya,* September 12, 1967.

Spiro Agnew engages in pan-Hellenic activities, or that Greeks were favored against Turks simply because the former were Christians.[51]

While American policies and actions were under fire, the principal target of anti-Americanism was the conspicuous presence of Americans in Turkey, where they constituted the principal alien element.

AMERICAN PRESENCE IN TURKEY

The number of American civilian and military personnel in Turkey (including their dependents) has varied between 15,000 and 30,000 in the last few years. In numbers they are even superior to another, more ancient group of aliens—namely, the Hellenic citizens in Istanbul (who are to be distinguished from the Turkish citizens of Greek tongue).

These Americans can be divided into two contingents—the civilians and the military. The civilian group primarily includes members of the United States diplomatic and consular missions, the United States Information Service (USIS), the Agency for International Development (USAID), the Peace Corps, and various private business or educational organizations. The two principal characteristics of this group for our purposes are their clustered settlement in the big cities and their relatively small size. There presently are far greater numbers of American military personnel in Turkey who live mostly in or around the military bases, which are officially (and more correctly) called "joint installations." The most important of these bases are in Western Turkey near Izmit (Karamursel air base) and Izmir (Ciğli); in the south and southeast near Adana (Incirlik) and Diyarbakır (Pirincilik) as well as those which are scattered in different parts of the country—in Manisa, Afyon, Konya, Iskenderun, Samsun, Trabzon, Erzerum, and also around Ankara. American contingents operate these installments as part, or as training units, of the Sixth Allied Tactical Air Force (SIXATAF) and of the First and Third Turkish Air Forces, all of which are committed to NATO in case of war. As mentioned earlier, the skeleton NATO command is "fictional" in peacetime. Accordingly, the United States officers in practice are restricted to command of the American units of the forces assigned to NATO.

---

[51] See *Hurriyet*, November 24, 1967; *Yeni Gazete*, August 11, 1968; *Cumhuriyet*, November 8, 1968; *Milliyet*, November 11, 1968. Even the marriage of Jacqueline Kennedy to the Greek shipowner Onassis has been given a political anti-Turkish meaning.

Another major subcommand of the United States Air Force in Turkey is the United States Logistics Group (TUSLOG), with headquarters in Ankara. Its mission is to provide logistical support for all United States forces in the area of the eastern Mediterranean and the Middle East, for the Military Assistance Advisory Groups, for the Joint United States Military Mission for Aid to Turkey (JUSMMAT), and for other American units and agencies. The NATO military maneuvers and war games held in Turkey are logistically supported by TUSLOG.

Contrary to the widespread belief in Turkey that these American bases are owned and exclusively controlled by the United States command, Turkish official spokesmen have pointed out that the joint defense installations are under the control of Turkey and are part of Turkish state property. Under the agreements in force, United States personnel could use these installations but would not be allowed to engage in any operations directed against other countries without the knowledge and consent of Turkish authorities.[52]

United States military forces, however, enjoyed a number of privileges generally accorded to foreign "visiting forces" under general international law or special agreements. Thus, supervisory or disciplinary authority over such visiting forces in foreign territory was reserved for their own commanding officers.[53] Naturally, the same privileges would accrue to Turkish armed forces abroad.

The prolonged stay of American military personnel on Turkish territory, equipped with their weapon systems, the establishment of their garrisons and military installations, and their movements and supply have necessitated the conclusion of agreements pertinent to the fulfillment of their military task as well as to their welfare and protection. It was, for instance, necessary to divide criminal jurisdiction between Turkish courts and the military service courts of the visiting armed forces. Exemptions under existing customs control had to be made for the equipment of these forces and goods delivered to them. Special passport regulations had to be introduced for servicemen. Furthermore, agreements had to be reached concerning the joint use of installations constructed under American or NATO plans, with regard to the use of training facilities, the

[52] See statement by the Turkish Ministry of Foreign Affairs in *Cumhuriyet*, July 20, 1968; Prime Minister Demirel in *Yeni Gazete*, November 27, 1968.

[53] For more recent development of international law relating to military forces stationed on foreign territory, see F. A. Váli, *Servitudes of International Law* (2d ed.; London and New York, 1958), pp. 208–17.

control of weapon systems, or the command structure at joint installations. Particularly important were arrangements with respect to the "double key" system to be agreed upon between the United States and Turkey.

Fifty-five agreements were concluded through 1964 relating to the military presence of the United States on Turkish soil. These agreements, some very significant, others of minor importance, were known as bilateral agreements, to distinguish them from the multilateral conventions of NATO. Most of these agreements have never been submitted for approval to the Turkish Parliament or even made public.

After the Cyprus crisis of 1964 and under the impact of rising anti-American sentiment, the opposition parties demanded publication, cancellation, or revision of the bilateral agreements which, they submitted, violated Turkish sovereignty, reintroduced the ill-famed capitulatory system of Ottoman days, or were inconsistent with the constitution. In addition, the Turkish military demanded greater operational control of joint installations and a larger share in the facilities, such as runways, hangars, and housing.[54]

Negotiations began in March 1966 for the revision of the bilateral agreements. But this proved to be a difficult task because many technical questions were involved and the topics were of a highly sensitive, political nature. When harassed by the opposition, the government of Süleyman Demirel pointed out that none of these agreements had been concluded under the Justice Party's rule. Foreign Minister Çağlayangil answered some charges by pointing out that eight of the "most dangerous bilateral agreements" had the signatures of his critics.[55] In fact, some of these arrangements had become obsolete or nonapplicable (as those concerning the handling of the Jupiter missiles), while others had to be completely renegotiated because of changed circumstances.[56] It was agreed between the negotiating parties that the provisions concerning the stationing of American forces should be consolidated into one "basic" agreement.[57]

In January 1969, Foreign Minister Çağlayangil announced that the

[54] See *New York Times,* March 28, 1966.
[55] *Cumhuriyet,* November 6, 1968.
[56] In February 1969, during the budget debates in the Senate, Çağlayangil revealed that some of the bilateral agreements were missing because of the confusion that followed the May 27, 1960, revolution; *Cumhuriyet,* February 3, 1969.
[57] *Yeni Gazete,* August 21, 1967; *Hürriyet,* November 15, 1968.

talks concerning the basic agreement had been concluded.[58] The main principles of the new comprehensive agreement included the following:

1. The joint defense installations were recognized as being the property of the Turkish republic. No new installations may be established without the consent of Turkish authorities.

2. The Turkish republic exercises full control over these installations and may station as many troops there as it wishes.

3. The number of American personnel stationed in or around these installations may be increased, decreased, or replaced, but the Turkish authorities have to be duly informed of any such moves.

4. The non-Turkish personnel are subject to the provisions of the Status of Forces Agreement of June 19, 1951, which divided jurisdiction between the territorial authorities and national command authorities of the visiting forces.[59] In contrast to earlier practice, it was agreed that the so-called duty document (a statement by the American command that the soldier suspected of having committed an offense was "on duty" at the time) was no longer automatically acceptable. This meant that the incriminated member of the armed forces no longer could be unilaterally removed from Turkish jurisdiction.[60]

On July 3, 1969, the Cooperation Agreement Concerning Joint Defense was signed in Ankara by Turkish Foreign Minister Çağlayangil and the American Ambassador William J. Handley. This agreement, which replaced the Military Facilities Agreement signed on June 23, 1954, revised some of the bilateral arrangements and attempted to clarify others. The new cooperation agreement sought to base American–Turkish relations concerning defense on a mutual respect for the sovereignty and equal rights of the two parties. In general, it was stipulated that any military installation in Turkey and its use must have the approval of the Turkish government; Turkey retains property rights of the land allotted

---

[58] See Çağlayangil's speech before the Mixed Budget Committee, *Milliyet*, January 7, 1969.

[59] The NATO Status of Forces Agreement was signed in London on June 19, 1951, and signed by Turkey in 1956. For text see NATO, *Facts*, pp. 217–29.

[60] In the case when both the military authorities of the forces of the foreign state and the local (Turkish) authorities have jurisdiction according to their respective legal regulations, the conflict of concurrent jurisdiction may be resolved by the claim of the American military authorities that the soldier was "on duty." The present change allowed the Turkish authorities to examine this and other circumstances of the crime before they agreed to waive their jurisdictional claim in the matter.

to joint defense installations. Her authorities have the right to inspect them and to assign her own military or civilian personnel to these areas. The joint management and utilization principle will be applied in these installations. The Turkish government was also authorized to restrict American utilization of bases in the event of a national emergency. American military and civilian personnel were bound to observe Turkish law. Furthermore, some of the bilateral agreements were to be revised regarding the implementation of the above agreed principles.[61]

The implementation of the consolidated basic agreement, while hardly satisfactory to the anti-American complex, was more acceptable to the moderates and removed the principal reason for the anxiety which grew from the alleged surrender of Turkish sovereignty to the United States.[62]

One may rightly question whether American participation in general was not overextended in Turkey and, therefore, whether a decrease of personnel would seriously compromise the defense of Turkey and commitments under NATO. To give one example, Turkish responses were highly favorable when the American-controlled "Site 23" communications base in Gölbaşı, 25 miles south of Ankara, was ceremoniously handed over to the Turkish armed forces in June of 1968.[63]

But anti-American complaints and accusations were by no means restricted to the complexities of the American military presence. Some justified resentment, which could be easily met, was confused with wholly

[61] On February 7, 1970, at his press conference, Prime Minister Demirel gave the most detailed information concerning the Military Facilities Agreement of July 3, 1969. He emphasized that the joint defense installations are under the joint control of the Turkish and NATO authorities and that the Turkish government will allow US forces to engage in any activity only after obtaining full information about the nature of these activities. By July 1, 1970, American military and civil personnel on these installations will be reduced to about 6000 men. The above agreement will not be submitted to the Grand National Assembly because under paragraph 3 of Article 65 of the constitution agreements concluded pursuant to an international convention do not require parliamentary ratification. *Cumhuriyet,* February 8, 1970.

[62] After the conclusion of the new Military Facilities Agreement, complaints were voiced that the important Incirlik Base remained under the exclusive control of the U.S. Strategic Air Force. It was suggested that its status be reduced to that of the Ciğli Base near Izmir which was operated jointly by Americans and Turks; see M. A. Kislali's article in *Tercüman,* July 10, 1969.

[63] *Cumhuriyet,* June 15, 1968. It was announced that by the end of 1968 the American radar stations along the Black Sea, in Samsun and Sinop, were handed over to the Turkish Air Force; *Milliyet,* December 31, 1968.

exaggerated or invented grievances. These varied from the belief that archeological treasures were being smuggled out of Turkey and that USIS or Peace Corps personnel were involved in espionage activities to an accusation that the "Turkish nation is being poisoned by American wheat."[64]

This climate of suspicion was fostered by both leftist nationalist and conservative-traditional groups and rendered fruitful cooperation in many fields difficult if not impossible. Research in various areas, especially anthropological, sociological, and economic field work, often has been thwarted by the resentment of local authorities, or by the reluctance of higher circles to cooperate for fear of provoking partisan accusations.[65]

The Turks expected American and other official visitors to have a solid knowledge of Turkish problems; any sign of ignorance was unfavorably recorded and interpreted as an expression of disdain toward Turkey.[66] The assassinations of President Kennedy, Martin Luther King, and Robert F. Kennedy were extensively exploited by the leftist press to prove American decadence and to compare it with conditions in the decaying period of the Roman Empire.[67]

The Vietnam War in particular stirred up anti-American feelings. Extremist-press organs explained to their readers that "Turkey is on the same parallel" as Vietnam and that she is being invaded and suppressed by the Americans in a similar manner. When Robert W. Komer, former chief of the pacification program in Vietnam, was appointed United States Ambassador to Turkey, he was described by one press commentator as "a notorious monster who ran torture affairs in the American intelligence

[64] *Milliyet*, August 7, 1967; Ilhami Soysal in *Akşam*, September 7, 1967; October 4, 1968. The Mexican "Sonora–64" wheat introduced from the United States to Turkey, which later proved to be an outstanding success, was mentioned as an attempt "to poison the Turkish nation"; *Tercüman*, May 22, 1968.

[65] See Edwin J. Cohn, "The Climate for Research in the Social Sciences in Turkey," *Middle East Journal* (Spring 1968): 203–12. For instance, a questionnaire circulated in the villages by researchers of The Johns Hopkins University on a health survey, in cooperation with the Institute of Hygiene in Ankara, was labeled as espionage. The questions included one as to whether there was a Koran course in the village and how many attended it; *Adalet*, May 17, 1968.

[66] When a group of leading American journalists and radio and television commentators visited Istanbul, they were briefed by the foreign ministry spokesman Oktay Işçen. According to press reports they surprised the official with such questions as: "In which part of Turkey is Cyprus?" "How long has Cyprus been under Turkish rule?" "How many Turks are living in Cyprus?" The report concluded that these visitors were very unfamiliar with Turkey and the Cyprus question; *Yeni Gazete*, October 22, 1967.

[67] Reşat Titiz in *Vatan*, June 7, 1968.

service in South Vietnam."[68] When he visited the Middle East Technical University in Ankara (established and maintained to a large extent by financial support from the Ford Foundation), his car, which bore a diplomatic number, was burned by a group of leftist students.[69] Some of the leftist organs excused this act of vandalism by labeling the ambassador's visit to the university a "provocation."[70]

Since 1964 anti-American demonstrations by students have become a matter of course.[71] Among the opportunities for demonstrations, visits by units of the Sixth Fleet have been the most popular. Turkish police (and occasionally other armed forces) have managed to restrain such demonstrations, although not without the use of force. There were often casualties among the demonstrators. The Turkish government has berated these outbursts of anti-American sentiment, and moderate press organs have joined in their condemnation.[72] There was no doubt, as official circles constantly pointed out, that these expressions of violent anti-Americanism emanated from a tiny minority; nonetheless, this was an elite minority with considerable influence among the press, universities, and students.[73]

[68] Ilhami Soysal in *Akşam*, November 1, 1968. Robert W. Komer previously served for fifteen years with the Central Intelligence Agency as a research analyst; *Milliyet*, November 29, 1968.

[69] *New York Times*, January 7, 1969; *Milliyet*, January 7, 1969. Prime Minister Demirel told the press this about the incident: "The incident . . . is regrettable from several aspects. Firstly, regardless of which country he comes from, an envoy is an envoy. The security of an envoy is under the guarantee of the country to which he is sent. Such actions . . . impair the country's prestige abroad. . . . It is also incompatible with Turkey's traditional hospitality. . . . This aggressive action of a small student group is aimed at weakening the Turkish–American friendship." *Milliyet*, January 20, 1969.

[70] *Cumhuriyet*, January 16, 1969. Another paper praised Ambassador Komer as an expert on arms analysis: "That such an expert has come to Turkey as ambassador is lucky for Turkey. . . . What has been burnt is not a black Cadillac but the traditional Turkish hospitality and national 'amour-propre.' " *Adalet*, January 8, 1969.

[71] At the time of the 1964 Cyprus crisis, there were widespread anti-American and anti-Greek demonstrations; *New York Herald Tribune*, August 29, 1964; *Neue Zürcher Zeitung*, August 31, 1964.

[72] For more recent such demonstrations, see the *New York Times,* February 11 and 17, 1969. The *Yeni Gazete* editorialist reminded its readers that twenty-three years have passed since the battleship *Missouri* received such a tumultuous welcome in Istanbul, while now American sailors are thrown into the sea; *Yeni Gazete*, July 19, 1968. Prime Minister Demirel declared that these visits by the Sixth Fleet were customary visits by a friendly navy. These calls by the American ships were used by the demonstrators as an "excuse to bring about unrest." He continued: "We cannot adjust the Turkish foreign policy according to such noise. We cannot allow the Turkish foreign policy to be governed by the street." *Cumhuriyet*, February 10, 1969.

[73] See C. L. Sulzberger, in the *New York Times*, August 9, 1968.

Even so, after twenty years of seemingly harmonious and productive collaboration, the militant, vituperative, and vociferous anti-American sentiment found in Turkey must be puzzling to any observer. Frustration and disillusionment because of the American refusal to support Turkey on Cyprus and an indifference toward Turkey's specific interests, or actual diplomatic blunders, understandably may have alienated Ankara. But it was not the responsible leadership which voiced the highly antagonistic noises—rather, it was those who were remote from the exercise of effective control in governmental affairs.

As far as they may be analyzed, the sources of anti-American sentiment are manifold; the motivations are both rational and irrational and rely both on tangible and intangible reasons. These can be summarized under the following six points:

1. It appears that the most powerful source of anti-Americanism is a conscious or unconscious national feeling. When American support was forthcoming to defend Turkey against a hereditary foe, the reception was enthusiastic; but after a number of years, especially when the Soviet threat faded away, the American presence, even American financial aid, became odious to many. The friend and supporter was looked upon as a usurper, an oppressor.

National pride characterizes the average Turk more than any other quality. The Turks are essentially a young nation; they have not forgotten their semi-colonial status during the late Ottoman times and are highly sensitive about national independence and national honor. For those who are convinced that the American presence is not needed, the United States is imagined as an imperialist power bent on subjecting Turkey to its will. Latent xenophobia and even religious fanaticism, often mixed with a subliminal sense of inferiority, operate in counterpoint with these feelings of national pride and frustration.

2. The meeting of the American and Turkish nationals was hardly felicitous. Their temperaments are, by and large, incompatible. Americans are often extroverts, whereas Turks are not. Americans speak frankly, act directly; such behavior is considered rude and primitive by Turks. On the other hand, when Americans tend to be reserved, they are open to reproach for haughtiness or duplicity. American affability or business-like manners do not mix easily with the dignity of the status-oriented Turk.

These incompatibilities and psychological impediments are found more frequently in Americans or Turks who have had no experience in meeting people of different cultures and different manners. The American military leadership was caught in a dilemma: if it discouraged contacts between American servicemen and Turks, as when the former separated themselves on a military base, they could be accused of aloofness and envied because of their superior way of living; on the other hand, if servicemen were encouraged to mix with the Turks, the differences of temper and habits might have caused friction. To reduce visibility and, as far as possible, the size of the American presence seemed to be the only workable solution.[74]

3. Certain aspects of domestic politics tended to foster anti-Americanism. Those circles which had vehemently opposed and overthrown the Menderes regime (intellectuals, lower-ranking army officers, and so on) opposed the government of the Justice Party. They regarded this government, as they did the Menderes government, as one supported by the United States or, directly, as an American stooge. Thus, their partisan antipathies were directed against the foreign "interloper," and in fighting the government, they fought the Americans as well.

4. Some Turks were incensed against the United States because they regarded American foreign policy as "imperialistic" or "neocolonialist." They were influenced in this attitude by the past policies of General de Gaulle, by the Vietnam War, or by any event which could be interpreted as American "bungling." Turks were often inclined to respect success only and showed impatience with failure. Protagonists of such attitudes were gloating over what they believed to be the loss of American "face" in the world. This sentiment was often coupled with the overestimation of Turkish strength and self-sufficiency in the face of a Soviet danger. One international event, however (the invasion of Czechoslovakia), caused a break in the ranks of these "neutralist" anti-Americans.

5. Economic frustrations also increased anti-Americanism. It was widely believed among intellectuals that strings attached to American economic aid have created a colonial dependency on the part of Turkey. As in some other developing countries, economic assistance by the richest country in the world was looked upon as the duty of the United States rather than as an act of generosity. Accordingly, any reduction in American aid is regarded as a failure to comply with a duty, or even as an

[74] *New York Times,* February 17, 1969.

affront. Persons ignorant of facts may even go as far as to decry United States economic or military aid as humiliating "handouts" which, in their view, it would be below Turkey's dignity to accept.

6. How far people are influenced by pro-Communist or pro-Soviet propaganda in their anti-American feeling is difficult to ascertain. No doubt, the Turkish Labor Party's propaganda had considerable impact outside the party ranks. One can only speculate about the number who listened to the vociferously anti-American *Bizim Radyo* (Our Radio), the Turkish Communist propaganda center broadcasting from East Berlin, and how great its impact was on such listeners. The relative importance of these propagandistic sources of anti-Americanism was probably much smaller than other motivations. The cumulative effect of the various antagonistic impulses was, however, enhanced by direct or concealed Communist propaganda. To play on ultra-nationalism has long been Moscow's method for stirring up anti-foreign feelings.

The American presence came suddenly to Turkey in the post-World War II period. It did not grow slowly as did the influence and prestige enjoyed in different epochs by the French, British, or Germans. Moreover, the roots of the American reputation were weaker than those of the Western European nations which had conducted relations with the Turkey of the sultans and thereafter. Whether these European nations were detested or admired, the point here is that contact with them was of some vintage and the Turks became accustomed over time to dealing with their numbers or representatives. Perhaps it was this "parvenu" or "upstart" nature of the American influence which was objected to by the older Turks.

RELATIONS WITH WESTERN EUROPE

Throughout the eighteenth and nineteenth centuries, Britain and France were the major naval powers in the Mediterranean. Their interests profited from the preservation of the Ottoman Empire and the exclusion of Russia from the Middle East. They had also developed commercial and cultural contacts with the subjects of the sultan. Occasionally, when Britain and France appeared as rivals or opponents in the affairs of the empire, the Sublime Porte contrived to play one against the other. On other occasions they cooperated as allies, as in the Crimean War, or as enemies of Turkey, as in World War I. Their respective weight on Turkey depended on the oscillation of international politics; on the whole, the French culture overshadowed any other Western influence, while British trade and financial interests often outranked those of France.

Germany, the other rival in the Ottoman scene, came to play a role in the destinies of the sultan in the last decades of the nineteenth century. Like the American presence in the mid-twentieth century, the kaiser's Germany made rapid headway in her involvement with the affairs of the empire. Germany's leading military power and her economic strength did not fail to impress the Sick Man of Europe.

Britain obtained important footholds in the Eastern Mediterranean when she occupied Cyprus in 1878 and Egypt four years later.[75] As mentioned earlier, Constantinople was almost abandoned to Russia in 1807–8 by France, and in 1915 was deserted by both Britain and France. German hegemony during World War I remained a transient phenomenon.[76]

After the liquidation of the Sèvres Treaty and the end of the Turkish–Greek War, French and British relations with Turkey greatly improved. As recalled earlier, Turkey, threatened by Italy, entered into an alliance with Britain and France in 1939. At the same time, the growth of German military power loomed threateningly over Turkey.

The vagaries of Turkey's relations with Britain, France, and Germany during World War II have been described. After the war, the Franco–British alliance with Turkey remained dormant and was subsequently absorbed by their common membership in NATO. When the Federal Republic of Germany also joined the Atlantic alliance, ties of friendship with Turkey were again re-established. Italy, now a friendly power, was also Turkey's ally in NATO. But all of these close relationships with countries of Western Europe were secondary to those between Turkey and the United States, whose protective umbrella overshadowed the members of the alliance. Only with the disaggregation of NATO in the early sixties did the profile of Turkey's ties with the individual countries of Western Europe become more pronounced.

---

[75] Turkish historians tend to believe that, with the acquisition of Cyprus and Egypt, London lost interest in the integrity of the Ottoman Empire, allowing Germany to gain dominating influence.

[76] See chapter I, pp. 15–17.

Britain

Britain has had a long acquaintance and experience with Turkey. As a naval power, she was more interested in the regime of the Turkish straits than any other country save Russia. The "infernal Straits"[77] had given her many a headache. She had unsuccessfully besieged the Dardanelles in 1915–16, although at the end of World War I she was able to take possession of Constantinople. She had to give up the Byzantine dream of Prime Minister Lloyd George but still dominated the Lausanne peace negotiations with Atatürk's new Turkey and managed to exclude Ankara from the Mosul district and its oil fields. Soon after 1925, however, Britain turned from an adversary into a friend and became in 1939 an ally of Turkey's. With the decline of German power at the end of World War II, Britain emerged as the most influential power in Ankara. By 1947, however, the burden of supporting Turkey economically and militarily against the threatening might of the Soviet Union became unbearable for her and she phased herself out, giving way to the United States as the new main protector of the Turkish state.

Since 1947 Britain's role with regard to Turkey has been that of a "silent partner" to the United States. London was hardly enthusiastic about Turkey's ambition to join NATO, for she had advanced another role for Ankara—namely, to become the leader of the planned Middle East Defense Organization.[78] Nevertheless, later the British were ready to sponsor Turkey's participation in the Atlantic alliance. In 1955 Britain still held a dominating role in the Middle East, and upon her suggestion Turkey joined the Baghdad Pact (which after the defection of Iraq became CENTO).

British–Turkish relations were heavily tested throughout the various phases of the Cypriote dispute. [79] The concern of the United Kingdom for Turkey was certainly one of the reasons which led Whitehall to refuse *enosis,* the unification of the island with Greece. As former Prime Minister Eden wrote: "I regarded our alliance with Turkey as the first consideration in our policy in that part of the world."[80]

[77] A *mot* by Admiral John T. Duckworth, commander of a British naval squadron which had almost been trapped inside the Dardanelles in February–March, 1807; Puryear, *Napoleon and the Dardanelles,* p. 140.
[78] See chapter VII below.
[79] See chapter VI below.
[80] Anthony Eden (Earl of Avon), *Full Circle* (Boston, 1960), p. 414.

Indeed, Eden exhibited greater interest toward Turkey than toward the desire of Greek Cypriots or the government of Athens.[81] Ankara responded by supporting Britain in her endeavor to have the United Nations recognize the Cypriote guerilla movement as a domestic issue; subsequently, London supported the idea of partitioning the island between Turkey and Greece, a plan eagerly seconded by Ankara.

The collapse of British influence in large parts of the Arab Middle East after the failure of the Suez invasion was hardly encouraging to Turkey. It took some time before Ankara became convinced that an independent Cyprus could satisfy Turkish interests. On the whole, however, the Zurich–London agreement was the result of difficult but nevertheless satisfactory cooperation between Ankara and London.

The rejuvenation of the defunct Baghdad Pact into the Central Treaty Organization was also the outcome of a common British-Turkish venture. After Iraq defected from the alliance, Turkey, together with the British, was to play the principal role in CENTO, with Ankara as the seat of the organization.

The gradual liquidation of British overseas commitments convinced the Turkish leaders that, in the future, they could not count on direct British support, even in a modest form. The British decision to withdraw from east of Suez was interpreted as the first step of a withdrawal from other overseas positions, such as from the eastern Mediterranean and from CENTO. Ankara would welcome an influential role for the British in European organizations but has not failed to record that while she is associated with the European Economic Community and may hope to reach full membership within a certain time, Britain's membership has been so far denied her. In other words, in one sense, Turkey is here regarded as "more European than the English."

Turkey's collaboration with Britain in NATO has not always been harmonious. The British predilection for "flexible deterrence," instead of "massive retaliation," did not quite coincide with Turkish strategical concepts. In the Turkish view, Britain's insular position, distant and immune from a conventional Soviet threat, was incommensurable with Turkey's strategic needs in an exposed location. Turkey has to rely on

[81] Cypriote Greek leaders are convinced that the British government instigated Adnan Menderes, the Turkish prime minister in 1954 to 1955, to interfere in the affairs of Turkey. See also Robert Stephens, *Cyprus: A Place of Arms* (New York, 1966), pp. 138–40.

a large army whereas Britain, partly for financial reasons, has abandoned mobilization strategy.

At the time of this writing, however, Britain is still a Mediterranean naval and air power; she still operates bases in Cyprus, 50 to 60 miles from Turkey's coastline. She is still a member of CENTO and a modest but nevertheless reliable contributor of military, economic, and technological aid to Turkey. Her past experiences in that part of the world enable her to analyze and evaluate developments with an expertise still denied to other powers. British diplomats observe with great interest the political and economic developments of Turkey; they are, however, somewhat skeptical about the ambitious goals set by Turkish statecraft. They fear that, in case of a fiasco of the Westernization policy, the ensuing frustration might lead the Turks to seek an imitation of Eastern–Communist models. Only the continued apprehension of possible Russian encroachments on their sovereignty might, in that event, restrain them from such a step. As an alternative, even a reversal of the historic trend and a return to Islamic ideal could not be excluded.

Nonetheless, in the field of diplomacy and, as far as their power potential allows in other areas, the British will remain staunch supporters of the present foreign policy line of Turkey. While remaining skeptical and cautious, they hope that their pessimistic prognostications of Turkey's future will eventually prove erroneous.

France

France is Turkey's oldest European ally; a treaty concluded between King Francis I and Sultan Suleyman the Magnificent in 1536 was believed to have been directed against the Holy Roman Empire. Thereafter, France often allied herself with the Ottoman Empire in her secular struggle against the Hapsburgs. France's alliance was also useful to the Ottomans in their battles against Spain and Venice in the Mediterranean. Thus, the Ottoman Empire, while culturally outside of Europe, served to maintain the European balance of power.

During the seventeenth and eighteenth centuries, French power increased and Ottoman power declined. Constantinople became a pawn in France's foreign policy, alternatively used against England, Austria, or Russia, especially at the time of Napoleon. In the nineteenth century, except when she supported Egypt against the Sublime Porte, France was generally friendly toward Turkey and cooperated with Britain to thwart Russian ambitions and to preserve her territorial status quo.

For a long time France represented all that was Europe in the Ottoman mind;[82] French cultural penetration greatly preceded that of any other European nation. French was the language through which European ideas entered the Ottoman Empire. After World War I, France became a neighbor of Turkey when she assumed control of the mandated territories of Syria and Lebanon. As described earlier, Turkish diplomacy skilfully used France's need for an ally in the eastern Mediterranean prior to World War I to obtain the retrocession of the Alexandretta District (Hatay). France's collapse during the war and her relative weakness in the postwar period greatly diminished French political influence in Turkey. Her cultural predominance also suffered as American penetration increased; within twenty years after World War II, French ceased to be the primary foreign language used by Turks, becoming replaced more and more by English.[83]

A revival of the French political and cultural impact occurred when General de Gaulle became the president of the republic. The general, as in other regions where French influence once predominated, undertook to restore France's image in Turkey. He must have been aware that he could not immediately compete with the overwhelming American influence; nevertheless, he could still compete with Britain or Germany, both of which had outdistanced French prestige during the Fourth Republic. The visit of Prime Minister Pompidou in July 1963 was the first of those exchanges which were to cement Franco-Turkish friendship. Prime Minister İnönü visited de Gaulle a year later.[84] In June 1967, at the centenary of the only previous French visit by a Turkish head of state,[85] President Sunay travelled to Paris on an official state visit.[86] The climax of this exchange of visits came in October 1968, when President

[82] The identification of anything French with Europe appears in the Turkish language: *frenk* means European; *Frengistan* stands for Europe; and *alafranga* has the meaning, "in the European style."
[83] See Geoffrey Lewis, *Turkey* (3d ed.; London, 1965), pp. 163–64.
[84] *New York Times*, July 2, 1964.
[85] In June 1867, Emperor Napoleon III received the visit of the Ottoman Sultan Abdul Aziz, a visit returned the following year by Empress Eugenie, who travelled to Constantinople (the Emperor was too ill to travel).
[86] *New York Times*, June 28, 1967.

de Gaulle received a ceremonious and cordial welcome in Turkey. Evidently, the whole range of questions of interest to both countries was reviewed on that occasion.[87]

Turkey expected France to play a more active role in a solution of the Cyprus conflict favorable to Turkish views. De Gaulle, however, hesitated to take sides and advocated the restoration of peace on the island as a prerequisite for fruitful negotiations.[88]

De Gaulle's resignation was received with mixed feelings in Turkey. Admirers of the general felt genuine sorrow; adherents of NATO felt some relief, hoping that the disaggregation of the alliance would thereafter be discontinued.

By far the most important topic of primary interest to both countries was the attitude of France and Turkey toward NATO, but it was difficult for them to find common ground. Turkey's objections to certain aspects of the Atlantic alliance differ from those of France. France liquidated all ties of military integration and retained only the skeleton of the political alliance; Turkey favored integration, but not necessarily that kind of integration existing in other geographical areas under the umbrella of NATO. Furthermore, Turkey never resorted to pressures or threats to obtain her demands but used friendly negotiations and persuasion with her partners in NATO.

While de Gaulle and Michel Debré, his foreign minister, who accompanied him on this tour, no doubt urged Turkey to pursue an "independent foreign policy."[89] they refrained from advising Ankara to follow France's example with regard to NATO.[90] France, in a much more fortunate geographical position than Turkey, may rely entirely on deterrence; Turkey, adjacent to the Soviet Union, cannot fail to develop a mobiliza-

---

[87] The Turkish press devoted much space to this visit: see *Cumhuriyet,* October 6, 1968; *Hürriyet,* October 25, 1968; *Milliyet,* October 29, 1968; *Cumhuriyet,* October 30, 1968; see also *New York Times,* October 30, 1968.

[88] *New York Times,* July 2, 1968; the Turkish press reported that de Gaulle had, at one time, advocated partition of Cyprus; *Cumhuriyet,* October 25, 1968. Before his visit to Turkey, at a press conference, he suggested a federal system for the island; *Tercüman,* October 24, 1968.

[89] *Yeni Gazete,* October 29, 1968.

[90] According to the Turkish press, de Gaulle told his cabinet after his return from Turkey that he had not visited Turkey to talk about relations with NATO. "Turkey has a very understandable attitude with regard to the future, and it is entirely normal that she should remain a NATO member. Turkey's situation is not the same as France's and in this respect France has no difference of opinion with Turkey." *Cumhuriyet,* November 1, 1968.

tion strategy of her own and, for this purpose, must receive conventional military backing. Also, observers have pointed out that had de Gaulle come to Turkey before Czechoslovakia's invasion he could have accomplished something concrete.[91] Accordingly, the net result of the visit remained symbolic rather than productive; as Foreign Minister Çağlayangil expressed it, the visit "contributed greatly to the vitality of our relations."[92]

In principle, Turkey favors European cooperation and includes herself when thinking of Europe. She favors political as well as economic cooperation by aspiring to full membership in the Common Market. Should the concept of European federalism be realized, Turkey would not hesitate to join. In this respect, Turkey would not see eye-to-eye with de Gaulle's European policy. On the other hand, the general's concept of nationalism is not alien to Turkish political thinking. It seems that, for the sake of Westernization, Turkey, unlike France, would not oppose political federalization, even if it meant a partial abandonment of complete sovereign independence.[93]

France's collaboration, in addition to the economic, technological, and cultural assistance she provides, may one day bring political dividends to Turkey, although it is at present difficult to ascertain how the "traditional friendship" might work in the future. It would be a logical extension of Turkey's foreign policy line to establish close links with the major European powers, which would not interfere with her other vital contacts and would not impede the flexible and realistic policy which she wishes to follow to attain her fundamental national objectives.

Germany

Although it did not originate in the sixteenth century, as did Turkey's friendship with France, Turks are likely to speak of their "traditional friendship" with Germany. Prussian officers trained the Turkish army from the time of von Moltke in the 1830's; Emperor William II declared

[91] *New York Times*, November 3, 1968.
[92] *Milliyet*, October 31, 1968.
[93] At his meeting with West German Chancellor Kiesinger in March, 1969, de Gaulle was reported to have expressed the view that Europe had to choose between two avenues: either the present six-nation community without new members, or the formation of a new and much more loosely organized group of states that might include not only Britain and Scandinavian countries but also—as the General expressed himself—"the Turks and the Swiss." *New York Times*, March 15, 1969.

himself the Defender of Islam in 1898; and the German *Drang nach Osten* (drive to the east) assumed the forms of economic penetration, the construction of the Baghdad Railway, and, last but not least, military assistance. The role of German influence in bringing the Ottoman Empire on her side in World War I and German hegemony during the war have been mentioned earlier. Atatürk himself had no liking for Germans, but in this respect, he was not followed by his countrymen. However, Turkey learned her lesson in the World War I and refused to place her bet on the German horse even when the Germans fought Russia in World War II. Upon the insistence of the Allies, Turkey finally severed diplomatic relations and even declared war on Germany, but only when the front was far away from Turkey's borders.

Two years after the conclusion of hostilities in Europe, those Germans who had been interned in Turkey were released and their property was returned. Ankara entered into trade relations with Bonn soon after the establishment of the Federal Republic of Germany and resumed diplomatic relations when West Germany regained her sovereignty. The German embassy building in Ankara, the Consulate General in Istanbul, and the German School, Hospital, and Archeological Institute were returned to German ownership earlier. In 1959 legislation was passed to compensate all German property owners who had left Turkey in 1944.[94]

Within the NATO alliance, the federal republic and Turkey developed another "special relationship." For example, only the military equipment of the United States was more impressive than that of Germany in strengthening Turkey's defensive power. Financial and technological assistance were no less important. Relations were also strengthened by the repeated visits of heads of government and foreign ministers of the two countries. Chancellor Adenauer was welcomed in March 1954; Chancellor Erhard came to Turkey in 1959; and Prime Minister Demirel visited Bonn in May 1967, in the company of his foreign minister. The German Foreign Minister Schröder returned the visit in July 1966; and in September 1968, Chancellor Kiesinger spent several days in Ankara. Both parties recognized that there existed "no open problems" between Ankara and Bonn.[95] Turkey, despite Soviet persuasion, refused to "up-

---

[94] Franz von Cancig, "Die Türkei, Griechenland und die deutsche Aussenpolitik," in *Deutschlands Aussenpolitik seit 1955,* ed. Helmut Reuther (Stuttgart-Degerloch, 1967), pp. 268–88.
[95] See *Die Welt,* July 9, 1966.

grade" the German Democratic Republic by granting her even a limited recognition.

Both the federal republic and Turkey possess border areas which are exposed to potential Soviet encroachments on their security. This circumstance has created a certain community of interest between the two countries and similar strategical answers to their respective defense problems. Both were reluctant to accept the abandonment of the massive retaliation concept. Both oppose a unilateral reduction of conventional forces and advocate strengthening the Atlantic alliance. At the visit of Chancellor Kiesinger in September 1968, talks were held for the purpose of "establishing closer military relations" between the two countries.[96]

Germany rates very high—probably the highest—on the scale of Turkish sympathies toward foreign countries.[97] In spite of her ultimate defeat in two world wars, Germany is considered a staunch friend, a reliable ally, and a leading nation. It is not difficult, though not always convincing, to explain this phenomenon on the basis of the similarity between the national characters of the two nations. It is often pointed out that both Turks and German are essentially "military peoples" with powerful imperialist traditions. They also share legalistic strains in their approach to international politics as well as a liking for romantic visions in their national life. Doubtless, an affinity may be found in the Prussian military organization and that of the early Ottomans; their concept of the state may also demonstrate certain similarities.[98] It seems clear that Turks are more likely to be impressed by German achievements in the fields of technology, economics, and the military than by that of any other Western nation. The presence of more than 200,000 Turkish workers in Germany who, upon their temporary or final return to Turkey, praise German efficiency and discipline, has greatly contributed to the rise of German prestige. The transfer of the savings of these workers

---

[96] See Kiesinger's interview with Turkish journalists before his departure to Turkey; *Tercüman,* September 4, 1968. Ismet İnönü revealed that, at the time of his prime ministership, the federal government of Germany sought to rent land in Turkey to be used as "training terrain" for military purposes. It was also reported that Kiesinger had renewed the request in 1968. This news was denied, however, by both the German and Turkish governments. See *Cumhuriyet,* September 18 and 19, 1968.

[97] See the results of popular opinion polls, chapter III, pp. 107–12.

[98] Lewis, *Turkey,* pp. 163–64. See also David Hotham, "The Curious Affinity of Germans and Turks," in *The Times* (London), May 11, 1967.

to their families in Turkey enhances the belief in German prosperity and ingenuity.

Although West Germany would be unable to replace, even partially, the military and economic assistance rendered at present by the United States, the role of the former in helping Turkey to strengthen her military and economic potential is likely to increase in the years to come. Although the Soviet Union dislikes the preponderant American influence in Ankara, it would hate to see West Germany firmly established as the protector of Turkey.[99] It is, however, questionable whether the federal republic would really be able or would aspire to play such a role. Ultimately, the Turks might become as apprehensive of German "hegemony" as they are now of that allegedly exercised by the United States.[100]

The Soviet menace had brought America to the shores of the eastern Mediterranean and was responsible for the present position of the United States in Turkey. Had this penetration from beyond the Atlantic not been necessary to restore an imbalance of power, Turkey would still have sought close contacts with the European West. In any case, she would have sought to become part of Europe. In other words, Turkey's links with Europe would remain permanent even if, by a change in the global balance of power, the United States decided to relinquish its interest in that part of the world.

Even if present relations with Europe had to yield before the compelling necessity of the American presence, the bond that Turkey wishes to establish between herself and Europe will, in the long run, prove to be more lasting than those with the transatlantic superpower.

Accordingly, the great question is whether and under what circumstances Turkey should continue her present status within the Atlantic

[99] According to *Hürriyet* (September 6, 1968), Kiesinger believes that "Turkey and Germany are the two doors open to Soviet danger . . . and Turkey and Germany should follow a more distinct policy toward the Soviets within NATO."

[100] Leftist press organs complained that, as a result of Chancellor Kiesinger's visit in September, 1968, "Uncle Hans" is to replace "Uncle Sam" in Turkey. "Why always look for an uncle?" asked *Yeni Gazete,* September 11, 1968. "One of our failings as a nation is that we do not regulate well the degree of friendship in our relations with others. . . . Our boundless friendship with France resulted in the Ottoman capitulations. Also the affinity we felt with Germany led to the disappearance from history of the Ottoman Empire in World War I. Paradoxically, whenever we set up such limitless friendships we shortly thereafter began to complain about it, realizing that what we receive is not as great as what we give. In short . . . creating an 'Uncle Hans' today is as harmful as the Uncle Sam we once created. The healthy path is to trust in our own might."

alliance, or whether NATO is a durable requirement of the balance of power in the eastern Mediterranean. This choice does not cease to occupy the minds of students of foreign policy in Turkey.

SHOULD TURKEY LEAVE NATO?

When Turkey acceded to NATO in 1952, the nuclear monopoly of the United States was still unchallenged; the possibility of a Soviet aggression across Germany or Austria, or against the Scandinavian or Turkish–Greek flank of Europe was still weighed. Neither the countries bordering the Soviet-controlled areas, nor those more remote from the Soviet threat, possessed sufficient conventional forces to repel aggression. The Korean War was in full swing and the outbreak of other wars "by proxy" were considered possible. Mutual guarantees of assistance, an integration of forces, and common strategical concepts were called for in order to forestall or repulse the aggression.

Nearly two decades later, the probability of Soviet aggression is believed remote. The conventional forces of the Atlantic alliance had been considerably strengthened to fight at least a delaying action—until nuclear weapons might be used should the aggression not be ended. The Soviet Union had, in the meantime, developed its nuclear arsenal and delivery system; in case of a reciprocal exchange of such weapons, a holocaust in both the United States and the USSR as well as in many homelands of their allies could be expected.

Since Khrushchev's time, "peaceful coexistence" rather than the Cold War has governed the relations between the two camps. Rapprochements have been worked out between the individual members of the Atlantic alliance and the Soviet Union, including Turkey herself. Furthermore, both NATO and the Warsaw Pact Organization have suffered internal disaggregation: France denounced military integration on the one side; Rumania became a doubtful ally on the other. Albania deserted the Warsaw Pact altogether.

In view of these changed conditions, leading foreign affairs specialists in Turkey wished to review their country's place in NATO. Such an examination was considered timely because, from August 24, 1969, member states were entitled to withdraw from the alliance after giving one year's notice. These studies and inquiries are to be distinguished from those highly prejudiced, ill-informed, or propagandistic pronouncements demanding that Turkey quit NATO. In contrast, the presentations to be examined hereafter are characterized by objectivity, scholarship, or expertise.

Fahir H. Armaoğlu, Professor of Diplomatic History of the Faculty of Political Science at the University of Ankara, suggested in late 1966 that the relations between Turkey and the United States should be reduced to a "certain minimum level." He wrote:

> We sincerely believe that *military ties* between Turkey and the United States should develop within the framework of the collective partnership of NATO, not within the narrow limits of bilateral relations. On the other hand, we strongly oppose the complete elimination of bilateral *military relations* with the United States.[101]

Armaoğlu refers to a change of objective conditions (from a bipolar to a polycentric structure in world politics) and a change in the subjective conditions of Turkey (the leftist movement, Cyprus, Turkish public opinion) to prove that the present rigid Turkish–American relationship should be transformed into a "flexible alliance" based less on material interests than on "common values and principles." He thinks that the classical balance-of-power policy is still valid in the world today and that geopolitical factors continue to play an important role. The de-emphasis of relations with the United States should do away with the "policy of influence." Turkey should try to emancipate herself from relying to a large measure on American aid, a circumstance which has become undesirable for both partners. Washington is "no longer eager to buy antipathies with her own money."

Whereas Armaoğlu suggested a transformation of the American and NATO alliances, another member of the Ankara Political Science Faculty, Halûk Ülman, advocated in 1967 a neutral status for Turkey.[102] In Ülman's view, the protection of the country and its social-economic development should not be mutually exclusive policy goals. Because of her

---

[101] Professor Armaoğlu delivered a lecture on "Turkey and the United States: A New Alliance" before the Turkish–American Association in Ankara in December, 1966. The lecture was developed into an article and published in the *Turkish Yearbook of International Relations, 1965,* pp. 1–15. (Italics added.)

[102] "Türk ulusal savunması üzerine düşünceler" ("Reflections on Turkish National Defense"), *Siyasal Bilgiler Fakültesi Dergisi* (Review of the Political Science Faculty) 21, no. 4 (1967): 197–225. See also by the same author: "Türk Dış Politikasına Yön Veren Etkenler" ("Controlling Factors of Turkish Foreign Policy"), *ibid.,* 23, no. 3 (1968): 241–73.

oversized army, required under the NATO agreements, Turkey is unable to use a considerable part of her own resources for economic development. Turkey entered NATO because of the Soviet threat, but now that Moscow has shifted its policy from direct menace to subversive activities, socio-economic reforms are the best defense against subversion.

Ülman believes that Turkey would be dragged into war under the NATO commitments should there be a conventional war anywhere in Europe. On the other hand, should Turkey be attacked by the Soviets, she would receive help even without NATO membership because the United States could not allow Russia to conquer the Middle East. In case of a nuclear war, and as a member of NATO, Turkey most probably would become a victim of nuclear devastation; if she were not a member and had neither nuclear nor radar detection devices on her territory, she would be spared.

Ülman concluded that it would be in Turkey's interest to withdraw from NATO. The Cyprus conflict demonstrated that she would not receive support from NATO or the United States when engaged in a struggle involving her individual interests. In the improbable case of a Soviet attack, she would be just as safe without NATO as within.

The argument advanced by Ülman resembles somewhat the tacit assumption of Gaullist France—namely, that the United States cannot afford to let her be invaded by Soviet forces and would come, in any case, to her rescue. The question remains, however, whether the rescue operation would not be thwarted by a liquidation of integrated forces and by the lack of a commonly conceived strategy.

Retired Admiral Sezai Orkunt discussed the advantages and disadvantages of Turkey's NATO membership in three articles published in April 1968.[103] In his view, Turkey would gain in the following respects by withdrawing from NATO: (a) leftist anti-Americanism would lose its target; (b) foreign dependence would be eliminated; (c) involvement in any local conflict outside Turkey would not arise; (d) the dismantling of American installations would reduce Turkey's exposure to nuclear attacks.

Admiral Orkunt listed the drawbacks of Turkish withdrawal from NATO as follows: (a) Turkey would be deprived of much of the eco-

---

[103] *Cumhuriyet,* April 10, 11, and 12, 1968.

nomic support she is receiving presently; (b) Turkey's regional interests might be harmed, and her position vis-à-vis Cyprus would be weakened; (c) the Soviets would try to exploit the isolation of Turkey to their benefit; (d) American military aid would be discontinued, while similar aid to Greece might be stepped up, a fact which would upset the balance of power in favor of Athens; (e) part of the military aid material would have to be returned to the United States or NATO; (f) a critical situation would arise concerning spare parts for Turkish war material, a shortage that would paralyze the armed forces; (g) while Turkey might still receive support from the West in case of a Soviet attack, she would not be helped in case of a regional war; (h) Turkey would be deprived of information and experience obtained by her participation in NATO and would have no voice in influencing developments within the Atlantic alliance.

The author concluded that "the Soviet Union would be the greatest beneficiary of Turkish withdrawal from NATO." The gains of such a move for Turkey were mostly psychological and these advantages could be obtained without leaving NATO. Turkey should therefore remain in the alliance and take measures to rectify her situation. For this purpose he made the following suggestions: (a) strategical nuclear weapons should be removed from Turkish territory; (b) tactical nuclear arms should be allowed to stay in Turkey only if the Turkish commander is authorized to use them; (c) a new Turkish national strategical concept should be worked out, and it should be fitted into the general NATO strategy; (d) NATO headquarters in Izmir should be disbanded (the Greek staff officers having already left), the Turkish forces to be placed directly under the Southern Europe Command at Naples; (e) the American installations in Turkey should be deprived of all aggressive capabilities in order to forestall retaliation; (f) Turkish war industry should be developed; (g) Turkish airfields should never be used for military operations (for instance, in the Middle East) in which Turkey does not participate; (h) it should be assured that, whenever the NATO wing states (Scandinavian members in the north, Turkey and Greece in the South) are attacked, the center would provide adequate protection with more than light mobile forces. If Turkey should have to remain under the "You die so that I may live" tacit understanding, she should seriously consider leaving NATO.

The Republican People's Party formed a committee of experts to report on the advisability of Turkey's remaining in NATO. The committee was chaired by Professor Nihat Erim; its other outstanding members were former Foreign Minister Selim Sarper and former Defense Minister Ilhami Sancar. The committee prepared a lengthy report and its basic findings were published in the press.[104]

The report also lists the advantages and disadvantages of Turkey's NATO membership. Among the former, the report mentions that NATO induced Turkey to follow a provocative policy toward her northern neighbor, that Arab countries turned their backs on Turkey, that national policy had been impaired, and that Turkey could be involved in a war in which her interests are not at stake. The report also expressed doubts whether NATO would function if Turkey became a victim of aggression.

As in Admiral Orkunt's evaluation, the report warned that Turkey would be deprived of political and economic support if she should withdraw from NATO, a loss which she can afford less than France can. American military aid to Greece will be to Turkey's disadvantage and the Cyprus question would also be unfavorably affected. The Soviet Union is likely to benefit from such a change, and the connecting link between NATO and CENTO would disappear.

Ultimately, the report recommended that Turkey should stay in NATO but that the application of the treaty should be drastically revised to conform to Turkey's national interests. The recommendations of the report for the revision of Turkey's ties with NATO and the United States ran along the same lines as those of Admiral Orkunt. The report, however, stressed the importance of a radical change in Turkey's military structure so that this country would be able both to cooperate with NATO and to safeguard its own national interests. In the opinion of the committee, NATO proved to be incapable of solving problems between its members —a clear allusion to the Turkish–Greek controversy about Cyprus.

In a series of articles on NATO published by *Milliyet,* Foreign Minister Ihsan Sabrı Çağlayangil added his contribution.[105] He began by mentioning that at the end of the tragic World War II Western statesmen asked themselves: "Would Hitler have risked aggression if European States had been determined to resist jointly the aggressive plans of Nazi Germany and had taken the necessary defense measures collectively?" The answer to this question was in the negative. It was admitted that omission was the main reason which allowed this calamity to descend on

[104] *Milliyet,* April 14, and July 5, 1968.
[105] *Milliyet,* April 8, 1968.

humanity. The rationale for the foundation of NATO was, therefore, to curtail the ambitions of a potential aggressor; the alliance maintained the power balance and played a major role in safeguarding European peace. But "it is unrealistic to regard the Alliance as an organization which prevents a détente in East-West relations." The minister continued:

To tie her security to the strongest safeguards, in the *geopolitical situation* she finds herself, is a matter of life and death for Turkey. In seeking its security, every country should use its judgment *in the light of political and military realities* by discarding sentimentalism, preconceptions, and academic speculations. The basic principle for this judgment should be not to leave national security, as much as possible, to chance. (Italics added.)

The minister explained that Turkey's security required her to have the capability "of countering a military power in her vicinity." Her individual power is insufficient to strike the balance against potential hostile forces, and, therefore, she must seek security "within a wider framework." This is why Turkey became a member of NATO and why all political parties, except one, support her membership in the alliance. He added:

Another reality is that Turkey would have to make very big sacrifices, cutting down her development effort, if she wished to maintain her defense power alone. It is common knowledge that many countries following a neutralist policy feel the necessity of devoting a much greater slice of their national income to military expenses than does Turkey.

In Çağlayangil's view, the real aim of collective security measures is to show the determination to resist aggression and to deter the potential hostile country from embarking on such an aggression. But belonging to an alliance entails making some sacrifices and also taking certain risks. The balance of mutual interests must be determined in a just and equitable manner. The burden NATO placed on Turkey is not excessive.

Turkey maintains a force of 15 divisions for the purposes of her NATO membership. Turkey's present level of armed forces is based on her needs as found after surveys and calculations. The dominating view holds that Turkey would have to increase and not reduce her forces should we have to leave NATO.

The minister emphasized that Turkey's foreign policy demonstrated that this policy is not burdened by "any mortgage" and that she can pursue her own national goals according to her own determination. He concluded:

The Alliance aims today at creating an atmosphere conducive to easing political tension and to solving conflicts, all this in addition to the achievement of collective security. No matter what some people might say, peace is being safeguarded in Europe, thanks to the balance of power provided by the Alliance.

The preceding considerations reveal that responsible leaders of Turkey were engaged in a soul-searching analysis of the measure of their NATO involvement, were rethinking the value of the alliance for their country, and also were engaged in a search for possible alternative solutions.

The first concern of those who were evaluating NATO and the American relationship was to preserve or restore the maximum freedom of action, compatible with the essential requirements of the alliance. They want their country to be an "ally" and not a "satellite." In this respect, emotional factors play a major role: intense national feeling, a wish to stress the "national personality," and the memories of past humiliations and dependencies. With some organizational changes, with greater tact concerning Turkish sensitivity, with a certain reduction in the American presence, and with a major substitution of American involvement by NATO, existing susceptibilities could be allayed and grievances met.

The second concern of Turkey in regard to NATO is the strategic conception of the alliance. There are serious doubts about the feasibility and wisdom of the "flexible response" strategy. At the bottom of these anxieties is the credibility problem: distrust in the promise made by the United States and European allies to provide massive and effective assistance to Turkey when attacked. The ultimate validity of the "One for all, all for one" axiom is questioned. There is really very little more which could be done to strengthen confidence. For the Germans, the American military presence provides the most plausible assurance that they will not be left alone, but in Turkey this argument has, so far, hardly been mentioned. Strategic planning, however, could be made more suitable and acceptable to the requirements of Turkish interests.

The present single "basic hypothesis" of NATO military planning is opposed by the Turks as being incompatible with their national interests. For them, NATO objectives or United States policy goals are no longer identical with the objectives or aims of Turkish national policy. What is good for America is not considered necessarily good for Turkey.

Despite all of these objections to the nature and implications of the Atlantic alliance, the other real alternative—a return to Kemalist neutralism—is judged unrealistic or harmful. It would jeopardize the nation's security, would endanger economic development, and would at least slow Turkey down on her road toward the fundamental goal of becoming an equal member of the Western society of nations.

Among these considerations, the care for national security is paramount. Could her security be assured without the commitments by and toward NATO and the United States? Would Turkey still be able to move toward her basic national goal? If she could become once more, without undue risks, a balancer instead of one weight in the balance of power, she might by skillful diplomacy obtain economic assistance and exert influence in European affairs. But, as her leaders realize, she cannot, unlike France, extend her "azimuth in all directions." Her geopolitical location predestines her to scrutinize the north with never-ceasing suspicion. To counter this "military power in her vicinity"—as Çağlayangil expressed it—remains the only final argument for her place in NATO. The uncertainties of Russian intentions and policies continue to weigh heavily on the decisions of the statesmen in Ankara, as they did on those who had served the Ottoman sultans on the Bosporus.

V

The USSR, the Straits, and the Balkans

Constantinople! Constantinople!
jamais! c'est l'empire du monde.
(Constantinople! Constantinople! never!
it is the empire of the world.)
Napoleon at Tilsit in 1807, after having
discussed with Tsar Alexander the
partition of the Ottoman Empire.
—M. A. THIERS, *Histoire du Consulat*
et de l'Empire (Paris, 1847),
Vol. VII, p. 654.

Su uyur, düşman uyumaz. (Water
sleeps but the enemy never sleeps.)
—Turkish proverb.

T HE RUSSIAN ADVANCE TO THE
Black Sea and, subsequently, along its western and eastern shores was
primarily responsible for the decline of external Ottoman power during
the eighteenth and nineteenth centuries.[1] The Russian moves were simultaneously prompted by the urge for geographical expansion and by an
ideological messianism. The Black Sea appeared to the Muscovites as the
natural southern border of their domain. They realized very early, however, that the navigational, commercial, and military uses of the Black
Sea were seriously hampered by its bottlenecked outlet to the Mediterranean which was jealously guarded by its Ottoman master. Although
tsarist imperialism wished to expand in every direction, its most insistent
drive remained directed toward the warm waters of the Mediterranean
Sea and the Persian Gulf.

The power politics of Russian expansionism was significantly inter-
mingled with ideological goals. Russian expansionism was to serve
Orthodox Christian coreligionaries, to remove the crescent from Constantinople, the Second Rome, and to restore Christian rule.[2] Furthermore,
under the motto of Panslavism, the Slavs of the Balkans—Serbs, Mon-

---

[1] In chapter I above the main events of Russian–Turkish relations have already
been listed; see especially pp. 8–9, 11–12, 16–17.

[2] Tsarina Catherine the Great conceived the grand design of restoring the
Byzantine Empire and placing at its head her grandson (named Constantine, after the
last Byzantine emperor). Russians (and Bulgarians) called Constantinople Tsargrad or
Tsarigrad.

tenegrines, and Bulgarians—were encouraged to revolt against their Ottoman overlords.

The 250-year-long struggle between the empire of the tsars and the Ottoman Empire was only part of the tercentennial war that Russia waged against Islam. Once Moscow had emancipated itself from the Tatar yoke in 1480, it fought and conquered Muslim–Turkic peoples: the Khanates of Kazan and of Astrakhan along the Volga, and the Crimean Khanate on the Black Sea. The Caspian Sea was reached in 1557, but Crimea (formerly a vassal state of Turkey) was annexed only in 1783. Russians fought Muslims in the Caucasus and beyond. By the middle of the nineteenth century, they had penetrated into Turkestan and conquered the Turkic-speaking peoples of that region. While absorbing the vastnesses of the southeast European and central Asian steppe, the Russian generals met organized resistance by Muslims, mostly of Turkic–Tatar stock. But the most formidable and tenacious adversary was the empire of the sultans; it was that capital that was the most coveted prize.

During this intercontinental struggle between Slavic Eastern Orthodoxy and Islam–Turkism, the principal enemy was the Ottoman Empire; at the same time, this empire was considered by its coreligionaries, who were threatened and later dominated by Muscovite power, as their only support and place of ultimate refuge. Thus, while the Ottomans had to sustain a life-and-death struggle against the northern menace, the threat was not entirely one-sided: the rulers of Russia could never discount the attraction that Ottoman independence and resistance exercised on their peoples of Turkic extraction. When the Russian empire disintegrated at the end of World War I, the peripheral Turkic nations (Azerbaijan and those of Turkestan) temporarily and precariously regained their independence. Only the simultaneous collapse of the Ottoman Empire prevented the Turkish support which might otherwise have been forthcoming.[3] At the time of this writing, the Soviet Union included among its population about forty million Turkic–speaking inhabitants, more than the population of Turkey herself.

It is natural that this struggle, continued through many ages, created

---

[3] In September 1918, nearly one month before the capitulation of Turkey to the Entente, Turkish forces occupied Baku, the capital of Azerbaijan, but withdrew after the Armistice of Mudros. Enver Pasha, who after the collapse in 1918 fled first to Berlin, then to Moscow, eventually led Turkestani Turks in their revolt against the Soviets and perished in battle in August 1922.

an atmosphere of traditional enmity between Turks and Russians. This is particularly true for Turks, who have been the losers in most of the 13 wars waged with Russia since 1677. Because Russia was the mightier power, the Turks had more to fear from her; thus, in the Turkish mind, Russia has come to be the archenemy.[4] This image became somewhat blurred after the Russian Bolshevik and Turkish Kemalist revolutions but regained its erstwhile character after the events following World War II.

SOVIET–TURKISH RELATIONS: COOPERATION AND CONFRONTATION

As far as Turkey was concerned, it appeared that with the Bolsheviki take-over in Russia a new page had been turned in the history of Russian–Turkish relations. The new government in Moscow repudiated the war-time inter-Allied agreements, giving the impression that its claims to the possession of Constantinople and the straits had been abandoned. Furthermore, it promised freedom and self-determination to the peoples of the Russian empire and in particular to the former Muslim subjects of the tsars.[5] During the war of independence, as recalled earlier,[6] Soviet backing proved to be extremely useful to the fledgling Kemalist regime. Also, that the pre-1878 border between Turkey and the Soviet Union could be restored seemed to prove that Lenin's Russia had changed its disposition.

Attitudes toward Turkey in the formative period of the Soviet state were dictated partly by opportunistic motives, partly by ideological considerations. For years after the Bolshevik take-over, the Russia of the Soviets was not only an international outcast but was seriously threatened

---

[4] The average Turk is aware that Russians have fought 13 wars against them. This writer heard many Turks in the late 1940's say, "My grandfather fought the Russians; my father did; and so shall I, and my son."

[5] On December 7, 1917, the Council of People's Commissars issued a proclamation: "To all Muslim Toilers of Russia and the East," addressed in particular to Turks, who were invited to revolt against their "robbers and enslavers." The manifesto assured Turks that the secret treaties providing for the annexation of Constantinople by Russia had been "torn up and destroyed." It also stated that "the Russian Republic and its government, the Council of People's Commissars, is opposed to the conquest of foreign territory. Constantinople must remain in the hands of the Moslems." The manifesto also announced that "the treaty for partitioning Turkey and 'depriving' her of Armenia has been torn up and destroyed." Alvin Z. Rubinstein (ed.), *The Foreign Policy of the Soviet Union* (2d ed., New York, 1966), pp. 357–58.

[6] See chapter I, pp. 19, 25.

by internal and external foes. The armies of the White Generals Denikin and Wrangel were supplied by the Western Allies across the straits and the Black Sea; the elimination of Allied occupation of Constantinople was, therefore, in the vital interest of Moscow. Kemalist Turkey, until the conclusion of the Peace Treaty of Lausanne, was another isolated regime and accordingly a natural ally of boycotted Russia.

Ideologically, the Communist theoreticians and revolutionaries of the Kremlin pursued a prolonged debate on the evaluation, from their party point of view, of the Kemalist movement and the new Turkey. They examined carefully whether the Turkish war of independence had a "class character." The more Kemalist Turkey evolved, the more these theoreticians became convinced that, although Kemalism was "progressive," it was producing a "national" not a "class" revolution. After 1923, the support provided for Turkey was no longer based on ideological grounds.[7]

In the first years of Soviet relations with Atatürk's Turkey, the well-known dualism of Soviet foreign ambitions was soundly tested in Moscow's attitude toward Turkey. Although the Comintern's objectives were frustrated by the interdiction of Communist parties in Turkey, the *Narkomindyel* (People's Commissariat of Foreign Affairs) was able to maintain close ties of cooperation with the only friendly foreign government.[8] Thus, it was ready to sacrifice the greater part of Armenia to please the Turks. Turkey was also supported in her struggle against Britain and the Greeks; in order to secure Russia's safety, Constantinople and the straits were to be restored to the absolute sovereignty of Turkey.[9]

The "special relationship" between the Soviet state and Turkey was

---

[7] See Walter Z. Laqueur, *The Soviet Union and the Middle East* (New York, 1959), pp. 25–29.

[8] The duplicity of the Comintern and *Narkomindyel* (which often operated at cross-purposes) was reciprocated by Mustafa Kemal. The Moscow-sponsored Communist movement was suppressed and only those who abandoned all international pretensions were tolerated. A group of die-hard Muscovite Communists led by Mustafa Suphi were "accidentally" drowned in the Black Sea near Trapezunt. In October 1920, Kemal set up an "official" Communist Party, staffed with some of his close collaborators, which operated for a short time. After 1925 communism was outlawed and only continued underground or in exile. See Harris, *Origins of Communism in Turkey, passim;* Edward Hallett Carr, *The Bolshevik Revolution, 1917–1923,* vol. 3 (Baltimore, 1966), pp. 299–304; Laqueur, *Soviet Union and the Middle East,* pp. 25–29.

[9] For the Soviet–Turkish cooperation during the war of independence, see Harry N. Howard, *The Partition of Turkey* (New York, 1966), especially pp. 262–64.

based on mutual interests. This relationship, which lasted until the outbreak of World War II, had as its objective the safeguarding of the peace and security of the Black Sea region and the Balkans. It was a relationship of trust rather than an alliance; while Turkey pursued a neutralist, uncommitted attitude, she was expected to prevent any hostile action in her region from being carried out against Moscow. The outward expressions of this rapport were the Treaty of Friendship of March 16, 1921, and the Treaty of Friendship and Neutrality of December 17, 1925.[10]

British hostility toward the Soviet regime prevented Moscow's full participation in the Peace Conference of Lausanne; the Soviets were invited to take part only in those sessions which dealt with the question of the regime of the straits. Moscow felt compelled to accept this humiliating posture because it wished to have an opportunity to appear at such an important gathering of states. Of more specific importance was its hope of closing the Black Sea to the warships of all nonriparian states.[11] As will be pointed out later in this chapter, Turkey failed to support the Soviet contentions; at that moment she felt unable to insist on her unrestricted right to fortify the straits and believed that an internatinal regime guaranteed by the League of Nations might contribute to her safety. Reluctantly, Soviet Russia signed the straits convention of Lausanne but never ratified it.

During the years following the Lausanne treaty, both sides must have realized that the relations between Ankara and Moscow were based on convenience rather than on sincere cordiality. Until Stalin put an end to the extravagant attempts by the Comintern to stir up the peoples of the Middle East, the idea of revolutionizing Turkey was not entirely abandoned.[12] Stalin, however, as a Georgian, had never lost his bias against Georgia's Muslim neighbor and was just biding his time before striking out against his "partner" across the Black Sea.

In the mid-1930's, official Soviet foreign policy still wished to be dis-

[10] By the Treaty of 1921 with Soviet Russia, Turkey had agreed to settle the question of the straits in a conference of the Black Sea riparian powers; this clause had to be overlooked when the problem of the straits was to be discussed by the Lausanne Peace Conference; *ibid.*, pp. 268–69.

[11] George F. Kennan, *Soviet Foreign Policy, 1917–1941* (Princeton, N.J., 1960), pp. 51–52.

[12] Laqueur, *Soviet Union and the Middle East,* pp. 50–52, 87–88.

tinguished from the traditional tsarist policy aims. Thus, Karl Radek, at that time editor of the government's official organ, *Izvestia,* wrote:

The attempt to represent the foreign policy of the Soviet Union as a continuation of Tsarist policy is ridiculous. Bourgeois writers who do so have not grasped even the purely external manifestations of this policy. It used to be *an axiom of Tsarist policy* that it should strive by every available means *to gain possession of the Dardanelles* and of an ice-free port on the Pacific. Not only have the Soviets not attempted to seize the Dardanelles, but from the very beginning they have tried to establish the most friendly relations with Turkey.[13]

When the Soviet Union entered the League of Nations and became a fervent advocate of collective security measures, its international political strategy coincided with Turkey's. The collapse of the League's collective peace-keeping system in the failure to curb Japanese, Italian, and German aggressive actions provoked somewhat similar reactions in Ankara and Moscow. The Soviet Union endeavored to safeguard its security and the balance of power by concluding defensive alliances with France and Czechoslovakia. Turkey first wished to improve its military position by strengthening its Achilles' heel, the straits. The demilitarization of that area under the Lausanne treaty, which was guaranteed by the League of Nations, no longer offered any realistic protection. The Soviet Union, conscious of its own unprotected southern flank, strongly supported Turkey's proposal for a change in the regime of the straits.

Although Moscow was again unable to attain its objectives at the Conference of Montreux, the new regime of the straits was more satisfactory to it than the previous one. Turkish–Soviet policy goals also coincided on some aspects of the Spanish Civil War. Moscow supported the Republican side, while Ankara objected to Italian violations of the nonintervention agreements and piratical acts in the Mediterranean. In 1938 and during the first half of 1939, complete harmony seemed to prevail in the general foreign policy concerns of Turkey and the Soviet Union: fear of aggression by Hitlerite Germany and her ally, Italy, and determination to resist such aggression. To this effect, they sought alignment with the status quo powers of the West—Britain and France.

The Soviet volte-face of August 1939 was felt as a heavy blow in

[13] Karl Radek, "The Bases of Soviet Foreign Policy," *Foreign Affairs* (January 1934): 193–206. (Italics added.)

Ankara. Still, even after war broke out and Moscow participated in the dismemberment of Poland and the occupation of the Baltic countries, Turkish leaders hoped that Soviet attitudes toward their country would not change. Foreign Minister Saracoğlu's frustration in Moscow, however, made it clear that Turkey had no other choice but to turn to Britain and France.[14]

Even if we admit some justification for Stalin's obtaining advanced strategical positions in Poland and in the Baltic against an expected German attack, the return to traditional tsarist power politics which aimed at the seizure of the straits cannot be explained by any reference to the safety of the Soviet Union. It was wholly unrealistic and hypocritical for the Soviets to believe that they could be endangered by any Franco–British aggressive act across Turkey. After the defeat of France in the summer of 1940, such a contention sounded ludicrous. Indeed, the crucial Soviet–German exchanges in November 1940 gave no reason for the Soviet claims to the straits and to the area "south of Batum and Baku" but the "delimitation of spheres of influence" or the "aspirations of the Soviet Union." Tsar Nicholas I could have used the same language.

The memorandum submitted by Molotov to the German foreign office on November 26, 1940, clearly reveals that Soviet entry into an alliance with Germany, Italy, and Japan depended, as far as Moscow was concerned, on Hitler's acceptance of the Soviet conditions, which included the guarantee of a "base for light naval and land forces of the U.S.S.R. on the Bosporus and the Dardanelles by means of a long-term lease." Furthermore, it was stated that, should Turkey refuse to join the Four Power Alliance, "Germany, Italy, and the Soviet Union agree to work out and to carry through *the required military and diplomatic measures*."[15]

The conclusion of this agreement on the delimitation of spheres of influence in the Near and Middle East would have sealed Turkey's fate. Subsequent developments—the German invasion of Russia and Soviet alliances with the United States and Britain—postponed but did not essentially alter Stalin's determination to achieve the grand design which had been unsuccessfully pursued by the tsars.

[14] The events leading to the outbreak of World War II and subsequent policy attitudes by Turkey have been discussed in chapter I, pp. 28–30.
[15] Rubinstein, *Foreign Policy of the Soviet Union*, pp. 160–62. (Italics added.)

Toward the end of World War II, Turkey realized that she would have to confront the Soviets as soon as the hostilities ended. This realization was her main reason for avoiding any involvement in the hostilities with Germany which would weaken her already outdated war potential. Given the open Soviet hostility prior to the German attack on Russia, it should be noted that Turkish governmental announcements and the press refrained from expressing delight over the German advance into Russia. The alleged Turkish–German collaboration for the secession of Turkic peoples from the Soviet Union remained restricted to conversations between refugee leaders and the German ambassador, von Papen, in Ankara and members of the German foreign office. Turkish army officers, many of them born and raised in the Caucasus or Azerbaijan, were denied permission by the Turkish government to volunteer in the German armed forces.[16]

At the victorious conclusion of the war against Germany, Soviet imperialism, already expanding in Eastern and Central Europe, began to direct its attention to Turkey. The demands submitted to Ankara were twofold: (1) that the Montreux regime of the straits be revised to secure the protection of these vital waterways solely to the Black Sea powers (that is, the USSR and Turkey) and to provide for a Soviet military base in the straits; (2) that certain territorial concessions be made, the effect of which would have been the demoralization of Turkish resistance. These demands were particularly stressed in 1945 and 1946 and were supported by demonstrative troop concentrations obviously aimed at breaking Turkish determination. As recalled earlier, at that time Turkey was surrounded on three sides by Soviet or pro-Soviet forces (in Bulgaria and Iran, while Communist guerillas were threatening the overthrow of the government of Greece).

Stalinist *hubris,* however, was stalled by Turkey's determined refusal even to enter into negotiations on the Soviet demands. This was the first overt diplomatic defeat of Stalinist Russia, which was "dizzy with success" after the defeat of Germany. This diplomatic setback preceded those suffered with Titoist Yugoslavia, in Berlin, and in Germany in general. Stalin's only remaining choices in Turkey were a military operation or a humiliating acceptance of defeat.[17]

[16] See Charles Warren Hostler, *Turkism and the Soviets* (New York, 1957), pp. 171–77.
[17] A rather clumsy Stalinist diplomacy also endeavored to leapfrog the Turkish

Evidently, Stalin was chary of risking a military confrontation which, most likely, would have precipitated another world war. On another level, the Turkish situation was so different from that of Greece that there was no chance of fomenting a guerilla uprising in Turkey. Nowadays, some Turks like to point out that they had "singlehandedly" faced the Soviet threat in 1945–46 and that the Truman Doctrine was announced only after the danger was over. The United States, however, demonstrated its interest in June 1946 by sending a unit of the Sixth Fleet, headed by the battleship *Missouri,* to Istanbul and the straits. This show of force was a warning which could not have escaped the attention of Moscow.

Thus, while Soviet expansionism was able to penetrate Central Europe and extend Soviet control over vast areas that were never controlled by the tsars, the status quo was fully maintained ante bellum along the Black Sea. Soviet attempts to obtain a foothold in the straits and, eventually, to destroy Turkish independence provided convincing proof that regarding the foreign policy of the Soviet Union as a continuation of tsarist policy was not—using Radek's words—"ridiculous." At least, such was the conclusion of all responsible Turkish leaders of that time.

Soviet–Turkish Relations: Relaxation and Reorientation

The Soviet note of March 19, 1945, had denounced the Turkish–Soviet Treaty of Neutrality and Non-Aggression of 1925 and proposed a new treaty "in accord with the new situation." The Soviet demands and the manner of their presentation left no doubt in the Turkish mind that their aim was not only control of the straits but also submission of Turkey to satellite status.[18] Against such an immediate danger, Turkey sought protection in the arms of the West, principally of the United States, through the political, military, and economic systems of the Atlantic area. Turkey thus became one of the most militant antagonists of the Soviets in the Cold War. She was denounced by Moscow as a country that had lost its independence, had become "Marshallized, a colony of Wall Street and a base for capitalist aggression against the Fatherland

---

position by obtaining a trusteeship territory in Tripolitania and Cyrenaica and by pressing the Greek government to surrender a base in the Dodecanese, in front of the Turkish coast on the Aegean. Both attempts were, however, thwarted because the Soviet aim to reach out into the Mediterranean in force was never overlooked.

[18] Turkish reactions to Soviet pressures are described in Kiliç, *Turkey and the World,* pp. 116–33.

of Socialism."[19] This state of extreme tension and bitterness ended only after Stalin's death in March 1953.[20]

The new Soviet regime under Malenkov speedily undertook a re-examination of Soviet Union's external relations, which had been left in considerable confusion and strain. It was soon realized that a major blunder had been committed in relations with Turkey. The icy, uncompromising stance of the Turks against Soviet claims offered no alternative but a complete reversal of attitude.

On May 30, 1953, the Soviet government issued the following declaration:

The Soviet Government has recently engaged in questions of relations of the U.S.S.R. with neighbors, and among these turned its attention to the state of Soviet-Turkish relations. As is known in connection with the expiration of the period of the Soviet-Turkish Treaty of 1925, the question of regulating Soviet-Turkish relations was touched upon in official talks of representatives of both States some years ago.

In these talks there figured certain territorial claims of the Armenian Republic and the Georgian Republic on Turkey, and also considerations of the Soviet Government relative to removal of the possible threat to the security of the U.S.S.R. from the side of the Black Sea Straits. *This was accepted badly* by the Government and public circles of Turkey, which could not but in certain degree be reflected on Soviet-Turkish relations. In the name of preserving good neighborly relations and strengthening peace and security, the Governments of Armenia and Georgia *have found it possible to renounce their territorial claims on Turkey.*

Concerning the question of the Straits the Soviet Government *has reconsidered its former opinion* on this question and considers possible the provision of security of the U.S.S.R. from the side of the Straits on conditions acceptable alike to the U.S.S.R. and to Turkey. Thus the Soviet Government declares that the Soviet Union *has not any kind of territorial claims on Turkey.*[21]

Despite the awkward language and semantic cosmetics used in this declaration, we should note not only the public retraction of a demand but the admission of its original wanton nature—both unusual actions for the

---

[19] Laqueur, *Soviet Union and the Middle East*, pp. 143–45. Molotov threatened again that Turkey would deeply regret this step; *Survey of International Affairs, 1951,* p. 36. The Turkish government replied on November 12, 1951, with a note explaining that she had to join NATO as a measure to secure her independence, a step necessitated by the Soviet menace; *Documents on International Affairs, 1951,* p. 69.

[20] A few days before the Soviet dictator's demise, on February 28, 1953, Turkey also entered into a Treaty of Friendship and Assistance with Yugoslavia and Greece, the so-called Balkan Pact, which had the avowed aim of mutual assistance against potential aggression by the Soviet Union and its satellites, Bulgaria, Rumania, and Hungary. See pp. 199–201 below.

[21] *Documents on International Affairs, 1953,* pp. 277–78. (Italics added.)

Soviet state, which was then, as always, self-righteous and conscious of its might. That such a diplomatic retreat had to be made before the much weaker Turkey must have been doubly painful. Still, the Kremlin preferred making an effort to "normalize" Soviet–Turkish relations to allowing the existing situation to freeze over. The prospects of loosening Turkish ties to the West and, ultimately, of detaching her from the Atlantic alliance, must have looked dim; still, the attempt had to be made in order to end Soviet isolation from her southern neighbor. Although the renunciation of territorial claims was unconditional, Turkey considered the text concerning the straits rather ambiguous.

The Turkish reply was late (July 18, 1953), frosty, official, and laconic:

The Government of the Turkish Republic notes with satisfaction the declaration in which the Government of the U.S.S.R. declares that the U.S.S.R. does not have any territorial claims against Turkey whatsoever. The Government of the Turkish Republic declares that the concern for maintenance of good neighborly relations and strengthening the peace and security to which reference was made in this declaration fully corresponds to the concern which Turkey has always manifested and will manifest. The Government of the Republic considers it necessary to emphasize in this connection that the question of the Straits, as is known to the Soviet Government, is regulated by clauses of the Montreux Convention.[22]

For another ten years, Turkish–Soviet relations remained cool—correct but not cordial. Turkish attitudes were dominated by an utter reserve and distrust, whereas Moscow thought that it could not afford any new gesture of rapprochment. There also were some crises and periods of tension. In September 1957, Moscow initiated a war of nerves against Turkey by accusing her of planning an invasion of Syria. Warning notes were sent to both Washington and Ankara. Turkey was threatened with Soviet retaliation in unmistakable terms should she undertake any of her alleged sinister activities. A Soviet military concentration was reported in the Caucasus, and Marshal Rokossovski was ostentatiously appointed commander of this military district. By late October, however, the erratic Khrushchev announced that there would be no war with Turkey; he alluded to an adventurous policy line supposedly pursued by the just-deposed Soviet Defense Minister, Marshal Zhukov.[23]

[22] *Ibid.*, p. 278.
[23] It was reported that Khrushchev used a forged document as evidence for the alleged Turkish plans to invade Syria; David J. Dallin, *Soviet Foreign Policy after Stalin* (Philadelphia, 1960), p. 101. See also Laqueur, *Soviet Union and the Middle East*, pp. 258–59.

A similar crisis was manufactured by Moscow in the summer of 1958 when Turkey was suspected by the Soviet leaders of preparing for aggressive action against Iraq, which had just overthrown its pro-Western royalist government. Moscow also objected to the assistance given by Turkey to American forces which landed in Lebanon on the invitation of the Lebanese president. But by early August 1958, this crisis had been quickly overcome.[24] Another broadside of Soviet threats was let loose against Turkey in May 1960 (as well as against Pakistan and Norway) when a U-2 high altitude reconnaissance aircraft was brought down in Soviet territory. It was revealed at that time that Turkey and these other countries had provided bases for U-2 flights.[25] The discontinuation of these flights saved Ankara from further Soviet recrimination on this issue.

The expulsion of Menderes and the Democratic Party by the revolution of May 27, 1960, prepared the ground for a significant improvement in Turkey's relations with the Soviet Union. On June 28, Premier Khrushchev, in a letter addressed to Prime Minister Gürsel, invited Turkey to embark on the road of neutrality but met with a determined refusal. The impetus for a real change only came in 1964.

In May 1963, a Turkish parliamentary delegation visited Russia and was received by Khrushchev. The Soviet leader told the delegation that Stalin's policy toward Turkey had been "idiotic" and that the Soviet Union desired friendship and neighborly relations with Turkey. This did not, however, prevent Moscow from dispatching another note to Ankara warning against anti-Kurdish actions allegedly undertaken jointly by Turkey, Iraq, and Syria.[26]

Ankara's frustration over the Cyprus issue and, in particular, the attitude of the United States as expressed in the letter of President Johnson (see chapter IV above) prompted the Turkish government to improve and intensify its rapport with Moscow. It should also be remembered that by 1964 the Soviet government had entertained close contacts with the government of President Makarios of Cyprus and was a supplier of mili-

---

[24] *Ibid.*, p. 338. See also Friedrich-Wilhelm Fernau, "Nachbarschaft am Schwarzen Meer," *Europa Archiv* (September 10, 1967), pp. 613–14. According to this source, Prime Minister Menderes was prevented by the United States from intervening militarily in Iraq.

[25] *Survey of International Affairs, 1959–1960*, pp. 62–63.

[26] *Neue Zürcher Zeitung*, August 16, 1963.

tary aid to the island. At that time, Ankara began wooing several un-committed governments in order to improve its stand in the United Nations, where the Cyprus issue was being fought. At that time it appeared that the Soviet Union might become the main champion of an independent Cyprus, if only to oppose both Greece and Turkey. It was naturally in the interest of Turkey to come to an understanding with her northern neighbor.

In October 1964, Prime Minister Inönü sent his foreign minister, Feridun Cemal Erkin, on an official visit to Moscow.[27] The avowed purpose of the visit was to end Turkey's one-sided role in the Cold War which had become outdated by ties other members of the Western alliance had established with Moscow. Ankara wished to dispel its image as NATO's unyielding and inaccessible bastion and to obtain elbow room for diplomatic maneuver outside the American aegis. This move was in-evitable, given the momentum toward a more independent Turkish foreign policy. The Johnson letter was simply the final catalytic agent which precipitated change.

Soviet attitudes toward Turkey had, since Stalin's death, alternated between invitations for closer and better relations and warnings or propa-ganda attacks. Moscow several times hinted that it wished to terminate the state of mistrust existing between the two countries and expressed hope that the mutually profitable policies of Atatürk toward the Soviet Union might be restored.

The Turkish effort to open high-level contacts with Moscow was accompanied by expressions of loyalty to Turkey's allies. On the other hand, it was hoped that the talks conducted by the foreign minister might lead to an agreement by which the Soviet government would be ready to support Turkey's efforts to establish a federal regime in Cyprus with full autonomy for the Turkish community on the island.[28]

Feridun Cemal Erkin's visit was not aimed at the conclusion of any formal agreement; it was intended to become the starting point of a more cordial and sincere collaboration in all areas not incompatible with the alliance systems to which Turkey belonged. Moscow had earlier ex-

---

[27] On September 30, 1964, a military aid agreement was signed in Moscow be-tween Cyprus and the Soviet Union; Fernau, *Nachbarschaft am Schwarzen Meer*, p. 616.

[28] Concerning the Turkish foreign minister's visit to Moscow, see *The Times* (London), November 2, 1964; *New York Times*, November 3, 1964.

pressed its view (inconsistent with declarations under Stalin) that Turkey's membership in the Western alliance would not be an obstacle to normal relations.[29] It was well understood by both participants that a new phase of Turkish–Soviet contacts had been initiated at this meeting in Moscow, even if no formal certification were offered. Henceforth, Moscow appeared to be ready to place its weight on the side of the Cypriote solution favored by the Turks. Violent attacks by the Soviet radio network also ended; however, the Moscow-sponsored *Bizim Radyo* (Our Radio) in East Berlin, the mouthpiece of the exiled Turkish Communist Party, continued to transmit, as did hostile broadcasts in the Turkish language from Sofia and Budapest.

The Turkish foreign minister's travel was quickly followed by the January 1965 visit to Ankara of a delegation of the Supreme Soviet, led by the Politburo member Nikolai Podgorny (titular Soviet president). In May 1965, Soviet Foreign Minister Gromyko returned the call of his Turkish colleague.

In the meantime, the Turkish protagonists changed places: Ismet Inönü became leader of the principal opposition party and Suat Hayrı Ürgüplü prime minister in his stead. The new head of the Turkish Cabinet selected Hasan Işık, then Turkish ambassador to Moscow (a choice that may not have been entirely accidental) as his new foreign minister. Gromyko expressed support for a "federal" solution in Cyprus. He must have noted with satisfaction that, some months before his journey, Turkey had renounced her participation in the MLF (Multilateral Force) project sponsored by the United States.

In August 1965, Prime Minister Ürgüplü journeyed to Moscow in the company of his foreign minister. In the fall of 1965, after the general elections, Süleyman Demirel, leader of the victorious Justice Party, assumed the prime ministership. For more than an entire year, the exchange of top leaders was discontinued. After a careful evaluation of the situation, however, the new Turkish government decided to pursue the course staked out originally by Ismet Inönü. Soviet Premier Alexei Kosygin, whose journey had been postponed several times, was asked to visit Ankara in December 1966.

Kosygin was the first head of the Soviet government ever to visit

---

[29] Soviet Foreign Minister Shepilov before the Supreme Soviet on February 12, 1957; Jäschke, *Die Türkei in den Jahren 1952–61*, p. 72.

Ankara. Although his reception was reserved at first, it warmed some-what later. No spectacular agreement was reached; the purpose of this and other visits was a general improvement in the atmosphere between the two countries, coupled with a search for possible meaningful con-tacts. Thus, most of the conversations between Demirel and Kosygin were restricted to the less political area of industrial planning and devel-opment, which was of interest to both statesmen.[30] Kosygin invited both President Cevdet Sunay and Prime Minister Süleyman Demirel to Mos-cow.

Demirel's journey to the Soviet Union was probably the culmination in the policy of "normalizing" relations with Moscow. His reception was extremely cordial (he was accompanied by a group of deputies), and his hosts eventually abandoned their attempts to give any anti-American tinge to the visit.[31] The Turkish party also travelled to other parts of the Soviet Union, including the areas of Turkic-speaking peoples in Central Asia and Azerbaijan.[32] The final communiqué expressed an understand-ing of the Soviet position on Vietnam and endorsed the demand for Israel's withdrawal from the territories occupied during the June 1967 war; in return, the Soviet side agreed that the independence of Cyprus should be preserved and that the legitimate rights and interests of both the Greek and Turkish communities on the island should be secured.[33] Accordingly, the communiqué reflected the approach of both sides toward the policies of the other.

After his return, the Turkish prime minister expressed the view that his visit had eliminated "the last traces of hostility" from Soviet–Turkish relations. He further said:

I think we have entered a new era in our dealings with the Russians. As it is known, there had been great strain between our countries over the years, and in the period after World War II we had no relations at all. Now that the gap has been bridged, *I am not suggesting that all the doubts are gone*, but I think the hostility is gone.[34]

[30] *New York Times,* December 25, 1966; Fernau, *Nachbarschaft am Schwarzen Meer,* p. 616.

[31] In his first address, Kosygin expressed critical remarks on American foreign policy; upon Turkish remonstration, all such further comments were discontinued (information conveyed to this author by a member of the Turkish delegation).

[32] In Baku the local Turks gave a rousing welcome to Demirel's party which amounted to a political demonstration.

[33] *Milliyet,* October 6, 1967.

[34] *Milliyet,* October 14, 1967. (Italics added.)

After Demirel's visit, the Turkish government emphasized that the rapprochement with the Soviet Union was simply Turkey's contribution to the policy of coexistence between the two camps and did not imply her abandonment of the Atlantic alliance, nor even a partial withdrawal from her participation in the Western system of integration. As Demirel said: "NATO is a collective defense system. It does not prevent us from having friendly relations with the Soviet Union."[35]

These visits did not at the time lead to any formal agreement concerning the political relations of the two countries. Except for an economic aid agreement signed on March 26, 1967, no other general treaty was concluded; however, negotiations were held, without concrete results, on cultural and trade agreements.[36] Foreign Minister Çağlayangil returned Gromyko's visit in July 1968; his talks with his Soviet colleagues were held "in mutual understanding and frankness," as the communiqué announced. As in the case of the communiqué following the Demirel visit, Ankara's official position on Cyprus and the Soviet views on Vietnam and the Israeli-Arab conflict were endorsed.[37]

In November 1969, General Sunay, president of Turkey, returned the visit made earlier by the Soviet titular head of state. This was to be considered a "protocol call," although Sunay was also received by Soviet Party Chief Brezhnev and all questions pending between the two countries were discussed.

The resumption of "normal" relations with Turkey's mighty neighbor was generally received with approval by the Turkish foreign policy elite. Rightist voices raised objections, however, and accused Demirel of being too complacent with Moscow. On the other hand, leftist commentators congratulated the "pro-American" prime minister for his initiative in visiting Moscow.[38] Moderates genuinely welcomed these

---

[35] *Cumhuriyet*, October 6, 1967.

[36] *Daily News* (Ankara), July 13, 1968. A cultural agreement signed in November, 1964, failed to receive ratification by the Turkish National Assembly; Fernau, *Nachbarschaft am Schwarzen Meer*, p. 618.

[37] The Turkish press reported that a long-term trade agreement, a highway agreement to facilitate Turkey's exports to Scandinavia, a consular agreement, and the long-pending cultural agreement were discussed; *Cumhuriyet*, November 22, 1969; *Milliyet*, November 24, 1969.

[38] At the same time, Demirel was reproached for pursuing conflicting policies: talking in different terms in Moscow and in Washington and Bonn; Halûk Ülman in *Ulus*, October 2, 1967.

developments but admitted that their distrust of the Soviets had not been fully dispelled.

Although the Turkish government did not accept the proffered hand of Moscow's friendship for almost ten years, it would not be accurate to characterize Ankara's move as one of a Dullesian "agonizing re-appraisal" of foreign policy. Even if accelerated by the disappointments over Cyprus, the renewal of cordial ties with the Soviet Union was a prudent and expedient step, one certainly in harmony with the well-considered interests of Turkey. Washington was kept constantly informed of all Turkish steps and voiced tacit approval. As one Turkish commen-tator observed, Washington must have felt better to know that the policy initiated by Inönü was being applied by Demirel.[39]

The value and credibility of Soviet friendship has been weighed care-fully in Ankara, but the main question has not been answered: has Moscow really abandoned plans of placing the straits under its control? The mounting interest of the Soviet Union toward the Arab world, started in the time of Khrushchev and brought to culmination after the Arab–Israeli war in 1967, appeared incompatible with genuine acquiescence to Turkish control of the narrow waterways leading from the Black Sea to the Mediterranean, where a Soviet armada operates from Arab bases. Once more, as so often in the past, the straits are the crux of Turkish–Russian relations.

THE SOVIETS AND THE TURKISH STRAITS

Constantinople and the straits have been described as the very "heart of the Ottoman Empire."[40] The malady of the Sick Man of Europe was not only domestic; his deadly sickness was also caused by Russia's ambi-tion to possess his "heart." The Eastern question, which for centuries worried the chancelleries of Europe, revolved around the problem of who should inherit the Bosporus and the Dardanelles after the collapse of the sultan's power.

While the straits were recognized as the "heart" of Turkey, it was also contended that they were "the door" to Russia or "the keys" to her

[39] Metin Toker in *Milliyet,* September 20, 1967.
[40] See Cemil Bilsel, "The Turkish Straits in the Light of Recent Turkish-Soviet Russian Correspondence," *American Journal of International Law* 41, no. 4 (October 1947): 732–33.

house.[41] Not only the tsars coveted the straits; Stalin complained at the Yalta Summit Conference that "Turkey's hand holds our throat."[42]

The geopolitical and strategical significance of the straits has been described earlier.[43] For tsarist Russia along the Black Sea—landlocked except for the narrow exit of the straits—seizure or control of those narrows had meant: (1) the satisfaction of the ideological urge to restore Constantinople to Christendom; (2) unimpeded navigation by both naval and commercial vessels to and from the Mediterranean Sea and the oceans beyond; (3) the geostrategical domination, from this vantage point, of the Near and Middle East; and (4) a forward position of defense against any potential aggressor wishing to attack Russia's "soft underbelly."

The value of the Turkish straits (significantly and consistently called the "Black Sea Straits" by Russians) in the hands of a powerful land and naval power was clearly recognized by Britain and France after the Treaty of Kuchuk Kainarji (Küçük Kaynarca) of 1774, which placed Russia in the position of the principal power along the Black Sea. As Napoleon's Ambassador Caulaincourt expressed it to Tsar Alexander I in 1808: "Constantinople is a point so important that its possession, together with the entrance of the Dardanelles, would make you [the Russians] masters of all the commerce with the Levant, even with India."[44]

The navigation on the straits or, as it is known, the *régime* of the straits, varied during the 450 years of Ottoman control according to the strength of whoever ruled the Black Sea, the power status of the Sublime Porte, the development of trade and technology, and, last but not least, the balance of power in Europe and the Near East.

In the year 1475, the entire Black Sea coast came under Ottoman domination; all foreign ships were excluded from this *mare clausum turcicum*.[45] When Russian power descended on the Black Sea coast, Tur-

[41] Tsar Alexander I expressed the classic Russian position in his conversation with Napoleon's Ambassador Caulaincourt: "Geography wills that I have it [Constantinople], because if it goes to another I would be no longer master of my house. . . . It is indispensable that I possess what geography assigns me." Puryear, *Napoleon and the Dardanelles*, pp. 325–26.

[42] U.S. Department of State, *The Conferences at Malta and Yalta, 1945* (Washington, D.C., 1955), p. 903.

[43] Chapter II, pp. 43–46.

[44] Puryear, *Napoleon and the Dardanelles*, p. 326.

[45] See Ahmed Şükrü Esmer, "The Straits: Crux of World Politics," *Foreign Affairs* (January, 1947), pp. 290–91.

THE SOVIETS AND THE STRAITS

key was forced to sign the Treaty of Kuchuk Kainarji (Küçük Kaynarca), Article XI of which provided:

For the convenience and advantage of the two Empires, there shall be a free and *unimpeded navigation for the merchant-ships* belonging to the two Contracting Powers, in all the seas which wash their shores; the Sublime Porte grants to Russian merchant-vessels, such as are universally employed by the other Powers for commerce and in the ports, a *free passage from the Black Sea into the Mediterranean, and reciprocally from the Mediterranean into the Black Sea*, as also the power of entering all the ports and harbors situated either on the seacosts, or in the passages and channels which join those seas.[46]

Although Russian commercial ships were granted free passage through the straits, the straits remained closed to warships of any power other than the Ottomans, under what was known as the "ancient rule of the Ottoman Empire."[47] Thereafter, as the liberty of navigation was extended to merchant vessels of other nations, the question of passage for warships remained the contested issue in which Russia maintained a consistent and vital interest.

Between 1774 and 1840, Russia three times succeeded in obtaining temporary rights for the passage of her warships for the duration of emergency situations and was once even invited by the sultan to establish a garrison on the Asian coast of the Bosporus. In all of these cases, as soon as the special conditions came to an end, the former regime was reinstated and foreign warships forbidden entrance to the straits in time of peace.[48]

These precedents, despite their short life and precarious nature, have

---

[46] U.S. Department of State, *The Problem of the Turkish Straits* (Washington, D.C., 1947), p. 14 (italics added). The text mentions the "White Sea" to which and from which Russian mercantile shipping is permitted: this is the literal translation of the Turkish name (*Akdeniz*) for the Mediterranean Sea. This writer felt entitled to replace "White Sea" by the proper translation of the Turkish equivalent: Mediterranean Sea.

[47] The "ancient rule of the Ottoman Empire" was recognized by several international treaties: the Treaty of July 13, 1841, between Britain, Austria, France, Prussia, Russia, and Turkey; the Peace Treaty of Paris of March 30, 1956, signed by Great Britain, Austria, France, Prussia, Russia, Sardinia, and the Ottoman Empire; the Convention of London, March 13, 1871, between Great Britain, Austria, France, Germany, Italy, Russia, and the Ottoman Empire.

[48] The political reasons for allowing passage of Russian men-of-war were the campaigns of Bonaparte in Egypt and Italy (the Ionian Islands were, for a number of years, protected by Russian forces), the Franco–Austrian–Russian war of 1805–7, and, finally, the insurrection by Mehmet Ali, Viceroy of Egypt, whose forces threatened Constantinople.

subsequently been distorted by Russian historians[49] and were invoked by Molotov at the Potsdam Conference of the summer of 1945.[50] Whatever the extent or interpretation of these pro-Russian concessions, it seems clear that they had been abrogated, if not earlier, by the Convention of London of July 13, 1841, entered into by Great Britain, Austria, France, Prussia, Russia, and the Ottoman Empire. The convention was held after the termination of the threat posed by Mehmet Ali and was to reconfirm the rights of the sultan to close the straits to warships. Its controlling Article I ran as follows:

His Highness the Sultan, on the one part, declares that he is firmly resolved to maintain for the future the principle invariably established as the *ancient rule of his Empire*, and in virtue of which it has at all times been prohibited for the ships of war of foreign Powers to enter the Straits of the Dardanelles and of the Bosporus; and that so long as the Porte is at peace, His Highness will admit no foreign ship-of-war into the said Straits.

And their Majesties the Queen of the United Kingdom of Great Britain and Ireland, the Emperor of Austria, the King of Hungary and Bohemia, the King of the French, the King of Prussia, and the Emperor of all the Russias, on the other part, engage to respect this determination of the Sultan, and to conform themselves to the principle above declared.[51]

Russian attempts to secure rights of passage for her warships into the Mediterranean had thus been thwarted by Britain and France. At the same time, the Western powers agreed to the closure of the straits to their own men-of-war, a prohibition strongly urged by Russia. During the Crimean War, British and French warships entered the Black Sea with the consent of the sultan and landed troops on the Crimean peninsula. The ensuing Treaty of Paris of 1856, while providing for the neutralization of the Black Sea and the demilitarization of the Russian coast, confirmed once more the ancient rule of the Ottoman Empire—namely, the closure of the straits to warships of all flags other than Turkish. Simultaneously, freedom of navigation for commercial vessels of *every*

---

[49] For the controversy relative to the text and interpretation of the Russian–Turkish agreements of 1798–99, of 1805, and 1838, see Philip E. Mosely, *Russian Diplomacy and the Opening of the Eastern Question in 1838 and 1839* (Cambridge, Mass., 1934); J. C. Hurewitz, "Russia and the Turkish Straits." *World Politics* (July 1962): 605–32; J. C. Hurewitz, *The Background of Russia's Claims to the Turkish Straits* (Ankara, 1964).

[50] See U.S. Department of State, *Foreign Relations of the United States, Diplomatic Papers: The Conference of Berlin (The Potsdam Conference), 1945* (Washington, D.C., 1961), vol. I, p. 1035.

[51] U.S. Department of State, *Problem of the Turkish Straits*, p. 17. (Italics added.)

nation was recognized. When Russia, profiting from the distraction caused by the Franco–Prussian War, denounced the demilitarization of her Black Sea coast in November 1870, the powers meeting in London condoned the act but, once again, reconfirmed Turkey's closing the straits to warships.[52]

The regime of the straits, as described above, remained in force until World War I. Renewed attempts by Russia to change the status quo in her favor were unsuccessful.

It has been recalled earlier[53] how, during World War I, Britain, France, and Italy agreed to Russia's annexation of the Turkish straits. This agreement amounted to a death knell for the Ottoman Empire but became a dead letter when Russia withdrew from the war. Under the abortive Peace Treaty of Sèvres, wide powers of authority over the straits were granted to an international commission; complete freedom of passage was to be guaranteed to both commercial and naval vessels.

The Peace Treaty of Lausanne of July 24, 1923, contained in its Annex the Convention Relating to the Regime of the Straits which regulated the navigation on these waters for thirteen years.

After the end of World War I, it was generally realized that the "ancient rule" relating to the straits had become anomalous and outdated, but opinions differed greatly on the question of what kind of international regime should be established. Soviet Russia wished to restrict participation in an international regime of the straits to the riparian powers of the Black Sea, thereby excluding warships of non-littoral states, while securing free exit for its warships into the Mediterranean.[54]

The Western maritime powers, primarily Great Britain, wished to guarantee complete freedom of navigation for all warships to and from the Black Sea. Turkey was less interested in the navigation of these waterways; she desired to maintain sovereignty and control over the straits

[52] See Esmer, "The Straits," pp. 292–93; Bilsel, "The Turkish Straits," pp. 735–37.
[53] Chapter I, pp. 16–17.
[54] In the Treaty of Friendship with Turkey of 1921, Moscow proposed the elaboration of an international straits agreement with the participation of the Black Sea states. Before going to Lausanne, Turkey insisted on Soviet participation in the forthcoming negotiations concerning the new regime of the straits. In its note of September 24/25, 1946, the Soviet government reproached Ankara for having violated its earlier commitment of 1921 when consenting that the statute of the straits should be worked out by the Lausanne conference together with states other than Black Sea powers; U.S. Department of State, *Problem of the Turkish Straits*, p. 57.

and her territorial waters; her concern was that the entry of warships should not jeopardize her security.

The Lausanne regime of the straits accepted a compromise between the conflicting interests of the principal powers. The maximum force which any power was to be allowed to send to the Black Sea was not to be greater than the most powerful fleet of any Black Sea power; however, under all circumstances, the non-Black Sea powers were permitted to dispatch a force of no more than three ships, the individual ships not exceeding 10,000 tons. Otherwise, except in time of war when certain restrictions were to be observed, complete freedom of passage was provided for both merchant and war vessels of all nations. A straits commission (considerably less powerful than the Sèvres commission) was set up to operate under the auspices of the League of Nations. The area on both sides of the Dardanelles and the Bosporus was to be demilitarized.

The Soviet government signed the convention but, finding many of its provisions unsatisfactory, refused to ratify it. Nevertheless, Moscow cooperated with the commission by furnishing the information required under the Lausanne regime.

In 1936, due to the failure of the League's security system, Turkey urged that the Lausanne convention be replaced by a more acceptable agreement. The Soviet government supported Ankara because it hoped that the new regime would better suit its interests. Moscow was now very much interested in securing protection for her vulnerable Black Sea coastline and the industrial region of the Ukraine against potential attack by Fascist Italian or Nazi German forces. The Kremlin believed that it would be easier to handle the straits issue by dealing directly with Turkey than through an international commission.

British, Turkish, and Soviet interests again clashed during the negotiations at Montreux. Moscow once more sought to have all warships of non-Black Sea powers excluded from the Black Sea, but in vain. Turkey failed to support the Soviet contention; her main ambition was to regain control over the straits area and end its demilitarization. Eventually, her point of view was accepted; the British–Soviet confrontation ended with a compromise which was somewhat more favorable to Moscow than the Lausanne results.[55]

---

[55] For the proceedings of the Montreux conference see: *Actes de la Conférence de Montreux concernant le régime des Détroits. 22 juin–20 juillet 1936* (Liège, Belgium,

The guiding policy of the Montreux convention regarding the regime of the straits, as set out in the Preamble, was "to regulate transit in the Straits in such manner as to safeguard, within the framework of Turkish security and of the security, in the Black Sea, of the riparian States." In its Article 1, it reiterated the principle already enshrined in the Peace Treaty of Lausanne:

The High Contracting Parties recognize and affirm the principle of freedom of transit and navigation by sea in the Straits.
The exercise of this freedom shall henceforth be regulated by the provisions of the present Convention.

Although the convention could be denounced with a two-year notice after twenty years (no notice of denunciation has been announced, although this has been possible since November 9, 1956), Article 28 provided that Article 1 should continue in force without time limit; in other words, it is not subject to denunciation.

In time of peace, *merchant vessels* were to enjoy unrestricted freedom of transit and navigation in the straits by night and day.[56] Only during a war involving Turkey would enemy vessels be forbidden to use the straits, and others only on the condition that "they do not in any way assist the enemy." Should Turkey consider herself "threatened with imminent danger of war, "merchant ships must pass by day and along a route indicated by Turkish authorities.

Warships, other than light surface vessels, minor war vessels, and auxiliary vessels (which are nevertheless subject to the notification clause and certain other restrictions), enjoy the right of transit to and through the straits under special conditions, which are the most controversial clauses of the Montreux regime. Black Sea powers, a concession to the Soviet point of view, were allowed to send warships of any size through the straits, provided they pass through the Straits singly, escorted by not more than two destroyers." On the other hand, non-Black Sea powers are not permitted to send through naval vessels with greater tonnage than the maximum permissible 15,000 tons; however, warships paying visits to a port in the straits (such as Istanbul) are not to be included in the above maximum tonnage.

1936). For the text of the convention, see *Documents on International Affairs, 1936,* pp. 643–67.
    [56] Merchant vessels are all those not covered by Section II of the convention dealing with warships and further defined by Annex II of the convention.

In time of war when Turkey is not a belligerent, warships enjoy freedom of transit under similar conditions as in time of peace. Nevertheless, warships of belligerents are only allowed to pass through the straits when acting under the collective security provisions of the Covenant of the League of Nations[57] or "in cases of assistance rendered to a State victim of aggression in virtue of a treaty of mutual assistance binding Turkey, concluded within the framework of the Covenant of the League of Nations."[58]

In time of war, when Turkey herself is one of the belligerents, the passage of warships is "left entirely to the discretion of the Turkish Goverment."[59] Similarly, Article 21 grants Turkey the right to close the straits under the threat of an imminent danger of war. Only warships which have passed through the straits before the Turkish government has made use of its discretionary powers may return to their bases. Turkey, however, may "deny this right to vessels of war belonging to the State whose attitude has given rise to the applications of the present article."

Another provision, much debated at the Montreux conference, was the question of the presence of warships of nonriparian powers in the Black Sea. The Soviet delegation, consonant with earlier Russian attitudes, wished to exclude or restrict entry of men-of-war of outside powers. They pointed out that the Turkish straits are not comparable to international canals or other straits because they do not lead anywhere but into the Black Sea, a dead end. The British representative maintained that the Black Sea should be treated as any other portion of the high sea, entry to which is free and unrestricted.

The conference, however, finally adopted a solution not unlike that reached in Lausanne, with some differences in the tonnage of warships of non-Black Sea powers permitted entry into that sea. Accordingly, the convention provided that the aggregate tonnage of nonriparian warships in the Black Sea should not exceed 30,000 tons in peacetime. If at any time the tonnage of the strongest navy of a Black Sea power (the Soviets) should exceed by at least 10,000 tons its tonnage at the time of the signa-

---

[57] The Covenant of the League of Nations has been replaced by the Charter of the United Nations; it is legally dubious whether enforcement action under the charter would be applicable under the Montreux convention.

[58] It is again questionable whether Turkey would be bound to allow passage to warships of states carrying out hostile operations by virtue of measure of collective self-defense under Article 51 of the charter.

[59] Article 20.

ture of the convention, the aggregate tonnage of non-Black Sea powers could then be increased to a maximum of 45,000 tons.[60]

The Montreux convention transferred the functions of the International Commission of Lausanne to the government of Turkey. Turkey was also authorized to fortify the straits area, a right of which she made immediate use. The Turkish government was also empowered to collect statistics and information concerning the passage of all foreign warships through the straits and the tonnage of warships in the Black Sea of riparian and nonriparian powers.

Many other detailed provisions concerning the navigation of warships were inserted into the convention. Briefly, non-Black Sea naval vessels were not to stay in the Black Sea longer than 21 days; transit of warships was to be preceded by notification to the Turkish government 8 to 15 days before entry into the straits; submarines were generally forbidden passage, except that newly constructed or repaired submarines of Black Sea powers were allowed to pass on the surface in the daytime; finally, vessels of war in transit through the straits were not permitted to make use of any aircraft which they carried.

Annex II to the convention contains the important classification of warships, taken verbatim from the Treaty for the Limitation of Naval Armaments concluded in London on March 25, 1936.[61] The treaty established seven categories for vessels of war, but its basis of classification has become outdated in many respects because of technological developments during and following World War II.[62] For reasons unknown, the seventh category of warships (small craft) was omitted from Annex II, causing differences of interpretation and application during World War II.[63]

The new regime of the straits worked satisfactorily until the last phase of World War II. After the outbreak of the German–Russian war, both Britain and the Soviet Union vowed to abide by the provisions of the

[60] See *U.S. Department of State, Problem of the Turkish Straits*, pp. 8–10; D. A. Routh, "The Montreux Convention Regarding the Regime of the Black Sea Straits," *Survey of International Affairs, 1936* (London, 1937), pp. 584–651; James T. Shotwell and Francis Deak, *Turkey at the Straits: A Short Story* (New York, 1940), pp. 122–27.
[61] See *Documents on International Affairs, 1936,* pp. 616–32.
[62] Missile-launchers, nuclear weapons, among others, were unknown at the time of the conclusion of the treaty; the categorization of war vessels is based on displacement and caliber of guns. The application of the Montreux convention, in view of many technological innovations, often places delicate decisions before the Turkish government.
[63] Bilsel, "The Turkish Straits," p. 739.

Montreux convention.[64] Because of the occupation of the Greek islands in the Aegean and the control of most of the Soviet Black Sea coast by the Germans, supplies to the Soviet Union could not pass through the straits until January 1945.[65]

When Moscow opened its campaign of nerves against Turkey and denounced the Treaty of Friendship of 1925, it referred to "changed conditions" which demanded the renegotiation of a new treaty. When asking for clarification, the Turkish ambassador was told by Soviet Foreign Minister Molotov on June 7, 1945, that, in addition to territorial demands, the Soviet government wanted a new regime of the straits which would provide for "effective guarantees."[66] In the meantime, Stalin had pressed at both the Yalta and Potsdam Summit Conferences for a revision of the Montreux convention. During all of these exchanges, the Soviet intention left no doubts: Moscow wanted bases in the straits.[67]

At Potsdam, the three heads of government agreed that the Montreux convention should be revised "as failing to meet present-day conditions." They also agreed that "as the next step, the matter should be the subject of direct conversations between each of the three governments and the Turkish Government."[68]

The ensuing exchanges of diplomatic notes started with the message delivered to the Turkish minister of foreign affairs by the American Government on November 2, 1945. Washington proposed the convocation of an international conference. The principles for an equitable solution to

[64] U.S. Department of State, Problem of the Turkish Straits, p. 36.
[65] Under the Montreux convention, merchant ships of any flag and with any cargo were entitled to pass through the straits. That included merchant vessels carrying arms and other war supplies. See Harry N. Howard, "The United States and the Question of the Turkish Straits," Middle East Journal (January 1947): 59–72.
[66] Eren, Turkey Today, p. 233; Esmer, "The Straits," p. 297.
[67] Characteristic of Soviet insistence is the story narrated by Prime Minister Churchill in his memoirs. At the Potsdam Conference, having emptied a glass of brandy in the company of Stalin, the latter unexpectedly burst out: "If you find it impossible to give us a fortified position in the Marmora, could we not have a base at Dedeagatch?" Triumph and Tragedy: the Second World War, vol. 6 (Boston, p. 572). Dedeagatch, now known as Alexandroupolis, is a seaport in Greek Western Thrace, not too distant from the entrance of the Dardanelles.
[68] The Soviet version of the Potsdam decision differed from the above-quoted British version. It ran as follows: "The three Governments agreed that as the proper course the said question would be the subject of direct negotiations between each of the three powers and the Turkish Government." This latter text omitted the words "as a next step," thus seeking to avoid any reference to another step; namely, the international conference. See U.S. Department of State, Problems of the Turkish Straits, p. 48.

the question of the straits suggested in the note did not differ from those in force since Lausanne and Montreux, except on the following points: first, certain unspecified "changes to modernize" were mentioned; next, the United Nations was to be substituted for the League of Nations; and, finally, Japan was to be eliminated as a signatory.[69]

On November 21, the British government sent a memorandum to Ankara approving the American principles. On December 6, the Turkish government accepted the American note as basis for discussion and expressed its readiness to participate in an international conference on the straits and to accept any decisions reached there, provided that "Turkey's independence, sovereignty and territorial integrity are not infringed."[70]

The long-awaited Soviet note was delivered in Ankara on August 7, 1946. It first referred to certain events which were adduced as evidence that the Montreux convention "does not meet the interests of the safety of the Black Sea Powers." The note referred to a number of incidents during World War II when Turkey allowed passage to a few German and Italian small vessels which Moscow considered in violation of the Montreux convention. The Soviet note proposed the following principles for a new regime of the straits:

(1) The Straits should be always open to the passage of merchant ships of all countries.

(2) The Straits should be always open to the passage of warships of the Black Sea Powers.

(3) Passage through the Straits for warships not belonging to the Black Sea Powers shall not be permitted except in cases specially provided for.

(4) The establishment of a regime of the Straits, as the sole sea passage, leading from the Black Sea and to the Black Sea, should come under the competence of Turkey and other Black Sea Powers.

(5) Turkey and the Soviet Union, as the Powers most interested and capable of guaranteeing freedom of commercial navigation and security in the Straits, shall organize *joint means of defense* of the Straits for the prevention of the utilization of the Straits by other countries for aims hostile to the Black Sea Powers.[71]

Turkey promptly replied on August 22, 1946, by refuting one by one the Soviet charges against her handling of certain wartime precedents. Nevertheless, the Turkish government admitted that the Montreux convention required adaptation to "technical progress and present condi-

[69] The note is printed in *ibid.*, p. 47.
[70] *Ibid.*, p. 37.
[71] *Ibid.*, pp. 48–49 (italics added).

tions." It declared its approval of the meeting of an international conference (which the Soviet note failed to propose) for a revision of the convention, with the participation of the signatories and the United States. As to the principles set forth in the Soviet note, Ankara declared itself unable to accept points 4 and 5. It refused to agree to a regime of the straits by the Black Sea powers only; any defense of the straits, jointly with the Soviet Union, was "not compatible with the inalienable rights of sovereignty of Turkey nor with its security, which brooks no restriction."[72]

The Soviet government replied swiftly. A lengthy note was handed to the Turkish Ministry of Foreign Affairs on September 25, 1946.[73] Moscow repeated its charges that "the Straits Convention did not prevent the enemy powers from using the Straits for purposes of the war against the Allied States." The note insisted that, owing to the special situation of the Black Sea (the straits leads only to the shores of a limited number of powers) and the fact that it is a closed sea, "it seems proper in this case to establish such a regime of the Straits which above all would meet the special situation and the security of Turkey, the U.S.S.R. and the other Black Sea Powers." Moscow also reminded Turkey that the Turkish–Soviet treaty of 1921 "is based on the recognition of the necessity of confiding the drafting of the international status of the Black Sea and Straits to a conference, composed only of the representatives of riverain countries." With regard to the "joint defense" of the straits, as proposed by Moscow, the diplomatic note said:

In declining en bloc, all possibility of joint study with the Soviet Union of this important problem, indissolubly linked with the security interests of the U.S.S.R. and the other Black Sea Powers, the Turkish Government is in complete contradiction with its declarations regarding its desire to reestablish friendly relations with the U.S.S.R., based on confidence, by considering it possible to give voice to such suspicions which had no basis at all and which moreover are incompatible with the dignity of the Soviet Union.

The Turkish Ministry of Foreign Affairs answered in an even lengthier note (the last in this exchange) on October 18, 1946.[74] It again defended

[72] Ibid., pp. 50–55. The wartime precedents are discussed and evaluated from legal point of view by Bilsel, "The Turkish Straits," pp. 741–42.
[73] Ibid., pp. 55–58.
[74] Ibid., pp. 60–68.

its position concerning certain vessels passing through the straits during the last war and concluded:

The Turkish Government has already strongly set forth and emphasizes once again that the essential difficulty in differentiating between warships or commercial vessels, as regards ships in transit, rested in the imperfections of Annex II of the Convention.

The Turkish note referred to the unanimously held doctrine that the Black Sea is an open sea. It also reminded Moscow that the passage of ships of riverain and nonriverain states was for a long time considered an exceptional right agreed to by Turkey and that the tsarist government had supported this rule as a general principle of European Public Law from the beginning of the nineteenth century. Turkey had accepted the provisions of the Montreux convention; these provisions, as laid down in the convention itself, may be modified only by an international conference of the contracting states. Any other procedure would be in violation of international law. The note further observed:

Turkey has a clear consciousness of her status as a Power of the Black Sea. But she cannot forget that she is also a Mediterranean country. Charged by a particularly delicate geographic situation, with assuring the liaison between two worlds separated by the restricted space of the Straits, she is conscious of the obligation which this situation imposes on her with respect to the two seas which bathe her shores. The Turkish Government can, therefore, not consider the question of the Black Sea and of the Straits as a problem interesting the riverain Powers of this sea only.

The Turkish government pointed out in its note that the closing of the Black Sea to warships of nonriparian powers "would put the other riverain States at the mercy of the maritime power which possessed the strongest land forces, in other words, at the mercy of the USSR itself."

The note recalled that Turkey had already discussed the question of "joint defense" with Moscow—namely, in 1939, when the Turkish Foreign Minister Saracoğlu met with Molotov. Thus, Turkey had already examined the Soviet proposals of a "mixed system of Turco–Soviet defense of the Straits" and considered this proposition incompatible with the sovereignty and security of Turkey.

The note rebutted the Soviet reference to the Turkish–Soviet Treaty of 1921 by stating that the two parties to this treaty had abandoned the idea of a meeting of Black Sea powers by their effective participation at Lausanne in the negotiation of the regime of the straits within a "considerably enlarged international framework." The note added that, in the view of Turkey, the direct conversation between the three Potsdam powers and Turkey having been completed, a revision of the Montreux convention by an international conference of the signatories may be attempted.

While Turkey and the Soviet Union exchanged these notes, both Washington and London called Moscow's attention to the fact that the Potsdam conference only envisaged preliminary talks with Turkey but otherwise the Potsdam protocol wished to reserve the revision of the Montreux convention to an international conference.[75]

No futher initiative by the Soviet Union for the revision of the regime of the straits took place thereafter. The declaration issued by Moscow after Stalin's death which renounced all territorial claims on Turkey contains only a vague reference to the straits, expressing the hope that provisions will be found to secure the interests of the Soviet Union on conditions acceptable to both Ankara and Moscow.[76]

We can only speculate on the reasons for the subsequent Soviet passivity in regard to the regime of the straits. The overbearing Soviet attitude pressed Turkey into the NATO camp; perhaps Moscow has decided that an international conference for the revision of the Montreux convention would result in a regime no more favorable to the contentions of the Soviets than the present one or—with the key country, Turkey, in the hostile camp—in an even less favorable regime. To wait for an appropriate time to take up the question of a new regime of the straits must have appeared to the rulers of the Kremlin the only proper course to follow—especially after Stalin had so unwisely played his cards and lost.

For the Western powers and Turkey, the change in the status of the straits was a matter of no urgency; since Turkey, their ally, was in control of these waterways, they could quietly wait and see. That the Montreux convention was outdated in many respects did not hurt them. It was for Turkey to implement the convention and, as long as the application rested with a friendly and allied power, it was better to leave things as they were.[77]

---

[75] *Ibid.,* pp. 49–50.

[76] See pp. 174–75 above.

[77] The Turkish press reported that the Assembly of the Western European Union (Britain, France, West Germany, Italy, and the Benelux states) in its session held in

THE SOVIETS AND THE STRAITS

Accordingly, Turkey is applying the convention of 1936 under the changed conditions of present-day international politics and applying it to warships carrying weapons developed by military technology in the more than three decades since its conclusion. The Turkish government is being closely watched by all maritime powers in its handling of the affairs of the straits; while Ankara is trying to be impartial as best it can in sometimes difficult situations, it cannot escape criticism by the press or even by interested governments.

Difficulties of applications arose, for instance, when warships of the United Arab Republic wished to pass the straits when professed to be in a state of war with Israel. On the other hand, anti-American elements questioned the right of the United States to send its men-of-war through the straits because it pursued an undeclared war in Vietnam. In both cases, the Turkish foreign ministry ruled that no belligerency exists in the meaning of the Montreux convention.[78]

Because of the large number of Soviet submarines in the Mediterranean since the Arab–Israeli war of 1967, accusations have been leveled at Moscow for sending submarines from the Black Sea to the Mediterranean and at the Turkish government for closing its eyes to this activity forbidden by the Montreux convention.[79] The Turkish authorities, however, have strongly denied these accusations and maintained that the Soviet submarines must have entered the Mediterranean Sea exclusively through the Straits of Gibraltar.[80]

The United States' Sixth Fleet, operating in the Mediterranean, in addition to sending some of its units on courtesy calls to Turkish ports, dispatched smaller units every six months into the Black Sea to show the flag—in other words, to affirm the right of nonriparian powers to enter the Black Sea with their warships as provided by the convention of Montreux.[81] In December 1968, the U.S. destroyers *Dyess* and *Turner* entered the Black Sea for a few days on such a routine voyage. Both had a displacement under 10,000 tons, and their guns were of a caliber not exceed-

---

December 1967 demanded the revision of the Montreux convention so as to cover modern ships and arms. *Cumhuriyet*, December 6, 1967.

[78] See Foreign Minister Çağlayangil's answer to a question addressed to him by Deputy Settar Iksel in the National Assembly; *Cumhuriyet*, February 5, 1969.

[79] *New York Times*, February 8, 1969.

[80] Information given to this writer in the Turkish Ministry of Foreign Affairs. See also *Milliyet*, February 11, 1969.

[81] *New York Times*, December 15, 1968; *Akşam*, December 11, 1968.

ing 8 inches or 203 mm. The *Dyess,* however was also equipped with an eight-missile ASROC (anti-submarine rocket launcher) which is 305 mm. Under the Montreux convention, warships of non-Black Sea powers are forbidden to carry guns of a caliber larger than 203 mm.[82] The Turkish government answered Soviet protests by pointing out:

New arms have been developed since the Montreux Convention. These weapons were not listed in the Convention because they did not exist at the time of its signature. The Turkish Government takes the view that carrying such weapons is not conflicting with the Convention if they are not of an aggressive nature.[83]

Ankara established that the rocket launcher in question was of a defensive nature to be used against submarine attack; therefore, it did not object to the passage of the American warship through the straits.

The application of the Montreux convention, as demonstrated by the cases described above, is not an easy or routine matter; it requires vigilance and consistent interpretations whenever the letter of the convention fails to provide clear-cut answers. Novel problems constantly come before the Ministry of Foreign Affairs in Ankara, which are not covered by the treaty. For instance, under the present regime of the straits, aircraft may not be launched from the deck of warships in these waters. Thus, when the American admiral in command of the aircraft carrier *Enterprise* was taken by helicopter over the head of demonstrating students in Istanbul for a courtesy visit to the governor of that city, should this action have been considered a violation of the convention? In other words, is the helicopter an "aircraft" in the meaning of the draftsmen of Montreux? Even the lawfulness of the bridge planned to be constructed over the Bosporus may be questioned as a possible artificial obstruction to free traffic along the straits.[84]

---

[82] Both destroyers have a displacement of only 3,500 tons and were armed with 127 mm. guns; *New York Times,* December 7, 1968. The Montreux convention permits the entry of outside warships of a tonnage not exceeding 15,000 tons. Whether the *Dyess* and *Turner* carried nuclear weapons was not disclosed nor questioned by the Turkish authorities.

[83] *Milliyet,* December 7, 1968. In September 1966, the Turkish government barred the entry of the U.S. destroyer *William V. Pratt* because she was equipped with ASROC launchers.

[84] According to *Akşam,* the Turkish foreign ministry denied having knowledge of a helicopter taking off the visiting ships of the Sixth Fleet; *Akşam,* February 19, 1969. As to objections to the bridge over the Bosporus, the Ministry of Foreign Affairs in Ankara denied that the United States or the Soviet Union had opposed the height of the future bridge; *Cumhuriyet,* March 26, 1968.

Soviet traffic through the straits has increased tremendously with the concentration of Soviet naval units in the Mediterranean. Government observers in Ankara appeared little alarmed over these developments, though they could not remain indifferent to the improved strategic position of the Soviet Union in what used to be an uncontested NATO "lake." Turkey no longer has to face the potential Soviet threat only along her northern borders and coastline; Soviet naval forces are now concentrated in strength in her back yard, along her southern coast. Although many of the Soviet craft had entered the Mediterranean from the Atlantic, substantive forces have come from the Black Sea and are constantly moving in both directions through the straits. Most of the supplies needed for these vessels are shipped through the Bosporus and Dardanelles; more than half of all the ships passing in full view of Istanbul carry the Soviet flag. It looks as if the waters of the straits serve largely for the transportation of Soviet bottoms. It is hardly conceivable that, in view of these circumstances, Moscow should not again raise the issue of the Dardanelles.

The invasion of Czechoslovakia, followed by the announcement of the so-called Brezhnev Doctrine (the alleged right to intervene in other "Socialist" countries) created fear of an attack on either Rumania or Yugoslavia and added fuel to the fire of renewed suspicion about the real Soviet intentions. Turkey, because of her geographical location at the southeastern tip of the Balkan Peninsula, not only watches the straits as a possible route of Soviet penetration but is also traditionally interested in the political and military situation of the Balkans and, indeed, in the entire Soviet satellite empire in East Europe. Any Soviet moves in that area are likely to impair Turkey's geostrategic position. Her relations with the peoples of these areas are linked with the historical reminiscences and practical experiences gained during the past 200 years.

Turkey's Western Flank: The Balkans and East Europe

Two centuries ago the entire Balkan peninsula belonged to the Ottoman Empire; sixty years ago the sultan's realm still extended to the Adriatic. Rumania, Albania, Bulgaria, Greece, and much of what is now Yugoslavia were once either integral parts of the empire or vassal states. Muslims in faraway Bosnia, in Albania and Bulgaria, and ethnic Turks in Macedonia, Rumania, and Bulgaria are vivid proofs of former Ottoman rule.

In the sixteenth and seventeenth centuries, the sultan's power spread over large portions of Hungary, Transylvania, and Moldavia; that is, beyond the geographical peninsula of the Balkans. Ottoman armies fought Poles and Russians in the Ukraine; however, the partition of Poland in the late eighteenth century created a community of interest between Turks and Poles and was read as a warning of what Russia had in store for Turkey. The suppression of the Hungarian war of independence of 1848–49 by the tsar strengthened bonds of sympathy with Hungarians.

The Russian military menace against Turkey was felt mainly in the Balkan regions of the Ottoman Empire. Twice in the nineteenth century Russian armies approached Constantinople across this peninsula. The protracted defensive action to prevent the disintegration of the empire was fought against the autochthonous peoples of the Balkans who were revolting against Ottoman rule. In 1912, when most of the Balkans had been lost to Turkey, the Bulgarians even threatened the outer defense line of the Ottoman capital.

Kemalist Turkey planned to pursue the same policy of friendship with the Balkan countries that she followed with other neighbors. It was definitely a status quo policy that concealed no territorial ambitions. In the Balkans, Turkey had to observe a neutral attitude toward the rivalry between France and Italy: the latter endeavored to set up a Bulgarian–Turkish–Greek bloc against Yugoslavia, the former supported Yugoslavia and Rumania and also wished to include Turkey in her system of alliances. Turkey was deterred from befriending Italy because of Mussolini's territorial ambitions along the Anatolian coast and the establishment of a naval base on Leros, in the Dodecanese archipelago.[85] Until 1938 she was unwilling to become a party to an alliance led by one of the great powers, but she strove to organize the Balkan states into an alliance system which could withstand the pressure of any great power. Atatürk later hoped to set up a federation of Balkan states, a kind of Third Force, between the confrontation of the Axis and Western powers.[86]

With the Turkish–Greek reconciliation articulated by the Treaty of Neutrality, Conciliation, and Arbitration of 1930, and the Cordial Friendship Pact of 1933, the way opened for a collective Balkan treaty. Although

[85] See Hans Kohn, "Ten Years of the Turkish Republic," *Foreign Affairs,* October, 1933, 153–54.
[86] Kiliç, *Turkey and the World,* pp. 50–51.

it proved impossible to obtain the accession of Bulgaria (because of the latter's claims to a revision of the frontier), the convention, known as the Balkan Entente, was signed in February 1934 by Turkey, Greece, Rumania, and Yugoslavia. The failure of the Balkan Entente to prevent the extension of the approaching war into the Balkans has been described earlier.[87] By May 1941, Turkey was once more threatened along her Balkan and Aegean border, but this time the potential enemy was Germany.

With the reversal of the fortunes of the war, Soviet forces descended on Bulgaria in late 1944; the nineteenth-century pattern of Russian pressure on Turkey seemed to have returned. This time Soviet–Russian control was to stay: Rumania, Bulgaria, Poland, and even the Central European countries of Czechoslovakia and Hungary had been converted into Communist client states of Mother Russia. Only Yugoslavia and, subsequently, Albania managed to extricate themselves from Moscow's hug. Greece, with Anglo–American assistance, was able to repel Communist attempts of take-over.

Turkey, having become the southeastern bastion of the Atlantic alliance in the post-World War II world, was anxious to put out her feelers in both the East and West to secure her flanks against the embrace of Moscow. The secession of Yugoslavia in 1948 from the Soviet orbit and Stalin's threat to her newly won independence turned Belgrade into a suitable partner, together with Greece, in a defensive alliance directed to pursue common policies in the protection of their security.

Evidently, Yugoslavia had a greater need for protection than either Turkey or Greece, countries which had joined NATO in 1952. But Turkish diplomacy, intent on strengthening anti-Soviet forces in the Balkans, was instrumental in overcoming Tito's hesitation to deviate from strict neutrality. Because of the Trieste question, Italy opposed the conclusion of any military alliance by NATO powers with Yugoslavia.

Nonetheless, the closure of the Balkan pact proceeded gradually: on February 28, 1953, Turkey and Greece signed a Treaty of Friendship and Assistance with Yugoslavia in Ankara.[88] In this instrument, only consultation, collaboration, and nonaggression were promised by the parties. To harmonize obligations under a treaty of assistance with those undertaken in the North Atlantic alliance provided a problem. After the principal

[87] See chapter I, pp. 25–26.
[88] *Documents on International Affairs, 1953*, pp. 271–73.

NATO powers became convinced, however, that a Soviet attack against Yugoslavia would eventually involve them in an armed conflict, the blessing for a military assistance pact with Yugoslavia was given. Accordingly, on August 9, 1954, the Balkan Defense Pact was signed in Bled, Yugoslavia, by Turkey, Greece, and Yugoslavia. The controlling provision of this treaty ran as follows:

The Contracting Parties have agreed that any armed aggression against one, or several of them, on any part of their territories, shall be considered as an aggression against all the Contracting Parties, which in consequence, exercising the right of legitimate individual or collective self-defense, recognized by Article 51 of the United Nations Charter, shall individually or collectively render assistance to the Party or Parties attacked, undertaking in common accord and immediately all measures, including the use of armed force, which they shall deem necessary for . . . efficacious defense.[89]

The obligation to assist under the Balkan pact does not, therefore, differ from that undertaken in the Atlantic alliance. Thus, indirectly, Yugoslavia was covered by the NATO commitments, provided that Turkey and Greece come to her assistance when attacked. The Balkan Defense Pact, like NATO, provided for the establishment of a permanent council composed of the foreign ministers of the signatories, or of other members of the governments concerned, and for "joint work" by the general staffs of the three countries.

This alliance "across ideological boundaries"[90] soon proved to have been stillborn. The ink was hardly dry on the ratification documents of this tripartite pact before Tito made his peace with the Soviet Union during and following the apologetic visit of Bulganin and Khrushchev to Belgrade in May 1955. Immediately thereafter, Yugoslavia began to de-emphasize the military aspects, the most important ones, of the Balkan Pact.[91] Although the treaty would not expire until 1974, it had in practice become vitiated by the reluctance of Yugoslavia to continue holding meetings of the permanent council and to collaborate with the military staffs of her co-signatories. While the Balkan pact is technically valid (it could not be legally denounced before the lapse of twenty years), it has practically turned into a dead letter: Yugoslavia considers herself a

[89] Article 2. For the text of the Balkan Defense Pact, see *Documents on International Affairs, 1954*, pp. 197–200.
[90] See John O. Iatrides, *Balkan Triangle: Birth and Decline of an Alliance Across Ideological Boundaries* (The Hague, 1968), *passim*.
[91] See Kiliç, *Turkey and the World*, pp. 162–63.

"neutralist" or "uncommitted" power.[92] Of course, simultaneously with the elimination of the Soviet threat to Yugoslavia, Moscow's pressure on Turkey relaxed. Another reason for the breakdown of the Balkan alliance was the estrangement of Turkey and Greece because of their differences over Cyprus.

From Moscow's vantage point, Soviet efforts had thus prevented the creation of an anti-Russian bloc in the Balkans that would have included the "revisionist" Communist state of Yugoslavia. Western and parallel Turkish policy goals clashed with the Kremlin's desire to strengthen Soviet presence in the peninsula—an area which tsarist Russian policy always sought to transform into its exclusive playground. Nevertheless, even after the Yugoslav–Soviet rapprochement of 1955–56, the Balkan peninsula remained divided, not only by the historical national antagonisms of their peoples but also by the ideological cleavages of its Communist components. The plan to return Yugoslavia to the Soviet-led camp, if it had ever been a realistic endeavor at all, failed in 1956; Albania, with the gradually widening Sino-Soviet rift, turned against Moscow and became a Chinese *pied-à-terre* in the Balkans. Rumania, which appeared for a long time to be Moscow's voice for the affairs of the Balkan peninsula,[93] also "deviated" from the Kremlin's footsteps and initiated a more or less independent foreign policy line. Among the Communist states of the Balkans, only Bulgaria remained the faithful servant of her Muscovite master.

After the disaggregation of the Balkan states in the mid-1960's, Turkey and the Western powers could pursue policies toward them which were geared to the interests and necessities of the individual countries and not dependent on the placet of Moscow. Aside from Greece, however, Bulgaria is the immediate neighbor of Turkey along her Balkan border, and her rapport with that country remained a most delicate and critical concern.

Turkish-Bulgarian relations slowly deteriorated when Turkey moved into the Western camp and reached their low point in 1952. The Bulgarian government, to put pressure on her neighbor and to eliminate

---

[92] C. L. Sulzberger maintained that the Balkan Pact is nowadays aimed only at Bulgaria; *New York Times,* November 1, 1968.

[93] The Rumanian Premier Chivu Stoica had become the prime promoter of the Moscow-born plan for a "nuclear free zone" in the Balkan area voiced in September 1957 and again in June 1959, a plan consistently rejected by Turkey and Greece.

intractable elements, began to expel citizens of Turkish descent. On August 12, 1950, a Bulgarian decree ordered the expulsion of 250,000 Turks within three months. Turkey only consented to take over her countrymen in an orderly manner and gradually. From 1950 to 1952, about 140,000 Turks were forced to leave. Turkey retaliated by recalling her diplomatic personnel from Sofia and threatening to sever all diplomatic relations. In November 1951, Ankara closed its border to further immigration because of the infiltration of undesirable elements and Bulgaria did likewise in December. By 1953 the Bulgarians refused to allow any further emigration and many members of Turkish families thus became separated.[94]

For years the Turkish–Bulgarian frontier was one of the most inhospitable border regions in Europe; innumerable border incidents marked the uneasy relations between the two countries. After Stalin's death, a cautious relaxation took place without, however, leading to really normal contacts. The significant improvement of relations, directed no doubt from Moscow, began in August 1966, when Bulgarian Foreign Minister Ivan Bashev visited his Turkish colleague in Ankara. The two ministers considered all outstanding problems between their countries: prevention of border clashes, improvement of communications and transportation, the construction of direct rail lines and a new highway, reciprocal aid in law enforcement, and others. Talks between experts on all these questions were to be taken up, but the really fundamental problem between the two governments remained the Turkish minority in Bulgaria.[95]

The exact number of Turks in Bulgaria cannot be ascertained with certainty. Turks constantly refer to one million of their co-nationals.[96] Bulgarian statistics admit the existence of 650,000 Turks, excluding from their number Tartars and the Pomaks.[97] Other sources estimate them to be 800,000 or 900,000. There are continuous complaints in Turkey about

[94] *Survey of International Affairs, 1951,* pp. 204–5; H. L. Kostanick, "Turkish Resettlement of Refugees from Bulgaria, 1950–53," *Middle East Journal* (Winter, 1955): pp. 41–52.

[95] *The Times* (London), August 13, 1966.

[96] According to the *Daily News* (Ankara), the Turkish population of Bulgaria increased between the years of 1934 and 1968 from 618,000 to 1,058,000, as estimated by economists; *Daily News,* May 3, 1968.

[97] *Neue Zürcher Zeitung,* August 20, 1966. The *Pomaks* are Bulgarian-speaking Muslims.

the discriminatory treatment of Bulgarian Turks; they are employed as unskilled heavy laborers in the process of industrialization. Before the collectivization of agriculture, they were mainly small landholders, especially in the richest wheat-growing area of the Bulgarian northeast (known under the Turkish name of Deli Orman); they have since been removed from their compact settlements.[98]

The visit of the Bulgarian foreign minister was returned by Foreign Minister Çağlayangil in May 1967. In February 1968, an agreement was signed between the two governments to allow the reunion of families broken up since 1952: about 15,000 members of the Turkish minority would be allowed to emigrate to Turkey in groups of 300 per week from April to November every year. It appeared that Turkey was ready to receive a much larger number of immigrants, but Bulgaria had refused any emigration other than that prompted by humanitarian motives. According to Turkish sources, practically all Turks in Bulgaria were ready for a mass exodus to Turkey, had they been permitted to do so.[99]

The next diplomatic visit took place in March 1968, when Todor Zhivkov, premier and first secretary of the Bulgarian Communist Party, travelled to Ankara. In addition to the agreement on "immigration," a number of other agreements had been concluded before that visit, covering communications and transportation, economic development, culture, and tourism.[100]

The most significant transportation agreement was that which would enable Turkey and Bulgaria to establish a direct rail line. Because of the border changes between Turkey, Greece, and Bulgaria since the Balkan wars of 1912–13, the southeastern section of the "Oriental Railway," constructed in the seventies and eighties of the nineteenth century, had been shared by all three of these countries. Accordingly, the railroad link between Istanbul and Sofia passed through a Greek section of western Thrace, entered Turkish territory near Edirne, and re-entered Greece before reaching the Bulgarian border at Svilengrad.[101] Under the agree-

---

[98] Neue Zürcher Zeitung, June 9, 1962; Cumhuriyet, August 25, 1967; this is a report by Osman Bölükbaşı, the leader of the Nation Party who visited Bulgaria.

[99] Milliyet, February 25, 1968; Cumhuriyet, March 18, 1969.

[100] East Europe, August 1968, pp. 3–4. See also the press conference by Prime Minister Demirel of March 23, 1968, following the Zhivkov visit; Cumhuriyet, March 24, 1968.

[101] See Váli, Servitudes of International Law, pp. 115–18.

ment signed in August 1967, Turkey agreed to build the railroad from Pehlivanköy via Edirne to the Bulgarian border, and Bulgaria would be responsible for the construction of the section between the border and Svilengrad. Thus, passage through Greek territory would be avoided.[102] Another highway (in addition to the Trans-Europe motor road) will be constructed linking the Bulgarian port of Burgas with Kìrklareli in Turkey.[103]

Premier Zhivkov's Turkish visit will, no doubt, be reciprocated in due time by a visit of the Turkish prime minister to Sofia. Such personal contacts between the leaders of the two nations could produce a rapprochement that would stabilize the Balkans as a whole and enable Turkey to render her European area more secure from possible menace. Foreign Minister Çağlayangil, however, pointed out after the visit of the Bulgaria premier that "Turkey's good relations with the Eastern Bloc countries would never affect her relations with the West."[104] The Turkish–Bulgarian relationship, as long as Bulgaria remains under Soviet control, will be dependent on the rapport which Ankara is able to maintain with Moscow. As long as there is cordiality between Ankara and Moscow, similar tendencies will dominate the relations between Ankara and Sofia; however, the same no longer holds true between Turkey and Rumania.

More normal Turkish–Rumanian relations and genuine rapprochement between the two countries started with the visit of the Rumanian Prime Minister Maurer to Turkey in July 1966. Previously, the contacts were rather frosty and—at times—even a rupture of diplomatic relations was in the offing.[105] Maurer's visit thus concentrated in general on smoothing relations and increasing commerce between the two countries.[106]

Next, in the series of visits, Turkish Foreign Minister Çağlayangil travelled to Rumania in May 1967. Prime Minister Demirel returned his

[102] *Cumhuriyet,* November 6, 1967. Turkish editorialists expressed the view that with this new railroad line Turkey obtained a "more reliable gate to Europe" than crossing Greek territory, "in view of the weekly changing Turkish-Greek friendship." *Yeni Gazete,* March 22, 1968.

[103] *Tercüman,* August 17, 1967.

[104] *Milliyet,* March 21, 1968.

[105] *Survey of International Affairs, 1947–1948,* p. 221.

[106] *The Times* (London), August 2, 1966.

Rumanian colleague's visit in September 1967. It was pointed out on that occasion that on most world problems Turkish and Rumanian views happened to coincide.[107] The independent path on which Rumania had embarked since the mid-sixties, together with Turkey's intention to pursue a more self-centered foreign policy, enable them to harmonize most of their views.

Apart from ideological differences, easily de-emphasized when national interests come to the foreground, there were actually few areas of conflict. The Turkish minority in Rumania is relatively small, and there have been few complaints about their treatment by Rumanian authorities.[108] In every respect, Demirel's stay in Bucharest was considered a great success by the Turkish press.[109]

Corneliu Manescu, the Rumanian foreign minister, spent a few days in Ankara in November 1968. The visit was to prepare for the journey to Turkey of Nicolai Ceauşescu, the Rumanian president and party leader. This event, culminating three years of increasing friendliness between the two countries, took place in March 1969. The Rumanian leader's visit was marked by an attempt to heighten Turkey's interest in a new Balkan pact that would turn that part of Europe into a "peace region." It was suggested that Ceauşescu had hinted at the possibility of Rumania's leaving the Warsaw Pact to join a regional system of Balkan states; however, Turkish leaders preferred not to engage in such an exchange of ideas, the precondition of which appeared to them to be a complete dismantling of the Western alliance. Indeed, the Rumanian suggestion was conceived within the framework of a new European security convention and the reciprocal abandonment of both the Warsaw treaty and NATO. These were thoughts which were entirely alien to the cautious and realistic Turkish leaders.[110]

The Rumanian foreign policy, emancipated from strict Soviet controls, must be most pleasing and reassuring to Ankara. Such a policy line tends

[107] *Milliyet*, September 22, 1967.

[108] The number of ethnic Turks living in Rumania is now about 50,000 (Rumanians also distinguish between "Tatars" and "Turks"). It was reported that 500 Turks living on a small island on the Danube, Ada Kale, will be allowed to emigrate to Turkey; *Milliyet*, September 15, 1967.

[109] *Cumhuriyet*, September 18, 1967; *Yeni Gazete*, September 14, 1967.

[110] *Milliyet*, March 24, 1969; *Yeni Gazete*, March 25, 1969; *Cumhuriyet*, March 28, 1969.

to isolate Bulgaria (land routes from the Soviet Union to Bulgaria have to pass through Rumania) and renders direct Soviet interference more difficult. Nevertheless, it was realized in Turkey, more than perhaps anywhere else, that Rumania's course of action is limited by her geographical proximity to the Russian giant; too much freedom could jeopardize all that Rumania has gained in sovereign independence during the last years.

Since Yugoslavia has been expelled from the Cominform and outlawed by Moscow, her relations with Turkey have developed normally and in a friendly atmosphere. Political differences between the two countries are practically nonexistent. Vis-à-vis their common neighbor and potential adversary, Bulgaria, they share the bonds of interest engendered by being a "neighbor of one's neighbor."

As has been described earlier, the threatening posture of the Soviet Union and its satellites induced Belgrade to enter into a defensive military alliance with NATO's two Balkan powers, Turkey and Greece. Ankara must have been rather unhappy when, following the Soviet-Yugoslav reconciliation, Tito inactivated the Balkan Defense Pact. In fact, he went even further: he acted as if this treaty, still valid until 1974, were nonexistent. Yugoslavia prided herself as being one of the leaders of the group of "uncommitted" nations. One may wonder whether under changed circumstances, such as a renewed Soviet menace (which one might have expected after Czechoslovakia's invasion in 1968 and the announcement of the Brezhnev Doctrine), Yugoslavia would not be ready to reactivate her alliance with Turkey and Greece. Evidently, an even greater shock or more proximate threat would be needed to remind Belgrade of the Balkan pact.[111]

In spite of the "ignored alliance," there was a frequent exchange of visits between leading Turkish and Yugoslav statesmen. Lately, Yugoslav Prime Minister Spiljak visited Ankara in April 1968, and in return, Turkish Prime Minister Demirel journeyed to Belgrade in May 1969. The conversations, for lack of acute controversial topics, concentrated on a mutual evaluation of world events: the Arab-Israeli conflict, Vietnam, and also

[111] Tito's report to the Ninth Congress of the League of Communists (the Communist Party) of Yugoslavia on March 11, 1969, while strongly condemning "the military intervention by five socialist countries in Czechoslovakia," emphasized Yugoslavia's policy of nonalignment and failed to refer to the Balkan Pact. *Yugoslav Facts and Views,* Yugoslav Information Center, New York, March 16, 1969.

Cyprus. Turkey registered satisfaction that Tito advocated the independence of Cyprus, while the plan for securing the status of the Turkish community on the island by a federative system appeared to have received the reserved approval of Yugoslavia.[112]

The condition of the Turkish minority in Yugoslavia has not presented reasons for particular complaint. According to official Yugoslav sources, the number of Turks was 183,000 in 1961. The number of all Muslims is, of course, considerably higher: there are nearly one million Bosnian Muslims and nearly as many Albanians of Muslim religion in Yugoslavia.[113]

The Ankara–Belgrade "axis," despite the de-emphasized military aspects of this relationship, remains the most stable and durable base for any possible coalescence of Balkan states. Although Yugoslav leaders were as reserved as the Turks about Rumania's plans for the establishment of a "Balkan Union," their aim was identical with that of Ankara: peaceful cooperation of all countries of the peninsula. It was, however, realized by both sides that the nationally, ideologically, and religiously fragmented character of that region permits only a slow and carefully prepared advance toward the genuine rapprochement among all its members.

Albania's exotic position—she closely cooperates with Communist China—isolates that country from other nations in the Balkans. Her irredentist tendencies against both of her neighbors, Yugoslavia and Greece, perhaps even more than her pro-Chinese Communist line, has contributed to this alienation. Nonetheless, after Albania's secession from the Soviet bloc, Turkey established friendly relations with Tirana. In 1966 ambassadors were exchanged, and a trade agreement was reached in 1967—although there has been practically no trade at all and no reciprocal tourist travel. On the occasion of a visit of a Turkish parliamentary delegation in the summer of 1968, it was just stated that "the already good relations have been improved still more."[114]

The majority of Albanians—as far as they are religious—are Muslims; Albanians had mostly served the Ottoman sultans faithfully. They estab-

---

[112] *Cumhuriyet*, April 3, 1968; *Yeni Gazete*, March 7, 1969.

[113] Federal Institute for Statistics, *Statistical Calendar of Yugoslavia*, Belgrade, 1969. Turkish sources also mention 180,000 Turks in Yugoslavia; 120,000 in Macedonia; and the rest divided in other parts of the country; *Yeni Gazete*, September 12, 1968.

[114] *Milliyet*, September 3, 1968.

lished their independence only when they became territorially separated from the rest of Turkey. Accordingly, there exists a residue of good will between the two countries which was not eliminated by the ideological allegiance of the Albanian regime.

For Turkey, her diplomatic mission in Albania mainly serves the purpose of a "listening post." She is one of the few members of the Western alliance that maintains contact with Tirana. Reports from the only Chinese satellite in Europe may be of considerable interest to other Western nations.

Turkey maintains diplomatic relations with the Chinese Nationalist government in Taiwan; but, since 1965, Ankara has considered following the example of France and other countries in recognizing the People's Republic of China. In view of the presumptive or actual American opposition to such a move, however, the Turkish government has so far refrained from such action.

Turkey has little direct political interest in the affairs of East–Central European Communist states outside the Balkans. But because Soviet affairs concern her directly, the diplomatic missions in the capitals of these countries are excellent observation stations for trends and events within the Soviet camp. Among these posts, the one in Hungary is considered the most useful listening post.

Turco-Hungarian relations had been "brotherly" since the eighteenth century. Hungarian patriots sought and found refuge in the Ottoman Empire. The awareness that the Turks, like the Hungarians, are of "Turanian" stock has contributed to the good feeling and sympathies felt toward Magyars. Of course, because official Hungary finds herself in the Soviet-controlled bloc, official contacts have tended to be cool and reserved. Turkish officials, however, can and do distinguish easily between "official" ties and those which they can establish with individual Hungarians.

The easing of tension between Turkey and members of the Soviet camp has finally affected Hungarian–Turkish relations. The Turkish legation in Budapest and the Hungarian legation in Ankara were reciprocally raised to the level of embassies in September 1967.[115] Further, the foreign ministers of Turkey and Hungary exchanged visits. Talks were

[115] *Cumhuriyet,* September 27, 1967.

most fruitful in the area of trade, and closer ties in science and culture were also considered.[116]

As with the suppression of the Hungarian revolution by Soviet forces in 1956, the invasion of Czechoslovakia created a deep-felt sense of indignation in Turkey. It was generally felt that the Soviet Union, which accused other powers of being imperialist, was the greatest imperialist of them all. Prime Minister Demirel considered the Czechoslovak events the most important developments of the year 1968. He added:

If this is regarded as an internal affair of the Eastern Bloc, the Pact which was supposed to safeguard the security of its members against those of another Pact is in fact putting its own members under pressure one by one. Thus the true purpose of the Pact can clearly be seen.[117]

Immediately after the invasion, Foreign Minister Çağlayangil declared:

Our Government viewed and evaluated the developments in Czechoslovakia from the viewpoint of Turkey's long-standing policy principles of peace, respect for the independence of states, non-interference in domestic affairs and non-utilization of force in settling disputes. It is impossible for one to find the situation in Czechoslovakia compatible with the principles or objectives of the United Nations Charter.

Meanwhile, the detente atmosphere which was developing between the East and West European countries and which gave hope for the future of humanity has gravely been impaired by the situation in Czechoslovakia.[118]

The Turkish government, constantly in search of evidence of the "real intentions" of Moscow, was bound to be impressed by these events in the heart of Europe which were hardly conducive to a strengthening of its ties with the Soviets. Developments indicative of the fluctuations in Soviet foreign policy are being closely watched by Turkish missions in Prague as in Budapest and in Warsaw.

Turkey's relations with Poland never reached such a low ebb as her contacts with other members of the Soviet bloc. Friendship between Turks and Poles dates back to the end of the eighteenth century and is essentially

---

[116] *Milliyet,* July 21, 1968. Hungarian Foreign Minister János Péter expressed readiness to support the Turkish position concerning Cyprus. He praised the frankness and sincere atmosphere which dominated the talks; *Milliyet,* July 24, 1968.

[117] *Hürriyet,* December 31, 1968.

[118] *Ulus,* August 23, 1968.

based on the animosity which both nations felt toward the common enemy Russia.

Accordingly, each of the political visits between the two countries was characterized by an emphasis upon the "historical friendship" of the two nations. During his visit to Turkey in May 1967, Polish Foreign Minister Rapacki referred to the fact that diplomatic relations between Turkey and Poland date back to 1414. Of even greater interest was his reference at a banquet given in his honor to the fact that Turkey "never recognized the partitions of Poland nor the pretensions of the Hitlerite aggressors to cross our country off the list of independent and sovereign states."[119] For the Turkish listeners and readers, this speech must have sounded ironic: they were well aware that the country most instrumental in the partition of Poland (including her partition during World War II) was Russia, whose name was tactfully omitted by the Polish foreign minister.

Turkey's endeavors to maintain friendly relations with all nations of the Balkan peninsula and East–Central Europe serve her own security interests. Except for the Yugoslav–Greek alliance (which proved abortive), she has been reluctant to support collective forms of cooperation. Bilateral contacts have been favored and individual schemes of collaboration stressed. Turkey's Balkan policy is not directed against Moscow, but those policies, especially toward Yugoslavia or Rumania, might be interpreted as anti-Soviet. Whether Turkey's policies will be seen as inimical to Soviet policy ultimately depends on the Kremlin's intentions. If the Soviet Union insists on preserving its power posture in the Balkans, it will have to rely on Bulgaria; but Bulgaria would not be enough. The possibility that Moscow will one day be induced to bring Rumania to her knees is dreaded by Ankara. Such a Czechoslovak-type move would immediately topple the present equilibrium in the Balkans and turn the area, once again, into a powder keg of European—even world—politics. In this respect the relationship between Turkey and the countries of the Balkans remains, as it had been through decades in the past, ultimately dependent on Russian foreign policy.

CAN RUSSIA BE TRUSTED?

The formation of modern Turkey coincided with the creation of the Soviet state on the ruins of tsarist Russia. Both countries underwent pro-

[119] Radio Free Europe, *Polish Situation Report,* May 8, 1967.

found and traumatic metamorphoses. Out of the feudalistic tsarist empire developed an industrialized superstate, dedicated to Marxist–Leninist messianism, surrounded by a cluster of client nations. The decrepit Ottoman Empire shrank into a sturdy Turkish nation-state bent on modernizing and becoming a European nation.

In the field of foreign policy, the Soviet Union, after abandoning the utopian dream of a speedy world-revolution, became a defensive fortress of "socialism in one country." It supported Turkey's endeavor to protect her independence and strove to prevent the entry of foreign warships into the Black Sea. Turkey, too, wrote off her territorial losses as well as the Pan-Islamic or Pan-Turkist ambitions of the Ottomans and concentrated her efforts on internal development and modernization. Thus, for almost two decades, the foreign policy goals of the two countries essentially coincided, perhaps almost complemented, one another.

With the advent of World War II, however, the USSR suddenly reversed its disposition. It actually took up where tsarist Russia had left off on the pretense of self-defense; it demanded a share in the military protection of the straits, nothing less than a euphemism for the control of these vital waterways, and sought to strangle Turkey into obedience. At the end of the war, Moscow found itself in an even stronger position; having expanded herself along the Baltic into Germany and other parts of Central Europe and established submissive governments in Rumania and Bulgaria, the Soviet state attempted to expand into the Aegean and believed the time was ripe for browbeating Turkey into submission.

Upon Stalin's death, the futility of this imperious posture was realized. For a number of years, Moscow still maintained that Turkey's membership in NATO prevented a renewal of friendship; peaceful coexistence was offered to the West but not to Turkey. Only after 1960 did Soviet policy toward Turkey become more realistic; only then was Turkey's participation in the Atlantic alliance no longer thought incompatible with a cordial relationship.

The relaxation of relations with the Soviet Union enabled Turkey to give up her one-track foreign policy; previously, her preoccupation with the Soviet threat had been so overpowering that her freedom of action had been impaired. NATO would no longer monopolize her attention. Nevertheless, while she was no longer solely absorbed by Soviet actions, she still closely observed Soviet foreign policy in general and initiatives toward the "general direction" of the Mediterranean and the Middle East in particular.

The Soviets have officially abandoned claims to Turkey's territory, but they have not abandoned their desire for a change in the status of the straits. Turkey is under constant subtle pressures in respect to these water lanes, and a sudden reopening of the question of the Dardanelles may be expected at some future time when Moscow believes it appropriate for Soviet interests. It is unlikely that Moscow would repeat its blundering campaign of intimidation against her southern neighbor unless a moment arises when a threat could be followed by effective action. In the meantime, instead of the previous clumsy Stalinist attempt to blackmail Ankara into concessions, Soviet foreign policy pursues a three-pronged, delicate diplomatic maneuver.

Moscow wished to establish a relationship of cordial friendship with Ankara which would permit a constant exchange of views. The ultimate aim of this policy was to persuade Turkey that she had no reason to distrust Russia and that neutrality would suit her interests better than membership in the Atlantic alliance. After France, whose decisions Moscow could hardly influence, Turkey was considered the most likely country to desert the Western camp. To push a hole in the *cordon sanitaire* set up by NATO around its western and southern European borders would be a most outstanding victory of Soviet diplomacy. Unlike the Stalin-Hitler pact, this would be one which would not boomerang. Domestic developments in Turkey, given exaggerated evaluation in the Kremlin, appeared to encourage Soviet foreign policy experts in their belief that attempts to sever Turkey's NATO ties were no longer entirely hopeless.

How can Moscow intensify the pro-neutral and leftist tendencies of Turkish domestic politics? It seems clear, at first sight, that noninterference would be the only wise and prudent attitude; any overt support given to the leftist wing of the Republican People's Party, to the Turkish Labor Party, or to anti-American intellectuals, is bound to have counterproductive results. Evidently, it is so believed in Moscow. The overtures and encouragements given by Soviet diplomats and representatives of Soviet satellite countries have been extremely tactful and cautious. What now matters to Moscow is to avoid making any more mistakes, and the Turkish experts of the Soviet Ministry of Foreign Affairs are sedulously being consulted about what to do and what not to do. This diplomatic "fraternization" may, of course, be speeded up should there be a suitable opportunity for exploiting Turkish disappointments in the West.

Not that Moscow does not encourage Turkish discontent. Although the alternation of threats and blandishments, so common in the time of Khrushchev, has been discontinued, the Kremlin cannot abandon support of clandestine Communist organizations in Turkey and, more overtly, the exiled Turkish Communist Party. Thus, at the Twenty-Second Soviet Communist Party Congress in 1966, Leonid Brezhnev, secretary-general of the party, greeted Yakup Demir, the leader of the banned Turkish Communist Party. This event was not well received in Ankara.[120] The Turkish press frequently reports arrests of "Communist couriers" and other agents and complains of Soviet radio broadcasts in Turkish, which often are transmitted on the same wavelength radio stations use in Turkey.[121]

Activities of Soviet diplomats are more closely scrutinized by official and nonofficial circles than similar moves by members of other diplomatic missions. Soviet Ambassador Smirnov, who helped to re-establish friendly contacts not only with governmental circles but also with the Turkish public and press, was replaced in the spring of 1969 by Vasily Fedorovich Grubyakov, an old Turkish hand who during World War II served as secretary in the Ankara embassy and became consul general in Istanbul in 1945. The Turkish press accused Grubyakov of having been responsible for subversive operations in those critical years; hope was expressed that he would be subjected to a treatment similar to that reserved for the American Ambassador Komer.[122]

The third Soviet action that might induce Ankara to turn away from its Western orientation is aimed at establishing Russian influence in the

[120] *The Times* (London), April 14, 1966. For the activities of the Turkish Communist Party, see Günther Nollau and Hans Jürgen Wiehe, *Russia's South Flank* (New York, 1963), pp. 85–90.

[121] For the arrest of Communist agents, see *Milliyet,* June 19, 1968 (the case of Leon Kegan Pulli, alias Manukyan, who was sentenced to death by a Military Tribunal for espionage but his sentence was commuted to life imprisonment); *Akşam,* December 17, 1968 (the case of Nahit Imre, an employee of NATO, arrested in Istanbul); *Hürriyet,* April 20, 1969 (the case of Necdet Mualla, a Syrian student who cooperated with members of the Soviet Consulate General of Istanbul). For the interference of Soviet radio stations (Erivan radio broadcasted on the same wavelength as the Turkish radio station of Erzerum), see *Yeni Gazete,* July 1, 1967; *Tercüman,* November 20, 1967.

[122] *Son Havadis,* March 25, 1969; *Tercüman,* March 27, 1969; *Son Havadis,* April 25, 1969.

Arab Middle East and would at first only indirectly affect Turkey. Soviet involvement in the United Arab Republic, Syria, Iraq, Yemen, South Yemen, and Algeria is dramatized by the presence of a strong naval force in the Mediterranean, one which has been built up by leapfrogging Turkey. So far the Soviet weaponry so lavishly supplied to the Arab states has only helped them to establish a balance of power with Israel. However, the Soviet naval concentration remains a cause of anxiety in the Turkish capital.

Before the concentration of Soviet naval forces, the Mediterranean Sea was under the sole control of the American Sixth Fleet, supported by the navies of other NATO powers. The massive increase of Soviet naval power occurred immediately after the Arab–Israeli war of 1967 when in six months most of the Soviet complement of 40 to 60 ships entered that sea, partly through the Straits of Gibraltar, partly through the Turkish straits.[123] The Russian fleet consisted of three squadrons with light cruisers, one helicopter carrier, destroyers, and an impressive number of submarines. They carried a battalion of marine infantry but few landing craft. According to Western sources, the Soviet fleet did not constitute a serious threat to the Sixth Fleet and other Allied navies, primarily because the latter retained their command of the air.[124] Nevertheless, it was believed in the West and in Turkey that this massive concentration of naval power constituted a serious element affecting the East-West balance of power.[125]

What was the ultimate reason for this costly move by Moscow? The immediate purpose was evidently psychological rather than strategical. The Soviet fleet was to act as a visible counterweight to the American Sixth Fleet in order to enhance Moscow's prestige among the Arabs. In April 1967, Brezhnev demanded the withdrawal of the United States fleet from the Mediterranean; at that time Moscow was already preparing to show the flag in those waters. It was part of the long-range strategy to deny the

---

[123] *NATO Letter*, November, 1967, p. 5. According to the official report of the Turkish Ministry of Foreign Affairs (regularly informed of naval ship movements in the Straits as provided by the Montreux convention), 152 Soviet warships passed through the Bosporus and Dardanelles in 1967 and only 90 of them returned to the Black Sea; *Cumhuriyet*, May 14, 1968.

[124] See the interview with Denis Healey, British Defense Secretary, as reported by the *New York Times*, February 11, 1969. Healey said that the entire Soviet fleet in the Mediterranean would be sunk within minutes in the event of war.

[125] *Yeni Gazete*, December 6, 1968.

Middle East to the United States and to establish a zone of Soviet influence there.[126]

The Soviet argument ran along these lines:

Our state, which is, as is known, a Black Sea and *consequently also a Mediterranean power,* could not remain indifferent to the intrigues of those fond of military ventures organized directly adjacent to the borders of the U.S.S.R. and other socialist countries. No one can be allowed to turn the Mediterranean into a breeding ground of a war that could plunge mankind into the abyss of a worldwide nuclear-missile catastrophe. The presence of Soviet vessels in the Mediterranean serves this lofty, noble aim.[127]

A similar geopolitical line of reasoning has been submitted by the Soviet Party newspaper:

Soviet ships entered the sea on the strength of the U.S.S.R.'s sovereign right to make free use of the open sea. . . . As a Black Sea and, in this sense, a Mediterranean Power, it is closely connected with all problems involving the interests of the peoples of this area of Europe, Africa, and Asia. *It is directly interested in insuring the security of its southern borders.*[128]

It is exactly this argument which Turks find most alarming. In a similar vein, the Soviet Union would consider the Eastern Mediterranean as its first line of defense; that means that "fortress Turkey" is behind this strategical line, encircled by the Soviet presence in the waters south of her shores. A Turkish commentator expressed this fear by writing: "The purpose is evident: to make a sandwich of the Anatolian Peninsula with Soviet navies both in the Mediterranean and in the Black Sea."[129]

It is not so much that a direct confrontation between the American and Soviet superpowers is feared; the unsettled and hazardous state of affairs in the Middle East, especially between Arabs and Israelis, does not exclude the outbreak of yet another local war. Should the Soviet fleet intervene in such a war, the United States could not remain indifferent. Also the Cyprus conflict between Turkey and Greece may be affected by

---

[126] See Marshall D. Shulman, "The Soviet Turn to the Sea," in *Uses of the Seas,* ed. Edmund A. Gullion (Englewood Cliffs, N.J., 1968), pp. 148–50.

[127] Statement by Vice-Admiral N. Smirnov, "Soviet Ships in the Mediterranean," *Krasnaya Svezda,* November 12, 1968. (Italics added.)

[128] *Pravda,* November 27, 1968, as reported and commented by the *New York Times,* November 28, 1968.

[129] Mumtaz Taik Fenik in *Son Havadis,* July 24, 1968.

the presence of the Soviet navy: so far, Turkey had been dissuaded by the United States from invading Cyprus; it is feared that next time the Soviet fleet might step in.[130]

Even after territorial demands were withdrawn and official friendliness was established, Turkey never felt assured that Moscow would not reopen the straits issue and urge a new regime detrimental, or even dangerous, to Turkey. The presence of a large Soviet fleet in the Mediterranean, passing to and fro through the straits, and essentially supplied from the Black Sea bases of the Soviet Union, forecast with even greater certainty Soviet pressures on Turkey in regard to the status of the Dardanelles and the Bosporus. Turks never cease to remind the West that they "know the Soviets." They are aware of the realism of Soviet strategical thinking, their strong geopolitical approach to international affairs, and also—despite their "turn to the sea"—their belief in the necessity of "contiguous land power." Under such circumstances it appears inconceivable that Moscow should feel anything but unhappy about being dependent on Turkey's control of the "umbilical cord" leading to its navy far out in the Mediterranean. Even if civilian leaders in the Kremlin did not realize the awkwardness of this situation, the military would not cease to press their point of view and demand more reliable security for the forces.

Surely, Turkey has no wish to interfere with Soviet passage through the straits. She wishes to conform to the letter and, if the text does not provide an answer, to the spirit of Montreux convention. She would undertake everything in her power, short of jeopardizing her own security, not to provoke, or in any way impair, Moscow's sense of security in regard to the use of the straits by its shipping or otherwise.[131]

But situations, yet unforeseen, may develop. Soviet leaders might be induced to undertake more risky steps to expand their influence in the Mediterranean area or to forestall a real or imaginary danger. After all, Khrushchev gambled on a more distant Cuba, which was certainly not deemed to be within the security zone of the Soviet Union. Under the threat of impending hostilities or imminent danger, Turkey would be entitled under the Montreux rules to close the straits to Russian naviga-

130 This is the line of reasoning set forth by Coşkun Kırca in *Yeni Tanin*, November 14, 1968. Similar conclusion has been reached by C. L. Sulzberger in the *New York Times,* November 29, 1968.

131 See Nihat Erim's warning to this effect in a lecture in the Black Sea Technical University in Trabzon; *Cumhuriyet,* October 25, 1967.

tion. Such a move, even if done in the extreme need for self-preservation, could in turn precipitate an unwanted Soviet reaction or would place humiliating alternatives before Moscow.

All this speculation leads to one query which emerges whenever significant thinking is done on Soviet Turkish relations: how far is Russia to be trusted? In view of her geostrategical status, past historical experiences, and even the experiences of the last quarter of a century, Turkey's survival hinges on this consideration. Any mistaken step could prove to be fatal. This is the only foreign policy issue where even the smallest risk is intolerable.

Turkey, so as not to displease Moscow, has almost completely muted her expressions of sympathy toward the Turkic peoples living in the Soviet Union. Pan-Turkism or Pan-Turanism has practically been outlawed. Only seldom are voices heard complaining of the oppression or attempts at denationalization of these peoples by the Soviets.[132] When Prime Minister Demirel and his entourage visited Tashkent, Samarkand, and Baku— all Turkic or Turkish cities—the empathy, normally repressed, became vocal:

Here is the Prime Minister, for whom Turks have waited for years—a Prime Minister whose heart is burning with the fire of Turkdom. After the rulers who jailed those who asked for freedom of the Turks abroad, it is a great relief to see Demirel's interest in the Turks who fled Red Chinese atrocities and hear his words.[133]

I have written several times that no sane Turk dreams of founding an empire by merging with the Turks under Communist rule. But every Turk desires their freedom and salvation from Communist oppression in this age of freedom when all the African tribes are becoming independent states. We demand that the plight of the Turks under Communist domination be brought to the attention of the United Nations and the necessary moves be made in their favor by the free and democratic world.[134]

Naturally, the delicate nature of Soviet–Turkish relations and the resolve not to jeopardize the present "good feeling" would dissuade any Turkish government from raising such an issue. In any case, Turkish

---

[132] Tekin Erer, writing in *Son Havadis*, was one of the few who raised this question: "Is friendship with the Russians possible? Only if they liberate the 60–70 million Turks under their yoke and respect the reality of the Turk." *Son Havadis*, October 2, 1967.

[133] In November 1967, seventy refugees from Chinese Turkestan did arrive in Turkey via Afghanistan. A year before, 425 had reached Turkey. They were settled near Kayseri; *Cumhuriyet*, November 6, 1967.

[134] Tekin Erer in *Son Havadis*, November 13, 1967.

irredenta in the Soviet Union remain excluded from the realistic goals of Turkish foreign policy. It is, nevertheless, the unspoken expectation of many Turkish leaders that the nationality question will one day expose the inherent internal weakness of the Soviet empire, and then, perhaps, the Turks beyond the borders of the Turkish republic might be allowed to establish their own nation-states.

There arose, however, another irredenta issue in the late fifties, one that was nonexistent in Atatürk's days. The ardent interest felt toward the Turks of Cyprus has been a new development in Turkish public affairs. It has brought Turkey into conflict once again with another neighboring nation whose destiny has been closely intertwined with Turkey's, both in the distant and recent past.

VI

Turkey, Greece, and Cyprus

The supreme interests of Turkey and Greece no longer oppose each other. It is correct that our two countries should find their security and force in a sincere mutual friendship.—ATATÜRK before the Turkish Grand National Assembly, November 1931.

When we consider
The importancy of Cyprus to the Turk,
And let ourselves again but understand,
That as it more concerns the Turk
    than Rhodes,
So may he with more facile question
    bear it;
. . . .
    If we make thought of this,
We must not think the Turk
    is so unskilful,
To leave the latest which concerns
    him first.—SHAKESPEARE, Othello I.iii.
19–30.

F OR MORE THAN NINE CENTURIES the Turks and Greeks have found themselves interlocked in war and in peace. After the Ottoman conquest, they lived together in Anatolia and in the Balkans, in the islands of the Aegean, in Cyprus and in Crete, but their different religious cultures—the Byzantine Orthodox Christian of the Greeks and the Islamic-Oriental of the Turks—continued to divide them. Dwelling together did cause them to assimilate to some extent each other's mores, cusine, costumes, and other habits of life. Occasionally, they learned one another's language, even to the extent of abandoning their own.[1] Although many may not agree with the historian Arnold J. Toynbee, who thought that the purpose of the Ottoman Empire was to provide the Orthodox Christian world with the universal state it was unable to achieve for itself,[2] it still may be stated that a partnership, though an unequal one, existed between the Ottoman regime and the Greek Orthodox community (*millet*) for the management of the affairs of the empire.[3] Nonetheless, in the nineteenth century a dream to resurrect the former Byzantine-Greek state, known as the *Megali Idea*, gained impetus from the

---

[1] For instance, the "Karamanli Greeks" (of the town and region of Karaman in Anatolia) spoke Turkish but wrote with Greek letters. Many Muslims ("Turks") in Greek Epirus and in Crete spoke only Greek.

[2] Toynbee, *A Study of History*, abridgment of vols. I–IV, pp. 130, 173, 244.

[3] See chapter I, pp. 5–6 above.

nationalism engendered by the French Revolution. It remained deeply ingrained in the minds of Hellenic leaders. Even if supported by Russia, however, a revolt against Ottoman rule could be successful only where compact Greek settlements existed—that is, in the region of ancient Hellas.

MEGALI IDEA

The revolt began in 1821, was subsequently supported by Russia, Britain, and France, and by 1832 resulted in the establishment of an independent Greek state which extended over the Peloponnesus Peninsula, central Greece, and some islands in the Aegean Sea. Thus, modern Hellas became the nucleus of the Panhellenic Movement, an elastic program which aimed at the union of all the Greeks. The Ionian Islands were ceded to Greece by Britain in 1864. The Greek Kingdom gradually increased its territorial domain by slicing off adjacent parts of the Ottoman Empire: Thessaly was surrendered by the Sublime Porte in 1881; following the Balkan wars of 1912–13, Greece obtained parts of Epirus and Macedonia, including the city of Salonika, most of the islands in the Aegean, and Crete. Under the unratified Treaty of Sèvres at the end of World War I, Greece was to extend over western and eastern Thrace and western Anatolia; during the war against the Kemalists, she even cherished the hopes of acquiring the city of Constantine.

The realization of the *Megali Idea* was utterly frustrated by the Turkish victory and subsequent expulsion of all Greeks from the soil of Asia Minor, the birthplace of Hellenic culture. The cataclysmic outcome of the Turco-Hellenic struggle of 1921–23 ended the half-millennial symbiosis of Greeks and Turks, except in certain areas of Turkey (Istanbul and surroundings, and the small islands of Imroz and Bozcaada) and in Greece (western Thrace). Turks also continued to live among the Greek majority in Rhodes, the Dodecanese Islands (which remained Italian until 1947), and, last but not least, in Cyprus.

Religious and national emotions and memories of bloody historic struggles created a deep-seated antagonism between Greeks and Turks. The average Turk and Greek nurtures a prejudiced image of the other: Turks view Greeks as degenerate, artful cowards, and Greeks consider Turks brutal and uncouth barbarians. Almost everywhere where they still live together, Greeks regard themselves as the autochthonous race and the

Turks as unlawful intruders. The expulsion of Greeks from Anatolia, and of Turks from Greek territory, certainly accentuated this ill feeling, although after nearly half a century the beneficial results of the drastic operation are being realized. Uprooting ancient and historically established populations is a cruel and tragic procedure which should only be resorted to when all other remedial actions have been exhausted. No doubt, this was the case after the murderous events of the Greek invasion and subsequent Turkish liberation of Anatolia, when the continued coexistence of the two races became impractical.

It is understandable that Greeks feel a nostalgia toward places that formerly were seats of Hellenic civilization or centers of millenary Greek settlements. They are bound to think longingly and resentfully of the areas of Asia Minor where only archeological sites bear witness to their past glory. Historical reminiscences, however, cannot change today's realities: the former Greek cities of Smyrna, Nicaea, Trapezunt, Caesarea, and Pergamon have become Izmir, Iznik, Trabzon, Kayseri, and Bergama. It was no less easy for Muslims, many of them ignorant of the Turkish language, to give up what had been their homeland on mainland Greece or the islands. Nor could other Turks be lighthearted about the loss of vast territories which for centuries had been parts of the Ottoman state.

Resignation to the accomplished facts has been made more difficult because of the frictions which often arise in the relatively few areas where Turks and Greeks continue to coexist. One such area is Istanbul, where a Greek minority dwells amid a Turkish majority.

The Treaty of Lausanne exempted the Greeks[4] in the former Ottoman capital from expulsion. In the times of the sultans, the Greeks of Constantinople played an outstanding role in commerce and industry and in its cultural and public life. While the sultan and his ministers resided in the ancient Seraglio, and later in the Dolma Bahçe or Yıldız palaces, the Oecumenical Patriarch of the Greek Orthodox Christian Church resided in his own palace area, called Phanar, along the Golden Horn and ruled over a Greek *millet,* which was almost a "state within the state."

After the collapse of the sultanate and the rise of the Turkish republic centered in Ankara, the significance of Istanbul as a center of political life

[4] The Turkish language ingeniously distinguishes between a Greek of Turkey and one of independent Greece. The former is known as "Rum" (Roman) while the latter is "Yunan" (Ionian).

receded; but its economic and cultural importance remained predominant. During the republican regime, however, Greek culture diminished in Istanbul both quantitatively and qualitatively: many leading members and younger elements in the community preferred to emigrate rather than accept the modernized Turkish administration. The overall population of Istanbul was 690,000 in 1927; by 1965, it had risen to 1,750,000. During the same period, the Greek element, estimated at 100,000 in 1927, declined to about 60,000 in 1965. Thus, the proportion of Greeks shrank from about 14 percent to about 3.5 percent of the total population.[5] The Greeks who were not citizens of Turkey were likely to emigrate more readily; in fact, a number of them were expelled by the Turkish government for retaliatory reasons, especially during the Cypriote crises.

The Lausanne treaty guaranteed the continued residence of the Orthodox patriarch in Istanbul, provided that he was an "established resident" —that is, not one liable to compulsory exchange under the Lausanne agreements.[6] The Turkish government also expected the patriarch not to indulge in politics, neither of Turkey nor of other countries.[7] It appears somewhat unrealitic that the residence of the traditional head of Eastern Orthodoxy should remain in a Muslim environment, especially given the constantly diminishing size of his flock; however, expectations that the court of the patriarch might be removed to Greece have thus far been unfulfilled.[8]

The Treaty of Lausanne guaranteed the rights of national and religious minorities in Turkey, especially in education, religion, and personal liberties.[9] During the Ottoman regime, Greeks and other minority groups

---

[5] To this writer, business and some professions in the Beyoğlu (Pera) and Galata districts of Istanbul appeared to be, to a considerable degree, in the hands of Greeks (and other minorities, such as Armenians and Jews) in the mid-1940's. A quarter of a century later Greek participation seemed to have diminished greatly or to have practically disappeared; the use of the Greek language was hardly noticeable.

[6] In 1924, after the death of Patriarch Gregorius VII, his newly elected successor Constantine VI was not accepted by Ankara and expelled from Turkey. Eventually, he had to abdicate in favor of an incumbent who complied with the requirements of the Lausanne treaty; see Harry J. Psomiades, *The Eastern Question: The Last Phase* (Salonika, 1968), pp. 97–105; Robert Stephens, *Cyprus: A Place of Arms* (New York, 1966), pp. 113–14.

[7] A special issue (December 1964–April 1965) of *International Relations* (Athens) is devoted to the history and present status of the Ecumenical Patriarchate.

[8] In 1969 the Turkish press reported that, after the death of Patriarch Athenagoras, the Patriarchate will be moved to Athens. *Yeni Gazete*, May 12, 1969.

[9] See Articles 37–45. Greece had undertaken similar obligations with respect to "Moslem" minorities on her territory.

profited indirectly from the capitulatory system, which placed non-Ottoman subjects beyond the reach of local law. This often only psychological sense of security was lost when the capitulations were abolished. Also, the modernization of the new Turkish state, the standardization of the administration and of the school system, and the institutionalization of the Turkish language in business and official transactions rendered the life of ethnic and religious minorities more difficult than before. For Greeks, who proudly considered themselves the original inhabitants of the city, their disestablishment was particularly painful. Nevertheless, during Atatürk's administration no serious complaint of discrimination was raised.

The traditional cleavage between Muslim and non-Muslim was not bridged, despite the secular state concept adopted by republican Turkey. Unlike other parts of the world where language is the main mark of distinction between different ethnic groups, in the Near and Middle East religious and cultural differences run much deeper than linguistic ones. They divide even family from family and even person from person. Only Muslims would really consider themselves Turks (including assimilated Kurds or Arabs); no Greek of Turkish citizenship would identify himself as a Turk.[10] Thus, national identification, as distinguished from the voluntary linguistic or religious assimilation with the majority ethnic group practiced in other regions, is hardly a practical proposition in the Middle East or in Turkey. Of course, the same is true for Muslim communities living among a Christian majority as, for instance, in Cyprus or in western Thrace.

Genuine discrimination against minority groups in Istanbul occurred during the darkest wartime years, in 1942 and 1943, when the ill-famed *Varlık Vergisi* (capital levy) was introduced. This extraordinary tax to cover Turkey's increased military expenses was so applied that it ruined the commercial and financial power of members of the minorities but spared Turkish trade interests. Those in default were deported to the interior and subjected to compulsory hard labor. When the conflict turned in favor of the Allies, the Turkish government was eager to eliminate the

---

[10] See Bernard Lewis, *The Emergence of Modern Turkey* (London, 1961), p. 350. The movement of Papa Eftim, the head of the so-called "Turkish Orthodox Church," who claimed that Anatolian Greeks were Turks converted to the Christian Orthodox Church, found no sympathy with the Greeks and no support among the Turkish authorities.

effects of this measure by releasing all those affected and cancelling their debts.[11]

In Greece, the counterpart of the Greeks who remained on Turkish soil, as provided for by the Treaty of Lausanne, are the Turks of western Thrace. At the time of the conclusion of the treaty, the Muslim population of this region numbered 155,000; there were 45,000 non-Muslims. Among the Muslims, about 115,000 spoke Turkish, and the rest were mainly of Bulgarian tongue (Pomaks). The non-Muslims were practically all Greeks.[12] Over the past 40 years, the number of Turks in western Thrace has decreased significantly. In 1951 there were no more than 118,000 (according to Greek sources), and in 1968 their estimated number was about 100,000. At the same time, the number of Greeks in western Thrace greatly increased. The cause for this demographic reversal was continued emigration to Turkey because of difficult living conditions, alleged discrimination (especially in the field of educational opportunities), the wartime German-Bulgarian occupation, and the postwar civil war in Greece.

At the time of the conclusion of the Lausanne treaty, the Dodecanese Islands were held by Italy. Several thousand Turks live on those islands, mainly in Rhodes. In 1947, under the peace treaty with Italy, the Dodecanese were ceded to Greece, and it is now a moot question whether the provisions of Lausanne for the protection of national and religious minorities are applicable to the Turks of these islands. The two governments have not, thus far, reached an agreement on this legal issue. Accordingly, the status of the Turkish minority remains in doubt.

The Cyprus conflict has greatly contributed to the acrimony of discussions on the treatment of Greek minorities in Turkey and Turkish minorities in Greece. The further developments in the relationship between the two countries will determine the fate of those historic ethnic communities—Greek or Turkish—which the two world wars left stranded among majorities in other nations.

TURKEY AND GREECE BURY THE HATCHET

There are moments in history when enlightened and farsighted states-

---

[11] See Davison, *Turkey,* pp. 146–47.

[12] Ümit Halûk Bayülken, "Turkish Minorities in Greece," *Turkish Yearbook of International Relations, 1963,* pp. 145–64. The author also refers to Greek official statistical data which, by and large, coincide with the data submitted by the Turkish Delegation to the peace conference in 1923.

men, often in opposition to the emotions of public opinion, determine the course of their nations according to reason. It was fortunate that both Greece and Turkey possessed such leaders less than a decade after the conclusion of their bitter struggle. Both Atatürk, the nationalist leader of new Turkey, and Eleutherios Venizelos, the Greek prime minister who led his country through the victorious Balkan wars, realized the futility and peril of continuing the ten-century-old feud between the two races.

In 1930 the Turkish government decided to reconstruct and modernize the famous World War I battleship *Goeben* (named *Yavuz* by the Turks), which had been given to Turkey by the Germans and became, indirectly, one of the inducements for Turkey's participation in the war. A modernized *Yavuz* would have rendered the Turkish navy far superior to that of Greece and would have upset the naval balance between the two countries. Venizelos, however, refused to burden Greece's fragile economy with the purchase or construction of a warship to match Turkish naval expansion; he advocated instead a peaceful arrangement with Turkey on all outstanding questions and trust in Ankara's peaceful intentions. On June 10, 1930, a detailed agreement was signed between the two governments which professed to settle the remnants of their former savage confrontation: the population exchange, questions of property arising out of this exchange, and the problems of the Turkish and Greek nationalities remaining in the two states.[13]

The road was thus opened for more intimate contacts. Years before, at the finish of the Turkish–Greek war, Atatürk was reported to have prophesied the eventual re-establishment of friendship between the two nations.[14] Now, Ismet Inönü, the Turkish prime minister, invited his Greek colleague to Istanbul and Ankara, where he was given a warm welcome. The visit led to the conclusion of a Treaty of Neutrality, Conciliation, and Arbitration, which included a protocol providing for a "parity of naval armaments" and the balance of power in the Aegean.[15]

The agreement was followed by a formal Friendship Pact, signed on

[13] *Documents on International Affairs, 1930,* pp. 155–65. This treaty is known as the "Establishment Convention" because it defined which Greek citizen was to be considered "established" in Istanbul, and also allowed the return of a certain category of Greek refugees to the city.
[14] "I could never myself keep on hating a nation for the mistakes of their government . . . and toward the Greeks I feel the same. I am confident that we shall soon be great friends." Quoted by Türkkaya Ataöv, "Turkish Foreign Policy: 1923–1938," *Turkish Yearbook of International Relations, 1961,* p. 121.
[15] *Documents on International Affairs, 1930,* p. 165.

September 14, 1933, in which both countries guaranteed the inviolability of their common borders and pledged to consult each other on questions of common interest and to pursue a policy of friendship, understanding, and collaboration.[16]

The Greek–Turkish bilateral entente was further strengthened when both countries joined the Balkan Entente in 1934 with Yugoslavia and Rumania.[17] By the middle and late 1930's, Turkey and Greece appeared to have finally broken with the tradition that had so long separated them.

The outbreak of World War II placed new strains on Turkish–Greek relations. As noted earlier, Turkish efforts failed to transform the Balkan Entente into a cohesive group of states which could resist pressures by Italy and Germany.[18] No combined actions were possible because each of the Balkan states pursued its own independent policies. When Greece was attacked by Italy, Yugoslavia and Turkey remained neutral. Rumania and Bulgaria (the latter had consistently opposed the Balkan Entente) allowed German forces to enter them; Yugoslavia, which had long flirted with the Germans, suddenly turned against them and was crushed. Greece was subsequently overrun.

The Greek government resented Turkey's neutral posture and even accused Ankara of secret dealings with Berlin aimed at occupying some of the Greek islands in the Aegean. Turkey did not maintain a regular diplomatic representative with the Greek government-in-exile. Some restrictive or discriminatory measures against minorities, such as the capital levy (mentioned earlier), were also objected to by the Greeks.[19] It should be emphasized, however, that Turkey tolerated Allied support of Greek guerillas from her soil.[20] She also sent food to Greece to relieve widespread starvation.

At the end of World War II, Ankara viewed the domestic convulsions in Greece with dismay; a Soviet-dominated regime would have imperiled Turkey's independence and rendered most difficult her resolute resistance

---

[16] Documents on International Affairs, 1933, pp. 407–8.
[17] See chapter V, pp. 25–26.
[18] See chapter I, pp. 28–30.
[19] Iatrides, Balkan Triangle, pp. 75–76.
[20] From the Turkish port of Çeşme, west of Izmir, communications were maintained across the narrow channel to the German-occupied Greek island of Chios used as a base for Greek guerillas. Turkey closed her eyes to the movement of persons and material from Çeşme to the Syrian border (information based on this writer's personal knowledge.)

to Moscow's demands. The Turkish government, therefore, turned over to Greek authorities Communist insurgents caught while crossing the border and supported the Greek complaints lodged before the United Nations.

Under the peace treaty with Italy, the Dodecanese Islands and Rhodes were ceded to Greece. Although this event had much in common with the subsequent demand for a union of Cyprus and Greece, the Turkish government considered it unwise to oppose the merger of these islands with Greece, despite some popular and military pressures. At that moment, Turkey still expected some Soviet action against her borders; and in view of her wartime neutrality, she did not feel diplomatically strong enough to object to an aggrandizement of Greece, a victim of Nazi aggression. Such an opposition also would have had the effect of weakening the Greek government, already in jeopardy because of Communist conspiracies and revolts. Ankara therefore resolved to show reticence. Subsequently, the Council of Foreign Ministers extended the demilitarization of other Greek islands in the Aegean to the Dodecanese.

Common foreign policy lines and mutual interests soon led to a re-establishment of collaboration between Ankara and Athens. Even before the two countries were simultaneously admitted to NATO (the Truman Doctrine had previously brought them together), the two governments and military staffs began to consult each other, and *de facto* cooperative activity preceded the official alliance in NATO. Both countries considered a mere military tie between them insufficient and impractical (Turkey viewed the British-sponsored Mediterranean or Middle East Defense Pact in the same way) and no substitute for full membership in the Atlantic alliance.

Common participation in NATO intensified Turkish–Greek contacts, in both the political and military fields. NATO headquarters in Naples, Izmir, Ankara, or Athens included permanent or visiting Greek and Turkish officers; in other NATO centers, Turkish and Greek representatives worked out common strategical and logistic plans and programs.

A particularly important diplomatic task in which the two chancelleries closely collaborated was the setting up of ties of alliance with Yugoslavia—a country threatened since 1948 by the Soviets and, even more recently, by the Soviet satellites of Hungary, Rumania, and Bulgaria. The possibility of aggression from Bulgarian soil by either Bulgarian or Soviet armies against the sensitive Thracian border of Greece and Turkey, or against the Macedonian corner where the Greek and Yugo-slav frontiers meet, was a matter of great concern for Athens and Ankara and demanded consultation with the military leadership in Belgrade.

It took considerable time before the existing suspicions were over-come between Ankara and Athens, on the one hand, and Belgrade, on the other. Without genuine cooperation between Turks and Greeks, it hardly would have been possible to establish the Balkan Defense Pact. As we have seen, the military alliance with Yugoslavia did not materialize to the extent expected by the Turkish and Greek governments. The main reason for this eventual failure was, no doubt, to be found in the Soviet volte-face which occurred after Stalin's death. Another con-tributive reason was the disruption of Turco–Greek relations following the dissension about Cyprus. The "family discord" between Yugoslavia's two Balkan allies must have dissuaded Belgrade from continued close collaboration, and a "neutralist stance" must have had a more attractive appeal to the "Socialist conscience" of Marshal Tito.

In early 1954, Turkish President Celâl Bayar was still able to refer to Turkish–Greek cooperation as "the best example of how two countries who mistakenly mistrusted each other for centuries have agreed upon a close and loyal collaboration as a result of recognition of the realities of life."[21]

For a considerable time the Cyprus conflict had taken the shape of a feud between the British colonial administration and the Greek popu-lation of the island, although it was also a matter of controversy between Athens and London. In the fall of 1954, however, the conflict was brought into the international arena when the Greek government decided to place the dispute on the agenda of the United Nations General Assembly. From that moment on, Turkey had to take an open stand on the question; this soon brought her into overt opposition to her neighbor along the coast of the Aegean Sea.

THE NEW APPLE OF DISCORD: CYPRUS

The island of Cyprus lies at the entrance of the Gulf of Iskenderun, the easternmost corner of the Mediterranean Sea. The channel that

[21] *New York Times,* January 30, 1954.

separates the island from Turkey is 40 to 44 miles wide; the Syrian coast-line is 65 miles distant. Turks like to point out that, in contrast, 500 miles separate Cyprus from the Greek mainland.

With an area of 3,572 square miles, Cyprus is the third largest island in the Mediterranean, following Sicily and Sardinia. In the north-south direction, the island's breadth is about 60 miles; the average distance in the west-east direction is 100 miles. The northern mountain range extends another 50 miles into a narrow peninsula (Karpas), pointing into the Gulf of Iskenderun.

The population of Cyprus numbers about 620,000; about 485,000 are Greeks, 114,000 are Turks; and the rest are mixed.[22] While the Turkish population is dispersed throughout the island, there are predominantly Turkish villages. The five major cities of Nicosia, the capital, the harbors of Famagusta, Larnaca, Limassol, and Paphos all have Turkish quarters.

Cyprus has had a long and varied history, during most of which the island was ruled by foreign powers. Colonized by Phoenicians and Greeks, Cyprus came under the sway of the great kings of Persia in the sixth century B.C. Liberated by Alexander the Great and inherited after Alexander's death by the Ptolemaic dynasty, the island became part of the Roman possessions. Cyprus was christianized under the Eastern Orthodox rite and, after the division of the empire, became a province of the East Roman (Byzantine) Emperor. During the Crusades, Cyprus passed under the rule of the French Lusignan dynasty from 1192 to 1489. During these years, the Greek Orthodox Church was oppressed and almost superseded by the Roman Catholic Church. In 1489 the Republic of Venice, already in control of the commerce of the island, annexed Cyprus. Venetian rule, however, together with the Catholic influence, came to an abrupt end when an Ottoman army conquered the island in 1571.[23]

For the next 307 years, Cyprus was ruled by the sultans from Constantinople. The Ottoman conquerors introduced their own political sys-

[22] According to the 1960 census, the population of Cyprus numbered 564,000. About 78% of the people spoke Greek; about 18%, Turkish. See Stanley Kyriakides, *Cyprus: Constitutionalism and Crisis Government* (Philadelphia, 1968), p. 1. The figures in the text are based on the estimated growth of the population since 1960.

[23] For the earlier history of Cyprus see: Sir George Hill, *A History of Cyprus*, 4 vols. (Cambridge, 1940–52); Sir Harry Luke, *Cyprus Under Turks, 1571–1878* (Oxford, 1921); same author, *Cyprus: A Portrait and Appreciation*, 2d ed. (London, 1964); C. Spyridakis, *A Brief History of Cyprus* (Chicago, 1964); H. D. Purcell, *Cyprus* (New York, 1969).

tem, the *millet*. The office of the Greek Orthodox Archbishop (suppressed under the Latin regime) was reinstated and was recognized as the head of the Greek *millet* of the island. Since the time of the East Roman Emperor Zeno (A.D. 488), the archbishop of Cyprus has enjoyed an autocephalous status; he only owes reverential allegiance to the Greek Orthodox Patriarch of Constantinople. As head of the Greek community, he also bears the title of *ethnarchos*.[24]

Members of the Ottoman army that conquered Cyprus remained on the island; they were followed by other Turkish immigrants from Anatolia. Although there were times when Turkish Muslims outnumbered Greeks, only one-fourth of the population was Turkish when Ottoman rule ended in 1878.[25]

Until 1878 Cyprus existed under a dual regime subject to the ultimate control of the Sublime Porte. From the middle of the seventeenth century to 1821, the archbishop and bishops ruling over the Greeks even had direct access to the sultan. On the other hand, the Muslim–Turkish population was ruled by its own pasha.[26]

During the Russo–Turkish War of 1877–78, Britain felt the need for a naval base in the eastern Mediterranean, a "place of arms" as characterized by British Prime Minister Disraeli.[27] Egypt was not yet available, since the British occupation took place only in 1882. It was a time of imperial expansion for Britain: Queen Victoria had assumed the title of Empress of India, the most precious jewel of her crown, and the commercial control of the Suez Canal was acquired to secure the shortest route to the Indian Ocean. Russia, by seeking to annex the straits, to partition the Sick Man of Europe, and penetrate into the Mediterranean, was deemed a threat to India and Britain's route to that subcontinent.

Disraeli acted as the savior of the Ottoman Empire: when Russian armies reached the outskirts of Constantinople, the British fleet was anchored at the entrance of the Bosporus. London managed to have the disastrous Treaty of San Stefano revised by the concert of European great powers that assembled at the Congress of Berlin. Before the session of the congress, Disraeli surprised the world by a Convention of De-

---

[24] See chapter I, p. 5.
[25] Kyriakides, *Cyprus*, p. 6.
[26] Spyridakis, *A Brief History of Cyprus*, pp. 54–59; Kyriakides, *Cyprus*, pp. 4–5.
[27] See Stephens, *Cyprus: A Place of Arms*, p. 18.

fensive Alliance, concluded with the Sublime Porte, on June 4, 1878. The convention contained two provisions: first, "His Imperial Majesty the Sultan . . . consents to assign the Island of Cyprus to be occupied and administered by England." Second, it was agreed:

If Batum, Ardahan, Kars, or any of them shall be retained by Russia, and if any attempts shall be made at any future time by Russia to take possession of any further territories of His Imperial Majesty the Sultan in Asia . . . England engages to join His Imperial Majesty the Sultan in defending them by force.[28]

The Congress of Berlin met on June 13, 1878, and while it reduced in size the Bulgarian empire created by the Treaty of San Stefano, it left Batum, Kars, and Ardahan to Russia. Notwithstanding, Cyprus remained under British "occupation and administration"; another treaty, signed on July 1, 1868, had provided "That if Russia restores to Turkey Kars and the other conquests made by her in Armenia during the last war, the Island of Cyprus will be evacuated by England and the Convention of the 4th of June, 1878, will be at an end."[29]

Soon after the acquisition of Cyprus, a new situation arose for England. In 1882 Egypt (and the Suez Canal) came under British military control. When Disraeli (later Earl of Beaconsfield) relinquished the premiership in 1880, the anti-Russian and pro-Turkish foreign policy underwent considerable modifications.[30] In fact, London lost interest in Cyprus. The island was looked upon as neither a colony nor foreign territory but as a stepchild of British colonial concerns. The residual sovereignty of the sultan remained ingrained in official handling of the island's affairs until its formal annexation nearly 40 years later.[31]

When the British took over the administration of Cyprus, the Greek community of the island was a self-governing entity under the archbishop and the bishops, a situation which was essentially left intact. The Turkish population was handled by the British as if it were another *millet*—that is, an autonomous religious community. But whereas the Greeks possessed a time-honored, self-governing status, the Turkish com-

---

[28] See Hurewitz, *Diplomacy,* vol. I, pp. 187–89.

[29] *Ibid.*

[30] In 1907 Britain patched up its differences with Russia, opening the road to the formation of the Triple Entente with France. In the same treaty, Persia was divided into spheres of influence (one Russian, one British, and a neutral zone between) which might have been seen as an ill omen for Turkey.

[31] Stephens, *Cyprus: A Place of Arms,* pp. 106–7.

munity was slow to adapt to being reduced from a ruling element into one of the self-governing communities.[32] After the British takeover, a large-scale emigration of Turks to the Turkish mainland ensued.[33]

The Christian–Greek and Muslim–Turkish elements of the Cypriote population, as in other parts of the Ottoman Empire, had lived a life apart. That the Turks had developed into a kind of *millet* under the British rule accentuated the cleavage between two communities.[34] This bi-communal development was intensified by British administrative measures and also by the divergent socio-political tendencies of Greeks and Turks. The former considered British rule the first step toward union (in Greek: *Enosis*) with Greece, while the latter at first regarded British occupation as provisional and subsequently as a fact that would prevent Greek unification.

The British administration was organized according to the traditional colonial pattern: there was a high commissioner (later to be called governor) and his staff and a legislative council that could initiate legislation but was controlled by the representatives of the Crown. The council consisted of twelve elected members—nine Christians, three Muslims—and six appointed members. In 1925 the number of elected members was increased to fifteen (twelve Greeks and three Turks) with six officially appointed members. The distributions permitted the official members together with the Turks to defeat Greek proposals (the high commissioner or governor casting the decisive vote). Still, the Turks opposed their proportionately lower representation in the legislative council,

---

[32] The Greeks ran their own schools, cultural and economic institutions, and courts. With the departure of the Ottoman governor, the Turks had only strictly religious leadership (Koranic courts and schools). The July 1, 1878, treaty provided that the Sublime Porte should appoint one director of the *Evkaf* (Muslim religious foundations which maintained mosques and schools) and also the chief *kadi* (judge) of Cyprus. Subsequent to 1915 (when Turkey was at war with Britain), the British administration appointed the leading officials of the Turkish community.

[33] See A. Suat Bilge, *Le Conflit de Chypre et les Cypriotes turcs* (Ankara, 1961), pp. 4–5.

[34] "Bi-communal differences were strengthened during the British rule in Cyprus from 1878 to 1960. The British colonial administration did not encourage communal cooperation. Indeed, the British, from the very beginning, accentuated bi-communalism when they placed the administration of education under bi-communal authorities. The Greek-Orthodox Church directed the schools of the Greek Cypriot community and thus enhanced Greco-Byzantine tradition. The Turkish Cypriots controlled their own school system and thereby strengthened their Turkish national tradition. Thus education served as a non-integrating factor. Moreover, it tended to fortify the historical and cultural bonds of the two Cypriot communities with their respective 'mother countries,' Greece and Turkey." Kyriakides, *Cyprus*, pp. 163–64.

while the Greeks considered it a "toy parliament" without real power. Communal antagonism was sharpened in the deliberations of the council.[35]

Although there was lack of foresight or concern for the future of Cyprus, the British administration certainly introduced order, honesty, and economic development to the island. As soon as the British arrived, however, the Cypriote desire for a union with Greece was expressed, and over the years, this wish became the *sine qua non* of all Greek endeavors.[36] The powerful ecclesiastical organization in Cyprus acted as the mouthpiece of Panhellenism or the *Megali Idea*.

The Turkish community reacted in an equally vocal manner, opposing union with Greece and advocating the return of Turkish sovereignty to the island. It also resisted self-government for Cyprus unless based on a complete equality of the two communities. It was a natural consequence of the antagonistic forces operating in Cypriote politics that British and Turkish interests often coincided, in particular when confronting the quest for *Enosis*. At the same time, the Turks continued to complain about the numerical preponderance of Greeks among the public functionaries and in the assemblies.[37]

When war was declared between Great Britain and the Ottoman Empire in 1914, the British government issued the Cyprus (Annexation) Order in Council on November 5, 1914, declaring that "by reason of the outbreak of war between His Majesty and his Imperial Majesty the Sultan the said Convention [of 1878], Annex and Agreement have become annulled and are no longer of any force or effect."

In the Peace Treaty of Lausanne, Turkey formally recognized the annexation; henceforth, British sovereignty over Cyprus was to be unrestricted. It should also be noted that, in the course of World War I, the British government offered to cede Cyprus to Greece in return for the latter's participation in the war against the Central Powers. King Constantine and his cabinet, however, turned down the offer.[38] At the end of the

[35] *Ibid.*, pp. 13–17; Stephens, *Cyprus: A Place of Arms*, pp. 107–8.

[36] When the first British High Commissioner, Sir Garnet Wolseley, landed in 1878 in Larnaca, he was greeted by the Bishop of Kition in the following words: "We accept the change of Government inasmuch as we trust that Great Britain will help Cyprus, as it did the Ionian Islands, to be united with Mother Greece, with which it is naturally connected." Luke, *Cyprus: A Portrait*, pp. 173–74.

[37] Bilge, *Conflit de Chypre*, pp. 14–19.

[38] See Spyridakis, *A Brief History of Cyprus*, pp. 63–64; Stephens, *Cyprus: A Place of Arms*, pp. 92–94.

war, Greek ambitions focused on Asia Minor and Constantinople and ignored Cyprus. After the catastrophic defeat in 1922, Greece could hardly have raised the Cyprus issue at Lausanne.

Following World War I, British administration continued to be based on bi-communality. Politically, both communities organized their respective representative bodies. The Greek Cypriotes operated their National Assembly, whose executive organ was the National Council, on which the archbishop and three bishops sat as ex-officio members. The Turks were late in forming their organization, but in 1945 they organized the Cyprus National People's Party (*Kıbrıs Millî Türk Halk Partisi*), which was renamed the "Cyprus Is Turkish" Party (*Kıbrıs Türktür Partisi*) in 1955.

In the late 1920's, Panhellenism in Cyprus acquired new momentum: it was said that the British now exercised full sovereignty over the island and could no longer refer to their limited sovereign rights (the obligation to return Cyprus to Turkey under certain conditions). In 1931 the pressures of Greek *enotist* feeling erupted in open rebellion, which was easily defeated by the British.

During World War II, the *Enosis* movement was muted; the Greeks of Cyprus watched the struggle of their co-nationals against the Axis powers with sympathy. The island itself was considered to be in danger after the fall of Crete. At the end of the war, however, the general climate favoring self-determination, as laid down in the Charter of the United Nations, rekindled aspirations for *Enosis*.

In 1950 the Ethnarchy Council organized an open plebiscite on union with Greece. As expected, the Greek population overwhelmingly endorsed *Enosis*. The Turkish Cypriotes, however, demanded that Turkish sovereignty be reinstated if London relinquished the island.[39] The British had offered a new constitutional system in 1948, but the offer had to be withdrawn in 1954 in the face of Greek opposition.

After 1951 political parties were again allowed in Cyprus. The clandestine Communist Party now openly operated as the Progressive Party of the Working People, known by the initials of its Greek name: AKEL. The nationalist Greek Party was the Cyprus National Party

---

[39] Spyridakis, *A Brief History of Cyprus*, pp. 66–67; Kyriakides, *Cyprus*, pp. 27–28; Bilge, *Conflit de Chypre*, pp. 19–44.

(KEK). The AKEL was supported by the labor unions and was considered one of the best-organized nonruling Communist parties.[40]

After World War II, the significance of Cyprus in the eyes of British strategists and political leaders underwent a change. Their withdrawal from India was followed by the withdrawal from Palestine, and by the early 1950's, even the abandonment of Egypt and the Suez Canal was envisaged. Cyprus remained the only British-held territory in the eastern Mediterranean. Thus, as the demand for *Enosis* was being pressed more strongly than ever before, the British hold on Cyprus became less negotiable. But Cyprus had obtained a determined and shrewd leader in the person of Makarios III, archbishop and ethnarch of the island.

Makarios received the religious and Hellenistic education of future leaders of the Greek Orthodox Church: he had been a novice in a monastery and attended the Church-directed Pancyprian Gymnasium in Nicosia and the Faculty of Theology and Law of the University of Athens. With a scholarship he came to the United States and enrolled at the School of Theology, Boston University. He was 35 years old when elected Bishop of Kition and 37 when he became archbishop of Cyprus in 1950. He was imbued with the Panhellenistic spirit and a determination to liberate his island from foreign domination. He failed, however, to exhibit political subtlety in dealing with parliamentary British leaders. Furthermore, he felt the disdain often found in Greeks toward Turkey and the Turks and thoroughly misjudged the strength of Turkish reactions in the island and in Turkey herself.[41]

Another Greek protagonist in the Cypriote drama was Colonel (later Lieutenant-General) George Grivas, a Cyprus-born Greek army officer who, together with Makarios, masterminded the revolt which terrorized the island for more than four years.

From 1951 onward Greece officially began to push *Enosis*. Greek Prime Minister Papagos made the first direct approach to Britain in the fall of 1953, but British Foreign Secretary Anthony Eden, who was visiting Athens at the time, refused even to discuss the question. Thereupon, the Greek government submitted the Cyprus question to the United Nations

---

[40] Stephens, *Cyprus: A Place of Arms*, pp. 118–19; Kyriakides, *Cyprus*, pp. 26–27.
[41] Luke, *Cyprus: A Portrait*, pp. 183–85; Kyriakides, *Cyprus*, pp. 29–30.

General Assembly in September 1954, and the green light was given to Colonel Grivas and Makarios.[42]

It is incorrect to assume that Turkey was disinterested in Cyprus until Greece raised the question of union. Ankara only wished to avoid drawing attention to the issue and hoped that the British would remain adamant in their determination to stay on the island. Furthermore, Turkey considered the question a domestic one between the government of the island and its Greek inhabitants. Only when Athens stepped in, by submitting the problem to the United Nations, did Ankara feel obliged to respond.

In June 1954, under an agreement with Egypt, British troops were withdrawn from the Suez Canal Zone and the headquarters of the British Land and Air Headquarters was transferred to Cyprus. Under such circumstances, it is not surprising that London vehemently opposed discussing the Cyprus issue in the United Nations. The Greek request was shelved by the General Assembly. A few weeks after the negative outcome of the Greek initiative in New York, Grivas and Makarios secretly formed what was to be known as the EOKA (initials which stand for "National Organization of Cypriote Fighters"), the underground guerilla organization that commenced its terrorist activities on April 1, 1955.[43]

In August, under the impact of widespread guerilla attacks and bomb explosions, the British government invited representatives of the Greek and Turkish governments to London. Much to Athens' dismay, Turkey was for the first time given an opportunity to participate in a conference on the Cyprus issue. The London conference floundered essentially because the proposal submitted by Foreign Minister Macmillan refused to accept the principle of self-determination for Cyprus.[44]

The amicable relations between Turkey and Greece had already suffered when Greece formally joined the fight of Cypriote Greeks for self-determination, and the London discussions further exacerbated the Graeco–Turkish rapport. Before the conference ended, on the evening of September 6, 1955, news spread in Istanbul that a bomb had been exploded at the Turkish Consulate in Salonika, Greece. The "Cyprus Is

[42] Stephens, *Cyprus: A Place of Arms*, pp. 130–34.

[43] *Ibid.*, pp. 140–42.

[44] The Macmillan Plan was to transfer responsibility for domestic matters to a Cypriote Cabinet where a proportion of portfolios was to be reserved to Turks. The Turkish Foreign Minister Zorlu asked that, if a change in the status quo of the island was to take place, Cyprus be returned to Turkey. Kyriakides, *Cyprus*, 38–41.

Turkish" association organized a protest demonstration which soon got out of hand: the mob looted or destroyed Greek (and also some non-Greek) shops, houses, churches, and schools, while police remained inactive. Only later that night was order re-established.[45] Greece immediately withdrew from joint NATO exercises and demanded "material and moral" indemnity. The Turkish government expressed regret and undertook several acts of redress. Former Foreign Minister Fuat Köprülü characterized the excesses as "Communist methods."[46]

The London conference ended a dismal failure, and discordant emotions dominated both coasts of the Aegean and Cyprus. While the Greek government ignored Turkish interests in Cyprus,[47] Britain in turn refused to accept self-determination as an answer for the island: the Turks would never allow *Enosis,* and Great Britain could not afford to lose Turkish friendship.[48] The necessity of retaining the island for strategical reasons was slowly slipping into the background.

Subsequently, negotiations for a new constitutional plan between the

---

[45] *New York Times,* September 17, 1955; Stephens, *Cyprus: A Place of Arms,* pp. 142–43; Purcell, *Cyprus,* p. 279. It appears that a "small demonstration had been planned by Prime Minister Menderes, and the police were ordered at first to remain aloof. A mob of dissatisfied elements, however, used the opportunity to seek vengeance and plunder. Following the May 27, 1960, revolution, Adnan Menderes and Foreign Minister Zorlu were convicted also for having masterminded the riots; Weiker, *The Turkish Revolution,* pp. 33–35.

[46] See Gotthard Jäschke, *Die Türkei in den Jahren 1952–61* (Wiesbaden, 1965), pp. 53–54.

[47] For instance, the application of the Greek government for the inscription of the Cyprus question on the agenda of the United Nations General Assembly did not even mention the existence of the Turkish community and its hostility toward *Enosis* but referred instead to the plebiscite organized by the Greek Orthodox Church almost unanimously favoring the union with Greece; *Documents on International Affairs, 1954,* pp. 230–35.

[48] Foreign Minister Eden (later Lord Avon) wrote: "The Cyprus dispute could never be settled until the importance of the Turkish position was understood and accepted. This meant that Enosis must be ruled out as a solution." *Full Circle,* p. 403. British representative Selwyn Lloyd, addressing the General Committee of the U.N. General Assembly on September 23, 1954, said, "Briefly the background of the question is as follows. Cyprus is an island off the Turkish and Syrian coasts. It can in no way be described as being geographically a part of, or even connected with, Greece. Indeed, the distance from either Turkey or Syria is about one-tenth its distance from Athens. One hundred thousand of the five hundred thousands inhabitants of Cyprus are Turkish by race and Moslem by religion. Historically the Island has never belonged to Greece except for a short period in the 4th Century B.C. . . . The Turkish-speaking Cypriots who are Moslems are bitterly opposed to Enosis. . . . We have responsibilities to many European countries including Greece and Turkey. We have great responsibilities under the Charter. Cyrus is vital to the discharge of those responsibilities." *Documents on International Affairs, 1954,* pp. 236–39.

British governor and Archbishop Makarios proved unsuccessful; in March 1956, Makarios was exiled and interned in the Seychelles Islands. The full-scale revolt of the EOKA was colliding with superior British forces; however, the struggle soon developed on intercommunal lines. Many Turks had enlisted as policemen, and in retaliation, the Greek terrorists began to attack members of the Turkish community. The Turks responded by killing innocent Greeks in reprisal. A new plan, drafted by Lord Radcliffe, an eminent jurist, was refused without discussion by the Greek government, by Greek Cypriotes, and by Makarios himself, who declined to make any comments as long as he was in exile.

A new element was introduced into the conflict when Turkey suggested that the island be partitioned between Greece and Turkey (known as *Taksim*, the Turkish word for partition, or "double *Enosis*"). The suggested division along the thirty-fifth parallel would have cut Cyprus in about two equal halves. Of course, the device employed by the Greeks was also used by the Turks: the Turkish community should exercise "self-determination"—that is, express a wish to be united with Turkey.

This partial retreat from the original Turkish position demanding retrocession of Cyprus in the case of British abandonment of the island was motivated by the fear that London might come to some agreement with Athens and the Cypriote Greeks, without the consent of Ankara. Fighting between the two communities now almost equalled that between British forces and the EOKA. In April 1957, Makarios was allowed to go to Athens, where he was given a triumphal reception.

Another suggestion, that Cyprus be given independent status, originated in London when it was realized that military bases would satisfy the strategical requirements of Britain. The second Macmillan plan, however, was based on continued British administration under a constitution that would provide for a "partnership" between the two communities and control machinery to be operated by Britain, Greece, and Turkey. This arrangement was to be in force for seven years and then be reviewed. In this form the plan was acceptable to the Turkish government, but both Athens and Makarios rejected it. The archbishop derisively called it the imposition of a "triple condominium."[49]

---

[49] Despite this rejection, certain steps were taken to implement the second Macmillan plan, announced on June 19, 1958. Separate Greek and Turkish municipal

The various proposals and official plans brought forth a solution acceptable to all parties. Archbishop Makarios, afraid of partition more than continued British control, and resigned to the realization that *Enosis* was not imminent, suggested to the Greek government that the independence of Cyprus under the aegis of the United Nations would be welcome. This idea was at first rejected by London, but later the British modified their position.

Various factors contributed to a changed atmosphere in which a settlement was realizable. By mid-1958 Khrushchev had become interested in the civil war which was raging on the island, and he made threatening noises to ensure that Russia's weight would be felt in the conflict. The overthrow of the pro-British regime in Iraq and the ensuing collapse of the Baghdad Pact persuaded Britain to ease her grip on Cyprus and content herself with military bases on the island. Greece and Makarios feared an arrangement between London and Ankara that would lead to partition along the thirty-fifth parallel and were apprehensive that the intercommunal assassinations would prove to the world that the Turks and Greeks could not coexist under a common government. Finally, Turkey was pleased to accept a solution that would satisfy her two basic contentions: that there should be no *Enosis* and that the security of Cypriote Turks must be guaranteed.

Direct negotiations were conducted beginning in December 1958 between the foreign ministers of Greece and Turkey: they were held at the NATO council meeting in Paris on December 18, 1958. In February 1959, the Greek and Turkish prime ministers, Karamanlis and Menderes, met in Zurich. The prime ministers and their foreign ministers thereafter went to London, where leaders of the Greek and Turkish communities of Cyprus were also summoned. The result of these short but dramatic negotiations was the birth of a new, independent state—the Republic of Cyprus. In view of the radically different standpoints, each supported by emotional and rational arguments, it was surprising that common ground was found at all. It can be surmised that all parties—except the British —accepted the agreement with reservations. This may or may not have

---

councils were set up, and Turkey appointed her representative to assist the Governor. Makarios could expect that the Turkish House of Representatives, as envisaged by the plan, might be convoked, leading to a *de facto* partition of the island; Stephens, *Cyprus: A Place of Arms,* pp. 153–56; Kyriakides, *Cyprus,* pp. 48–50.

been the case; however, it is certain that neither Greeks nor Turks wished to abandon their views finally and unconditionally.[50]

It is certainly true that the Cypriote Greeks feel like "Greeks," just as the Turks of Cyprus consider themselves part of Turkey. As is often the case with isolated elements of a people, national consciousness is more highly developed among them than among the members of the parent ethnic group. Indeed, the language of the Cypriote Greeks includes more Homeric words than other Greek dialects,[51] but more important from the point of view of present-day politics, the Graeco-Byzantine ideology had been better preserved in the life of the Cypriote Greeks than anywhere else. They have kept their identification with the Eastern Orthodox Church, the symbol of a Graeco-Byzantine traditions, not only by means of the *millet*-autonomy they enjoyed under the sultan (and, thereafter, the British) but also by virtue of their own ethnarchical system.

The Greek argument on Cyprus was short and simple: self-determination for the people of the island. It was assumed (and rightly so) that the overwhelming majority of the Greek population wanted union with Greece. In a plebiscite, it was thought that only the Turkish 18 percent and possibly many of the Communists (who would vote for independence) would oppose *Enosis*.[52]

Thus, the end of British rule was demanded under the guiding principles of this epoch which together were enshrined in the Charter of the United Nations—anticolonialism and self-determination. Promoters of *Enosis* asked why the people of Cyprus should not be given the right to join their "mother country" when other nations of Asia and Africa were entitled to such benefits. All Greek territories (Cyprus included, being considered by the *enotists* as an ancient homeland of Hellenism) should

[50] Among the many publications on the Cyprus question, in addition to most of the works cited above, see: Charles Foley, *Legacy of Strife: Cyprus from Rebellion to Civil War* (Baltimore, 1964); E. N. Dzelepy, *Le complot de Chypre* (Brussels, 1965); Institute of Greek-American Historical Studies, *The Cyprus Question* (Chicago, 1965); T. W. Adams and Alvin J. Cottrell, *Cyprus between East and West* (Baltimore, 1968); Lawrence Durrell, *Bitter Lemons* (London, 1959); Department of Information, Ministry of Foreign Affairs, Ankara, "The Question of Cyprus," *Turkish Yearbook of International Relations, 1963*, pp. 165–200; Publication Department of the Greek Communal Chamber, *Cyprus: A Handbook of the Island's Past and Present* (Nicosia, 1964); Stephen G. Xydis, *Cyprus: Conflict and Conciliation, 1954–1958* (Columbus, Ohio, 1967); Linda B. Miller, *Cyprus: The Law and Politics of Civil Strife* (Cambridge, Mass., 1968).

[51] Kyriakides, *Cyprus*, p. 3.

[52] Foley, *Legacy of Strife*, p. 185.

be united under the roof of the same state. Eastern Orthodoxy and the Graeco-Byzantine mystique formed the genuine wellspring of the drive for unification with Greece although—it was asserted—the *Megali Idea* was no longer to be relied on.[53]

It had always been expected, particularly after Lausanne, that London would hand over Cyprus to Greece. The Greeks considered the future of the island a matter between themselves and the British. The Turkish intervention was an unpleasant surprise for them. They firmly believed that the British instigated the Turkish government's interference in Cypriote affairs to prolong their domination over Cyprus. Without such British intrigue—so they thought—Turks would not have opposed *Enosis*. They also believed that Turkish nationalist emotions have been artificially stirred up by Ankara and the Turkish press. Menderes only wished to distract public attention from the deplorable economic situation and other sources of discontent by focusing it on Cyprus, or so this line of reasoning went.

Turkish thinking on the subject was highly diversified, and emphasis on individual points changed according to the spokesman or the opportunities for speech. Some combination of the following five arguments was most often employed.

1. Turks in Cyprus and on the mainland relied heavily on historic reasoning to support their claim. The Ottoman Empire had conquered the island to protect its naval interests. At that time, the Cypriote Greeks were serfs under the oppressive rule of their Venetian and Frank masters; the Ottomans liberated them and gave them land to cultivate. They also restored the Greek Orthodox Church and made the archbishop the head of the Greek *millet*. The rank and title of an *Ethnarchos* was conferred by the sultan (earlier the archbishop was only "independent" from the rest of the Orthodox Church). During the British administration, it was always recognized that there were two equal communities on the island. The Turkish people of Cyprus form, therefore, no "minority" (at one time, they were the majority) but a *community* (in Turkish: *cemaat*), irrespective of their numbers, with rights that could not be overruled by the Greek "majority."

It was also emphasized that the island, originally given "in administra-

<hr/>

[53] For the *Megali Idea*, see pp. 8, 219–21 above. On February 20, 1956, Radio Athens officially denied that *Enosis* is based on the *Megali Idea* "which does not exist any more"; Jäschke, *Die Türkei in den Jahren 1952–61*, p. 60.

tion," with the right of reversion, was ceded by the Treaty of Lausanne to Britain with the natural understanding that it should remain British, unless returned to Turkey. Should, therefore, London decide to abandon the island, Turkey would have the historic right to claim it as her own.

2. The Cyprus question was widely regarded in Turkey as a point of national prestige and honor. The memory of an imperial heritage occupied a major part of the image Turks had of themselves: modern Turkey was no longer a sick man whose just claims could be ignored. Turks recalled that the island of Crete was gradually weaned away from Turkey under the pretext of "self government" and finally surrendered to Greece; they did not want that precedent repeated with Cyprus. The surrender of Cyprus against Turkey's will would be inconsistent with national "self-esteem."

It was maintained that Cyprus was not only a national but also a popular issue for the Turks, and that Turkey's foreign policy could no longer be "managed" by a cabinet of a few. Indeed, there was much less popular interest shown in questions such as membership in NATO or even relations with the Soviet Union than in the issue of Cyprus—an issue viewed through popular eyes as identical with the question of Graeco-Turkish antagonism.

3. In the leading circles of Ankara the strategical reasons for preventing Greek sovereignty over Cyprus were regarded as being of prime importance. It was submitted that the Lausanne treaty did divide the Aegean and Mediterranean area between Turkey and Greece. The unfavorable Turkish geopolitical position (practically all the islands adjacent to the Aegean Turkish coast had been assigned to Greece) was counterbalanced by the demilitarization of the Greek islands near the Anatolian shore. Turkey's exposed strategical position as well as the accepted Aegean and eastern Mediterranean balance of power (distribution of lands and forces) would be tilted into Greece's favor by the cession of Cyprus.

Furthermore, it was pointed out that Cyprus controlled the approaches to Turkey's most important harbors in the Mediterranean, Mersin, and Iskenderun; in case of a blockage of the straits and of the Aegean, these harbors would be the only access to and from Turkey. Ankara, it was said, would have opposed *Enosis* for strategical reasons even if there had been no Turks on Cyprus. Turkey had had great misgivings about handing the Dodecanese Islands over to Greece, but the time was consid-

NEW APPLE OF DISCORD: CYPRUS

ered inopportune for her to oppose the cession openly.[54] The incorporation of these islands by Greece, however, had already weakened Turkey's strategical position, and, thus, it was necessary to oppose by all means the creation of a similar situation in Cyprus.

4. The strategical-geopolitical reasoning was allied with political apprehensions concerning *Enosis*. In 1945–47 a Communist takeover in Greece was just around the corner. Turkish leaders justifiably considered Greek internal politics rather unstable. The strength of the Communist Party in Cyprus was well known. Should Cyprus join Greece, any change in the Greek domestic political status would automatically affect the island. A Communist or even neutralist regime in Greece would create considerable difficulties for Turkey, for it was well-nigh impossible to cross the Aegean without passing through Greek territorial waters, especially along the Anatolian coastline. Airplanes could not avoid flying over Greek-controlled territories when using the direct route from Italy or the Mediterranean to Istanbul or Izmir. Access to and from the straits could easily be mined or otherwise blocked in the narrow channels among the Greek islands, or between these islands and the Anatolian shore. In such cases Cyprus, if ruled from Athens, would significantly detract from Turkey's military position as a member of NATO.

It is well known that AKEL, the Cypriote Communist Party, was never enthusiastic about *Enosis*. Such a solution would have resulted in a ban on the Communist Party, which was outlawed on the mainland under Greek legal provisions.[55] An independent Cyprus, without sufficient guarantees, would also expose Turkey to dangers should the island fall under Communist or leftist rule. A Mediterranean Cuba was the last thing that Ankara wanted to see established 40 miles from her shores. Accordingly, the local balance of power, said to be jeopardized by *Enosis*, had a meaning in Turkish eyes which transcended purely military considerations. The entire Western orientation of Turkey and her ties with Europe and her Atlantic allies would have been threatened if Cyprus had been joined to a foreign power over which Turkey could exercise no direct influence.[56]

[54] See p. 227 above.

[55] In Cypriote Communist circles, *Enosis* was known as the "NATO solution" for Cyprus and was therefore objected to.

[56] See the analysis by Feridun Cemal Erkin, *Les relations Turco-Soviétiques et la question des Détroits* (Ankara, 1968), pp. 401–4.

5. Lastly, the life and prosperity of the Turkish community was considered endangered by *Enosis*. A situation somewhat similar to that which existed in Anatolia during and after the Turkish-Greek war of 1919–22 had developed in Cyprus. The average Turk became convinced that any Greek control over the Turkish Cypriote people would expose them to all sorts of hardships, even to the peril of extermination. Thus, it became a principle of Turkish Cypriote policy never to permit the Turks on the island to live under Greek sovereignty. United Nations or treaty guarantees were believed to be unrealistic and unreliable. Furthermore, the concept of "two equal communities" excluded any arrangement by which Greeks could rule over Turks on the island.

Because the Turkish government soon realized that a retrocession of Cyprus to Turkey by the British was not feasible, it began to insist that the island be partitioned between the two countries. While the halving of Cyprus along the thirty-fifth parallel was officially demanded, a smaller portion of the island probably would have been acceptable to Ankara. The northern coastline, with the Turkish quarter of Nicosia, would have satisfied strategical needs and also included a high proportion of Turkish Cypriotes. It should be mentioned that no resettlement of Turks and Greeks in the divided portions of the island was contemplated; Greeks living in the Turkish part of Cyprus might have provided a sufficiently "real" guarantee for the welfare and security of the Turks in the Greek sector of the island. It was believed, and still is, that the Greek government essentially would not have been hostile to partition. Those who were said to be better acquainted with local conditions maintained, however, that Cypriote Greeks would fight *à outrance* any attempt to divide their island politically and would have submitted to it only if forced to by the Greek and Turkish governments—an unlikely possibility.

If one thus excluded *Enosis*, on the one hand, and *Taksim*, the Ireland-like solution for Cyprus, on the other, the only remaining alternative to British rule was an independent Cyprus that would vouchsafe the existence of both communities. It has, however, been admitted by both Turks and Greeks that there is no Cypriote nation; there are only Greeks, part of the Greek nation, and Turks, part of the Turkish nation. This was exactly the argument submitted by Turkey against the self-determination demanded by Greece. If there should be self-determination—so Ankara said—the votes of *all* Turks (in Turkey and Cyprus) should be opposed to the votes of *all* Greeks (in Greece and on the island)—that is, 35 million compared to less than 10 million. Nevertheless, the solution adopted did create the Republic of Cyprus. As a commentator observed: "A Cypriot State may have come into being but not a Cypriot nation."[57]

CYPRUS: SETTLEMENT AND DEADLOCK

The settlement reached at the Zurich and London negotiations in February 1959 was a working arrangement which still had to be implemented by the drafting of the relevant treaty and constitutional texts. The basic provisions of the constitution, however, had been agreed upon by the Turkish and Greek prime ministers in Zurich and approved by Archbishop Makarios and Dr. Fazıl Küçük, representing the Greek and Turkish communities of the island. It took more than a year before the preparations for the transfer of government by the British to the authorities of the new Republic of Cyprus could be achieved; the formal constitution had to be drafted and three treaties signed. The signing of these documents took place on August 16, 1960, the day Cyprus became an independent state.

Under the Treaty Concerning the Establishment of the Republic of Cyprus,[58] Britain, Greece, and Turkey agreed to recognize the Republic of Cyprus, which was to comprise the island with the exception of two areas, the Akrotiri Sovereign Base Area and the Dhekelia Sovereign Base Area, which were to remain under the sovereignty of the British Crown. The three signatories, furthermore, undertook to consult and cooperate in the common defense of Cyprus.

A Treaty of Guarantee, signed by the representatives of the three interested powers (known as the Guarantor Powers) and the representatives of the Republic of Cyprus sought to ensure the independence, territorial integrity, and security of Cyprus. Greece, Turkey, and Britain undertook "to prohibit, so far as concerns them, any activity aimed at promoting, directly or indirectly, either union of Cyprus with any other State or partition of the Island."

Similar obligation had been assumed by the republic, which promised "not to participate, in whole or in part, in any political or economic union with any State whatsoever. It accordingly declares prohibited any activity

[57] Spyridakis, *A Brief History of Cyprus,* p. 73.
[58] The Cyprus documents were published in the *United Nations Treaty Series,* vol. 382, 1960, nos. 5475–5486, pp. 2–253. See also *Documents on International Affairs, 1960,* pp. 422–27; *Turkish Yearbook of International Relations, 1963,* pp. 201–305.

likely to promote, directly or indirectly, either union with any other State or partition of the Island." Furthermore, the Republic of Cyprus undertook "to ensure the maintenance of its independence, territorial integrity and security, *as well as respect for its Constitution.*"[59]

The three Guarantor Powers promised to consult and take the necessary measures to ensure the observance of this treaty. In the event of a violation of its provisions, "Insofar as common or concerted action may not be possible, each of the three guaranteeing Powers reserves the right *to take action with the sole aim of reestablishing the state of affairs* created by the present Treaty."[60] The above right of intervention subsequently was invoked but never applied by the Turkish government.

Another document simultaneously signed by Turkey, Greece, and the Republic of Cyprus (Britain was no party to this treaty) was the Treaty of Alliance. The signatories agreed to cooperate for common defense and to resist any attack or aggression against the independence or territorial integrity of Cyprus. For this purpose, tripartite headquarters were to be established on the island. Greek and Turkish contingents were to be attached to the headquarters to the number of 950 Greeks and 650 Turks. The ministers of foreign affairs of Cyprus, Greece, and Turkey were to constitute the supreme political body of the tripartite alliance.

The Zurich–London agreements provided Turkey with a legal status equal to that of Greece in the affairs of Cyprus—a status which she had been sorely missing to that point. Her participation in the exchange relative to Cyprus was possible only because London wished to consult her, very much to the displeasure of Athens and the Cypriote Greeks. They characterized Ankara's involvement as an unwarranted intrusion into a matter which was none of her concern. It was a significant success for Turkish diplomacy to have achieved full partnership in the treaty arrangements agreed to in Zurich and London.

The crux of the settlement on Cyprus was to be found in the constitutional provisions which were to govern the internal workings of the new state. The constitution was drawn according to the basic principles accepted in Zurich and incorporated the three treaties listed above.

The Cypriote Constitution of 1960[61] was based on the concept of two

---

[59] Article I. (Italics added.)

[60] Article IV. (Italics added.)

[61] The Constitution of Cyprus is to be found in *Cyprus,* Cmnd. 1093 (London, 1960).

communities and sought to prevent Greek majority rule in all important public affairs. The bi-communal nature of the Cypriote population was thus recognized:

> For the purposes of this Constitution
> (1) the Greek Community comprises all citizens of the Republic who are of Greek origin and whose mother tongue is Greek and who share the Greek Cultural traditions or who are members of the Greek-Orthodox Church;
> (2) the Turkish Community comprises all citizens of the Republic who are of Turkish origin and whose mother tongue is Turkish or who share the Turkish cultural traditions or who are Moslems.[62]

The official languages of the republic were to be both Greek and Turkish. The two communities would celebrate their respective national holidays and have the right to fly Greek or Turkish flags.

The constitution gave an institutional standing to the two ethno-religious communities. More so than ever before, in all spheres of public life, power was divided in prescribed proportion between Greeks and Turks. The ratio gave Turks greater weight than their representation according to popular census would indicate. Even so, the ratio varied according to the matter in question.

Thus, in the Cypriote House of Representatives, Greeks were entitled to 70 percent and Turks to 30 percent of the seats, with the two communities voting separately. In addition to the one-chamber legislature, the two communities formed communal chambers to legislate strictly communal matters.

The form of government was described by Article 1 of the constitution: "The State of Cyprus is an independent and sovereign Republic with a presidential regime, the President being Greek and the Vice-President being Turk, elected by the Greek and the Turkish Communities of Cyprus respectively." The executive power was thus to be exercised by the president and the vice-president in such manner that in all important questions they would have to act jointly. They were to possess a right of final veto, separately and jointly, over a long list of topics on which legislation was passed by the house.

The Council of Ministers was to be composed of seven Greek and three Turkish ministers, designated respectively by the president and vice-president but appointed by both.[63] The decisions of the Council of Min-

[62] Article 2.
[63] Article 46.

isters were to be passed by an absolute majority, except on matters concerning foreign affairs, national defense, and security, where both the president and the vice-president could use their veto powers. Also in matters other than those enumerated above, decision-making depended largely on the consent of both officials; they were to convoke the ministerial meetings and, by joint consent, establish the agenda. The constitution's presidential system was thus conceived on the basis of dual power, representing the bi-communal nature of the state.

The competence of communal chambers extended over a wide range of affairs: religious, educational, and cultural matters; questions of personal status and of civilian courts dealing with personal status; and the financing of these and other communal needs. The courts were also to be divided according to communal requirements: in civilian cases where the parties to the dispute belonged to the same community, the court was to be composed of a judge or judges of the same community; in criminal matters when both the accused and the plaintiff belonged to the same community, the judges were also to belong to that community. Only when the parties in a case were members of different communities was the court to consist of members of both communities. Only the high court, the highest court of appeal, was to be composed of two Greek Cypriote judges and one Turkish Cypriote judge, although it was to be presided over by a neutral (foreign) judge with the right to cast two votes.

The constitution also set up a Supreme Constitutional Court to rule over constitutional and bi-communal disputes. It was to consist of one Greek and one Turkish justice and a neutral president, all of them to be appointed jointly by the president and vice-president of the republic.

Communal participation in the public service was to be reflected in the ratio of 70 percent Greeks and 30 percent Turks. On the other hand, the ratio in the army, police, and gendarmerie was to be 60 percent to 40 percent.

The 1960 constitution accordingly introduced a rigid, bi-communal method of government which carried within it the possibility of confrontation in all branches of government and administration between representatives of the two communities. In fact, the constitution "communalized" every aspect of public affairs in order to prevent the smaller community's being overruled or dominated by the larger. Under the former Ottoman or British rule, the paramount power acted as an arbiter between the two ethnic communities. Lacking such a neutral superior power, the constitution was to force both communities to find compromise by themselves. However, the inclination to accept compromises presupposed a spirit of mutual trust, a reliance on the good faith of the partner, and a sense of benevolent equity. This spirit was blatantly absent from the relationship of both communities.

The constitution offered a very complex and inflexible legal structure which, even with the best will, would have been difficult to implement. With a maximum of effort, it might have been possible to convert this clumsy constitutional instrument into a smoothly working mechanism; however, Cyprus did not have a tradition of two communities cooperating, as in Lebanon where Christian and Muslim elements of the population (being about equal in numbers) have set up a satisfactory partnership. The communal differences in Cyprus were so deep-seated that a constitutional framework, based on separation and the protection of one community against the other, was hardly conducive to eliminate or diminish ethnic rivalries.[64]

We must add that the majority of the Cypriote Greek community was highly disappointed by the outcome of the negotiations. Instead of the hoped-for *Enosis,* they received "independence" which enhanced disproportionately the power and influence of the Turks. Indeed, the constitution was a victory for the Turkish point-of-view: instead of majority rule there was essential equality between Greeks and Turks; the status of Turks within government, administration, and the armed forces was solidified; and an international (that is, Turkish) guarantee protected their constitutional and social position.

Makarios had to overcome opposition to the accepted agreements and his own public position; he did so with his usual skill and the authority of his ecclesiastical office. He created the Patriotic Front to back his policies and gained support even from the Communist side, although strong opposition to the agreements continued. Makarios himself stated that since a *fait accompli* was placed before him in London, he had no other alternative but to consent to the accords reached.[65] In Cyprus it was widely held that the basic principles of the constitution were laid down without Cypriote participation.

[64] For a detailed analysis of the Cypriote Constitution, see Kyriakides, *Cyprus,* pp. 53–71.
[65] Makarios later announced that in February 1959, he tried in vain to have the thirteen points changed (which he raised again in 1963). He was given an ultimatum

The Cypriote Turks were quick to profit from their newly enhanced status. More homogeneous in their outlook and ready to follow Ankara's lead, they took over their share of governmental and administrative duties. Only later, when the constitutional structure was declared inoperative by the archbishop's fiat did a rift within the Turkish Cypriote leadership become perceptible. Their recognized leader, Dr. Fazıl Küçük, a medical doctor by profession, had become the vice-president of the republic. He was generally considered "soft" in the eyes of more militant Turks. The second leader of the Turks, shortly to surpass Küçük in significance, was Rauf Denktaş, who had studied law in London and had given up his legal profession to become the chairman of the Turkish communal chamber. Among the three Turkish ministers, appointed under the constitution, the minister of defense, Osman Örek, played an important role.

The Greek leaders of the republic of Cyprus were chosen mostly from among the ranks of the EOKA: Glafkos Clerides, like Rauf Denktaş, an English-trained barrister, became the president of the House of Representatives and thus Makarios' deputy under the constitution in the latter's absence from the country.

The psychological atmosphere between the leaders of the two communities was unfavorable to the promotion of sincere collaboration. The Turks pressed to have the constitution applied "to the letter," especially the appointment of 30 percent Turks to public posts. The Greeks objected that there was not a sufficient number of qualified Turks and were reluctant to dismiss Greeks in order to create vacancies.[66] Relations between Greek and Turkish officials, including within the cabinet, were characterized by mutual animosity. The Turks felt that they were being treated condescendingly; the Greeks thought of the Turks as stubborn, unsophisticated, and obstructive. English was used at the meetings of the ministry;[67] but Greek witticisms were frequent—to the displeasure of the Turks, who often felt like "poor relations."

The Cypriote army was to be created on the basis of a 60 and 40 per-

---

"to take it or leave it." He explained: "I was sure that, if I did not sign the agreement, there might be partition. Cyprus would be divided as a colony and we should not be able to raise the question again. The less bad thing was to sign." Stephens, *Cyprus: A Place of Arms,* pp. 165–66.

[66] Stephens, *Cyprus: A Place of Arms,* pp. 174–75; Kyriakides, *Cyprus,* pp. 77–83.

[67] Unfortunately, Fazıl Küçük, the vice president, was one of the older-generation Turks whose education was in French rather than in English. This circumstance rendered communication between him and Greek officials more difficult.

cent ratio between Greeks and Turks, although the constitution contained no specific provision as to how the army was to be formed. Greeks proposed armed forces in which the members of the two communities would be mixed; Turks insisted on separate Turkish and Greek contingents. A compromise solution submitted by Defense Minister Örek proposed the establishment of five battalions, each battalion to consist of three companies, the latter either Greek or Turkish. The Council of Ministers adopted a bill providing for completely mixed army units, which was vetoed by the vice-president. As a consequence, no real bi-communal Cypriote army could be set up. The Greeks began to organize their own army secretly, and the Turks retaliated by setting up their own secret military organization.[68]

The most virulent dissension arose in regard to the organization of municipalities. Under the constitution: "Separate municipalities shall be created in the five largest towns in the Republic, that is to say, Nicosia, Limassol, Famagusta, Larnaca, and Paphos by the Turkish inhabitants thereof."[69]

During the internal troubles in 1958, separate Turkish municipal councils were established in these five towns with the approval of the British authorities. The above constitutional provision only confirmed the existing status, but the geographic separation within the municipalities concerned was not clearly drawn. Makarios, however, wished to eliminate the existing division; when the Turks insisted on applying the constitution, he suggested a compromise proposal under which joint committees of Greek and Turkish members would perform the functions of municipal councils. But Vice-President Küçük rejected this formula as conflicting with the constitution. Since the House of Representatives failed to act, the Turkish communal chamber passed a statute defining and legalizing separate Turkish municipal councils. The Council of Ministers, disregarding the votes of its Turkish members, then set up development boards to run these towns; the Turkish municipal councils refused to surrender their power to the newly established boards. The Supreme Constitutional Court, with the casting vote of its neutral president, rejected both the legality of the development boards and the action by the Turkish communal chamber as inconsistent with the constitution.

[68] It was named *Türk Müdafaa Teşkilâtı* (Turkish Defense Organization) and its members were generally referred to as *muharib* (fighters).

[69] Article 173, par. 1.

TURKEY, GREECE, AND CYPRUS

The Turks, to force through legislation which would conform with the constitution, refused to extend tax legislation beyond a period of two months. The Greeks asked for a longer extension or a new tax law, but the Turkish members of the House of Representatives were able to block legislation on this matter.[70] Thus, the Cypriote government was not legally authorized to collect taxes after December 1961. Taxation then reverted to the communal chambers, which passed the necessary legislation with regard to their own ethnic communities. The Supreme Constitutional Court approved communal taxation, leaving the island divided on the important matter of revenue.

Both communities insisted on maintaining their points of view in many controversies. In late November 1963, the existing deadlock induced President Makarios to propose a number of constitutional amendments. His Thirteen Points were submitted to the guarantor powers and to the Turkish vice-president.

The Thirteen Points, if adopted, would have eliminated the right of the Turkish community to protect itself against a majority rule by the Greeks. The vice-president's right of veto was to be abolished (together with the similar right of the president, but the latter had no reason to fear legislation by the majority of the house or of the Council of Ministers); constitutional provisions concerning separate Greek and Turkish majorities for the enactment of certain laws (such as tax laws) were to be abolished; unified law courts were to be set up; the army was to be organized on a unified basis; municipalities were to be unified; the proportion of Greek and Turkish civil servants was to be accepted according to the numerical strength of Greeks and Turks in the island.

These constitutional revisions, if accepted, would have essentially abrogated the bi-communal character of the Cypriote state and were understandably unacceptable to the Turkish leadership. The Turkish government, for its part, most energetically objected in a note submitted on December 16, 1963, to any attempt to change the constitution. Five days later, fighting broke out in Nicosia when Greek police attempted to search a Turkish car near the Turkish quarter of the city. Thereafter, shooting

[70] Article 78, par. 2, of the constitution declared that laws "imposing duties or taxes shall require a separate simple majority of the representatives elected by the Greek and Turkish communities, respectively, taking part in the vote." This provision gave equal rights to the representatives of the Turkish Community with those of the Greek representatives in passing tax legislation.

and killing continued in Nicosia and many other places throughout the island.

Each party accused the other of having started the fight. It seems to be well substantiated that the Greeks had been preparing for months to subdue any Turkish resistance, perhaps to force acceptance of their demands on them. It also seems likely that the Turks were only preparing for self-defense, since they could not hope to defeat the Greeks without direct assistance from Turkey. That Makarios believed he could defeat all Turkish opposition became evident when, on January 1, 1964, he announced that the Zurich–London agreements together with the constitution had been "abrogated."[71]

British forces from their bases on Cyprus were called to restore peace but were unable to prevent bloodshed except in specific areas. In February 1964, the Turkish government threatened to land its forces on the island.[72] Previously, talks in London between representatives of the two Cypriote communities and the Turkish and Greek foreign ministers had ended in a stalemate. The United States then urged sending a NATO force to Cyprus, a plan accepted by Britain, Turkey, and Greece. Makarios, however, adamantly refused to cooperate with NATO and instead demanded action by the United Nations Security Council.

After Cyprus gained independence, she had been admitted to the United Nations. Although the island-state was also a member of the British Commonwealth, Makarios insisted on pursuing a neutralist policy and, despite the fact that British bases were functioning for the benefit of the Atlantic alliance, opposed all dealings with NATO. Supported by the Soviet Union, the archbishop succeeded in having the case of Cyprus submitted to the United Nations.

The world organization previously had been confronted with the Cyprus crisis when Greece had sought self-determination for the island.[73] But this time, Cyprus, as a member state, as well as the British govern-

[71] Duncan Sandys, the British Secretary for Commonwealth Relations, who was present in Nicosia, immediately enjoined Makarios to retract his announcement. Makarios corrected himself in a second statement by declaring that he only intended to convey his desire to secure the termination of the treaties. See Stephens, *Cyprus: A Place of Arms,* pp. 185–86.

[72] Turkey, this time and later, wished to rely on Article 4 of the Treaty of Guarantee which gave her a right of independent action. It was, however, maintained that the official Turkish contingent was to be strengthened; *Neue Zürcher Zeitung,* February 3, 1964.

[73] See Xydis, *Conflict and Conciliation, passim.*

ment, appealed to the Security Council for the dispatch of a peace force and a United Nations mediator to re-establish order and security. At a time when Turkey was again preparing to invade Cyprus in order to protect her co-nationals, the first contingent of the United Nations Peacekeeping Force in Cyprus (UNFICYP) arrived on March 14. Eventually, a force of 5,000, consisting of Swedish, Danish, Finnish, and Irish units, was placed on the island, in the language of the Security Council, "to use its best efforts to prevent a recurrence of fighting and, as necessary, to contribute to the maintenance and restoration of law and order and a return to normal conditions."[74]

The United Nations' peace enforcement did not end communal strife or fighting, though it did reduce its intensity. Substantively, it did not promote the solution of the problem at all. The Greek Cypriote government (the Turkish members having refused to recognize the legality of Makarios' actions) considered the Turks rebels. The Turkish community insisted that the 1960 constitution was still in force and that the government had acted illegally. President Makarios refused to meet with Fazıl Küçük as vice-president, but only as a representative of the Turkish community. The Turks continued to regard their leader as the constitutional vice-president, and the three Turkish ministers continued to fulfill their function, although their authority was now restricted to the Turkish-controlled areas of the island.

Most of the foreign powers acted with greater or lesser caution in regard to the confused situation: they maintained contacts with Makarios but continued to consult the Turkish leadership, as did the British and the United States.[75] The Turkish government kept only a chargé d'affaires in Nicosia because an ambassador should have presented his credentials to both the president and the vice-president, acting jointly. Ankara accepted,

[74] The Security Council resolutions are printed in Miller, *Civil Strife*, pp. 80–81.

[75] During the meeting of the United Nations Security Council in February 1964, when the sending of an emergency force to Cyprus was discussed, Kyprianou, the Cypriote ambassador, asked for a resolution that, by implication, would have acknowledged the abrogation of the Zurich–London Agreements. On the other hand, the Turkish ambassador, Turgut Menemencioğlu, submitted that the Makarios government was not the representative of Cyprus as a whole. The council also heard Rauf Denktaş who spoke on behalf of the Turkish community. In its resolution the council refrained from taking a stand on the legal and constitutional issue. See a detailed account in "The Question of Cyprus," *Turkish Yearbook of International Relations, 1963*, pp. 181–84. For a different interpretation, see Dzelepy, *Complot de Chypre*, pp. 144–67.

however, a new Cypriote ambassador, after having obtained from the vice-president his approval of the appointment.

The Greek leadership felt that the United Nations presence would protect it against Turkish intervention; Turks of the island expected that the international force would prevent Greek atrocities. The two communities, however, sought security in measures of self-defense; Greece and Turkey supplied them with arms and with military instructors. Because the official access routes to the island were controlled by the Greeks, a number of Greek regular forces (the estimate ranges from 2,000 to 5,000) easily infiltrated Cyprus; Grivas, now a general, came to take over command of the Greek forces. Makarios had ordered an economic blockade against the Turks which caused much hardship but did not break their will to resist.

The international conflict surrounding Cyprus has been widened by the interest which the Soviet Union displayed toward the island. It had to be a delicate operation: AKEL, the Communist Party of Cyprus, did not favor *Enosis*, since supporting Greek rule would have been suicidal; prior to 1960, Makarios could be approached only by supporters of his endeavors for union with Greece. Consequently, after 1960 Moscow became an advocate of independence for Cyprus. Soviet arms were made available to Makarios and Soviet representatives in the United Nations condemned "NATO encroachments" on the sovereignty of the republic.[76]

Despite the temporary Turkish–Greek reconciliation which led to the Zurich–London agreements, the renewed flare-up of the Cypriote domestic struggle, the massacres which were committed, and the armed support provided to their respective co-nationals brought relations between the two nations to another low. Ankara responded to the economic blockade set up against the Turkish community in Cyprus by expelling Greek citizens from Istanbul. In August, when the Cypriote Greek National Guard, led by Grivas, threatened to wipe out a Turkish enclave near Kokkina, Turkish jet-fighters bombed the Greek positions and Greek villages. Two months earlier, Turkey already had informed her allies, including the United States, that she intended to place additional regular Turkish forces on the island. The result was President Johnson's letter of June 5, 1964.[77]

[76] See Adams and Cottrell, *Cyprus between East and West,* pp. 32–37.
[77] See chapter IV, pp. 130–33.

Athens and Ankara each considered the other ultimately responsible for the violence on the island. A Turkish military invasion would have brought the forces of both countries into combat; it also was assumed that fighting would have started along the entire land and sea border of Turkey and Greece. The Turkish and Greek governments were in contact on the issue of Cyprus through the United Nations mediator. The first mediator was Sakari Tuomioja, a Finnish diplomat; he died following a heart attack during the negotiations conducted in Geneva and was succeeded by Galo Plaza Lasso, an Ecuadorian diplomat.

In Geneva, where Britain and the United States were also represented, Dean Acheson, special representative of President Johnson, submitted a plan which took notice of Turkey's renewed demand for a partition of the island. Under this proposal, Cyprus would be united with Greece, except for the northeast Karpas peninsula, which would become a sovereign Turkish military base. As another token concession, Greece would cede to Turkey the tiny island of Castellorizon (Meis) off the Anatolian coast. One or two Turkish "cantons" inside Cyprus would enjoy local autonomy, and Turks would be free to leave the island under adequate compensation. Although the Turkish government accepted the plan as a basis for discussion, the Greek government and Makarios rejected it out-of-hand. A second Acheson plan, providing for a Turkish military base to be leased to Turkey for 25 years, was unacceptable to all three parties.[78]

During 1965 the positions of the Greek and Turkish sides became more outspoken: Makarios now insisted not only on the abrogation of the Zurich-London agreements and annulment of the constitution but claimed "unfettered independence" for Cyprus, which evidently also meant possible *Enosis*. Ankara renewed its demand for either the maintenance of the agreements and the constitution or a measure of partition; alternatively, there were hints of a "cantonal" or "federal" system.

Mediator Galo Plaza Lasso resigned his position when Ankara lost confidence in him. In March 1965, he submitted to U Thant, the United Nations Secretary-General, his final report, in which he was unable to demonstrate any material progress. He did outline his personal suggestions, which entailed the recognition of an independent Cyprus, as a unitary state, with minority protection afforded to the Cypriote Turks.

[78] Stephens, *Cyprus: A Place of Arms*, pp. 200–204.

Such a proposal was anathema to both the Turkish government and the Turkish leaders of Cyprus.

Makarios was able to make some headway for his concept of complete independence,[79] but rapprochement between Turkey and the Soviet Union deprived him of Moscow's overt support. Nevertheless, the increase in the size of the Greek National Guard, now also supplied with arms from Czechoslovakia, showed that eventually a settlement by force would be sought. This was certainly the aim of Grivas, the motivating spirit behind the concept of an armed solution.

In April 1967, a military junta took over the government of Greece. The intentions of the new military government toward Cyprus were unknown at first. In Ankara it was hoped that it would be easier to come to terms with a regime no longer dependent on popular support.[80] In September 1967, the new Greek Prime Minister Kollias met Turkish Prime Minister Demirel on a bridge of the Efros River, at the Thracian Turco–Greek border. The talks took place first in Kesan, on the Turkish side of the frontier; then in Alexandroupolis, on the Greek side. Turkish and Greek heads of government had last met eight years before in London. But concerning Cyprus, the discussion proved futile: the Greeks proposed *Enosis,* and the Turks invoked the Zurich-London agreements.[81]

Two months later the Cypriote powder-keg exploded again. Greek Cypriote units tried to force their way into a village controlled by Turks which lay astride an important road from Limassol to Nicosia. Before the United Nations forces could stop the fighting, thirty Turks had been killed. Turkey immediately mobilized her forces to invade the island and, if necessary, to fight Greece in Thrace. Ankara presented Athens with an ultimatum demanding the removal of the illegal Greek army from Cyprus, the recall of General Grivas, disbandment of the Greek National Guard,

---

[79] On December 18, 1965, the General Assembly of the United Nations passed a resolution by 57 votes for, 5 against, and 54 abstentions, which appeared to give recognition to the claim that Cyprus should enjoy complete independence without any foreign intervention or interference. The Turkish government declared this resolution (which under the Charter of the United Nations was a recommendation only) contrary to justice, law, and international agreements and for this reason inapplicable; *Turkish Yearbook of International Relations, 1965,* pp. 264–65. The Makarios government had taken the position that the restrictions on the sovereignty of Cyprus, including the right of the guarantor powers to enforce the treaties, had ended by virtue of the admission of Cyprus to the United Nations; Miller, *Civil Strife,* pp. 14–21.

[80] *New York Times,* May 20, 1967.

[81] *New York Times,* September 11, 1967.

compensation for the Turkish Cypriotes, and greater security for the Turkish community.[82]

The "unthinkable" Turkish–Greek war was closer than ever before. President Johnson sent former Deputy Secretary of Defense Cyrus Vance to Ankara; United Nations Special Representative José Rolz-Bennett and NATO Secretary General Manlio Brozio rushed to the scene. Turkish military strategy planned to establish a beachhead or occupy a port in Cyprus. Meanwhile, the Turkish army in Thrace would await possible aggression from the Greeks. The overwhelming opinion was that the First Hellenic Army would not budge. In that case, the military actions would be limited to Cyprus.[83] After the unpleasant repercussions of the Johnson letter affair, the expectation was that the United States would not interfere with its Sixth Fleet.

As a result of mediation and under the threat of Turkish action, the Greek government grudgingly gave way. Grivas was immediately recalled and the Greek forces were to follow. Makarios, however, refused to dismantle the National Guard and consented to its reduction only when U Thant offered to expand the United Nations forces.

By January 16, 1968, the Greek regulars had been withdrawn. A relative calm slowly descended on the island. During the next months barricades were removed; some limited contacts between low-echelon Greek and Turkish officials were renewed; and the economic blockade was lifted. But Cyprus remained divided. To give greater authority to their independent existence, the leaders of the Turkish community announced on December 29, 1968, the formation of a Temporary Turkish Administration in Cyprus to run the affairs of their community. It was also declared that this body was just the merger of already existing administrative services. Fazıl Küçük was elected president of the new administration and Rauf Denktaş (who had earlier been expelled from Cyprus) became his deputy. Portfolios were given generally to those Turks who had been ministers in the Cypriote cabinet or high ministerial officials.[84]

Thus, the Turkish community established its *de facto* separation from

[82] Adams and Cottrell, *Cyprus between East and West*, pp. 70–73.

[83] The declared purpose of the Turkish action was to place as many Turkish forces on the island as there were Greek forces. Turks were confident that they would easily defeat the Greek army, but it was admitted that the invasion of Cyprus might be costly. In January, 1968, the *Hürriyet* daily published a series of apparently well-informed articles on the November crisis: *Hürriyet*, January 8–12, 15–17, 1968.

[84] *New York Times*, December 30, 1968.

the rest of the country and consolidated a partition which already existed in spirit. The separation of the two communities under the 1960 constitution was *personal* and similar to the *millet* system. The new division began to assume *territorial* or *geographical* forms. The Turks, though dispersed into 43 enclaves of varying sizes, did manage to partition the island. The Greeks, by their intolerant attitude, helped them or forced them into a condition that was economically unfavorable but provided at least relative security. This partition was achieved at the cost of resettling thousands of Turks who had to live as refugees in larger enclaves, most of them in the Nicosia Turkish quarter and north of it, along the scenic Kyrenia highway, which was controlled by the Turkish fighters and where Greeks were allowed to travel only twice a day under the protection of the United Nations forces.

As Cyprus was divided, so were Turkey and Greece. The island had become the symbol and epitome of the division between these two nations.

TURKEY AND GREECE: THE INTERLOCKED NATIONS

A glance at the map reveals the geostrategical interdependence of Turkey and Greece. Geography is a constant factor, whereas ethnic distribution may be altered, although painfully. The Lausanne conference attempted to reduce the tragic entwinement of the Greek and Turkish populations but had to accept these geographical determinants. The islands in the Aegean, alongside the Anatolian coast, had been allotted to Greece because of their overwhelming Greek population. The only exceptions, made for strategical reasons, were Imroz (Imbros) and Bozcaada (Tenedos) at the entrance to the Dardanelles. To compensate Turkey for facing these Greek islands from its shore, they were demilitarized under the Lausanne provisions. Thus, they remained within the easy reach of Turkish military power. Turkey felt the adverse effects of the cluster of Greek Cyclades and Sporades, which could close the narrow channels across the Aegean to navigation and prevent access to the straits and Istanbul. In any case, the membership of Turkey and Greece in hostile alliance systems or other potential confrontations between the two countries would be replete with unforeseeable dangers to both and would be unbearable in the long run.

It follows that the geostrategical proximity of the Turkish and Greek nations is such that if they do not peacefully embrace, they will strangle each other.[85] Since there appears to be no compelling reason to do the latter, it seems reasonable to do the former.

The *Megali Idea* is dead; it died in 1922 on the Anatolian battlefield. There is no Turkish irredenta in former Ottoman, now Greek, territories. It would be incorrect at any rate to view the Cyprus issue in this fashion because Cyprus is not and never has been part of modern Greece. Despite ethnic differences and incompatibilities, and in the face of tragic historic reminiscences, the national security of Greece and Turkey remains interdependent because of common Western orientations and the geographical realities. A Communist regime in Athens would achieve Turkey's encirclement; an anti-Western policy in Ankara would be a vital blow to Greece's security. It is an essential of elementary self-interest and political-strategical rationale that these two countries continue to collaborate. Turkish–Greek cooperation remains a postulate of the Atlantic alliance and a prerequisite of its defense policy in the eastern Mediterranean.

Lausanne did not entirely disengage Turco–Greek ethnic entanglements. The historic presence of Greeks in former Constantinople was to be maintained. The Oecumenical Patriarch of the Eastern Christian Church was then inconceivable apart from his ancient see. The autochthonous Greek population on the two Turkish islands in the Aegean was not to be subjected to compulsory exchange. Similarly, the compact Turkish settlement in Greek western Thrace was exempted from this exchange. Turkey and Greece mutually voiced often well-founded complaints concerning the status of these minorities. Injustice and ill treatment were generally the consequence of a political crisis in the Greek–Turkish relationship. Failing such crises, all the differences could be and should be negotiable and reconcilable.[86]

The Dodecanese Islands present another type of conflict. The Turkish minority (about 25,000, mostly on the Island of Rhodes) was not mentioned either in the Peace Treaty of Lausanne or by the Convention Concerning the Exchange of Greeks and Turkish Population

[85] This idea was succinctly expressed by Deputy Kasim Gülek in the Turkish National Assembly: "The geopolitical situation necessitates Turkish–Greek cooperation. The existence of a new [Soviet] navy in the Mediterranean makes this cooperation a must." *Cumhuriyet*, February 15, 1969.

[86] Turkish and Greek chancelleries are constantly in contact on reciprocal minority questions. Complaints of discrimination are frequently examined in regular sessions. Most of the complaints are submitted by the Greek inhabitants of Istanbul and the Turks of western Thrace. There were relatively few cases of discrimination presented by the Greeks of Imroz and Bozcaada (a population of about 4,000).

of January 30, 1923, because these islands passed under Italian sovereignty after World War I. After their cession by Italy to Greece in 1947, the Greek government maintained that no Turkish-Greek agreement applied to that ethnic minority, whereas the legal view of the Turkish government was that they were entitled to protection under the Lausanne treaty as nonexchangeable Muslim-Turks. It appeared that, leaving aside the juridical side of the question, a *de facto* solution for their nondiscriminatory treatment could easily be reached.

The Turkish press occasionally complained that the Greeks had violated their international commitments concerning the demilitarization of the Aegean Islands of Mytilene, Chios, Samos, and Rhodes. Construction of military jet airfields was also protested.[87] The Turkish government at first denied having information confirming such statements. In April 1969, Greek Prime Minister Papadopoulos spoke of these airfields as serving tourism and denied hostile intentions.[88] But in July 1969, Ankara protested to Greece against "illegal military preparations" in the Aegean Islands under the pretense of building tourist airfields.[89]

These and other frictions were inevitable, but there was no reason to believe that they could not be settled by patient negotiation and a modicum of good will. There remained only Cyprus, a thorny issue that did not lend itself to compromise.

The denunciation of the Zurich-London agreements by Makarios, the renewed fighting and massacres on Cyprus, the *de facto* Greek-Cypriote government, and the temporary Turkish administration of Turkish Cypriotes created additional problems and attitudes.

In the view of the Turkish government (and political parties in Turkey) and the Turkish Cypriote community, President Makarios blatantly had violated the international agreements entered into by Cyprus and the constitution adopted in 1960. Ankara insisted throughout that the treaties which it had concluded with Britain, Greece, and the Republic of Cyprus

---

[87] See *Hürriyet*, January 5, 6, 1969; *Cumhuriyet*, July 23, 1969. The press reports also referred to the alleged remilitarization of the Island of Lemnos, though this island was not listed in Article 13 of the Treaty of Lausanne as one to be demilitarized.

[88] Papadopoulos said in an interview: "True, we have a military base in Rhodes. It is common knowledge. We have military schools in the islands of Samos and Chios. New recruits are trained there. But they do not stay there constantly. . . . The jet airfields are entirely for civil aviation, for tourism. . . . When these airfields are built you will be able to come and see them. We sincerely believe that we cannot solve our problems with Turkey with soldiers and airfields." *Hürriyet*, April 13, 1969.

[89] *Zafer*, July 29, 1969.

continued to be the valid international instruments governing the relations of these powers with Cyprus, and the constitution remained the basic law of the Cypriote republic.

Turkey invoked the basic norm of international law, *pacta sunt servanda*, that treaties have to be observed. In particular, the reasons Makarios gave for invalidating the agreements were described as wanton, unfounded, arbitrary, and irresponsible.[90]

The Greek Cypriotes maintained that the rules accepted in Zurich and London, to which the constitution was adapted, had been worked out without consultation with "local experts." After years of attempts to operate on the basis of the constitution, the document had proved to be "inapplicable, unenforceable, and unworkable." It had to be set aside when a revision, according to its own provisions, became impossible. Yet, the treaties and constitution were concluded in the hope that they could meet the political requirements—*rebus sic stantibus* (as circumstances presented themselves at that time). Subsequently, their inadequacy and inapplicability had become evident; this justified—according to this view—the Cypriote government's not considering them binding any longer.[91]

In this way, the two international legal maxims, *pacta sunt servanda* and *rebus sic stantibus*, inexorably opposed each other in the assertions of the Turks and the Greeks.

To an impartial observer it must rather be clear that Makarios, by unilaterally releasing himself from the obligations of international treaties and a constitution freely accepted, had acted as a judge in his own case. He had failed to show patience and flexibility in applying the constitutional provisions and had proceeded, in any case, with undue haste. It was

---

[90] See the speech of Feridun Cemal Erkin, foreign minister of Turkey, before the United Nations General Assembly on January 25, 1965; *Turkish Yearbook of International Relations, 1965*, pp. 173–93.

[91] The Supreme Court of Cyprus (following the inactivation of the constitution, the Supreme Constitutional Court and the High Court of Justice, their neutral presidents having withdrawn, were merged into a Supreme Court) never held that the constitution was no longer valid; it only held that it could not be applied for physical or other compelling reasons in certain respects. For instance, the constitution did provide that all laws be promulgated in both Greek and Turkish; because there were no Turkish print-setters available, the Turkish texts could not be printed but the laws would still be valid, despite this deficiency in their publication. Information provided to this writer by Michael A. Triantafyllides, acting president of the Supreme Court of Cyprus.

open to him to submit his case to either the Security Council or the General Assembly of the United Nations or, with the consent of the other parties, to the International Court of Justice. But he preferred to act arbitrarily and only asked the General Assembly *ex post facto* for a confirmation of his unilateral act.[92]

Although the United Nations was not authorized by its charter to invalidate international agreements, a discussion of the topic in the world arena might have led to a consensus among the parties on revising the original texts. The Turks were certainly within their legal rights when they considered this action illegal and a violation of international agreements. No wonder they were surprised when the major Western powers did not rally to their side. Nor was the honor of the Afro-Asian majority in the General Assembly enhanced when they, at least implicitly, expressed sympathy for this breach of international and constitutional law. The loss of faith in the sanctity of treaties is bound to haunt relations between Turks and Greeks, and it is difficult to foresee how and under what conditions new agreements can be reached now that existing arrangements have been unscrupulously discarded.[93]

Ignoring or invalidating the Zurich–London agreements and the constitution based on those arrangements has led to a reversion to former political positions. In this respect, Makarios' stand appeared uncertain. Did he wish to attempt *Enosis* or, as he openly stated, to accept the statehood of a completely independent Cyprus operating with a unitary constitutional system? The reappearance of Grivas and the resumption of his activities, carried out with at least the passive approval of the archbishop-president, may lead one to believe that the goal was again union with Greece. Grivas, no doubt, was an uncompromising believer in a

---

[92] See the article by Christian Heinze, "Der Zypern-Konflikt, eine Bewährungsprobe westlicher Friedensordnung," *Europa-Archiv*, 1964, pp. 712–26 (the article was also published under the title, "The Cyprus Conflict: The Western Peace System Is Put to Test," in the *Turkish Yearbook of International Relations, 1962*, pp. 44–62). Heinze was assistant to Professor Ernst Forsthoff when the latter was president of the Supreme Constitutional Court of Cyprus.

[93] The Greek Cypriote argument that the restrictions on the sovereignty of Cyprus, imposed by the Zurich-London Agreements, were incompatible with the Charter of the United Nations and, therefore, became void when Cyprus was admitted to the World Organization, is more specious than correct. Admission cannot be an excuse for jettisoning burdensome treaty commitments; one of the conditions for membership is willingness to comply with international obligations (Article 4).

solution by force. In this he had failed and Makarios can now be credited with striving to maintain an independent Cyprus—of course, according to his lights. However, he may have not quite abandoned the concept of *Enosis* (which would deprive him of his post as a president or ethnarch); as ironic commentators suggested: Makarios would only stand up for *Enosis* on his deathbed.

Many leaders in Turkey, always discontented with the compromise settlement accepted by the Menderes government, reverted to the demand for partition as the only realistic and, for Turkey, acceptable solution.[94] The government as well as the main opposition party, however, found it more prudent to rely on the treaties of 1960 (which had given Turkey extended status in the affairs of Cyprus, including the right of intervention) but, at the same time, to advocate intercommunal talks for a domestic settlement, possibly within the framework of an independent Cyprus.

Since the "dual" government adopted by the 1960 constitution was declared unworkable by the Greeks, and the unitary type of government, even with the most liberal charter of minority rights for Cypriote Turks, was unacceptable to the Turkish community and Ankara, the only remaining alternative was a kind of federal or cantonal system with complete autonomy for the Turkish and Greek communities and a central governmental structure for foreign affairs, economics, and perhaps, defense.[95] Whether the autonomous Turkish area should cover 38 percent of the island, as earlier demanded, or only 20 percent or even less, was to remain a matter for bargaining.

Originally, the implementation of a federal or con-federal plan would have been more difficult and would have required relocating much of the population (if a resettlement had to be a necessary element of the

[94] In January 1969, the Turkish National Assembly discussed the problem of Cyprus. Nation Party chairman, Osman Bölükbaşı, asked for *Taksim*, "the most suitable solution in order to prevent future clashes between Turkey and Greece." Leaders of the National Action Party (former Republican Peasant Nation Party) and of the New Turkey Party also suggested partition, while Mehmet Ali Aybar, chairman of the Turkish Labor Party, opposed it. *Cumhuriyet*, January 23, 1969.

[95] During the January 1939 debate on Cyprus in the National Assembly, Foreign Minister Çağlayangil said: "The Turkish Community emphasizes the necessity of local autonomy." Ismet Inönü, chairman of the Republican People's Party, noted: "The other side refrains from using the word 'federation' as it does with 'partition.' The federal system is inevitable. We hope the Government is working for federation." *Cumhuriyet*, January 23, 24, 1969.

plan).[96] But, due to the internecine war, the intermingling of Greeks and Turks had ended, to a considerable extent, and the two ethno-religious communities were more separated physically by the events than ever before.

If it came to the adoption of a federal system of goverment with geographical separation, Makarios might find that he had exchanged the better for the worse. Instead of the "dual" governmental structure that was abhorrent to him, he might have to accept a topographically separated Turkish community, a possible prelude to partition. The unilateral action of the Greek Cypriote leaders, as well as the renewed violence, has led to an estrangement (and physical separation) of the two communities never experienced before; this almost amounts to a *de facto* partition of the island.

The establishment of the temporary or provisional Turkish administration in Cyprus, announced as an "emergency measure," was the direct consequence of the factual separation of the Turkish ethnic element from the rest of the population.

Since about mid-1964, the Turks have set up and organized their enclaves and surrounded them with makeshift fortifications and barricades defended by Turkish policemen, gendarmes, and the *muharib* of the Turkish Defense Organization. Army instructors and specialists from Turkey advised or led them. Exclusive control was exercised by the Turkish leadership over these enclaves, and all Greeks—officials, armed forces, and civilians—were refused entrance. Some of these Turkish positions were facing or were surrounded by Greek Cypriote forces; in some areas United Nations forces had interposed themselves to prevent fighting.

The principal Turkish enclave consisted of Nicosia's Turkish quarter and a considerable country area north of it, including the now-famous road to Kyrenia, almost to the gates of that Greek-controlled harbor. Greek convoys were allowed to pass only when escorted by United Nations units. Most of the Turkish refugees were provisionally settled in the area of Nicosia.

Other important Turkish enclave centers were the Turkish quarters of the towns of Famagusta and Larnaca, and about forty smaller enclaves or

---

[96] Before the guerilla war, out of 619 villages, 393 were entirely or predominantly Greek, 120 Turkish, and 106 were mixed; Stephens, *Cyprus: A Place of Arms*, p. 213. In the towns, there were Turkish quarters, although Greeks and Turks often worked together.

beachheads along the coast. Even in towns and villages where there was no major fighting and where fortress-like separation had not been established (as, for instance, in the port of Limassol, where the Greek district commissioner maintained a relative peace), the Turks put themselves under the control of the Turkish administration.

The Turkish army contingent was also stationed in the Nicosia enclave, the seat of the Turkish administration. Not only was the Turkish embassy located in that area, permitting easy and swift consultation with the head of the Turkish mission, but also some government buildings, among them the Ministry of Justice, containing all the official records, including the personal registers of the population of Cyprus.

By separating itself from the rest of the island, the Turkish community incurred great hardships and material losses. The refugees, mostly villagers, left their farms behind; they had to live on relief provided by financial help from Turkey. It was estimated that the Turkish government subsidized the Cypriote Turkish community with annual amounts of $15 to $20 million in hard currency (the Cypriote pound was tied to the British pound sterling). Although much of the earlier economic pressures imposed by the government had been relaxed, Turks were still dependent on Greek permission to receive essential deliveries, including mail. Turks did not pay governmental taxes, but some indirect taxes were collected from them (by adding to commodity prices or deducting from their wages, as in the case of Turkish miners working in the copper mines). The taxes collected by the Turkish community, due to the widespread unemployment and financial distress of their members, did not come close to covering their administrative expenses. The salaries the Turkish administration could afford to pay their employees were equally modest. Nevertheless, the "provisional" state of affairs may last indefinitely.

The *de facto* partition of Cyprus, though probably more tolerable for Greeks than for Turks, was still most inconvenient to the Greek government of the island. It visually and palpably demonstrated what the Turks had always contended: that the two communities cannot coexist if one of them rules over the other. It also showed that a partition along territorial lines is not inconceivable. No doubt the Turks have proved their point: they could, though with great difficulties, live and administer themselves without the Greeks, or even against them. The Turkish enclaves also blocked communication between Greek-controlled areas, and it was a source of constant humiliation for the government that it could not subdue or come to terms with those who had destroyed the administrative unity of the island.[97]

By spring 1968, both Ankara and Athens, unable to find a solution for Cyprus, agreed to induce the two communities to attempt a solution for themselves.[98] The unexpected turn of events, based on a realization of Turkey's strength, made Makarios more flexible and ready to accept a form of compromise. The parties agreed to leave the negotiations to their most capable and flexible representatives who, at the same time, happened to be personal friends.

As noted earlier, Rauf Denktaş and Glafkos Clerides had studied law in London. They were colleagues and both began practicing law in Cyprus. When Denktaş had to flee in late 1963, Clerides looked after the family of his friend and saw to it that they joined Denktaş in Turkey.[99] In April 1968, the exile was allowed to return to his homeland and was assigned to conduct the crucial negotiations with his Greek counterpart, Clerides. It was rightly thought that such talks between Archbishop Makarios and Fazıl Küçük[100] would be doomed to failure. Still, there were almost insurmountable obstacles because of the exaggerated mutual suspicion which existed between the two communities. The opening talks had to be held outside Cyprus, in Beirut.[101] But the atmosphere improved, and in June 1968 the negotiations were moved to Cyprus.

The two representatives began their conversations from diametrically

[97] Rauf Denktaş revealed in an interview that "the Turks ruled over 12–13 percent of the total surface of Cyprus as an independent community with its independent administration, security forces, courts, tax system and everything else." *Cumhuriyet,* March 12, 1970.

[98] In February 1968, Makarios was still contemplating the introduction of a "constitutional amendment" based on his Thirteen Points. The Turkish foreign ministry stated that any change of the constitution without the participation of Turkey and the Turkish Cypriote community would be considered "null and void." *Tercüman,* February 10, 1968. In April 1968, Greek Prime Minister Papadopoulos hinted that the two Cypriote communities may find the possibility "of living better days on the island." *Hürriyet,* April 13, 1968. In May 1968, Turkish Foreign Minister Çağlayangil said that "the two communities should come together in stages" and that their representatives will soon commence talks. *Yeni Gazete,* May 10, 1968.

[99] In October 1968, Denktaş attempted a clandestine entry to Cyprus but was captured. However, he was soon allowed to return to Turkey due to the mediation of the American ambassador, Taylor G. Belcher, and with the help of Glafkos Clerides (personal information given to this writer by Ambassador Belcher and Mr. Clerides).

[100] Dr. Küçük was considered rather a symbol by 1968. There was, however, no question of his replacement because he was regarded as the legal vice-president of Cyprus under the 1960 constitution.

[101] *Cumhuriyet,* June 4, 1968.

opposite poles: the Turkish delegate took the Zurich-London agreements and the 1960 constitution as a starting point, whereas the Greek wanted a pragmatic approach—how to settle the most urgent problems of the two communities.[102] They soon met halfway and by late July 1968 were able to reach agreement on some constitutional points. When the second round of talks opened in August 1968, it became known that Clerides and Denktaş were attempting to prepare the draft of a new constitution.[103]

There was understandable impatience in Ankara over the extension of the talks. In November, the Turkish foreign minister was able to report for the first time since the outbreak of the crisis "the two sides have agreed to seek a peaceful formula based on the independence of the island."[104] As a sign of relaxation, the military service of Turkish Cypriotes was reduced from three to two years.[105]

The third phase of the talks began in January 1969, when all the constitutional points were reviewed. The regional autonomy demanded by the Turks presented the greatest stumbling block in the negotiations.[106] As a sign of further relaxation, a regular ferryboat service was opened between Mersin in Turkey and Kyrenia in Cyprus, with the approval of the Turkish administration and the Cypriote government.[107] By the summer of 1970, a draft agreement was completed which, however, left important points still open. The fourth stage of intercommunal talks, evidently initiated to fill existing gaps, began at the end of September 1970.

Should the leaders of the two communities in fact reach an agreement on an amended constitution, the guarantor powers would be only too glad to give their blessing to such a transaction. Whether the new version of the constitution proves to be workable will depend on the cooperative

---

[102] Information provided to this writer by Mr. Denktaş and Mr. Clerides.

[103] Denktaş said that a draft of a new constitution would be prepared at the talks. "The states which signed the Zurich Agreement will review our work and a new agreement will be signed concerning the international status of Cyprus. Therefore, our path is a long one." *Hürriyet,* August 2, 1968.

[104] *Hürriyet,* November 4, 1968.

[105] *Hürriyet,* October 10, 1968.

[106] "There is a difference of opinion between Turks and Greeks about regional autonomy in Cyprus. We want a two-level administration on the island. The first should be a central government, the other an autonomous administration, that is, self-government of the two communities. There are disagreements on this topic." Denktaş' statement on December 19, 1968; *Yeni Gazete,* December 20, 1968.

[107] *Cumhuriyet,* March 13, 1969.

spirit, mutual trust, fairness, and diplomatic-pragmatical skill of its oper-
ators and, indeed, on the collaboration and good will of the two ethnic
communities of Cyprus. In such a case, all that the two closely interested
countries, Turkey and Greece, could usefully do would be to abstain
from interferring in the affairs of the island. It was frequently hinted in
Cyprus, particularly by Greeks, that if the two communities would be
left alone by their protecting powers, they would be able to find a solution to their problems.[108]

Cyprus is not only a microcosm of Turkish-Greek relations, it is also a
testing ground of their mutual relations. Menderes and Karamanlis, the
two prime ministers of the Zurich–London agreements, were supposed
to have regarded Cyprus as a kind of Turkish–Greek condominium
which could have paved the way for a con-federal relationship between
the two countries. They were interlocked in Cyprus more than in any
other area of mutual interest. At this juncture, it will depend on the
developments in Cyprus whether this contact will bring them nearer to
each other or estrange them even more.

Since the end of World War II, the international status of Turkey
and Greece has developed along remarkably parallel lines: both were
subjected to Soviet-Communist pressures; both sought assistance from
the Western powers; the Truman Doctrine was simultaneously applied
to both of them; they were admitted to NATO on the same day; together
they concluded the Balkan Defense Pact with Yugoslavia; and both obtained an associate status in the European Economic Community. But
the same "geographical fatalism" that drove them along on a parallel
track brought them once more to a collision course over Cyprus.

There appears to be a paradox in Turco–Greek relations, both ethnic
and politic: logic and reason compel them to collaborate; tradition and
emotions separate them. They display hatred and contempt toward each
other, yet they are drawn together by self-interest, rivalry, or the admiration of what is different between them. Like a feuding couple they are
enthralled by the "I cannot live with you nor without you" syndrome.
If one would examine this relationship by the Bogardus method of ethnic

[108] It was felt in Turkey that should the talks fail to produce positive results Turkey
would again be compelled to take some action. This time, it was believed that Athens
would not bring pressure on Greek Cypriotes and failure to agree would be attributable
entirely to the stubbornness of Archbishop Makarios; *New York Times,* April 14, 1969.

distance, one would be bound to find an extremely wide and often shifting range of ethnic distance scales.[109]

Turkish and Greek leaders, whenever they meet, generally understand each other well and easily agree on matters relating to third nations or outside events. They are less ready to agree on matters directly affecting their own nations. Even in such a case, the atmosphere in which they negotiate, the personalities of the negotiators, and the realization of the need to reach compromise solutions would mostly induce them to reconcile their views. They might not part in full agreement, but they would not part as enemies.

Arnold J. Toynbee drew attention to the circumstances of the miraculous reconciliation of two famous statesmen: Eleutherios Venizelos and Mustafa Kemal Atatürk, the protagonists of Graeco–Turkish reconciliation of 1930. Despite the enormous differences in their careers, they shared common memories and common historic experiences. Venizelos was born in Crete, as an Ottoman subject; Atatürk was born and brought up in Salonika, then a town in Turkey, later the second city of Greece. They were the leaders of two nations which had fought a life-and-death struggle in the early 1920's. Less than ten years later they managed to unite their nations in friendship.[110]

Although they stem from different cultures, Turks and Greeks are both territorial descendants of an empire which was first Byzantine–Christian and then Ottoman–Muslim.[111] It required centuries and enormous sacrifices before it was possible to disentangle the ethnic-religious conglomeration of these succeeding empires. In Cyprus the ghost of the Roman–Ottoman imperial heritage still survived; it remains for the successors of Venizelos and Atatürk to exorcise this last remnant of theocratic-ethnic obsolescence.

The conflict over Cyprus which made Turkey and Greece once more fall apart came at a time when the two nations could "afford" to feud. In the late 1950's, Soviet pressures had given way to peaceful coexistence. As noted earlier, the case of Cyprus speeded Turkey's momentum toward

---

[109] Emory S. Bogardus, *The New Social Research* (Los Angeles, 1926), especially pp. 200–216; same author, *A Forty-Year Racial Distance Study* (Los Angeles, 1967), *passim.*

[110] In *Survey of International Affairs, 1930*, p. 167.

[111] *Ibid.*, p. 168. Toynbee also recalled that the Ottomans had been called *Rumi's* (Romans) by their Islamic neighbors of Iran and Hindustan, while Greeks were known as *Rumi's* by the Turks themselves.

gradual depolarization of her foreign policy. She needed Soviet sympathies in order to divert Moscow's support for Makarios, but Ankara could not remain unmindful of its need also to gain aid in the United Nations from Asian and African countries for its case on Cyprus. The image of Turkey as a faithful and servile follower of the Atlantic powers had to be dispelled for that reason. Turkish diplomacy went to work in an area where Ottoman influence was once paramount—the Middle East.

VII

Turkey and the Middle East

... Come along, follow me,
Sail to the West, and the
East will be found.—ARTHUR HUGH
CLOUGH, *Say Not the Struggle Naught
Availeth*

O true believers, take
your necessary precautions against
your enemies, and either go forth
to war in separate parties, or go forth
all together in a body.—THE KORAN,
Chapter 4.

T HE OTTOMAN EMPIRE ENCOM-
passed the general geographical area formerly held by the Byzantine
emperors, but the Ottomans extended their boundaries in the east beyond
those reached by the Romans. In what is now known as the Middle East,
the Ottoman sultans in large measure superseded the Arab empire of the
caliphs in their rule over Syria, Palestine, Mesopotamia, Egypt, and Hejaz,
including the Holy Cities of Mecca and Medina. The sultan's writ ran
along the northern shores of the Mediterranean to the Moroccan border,
to the Persian Gulf, and, at one time, even to the Indian Ocean at Aden.
For over four centuries, all of the ancient lands of Islam were governed
from Istanbul. These Arab regions were lost only at the end of World
War I. Former Ottoman rule has left its imprint on many aspects of
public or private life in these Arab countries.[1]

TURKS, ARABS, AND PERSIANS

The Ottoman Empire was Islamic in character; allegiance given to
the sultan-caliph was religious and dynastic. Arabs and other Muslims

[1] "The major contribution of the Ottomans was to give the Middle East a legal and
administrative system. Ottoman law influences the region to such an extent that even
today large sections of the law codes of many Middle Eastern countries bear the imprint of the Ottoman system." Benjamin Rivlin and Joseph S. Szyliowicz, *The Contemporary Middle East* (New York, 1965), p. 23.

felt that they were attached to the Ottoman system by a natural bond not dissimilar to that which in earlier centuries led them to live under the Omayyad or Abbasid dynasties.[2] Since the Ottoman sultans professed the Sunni form of Islam, they opposed the Shiites and their principal protector, the shah of Persia, the only formidable adversary of Ottoman power for centuries in the Middle East. As noted earlier, Islam has for the most part supplanted former ethnic Turkish elements, and Arab and Persian words and linguistic forms have invaded the Turkish language.

Ottoman nationalism, the concept both adopted and dropped in the nineteenth century, attempted to include both Muslims and non-Muslims in a form of secular allegiance to the dynasty. In the late nineteenth century, Sultan Abdul Hamid II revived Pan-Islamism, with some success in Muslim countries outside the empire but with meager results among the Arabs. At that time, Arab nationalism turned against Turkish–Ottoman rule. During World War I the Arab provinces seceded from the Ottoman Empire, which subsequently disintegrated.

By its very nature, the new Turkish republic was antithetical to the former universal Islamic state. The ties which bound the latter to all Muslims, especially the people of the Prophet, were severed. Still, past history and the former symbiosis of Turks and Arabs could not be so quickly effaced. The common religious background remained a connecting bridge between Turks and Arabs.

The ambivalence which thereafter governed the relations between the two nations grew out of this cleavage between past and present. Arabs were inclined to resent Turkish secularism, which they regarded as a kind of treachery against the ancient faith and culture originally imparted by them to the Turks. They also remembered with resentment their centuries-old domination by the Ottomans. On the other hand, modernist Turks were proud that they had advanced toward Western civilization and looked down on the backwardness of the Arabs. Ankara fought hard to discard much of the Arab influence on Turkish culture and language: it dropped the use of the Arab characters and successfully introduced in their stead Latin script, an action most displeasing to Arab pride.

Differing national characters lent themselves to disparaging comparisons between Turks and Arabs. The former considered the latter

---

[2] See Bernard Lewis, "Turkey: Westernization," in *Unity and Variety in Muslim Civilization,* ed. Gustave E. von Grunebaum (Chicago, 1955), p. 314.

undisciplined and unreliable; they recalled their poor military performance in service with the Ottoman army. The Arabs, in return, were
likely to regard Turks as domineering, brutal, and slow-witted. National
incompatibilities, especially in the early stages of political severance,
weighed heavily on the Arab–Turkish rapport.

As was the case in the rest of the Near and Middle East, it proved impossible to draw strictly ethnic lines between the Arab and Turkish
populations along the Anatolian and Syrian and the Anatolian–Iraqi
borders. The ensuing conflicts have continued to impair relations between
Turkey and the two Arab states bordering her in the southeast.

At the end of World War I, Turkey failed to hold on to the oil-rich
Mosul district, an ethnically mixed area in which Kurds were in the
majority.[3] She was able to make good her claim to the district of Alexandretta which, under the name of Hatay, she incorporated in 1939. The
Iraqi border region, the area of Kurdish uprisings (later of the *de facto*
Kurdish "state"), continued to be a trouble spot not only for the rulers
of Baghdad but also their Turkish neighbor (see below, p. 301). Furthermore, the annexation of Hatay created a lasting Syrian irredenta
feeling.

In the interwar period, the formerly Ottoman-ruled Arab regions,
with the exception of Hejas, were administered as mandated territories
by Britain and France under the supervision of the League of Nations.
Only Iraq was granted independence in 1932, although British forces continued to garrison the country. Even if she had wished, Turkey could not
have pursued a particular foreign policy toward these colonial or semi-
colonial countries; her relations with Britain and France determined her
attitude toward territories under mandate or controlled by one or the
other European power, such as in the case of Egypt. In any event, the
Turkey of Atatürk hardly desired involvement in the politics of the Arab
countries, in their ambitions for independence, or in their struggle against
the colonial powers.

The eastern neighbor of Turkey is Iran (Persia), which, like Turkey,
has never been subjected to colonial rule but has gathered considerable
historic experience in her dealings with European powers, including
Russia. Her contacts with the expansionist Muscovite empire paralleled
those of the Ottomans; for over two hundred years Moscow managed to

[3] See chapter I, pp. 20–21.

slice off territory after territory from Persia or to occupy Persian territories for shorter or longer periods of time.

Previous to the Russian danger, the Ottoman Empire and Persia had fought each other since the sixteenth century; their reciprocal boundaries were settled in 1732 and did not change significantly thereafter. No ethnically Persian area was ever annexed by the Ottomans; perhaps, for this reason, Turkish popular evaluation of Persians differed from that of the Arabs. Persians were considered refined, somewhat haughty, brave, but unsteady. Turks would remind the listener that many of their kinsmen lived in Persia and that Persians had frequently been ruled by Turkish dynasties or had followed Turkish generals into battle.

The Persian culture (language and literature), like the Arab, made great inroads into the Ottoman mind. In fact, Ottoman cultural life rested on an amalgam of Arab, Persian, and Turkish influences; the knowledge of these three tongues was the test of being educated, just as the knowledge of French was the hallmark of culture for Europeans of the eighteenth century.

Because of her closer geographical location to Europe and more intimate contacts with the West, Turkey, more than Persia, entered much earlier and more intensely upon the path of modernization. When the Kemalist reforms were introduced in Turkey and adopted by the educated classes, their cultural community was severed from not only the Arab but also from the Persian world. Although the Persians, unlike Turks and Arabs, speak an Indo-European language, the Europeanization attempted by Turks would have been impossible for them.

The foundation of Persian national self-consciousness is an outstanding pre-Islamic culture and a glorious ancient history. Arabs were the people of the Prophet and the ones who carried his teachings into three continents. Turks, however, had a scanty pre-Islamic history and a relatively small cultural heritage from that period (except, of course, their language, which essentially differentiated them from their non-Turkic neighbors). Less burdened by the Islamic or pre-Islamic past, they were freer to seek assimilation with the European West. Arabs or Persians could not readily follow this road without relinquishing cultural and national identity.

During the Turkish war of independence, the non-Arab Muslim nations generally sympathized with the cause of new Turkey. One of the first countries with which the new government in Ankara concluded a treaty was Afghanistan, but after the end of this war, and due to Atatürk's secular and often anti-Islamic reforms, the Muslim communities all over the world expressed coolness or even outright hostility. From India to Morocco, the abolition of the caliphate was considered a blow against Islam.[4]

These drastic reforms even created obstacles to Turkey's relations with Muslim powers. For instance, the interdiction regarding headgear caused diplomatic incidents;[5] Muslim pilgrims to Turkish shrines were prevented from wearing their traditional turbans; and Turks were dissuaded from participating in the Hajj, the pilgrimage to the Holy City of Mecca, an act which strained relations between Ankara and Saudi Arabia.

The independent Muslim states of Persia (since 1935 officially known as Iran) and Afghanistan soon attempted to follow Turkey's lead at least partially. The ruler of Iran, Riza Shah Pahlevi, was a great admirer of Atatürk and undertook to copy his work, but conservatism and religious forces in Iran prevented any consistent modernization containing anti-Islamic tendencies. The shah "provided no substitute for traditionalism. . . . There was no counterpart in Iran to the Kemalism in Turkey."[6] The attempts at reform undertaken by Emir Amanullah, ruler of Afghanistan and another admirer of Atatürk, led to his deposition. The initial hostility with which Kemalism was received in the Muslim world had thus given way to appreciation in both Iran and Afghanistan.

Good neighborly relations did develop with a third Muslim country bordering Turkey—namely, Iraq. Soon after gaining independence, King Feisal visited Ankara to reassure himself that the Mosul dispute was genuinely closed. When the danger of war appeared on the diplomatic horizon, as a consequence of Hitler's and Mussolini's aggressive policies, Turkey became feverishly engaged in securing her borders against a potential attack by concluding alliances and treaties of nonaggression, an activity which at that time already was characterized as "pactomania." Under the impact of a threatening war, Turkey turned her attention to the

---

[4] See *Survey of International Affairs, 1925,* vol. I, pp. 51–91. Comments written by Arnold J. Toynbee.

[5] The Egyptian ambassador who was wearing a fez at one of Atatürk's receptions was told by the Turkish president to remove his headgear. Atatürk also told him: "Tell your King I don't like his uniform." This incident almost led to a rupture of diplomatic relations between the two countries. See Kinross, *Atatürk,* p. 525.

[6] Richard H. Pfaff, "Disengagement from Traditionalism in Turkey and Iran," in *Contemporary Middle East,* eds. Rivlin and Szyliowicz, p. 422.

east but only after solidifying treaties with Russia, an alliance with Greece, and the Balkan Entente. The immediate motivation for this search for cordial relations with Asian countries was Mussolini's chimerical plan of expansion into Africa and Asia.[7] No doubt, the successful conclusion of the Ethiopian campaign led Turkey's leaders to overestimate the Italian military potential. The hollowness of the Fascist threat was recognized only during World War II.

Under Turkish initiative, the independent governments of western Asia—Turkey, Iran, Iraq, and Afghanistan—concluded in Teheran on July 8, 1937, the Middle Eastern Pact, otherwise known as the Saadabad Pact, named after the palace where the signing took place.[8] It would be an exaggeration to consider this diplomatic instrument anything more than a weak nonaggression treaty. Nevertheless, because it was the first collective treaty among the nations of the northern tier, it gained distinction as a far-reaching precedent.[9]

World War II and its aftermath rendered the Saadabad Pact as meaningless as Turkey's western reinsurance treaties proved to be. The Middle East became involved in the war, whereas Turkey managed to stay out.

Unmindful of Syrian protests, the French surrendered Hatay to Turkey shortly before the outbreak of hostilities. Between France's collapse and the take-over by British forces in 1941, Syria and Lebanon were controlled by the Vichy government and infiltrated by German agents. In 1941 a pro-German government in Iraq was suppressed by Allied forces. In August 1941, Soviet troops from the north and British troops from the south penetrated Iran and established contact. The unstable Middle

[7] On March 19, 1935, Mussolini outlined his program: "The historical objectives of Italy have two names: Asia and Africa. . . . These objectives are justified by geography and history. Of all the great Western Powers of Europe, the nearest to Africa and Asia is Italy. . . . There is no question of territorial conquests . . . but of a natural expansion which will lead to a close cooperation between Italy and the nations of the Near and Middle East. . . . Italy can do this: her position on the Mediterranean, a sea which is resuming its historic function as a link between East and West, gives her this right and imposes on her this duty." Quoted from Türkkaya Ataöv, "Turkish Foreign Policy: 1923–1938," *Turkish Yearbook of International Relations, 1961*, pp. 135–36.

[8] For the text of the treaty, see *Documents on International Affairs, 1937*, pp. 530–33.

[9] The Saadabad Pact was never denounced and so, technically, is still in force. After World War II, it was simply "forgotten." See Mehmet Gönlübol and Cem Sar, "1919–1938 Yılları arasında Türk Dış Politikası" (Turkish Foreign Policy Between 1919–1938) in *Olaylarla Türk Dış Politikası (1919–1965) (Events of Turkish Foreign Policy, 1919–1965)* (Ankara, 1968), pp. 101–2.

East caused almost as many anxieties for Ankara as the developments in the Balkans.

For Turkey, however, the most critical events in Iran took place after the war, when Moscow refused to withdraw its forces from that country. The establishment of the Soviet-sponsored governments in Iranian Azerbaijan and Kurdistan, at the very doorsteps of Turkey, threatened her with being outflanked by the Soviets from the East, as she was threatened by a similar Soviet move on her west in Greece. The common interests of Turkey and Iran in thwarting Soviet expansion were very much in evidence in the postwar years and the memories of this common danger have not faded away.

Iran's response to Soviet encroachments on her territory at that time were different from the adamant attitude Turkey could display in 1945 and 1946. There were no Soviet forces on Turkey's soil, while Iran, militarily helpless, had to rely fully on Western assistance and on her own diplomatic subtlety. For Ankara, it was a profound relief when Soviet forces finally were withdrawn from Iran, pressured to do so by the United States and Britain, and persuaded by brilliant Iranian statecraft.[10] The Iranians could pride themselves, as do the Turks, that they know "how to handle the Russians"; only their methods are different.

The postwar situation in the Middle East differed essentially from the situation Turkey faced after World War I. It was no longer permissible for her to regard her Middle Eastern border as an area of third-rate diplomatic interest. All the mandated territories of World War I vintage had become independent states; Palestine was divided between the new states of Israel and Transjordan (which assumed the name of Jordan). The British (as the French had earlier) pulled out of Syria and Lebanon and were withdrawing from Iraq, Jordan, and Egypt. Affairs relating to the vast Arab territories could no longer be handled via London or Paris.

In the Middle Eastern area, Turkey is the most populated and most powerful state. Despite being a secularized Muslim nation, she was credited with having greater affinities with the peoples of the area and a better capability of dealing with them than the European West. Britain,

---

[10] Six months after the Soviet withdrawal, Iranian troops moved into Iranian Azerbaijan and the "Democratic National Autonomous Government" collapsed. It should be mentioned that the Azerbaijani pro-Soviet leaders were local Turks; nevertheless, Ankara disclaimed any interest in their political survival. The "Independent Kurdish Republic of Mahabad" was also easily suppressed by the Iranian military in December 1946.

particularly, urged Ankara to initiate diplomatic moves in order to co-alesce and organize these regions into a group of countries friendly to the principal political objective of the West: the containment of the Soviet–Communist danger.

Since the end of the war, the idea of Arab unity had gained consider-able ground among Arab leaders. The outward manifestation of this goal came in 1945 when the pact of the Arab League was signed on March 22 by Syria, Transjordan, Iraq, Saudi Arabia, Lebanon, Egypt, and Yemen.[11] The members of the league entered into an Arab Collective Security Pact in 1950, which bound them to provide armed assistance to any of them if attacked.[12]

The Arab League was originally founded with the approval of the British government. Less than ten years later, however, under the influence of nationalist Egypt, it became the main instrument of anti-colonial and anti-Western antagonism. By 1951 both London and Ankara realized that Middle Eastern collaboration had to be sought outside the framework of the league.

London and Washington approached France and Turkey to sponsor the establishment of a Middle Eastern Command. Turkey agreed only after her admission to NATO had been secured. Egypt was the first Arab state to be invited to join this defense organization; in October 1951, Cairo responded with a final "No" to the invitation, a gesture which killed the entire project.[13] A new attempt was made to seal off the Middle East from potential Soviet aggression and to set up a connecting link be-tween NATO and the Southeast Asia Collective Defense Treaty group (SEATO), which came into being at Manila on September 8, 1954. The structure of the parallel Middle Eastern defense organization was to be built step by step. Its principal promoter was the American secretary of state, John Foster Dulles, whose lightning-like journeys into the area served to persuade the interested governments to join the scheme; United States military and economic assistance provided another, in some cases perhaps the most persuasive, inducement.

Once it was clear that the bulk of Arab states would not join, the northern tier concept was thought to be the most promising path toward

---

[11] For text see Hurewitz, *Diplomacy*, vol. II, pp. 245–49. Subsequently, Libya, Sudan, Morocco, Tunisia, Algeria, Kuwait, and South Yemen joined the Arab League.
[12] *Ibid.*, pp. 311–14.
[13] John C. Campbell, *Defense of the Middle East* (New York, 1958), pp. 39–48.

establishing a chain of allied powers along the southern border of the Soviet Union. The new alliance was a geographical scheme similar to the Saadabad Pact except that Afghanistan was excluded and Iraq was included. Although the Saadabad Pact was in no way directed against Moscow, there was no doubt in the minds of the signatories of the Baghdad Pact that, this time, it was the fear of Soviet-Communist expansion or aggression that prompted their action.

FROM THE BAGHDAD PACT TO CENTO

Before the signing of the SEATO pact, two bilateral treaties led to the conclusion of a collective defense instrument in the Middle East. In both cases, Turkey acted as the promoter of a plan masterminded by Washington and London.

The first was a Treaty of Friendly Cooperation between Turkey and Pakistan dated April 2, 1954.[14] The second treaty, much stronger in its terms, stipulated cooperation for mutual security and defense and was concluded on February 24, 1955, between Turkey and Iraq. Both agreements were preceded by preliminary negotiations conducted during various state visits. The Turco–Iraqi document was signed by the Turkish prime minister, Adnan Menderes, and by the prime minister of Iraq, Nuri as-Said, as well as by the two ministers of foreign affairs, assembled in the city of Baghdad.[15]

At the time of the talks which resulted in the signing of the two treaties, strategical and political considerations determined the selection of the two states invited to join the Western anti-Communist camp. In the case of Pakistan, her participation was essential in completing the connecting chain between SEATO and the Middle East. Pakistan was ready to join both defense organizations; more to gain strength in her rivalry with India over Kashmir than because of apprehension of possible Soviet aggression. Previously, Washington had vainly tried to include India in a defensive alliance; Nehru, like Nasser, rebuffed any such offer. Afghanistan—another member of the northern tier—had to be excluded

---

[14] For text see *Documents on International Affairs, 1954*, pp. 185–86.

[15] The text is published in *Documents on International Affairs, 1955*, pp. 287–89. Regarding the circumstances of the history and signature of this treaty, see Waldemar J. Gallman, *Iraq Under General Nuri* (Baltimore, 1964), pp. 21–65. For Iraqi politics until 1958, see Khadduri, *Independent Iraq*, 1960.

because of her quarrels with Pakistan over the so-called Pushtunistan border area.

Iraq's candidacy was sought partly because of her geographical location and partly because of the likelihood that she would act as a counterweight to Egypt. Turkey particularly favored Iraq's inclusion. She saw that a Soviet thrust into the Iranian–Turkish border region could, with the use of tactical atomic weapons, be stopped along the range of the rugged Zagros Mountains in the border area of Iran, Iraq, and Turkey.[16] The Turco–Iraqi Pact, like that concluded between Turkey and Pakistan, contained an accession clause:

This Pact shall be open for accession to any member of the Arab League or any other State concerned with the security and peace in this region and which is fully recognized by both of the High Contracting Parties. Accession shall come into force from the date on which the instrument of accession of the State concerned is deposited with the Ministry for Foreign Affairs of Iraq.[17]

In order to increase the prestige of Iraq and to make the new defensive alliance more acceptable to other Arab states, it was decided that Pakistan, Britain, and Iran should accede to the Turco–Iraqi Pact instead of the somewhat weaker agreement signed with Pakistan. On April 4, 1955, Britain adhered to the pact, thereby terminating at the same time her Treaty of Alliance with Iraq of 1930 and relinquishing her right to maintain bases in that country. Pakistan joined on September 23, 1955, and finally Iran signed on November 3, 1955.[18] The first meeting of the Permanent Council of the alliance resolved to call it the Baghdad Pact Treaty Organization.

The triumph of Turkish and Western diplomacy in creating the Middle Eastern version of NATO was, however, far from perfect. Already the Turco–Pakistani Treaty, followed by American military assistance to Pakistan, had elicited heavy criticism from India, where it was regarded as a hostile action. For many years thereafter Nehru's India was inclined to look upon Turkey as a tool of the "imperialist" West, and the relations between the two countries remained cool and restrained.

---

[16] See *Survey of International Affairs, 1954*, pp. 206–7. This strategical consideration which suggested the inclusion of Iraq in 1954 is the source of the belief widely held in Turkey that the eastern portion of her country would be evacuated under NATO plans in case of a Soviet invasion.

[17] Article 5, par. 1.

[18] Texts in *Documents on International Affairs, 1955*, pp. 293–309.

Even more vehement were the reactions of the Arab states to Iraq's "traitorous" act. India charged Pakistan with deserting the neutralist camp; Nasser and other Arab nationalist leaders accused Baghdad of having violated Arab solidarity, for no member of the Arab League was allowed to enter into an alliance with non-Arab states. The force of Arab nationalism, significantly underrated by the West and Turkey, as well as by the leaders of Iraq, began to challenge the "renegade" Arab country that dared to join this "colonialist" alliance. Iraq and her pro-Western leader, Nuri as-Said, were even accused of playing into the hands of the Zionists, the arch-enemies of the Arabs, by trying to disrupt a "united Arab front."[19]

Under such unfavorable psychological pressures, it proved impossible to persuade other Arab states, even Jordan, to join the Baghdad Pact. Ankara tried in vain to influence Syria by measures which ran the spectrum from all the tools of diplomacy to troop concentrations. In a like manner, Lebanon declined. The Jordanian leaders were dissuaded from adhering to the Baghdad Pact by popular demonstrations. Nasser, in his counter-offensive, formed a new security pact with Syria, Saudi Arabia, and the Yemen, with plans for joint military command and common foreign policy.

Nasserite anti-imperialist propaganda was directed against Turkey as well. From early 1954, diplomatic contacts between Cairo and Ankara were almost totally eliminated when Egypt expelled the Turkish ambassador, Hulûsi Fuat Tugay, for having "offended the Government." The Egyptian press inveighed against Turkey's "anti-Arab policy."[20]

Another, and perhaps the most important deficiency of the Baghdad Pact was the formal absence of the United States. Although John Foster Dulles was one of the principal protagonists that brought the pact into being, Washington preferred to stay outside, at least for the time being. This caution was prompted by the desire not to antagonize either Egypt and Saudi Arabia, or Israel. The American administration evidently feared that the pact would have a very rough passage in the Senate.

---

[19] The Baghdad Pact was certainly not pro-Israeli. The government of Israel considered it hostile. Accession by Israel was ostentatiously barred; it was open only to governments recognized by both (Turkey and Iraq) parties. Nuri as-Said was used to refer to two dangers: communism and zionism, which threatened Iraq (see Gallman, *Iraq*, p. 169). During the Israeli campaign against Egypt in 1956, Iraq sent troops to protect Jordan.

[20] Jäschke, *Die Türkei in den Jahren 1952–1961*, p. 27.

The most unpleasant by-product of the Baghdad Pact was the rather unexpected involvement of the Soviet Union in the affairs of the Middle East—an involvement which might be dated from the year 1955. At that time Moscow sent notes of protest to all participants in the new pact. What was worse, it began sending arms to Egypt. It soon became clear that the fear of communism meant very little to Arab nationalists compared to the fear of zionism.

The year 1956 marked the turning point for Western and Turkish politics in the Middle East. The diplomatic offensive, which led to the conclusion of the Baghdad Pact, was to be transformed into a rear-guard action. The abortive Suez expedition of Britain and France (which temporarily made Washington and Moscow seem to act jointly against America's allies), the military victory of Israel, the sad picture of dissension in the West, and, finally, the protection which Moscow professed to have offered to a beleaguered Egypt, turned the Muslim members of the Baghdad Pact into bewildered spectators and presaged the collapse of this alliance.

The failure at Suez greatly reduced British prestige in the Middle East and enhanced Nasser's influence. The Baghdad Pact powers, with Turkey prominent among them, besought Washington to join the alliance; other NATO powers were also encouraged to join. After the inglorious experience of Suez, however, Washington was even less willing to assume formal membership. Instead, it produced the Eisenhower Doctrine to allay anxieties of pro-Western Arab leaders, to give encouragement to members of the Baghdad Pact, and at the same time to please Israel—all without provoking Arab nationalists or giving offense to neutralists, like Nehru. In a special address to Congress, President Eisenhower stated on January 5, 1957, that recent events indicated that the purpose of Soviet activity in the Middle East was to dominate or communize that area. The president invited Congress to authorize economic cooperation and programs of military assistance, including the deployment of United States forces to nations requesting such aid. The proposals contained in the presidential message were endorsed by a Joint Resolution of Congress on March 9, 1957. What was then known as the Resolution on the Middle East is more currently called the Eisenhower Doctrine.[21]

[21] For the President's address, see *Documents on International Affairs, 1957*, pp. 234–39; for the Joint Resolution of Congress, *ibid.*, pp. 267–69.

The Eisenhower Doctrine only partially and temporarily satisfied the need to fill the "vacuum" created by the withdrawal of British influence. Only Lebanon and Iraq formally accepted the assistance offered by the United States; Jordan accepted American financial aid later, without reference to the Eisenhower Doctrine.[22]

In the Arab world the post-Suez developments were influenced by Nasser's attempts to extend his authority over other Arab countries. Syria appeared to be most willing to go along with Egyptian leadership; others refused to become subservient to Nasser's wishes. Several minor crises, such as the internal convulsions of Jordan and the jockeying for position in Syria, kept Turkey and other Baghdad Pact members alert. In September 1957, Moscow accused Turkey of having aggressive designs on Syria.[23]

The year 1958 was the closing chapter of Turkey's post-World War II involvement in the affairs of the Arab countries. The dramatic events of that year started with the announcement of a union between Egypt and Syria on February 1, 1958, to be named the United Arab Republic. Nasser characterized this move as the first step toward the unification (evidently under his authority) of all Arab lands.[24] Following quick consultation with Ankara, Iraq and Jordan countered this action on February 12 by establishing their own federation known as the Arab Union. Turkey predictably recognized the federation a scant six days later.[25] It was a clear confrontation between Nasser, backed by the Soviet Union, and Nuri as-Said, who again became prime minister of Iraq, supported by the Baghdad Pact nations and the United States.

In the spring of 1958 internal strife erupted in Lebanon, fomented by pro-Nasserite elements. A civil war developed, supported from Syria. Neither appeals to the United Nations nor to the council of the Arab League helped end the crisis. Lebanon was threatened with being engulfed in a revolutionary struggle and, eventually, with being taken over by pro-Nasserite nationalists. In July 1958, while President Eisenhower was considering an appeal for assistance made by the Lebanese president, Nuri as-Said sought to organize aid by the Muslim members of the Bagh-

---

[22] Campbell, *Defense of the Middle East*, pp. 120–28; *Survey of International Affairs, 1956–1958*, pp. 161–82.

[23] See chapter V, p. 175.

[24] *Survey of International Affairs, 1956–1958*, pp. 364–69.

[25] Jäschke, *Die Türkei in den Jahren 1952–1961*, p. 83.

dad Pact which were to hold a meeting in Istanbul. Turkish President Celâl Bayar had already sent a message on July 12, 1958, promising help to the president of Lebanon, Camille Chamoun. While the Turkish leaders were waiting at the Istanbul airport for the arrival of the Iraqi delegation, news reached them of the overthrow of the royal government, the murder of King Faisal II, the Crown Prince Abdul-Illah, and—as was confirmed later—the assassination of Prime Minister Nuri as-Said.[26]

Simultaneously with the crisis in Lebanon, Jordan found herself in a critical situation. In fact, Brigadier Abdul Karim Kassem, the revolutionary leader of Iraq, was one of the officers in command of the Iraqi forces assembled to move into Jordan to defend the royal regime against Nasserite revolutionaries. Jordan dissolved the federation with the new government of Iraq, which failed to continue cooperation with the Baghdad Pact secretariat. On October 23 the headquarters and secretariat of the alliance were transferred from Baghdad to Ankara.[27]

On July 15 American forces landed in Beirut (Lebanon) without incident. Two days later British airborne troops landed in Amman (Jordan). It took several months for the situation in both countries to return to normal. American forces were withdrawn by October 25, 1958, and British withdrawal was completed by November 2. Contrary to expectations, the Kassem regime refused to prostrate itself before the United Arab Republic. Thus, the Arab imbroglio did not undergo any essential changes and Nasser's union with Syria came to a dismal end in September 1961. The Eisenhower Doctrine was never employed after the Lebanese intervention, but the Baghdad Pact had to be renewed in some other form if a defense alliance east of the borders of Turkey were to be maintained.

Soon after the Iraqi revolution, representatives of the Baghdad Pact nations (except for Iraq) met on July 28 at a ministerial conference in London which was also attended by United States Secretary of State Dulles. The conference issued a declaration which concluded that

the need which called the Pact into being is greater than ever. . . . The question whether substantive alterations should be made in the Pact and its organization or whether the Pact will be continued in its present form is under consideration by the Governments concerned. However, the nations represented at the meeting

[26] For details of the Iraqui coup, see Gallman, *Iraq,* pp. 200–206.
[27] See Halûk Ülman, "İkinci Dünya Savaşından sonra Türk Dış Politikası" (Post-World War II Turkish Foreign Policy), in *Olaylarla Türk Dış Politikası, 1919–1965,* ed. Siyasal Bilgiler Fakültesi Dış Münasebetler Enstitüsü, pp. 263–69.

in London reaffirmed their determination to strengthen further their united defense posture in the area.[28]

In London the United States was again approached to join the pact. Although formal accession was again excluded, Secretary Dulles did sign the declaration containing the following commitment:

the United States, in the interest of world peace, and pursuant to existing Congressional authorization, agrees to cooperate with the nations making this Declaration for their security and defense, and will promptly enter into agreements designed to give effect to this cooperation.[29]

Pursuant to this announcement, Washington opened bilateral talks with Turkey, Iran, and Pakistan for the purpose of entering into closer association with them without fully adhering to the pact. The apparent collapse of the Baghdad Pact encouraged Moscow to open a diplomatic campaign, particularly directed against Iran, which was the most exposed member because she lacked formal commitments of assistance by the United States. Ankara, much involved at that time in the Cyprus question, was not at all pleased that the Soviet government had invoked the Persian–Soviet treaty of 1921, which gave Moscow certain rights of military intervention.[30] After having had to abandon her diplomatic inroads into the Arab Middle East, Turkey was concerned that the alliance with Iran, protecting her eastern flank, would also be lost.

Soviet attempts to frighten Iran away from closer ties with the United States speeded up negotiations. On March 5, 1959, Turkey, Iran, and Pakistan signed separate Agreements of Cooperation with the United

[28] *Documents on International Affairs, 1958*, pp. 369–70.
[29] *Ibid.*
[30] The Soviet government handed a note to Iran on October 31, 1958, warning her not to extend further her military cooperation with the United States. The note went on to say that "if anyone in Iran tries to look for security under the collapsing roof of the Baghdad Pact and under the dubious protection of foreign powers situated thousands of kilometers from Iran, such attempts, as has been shown by the experience of Iran's recent allies under the Baghdad Pact, can least of all serve this purpose." *Documents on International Affairs, 1958*, pp. 330–32. The Treaty of Friendship of 1921 contained a clause (Article VI) providing that "if a third party should attempt to carry out a policy of usurpation by means of armed intervention in Persia . . . and if the Persian Government should not be able to put a stop to such a menace . . . Russia shall have the right to advance her troops into the Persian interior." This provision was to protect the Soviets against counter-revolutionary armed attack from Iranian territory. The Iranian government, therefore, considered this clause obsolete and no longer applicable. For the text of the treaty, see Hurewitz, *Diplomacy*, vol. II, pp. 90–94.

States in Ankara.[31] The agreement with Iran included an understanding that Washington would assist her in the event of aggression; similar commitments were repeated in regard to Turkey and Pakistan, which were already covered by NATO and SEATO, respectively. Article 1 of the agreement with Turkey ran as follows:

The Government of Turkey is determined to resist aggression. In case of aggression against Turkey, the Government of the United States of America, in accordance with the Constitution of the United States of America, will take such appropriate action, including the use of armed forces, as may be mutually agreed upon and as it envisaged in the Joint Resolution to Promote Peace and Stability in the Middle East, or order to assist the Government of Turkey at its request.

Washington further undertook (Article 4) to continue furnishing military and economic assistance to Turkey, Iran, and Pakistan:

The Government of the United States of America and the Government of Turkey will cooperate with the other Governments associated in the Declaration signed at London on July 28, 1958, in order to prepare and participate in such defensive arrangements as may be mutually agreed to be desirable.

The United States liked to style itself as an "observer" in the Central Treaty Organization (CENTO), the new name adopted in August 1959. In fact, American delegates have participated in the work of all committees dealing with questions of defense, and United States forces have taken part in CENTO military exercises. Economic projects undertaken under the aegis of CENTO have been financially supported by Washington and London.

Soon after the reorganization of CENTO headquarters, its ministerial council met in October 1959 in Washington; the military weaknesses of its Middle Eastern members were particularly examined by American representatives. The next years were years of planning and building, and CENTO's refurbishment was carried out smoothly, as one astute observer noted, "without the incubus of Arab affiliations."[32]

CENTO's structure somewhat resembles NATO's, but because of British and American reluctance to develop CENTO into a "little

[31] See Ruth C. Lawson, *International Regional Organizations* (New York, 1964), pp. 246–48. These agreements, from the United States constitutional point of view, were Executive Agreements which were not submitted to the Senate for approval.

[32] John C. Campbell, *The Middle East in the Muted Cold War* (Denver, 1964–65), p. 13.

NATO," there was never an attempt to set up "integrated" forces or a joint command.

The supreme body of CENTO is the Council of Ministers, which meets annually to outline the general tasks of the organization and also serves as a forum for consultation on political, economic, and military matters. The member countries are represented at such meetings by their prime ministers or foreign ministers and other cabinet ministers. The meetings of the council have alternated among the capitals of participating states: Ankara, London, Teheran, Karachi (Rawalpindi), and Washington. The Council of Deputies meets fortnightly at CENTO headquarters in Ankara; it is formed by the ambassadors of CENTO countries accredited to Turkey and a leading official of the Turkish Ministry of Foreign Affairs.

The activities of the organization have been guided by four major committees: the Military Committee (usually composed of the Chiefs of Staff), the Economic Committee, the Counter-Subversion Committee, and the Liaison Committee (a clearinghouse for the exchange of information). The committees often form subcommittees which report to the parent committees.

The day-to-day work of the organization was carried out by the secretariat in Ankara, headed by the secretary-general, who also served as the chairman of the Council of Deputies. The Permanent Military Deputies Group (composed of Lt. Generals from the five nations) was located at the secretariat. A Combined Military Planning Staff studied and submitted defense plans for the region covered by CENTO. Each year joint training exercises were held by armed forces of CENTO countries. The organization supported various development projects which strengthened the defense and economic status of the countries concerned.

There is no doubt that from the outset CENTO was less significant and less meaningful in international politics than NATO, and contacts between Turkey and the two eastern members of the organization were and are still less intimate than those between Turkey and most of her European allies. The reasons for this reduced interest, which is reciprocated, are to be found in history, geography, and in diverging foreign policy goals. Despite the centrifugal tendencies in the relations among these three Middle Eastern nations, however, CENTO gave meaning and purpose to their association. They were also bound together by the assistance promised to them, jointly and severally, by their Western partners, the United States and Britain.

IRAN, PAKISTAN, AND CENTO

Turkey's participation in the abortive attempt to establish a military-political alliance in the Middle East with as many Arab states as might be willing to join backfired in the sense that it made her appear as a tool of "Western colonialism." In retrospect, Ankara realized that membership in the pact by one or more Arab countries would have been, in any case, a permanent burden on the alliance. The three regional powers which eventually formed CENTO—Turkey, Iran, and Pakistan—were all ethnically "loners" in the Muslim world; their people were Muslims, like the Arabs, but linguistically and ethnically they differed from the Arabs and from one another.[33]

The distance from Istanbul to Islamabad, the new capital in Western Pakistan (Eastern Pakistan is distant by another thousand miles) is nearly three thousand miles and broken by high mountain ranges, salt deserts, and arid plateaus which divide the three states. Yet, despite this, they are historically, culturally, and economically related. Historians point out that this region once belonged to the Persian Empire and was crossed by the army of Alexander the Great. For centuries this was also the great trade route between east and west; along this route economic, cultural, and hostile interactions were frequent.

All three countries have common defense problems, for which they all need assistance. If combined, their economic efforts could be crowned with greater success. Although the danger of an attack from the north seems remote at present, it cannot be entirely ignored. Even as a potential instrument, the alliance is therefore neither artificial nor purposeless.

Each of the three CENTO members, while having common interests, is intent upon pursuing foreign political goals of its own. Pakistan is disenchanted because the alliance has not brought her closer to her coveted objective: a favorable solution of the Kashmir dispute with India. Iran, with a long experience of keeping a balanced relationship with Russia in

---

[33] Like Turkey, Iran has no ethnic-religious relative among sovereign states. Pakistan, while geographically and linguistically divided, is *the* Islamic state in the subcontinent of India.

the north and Britain in the south, is more reluctantly committed to an anti-Soviet alliance than Turkey. The latter, already protected by the NATO shield and striving to be recognized as a European rather than an Asian power, considers CENTO an additional, not a primary, means of protection. Institutional divergencies in their state structures, personal motivations, and prestige questions play a much greater role in the intercourse of these three Middle Eastern powers than among the members of the Western alliance.[34] Even the religious community among the three nations may not always operate in favor of understanding.[35]

During the past few years of CENTO's existence, several plans have been worked out to facilitate military cooperation or, in case of an emergency, joint military action by the four full members of the alliance, with the active participation of the United States.[36] One may assume that at least some measure of strategical and logistical planning has been achieved. Because of the longitudinal sprawl of their national territories and the distances between their capitals, communication and transportation appeared the greatest obstacles to be overcome. In 1965 the CENTO Microwave Telecommunications Network, with 88 stations between Turkey, Iran, and Pakistan, came into operation. In the same year a high-frequency teleprinter and radio-telephone service connecting London and the three regional capitals was opened.

To improve transportation major road construction has been undertaken, which includes a northern road connecting the Turkish port of Trabzon with Teheran and a southern road to connect Iran with Iskenderun harbor. Two roads are also under construction between Iran and Pakistan. A railroad linking the Turkish network with the Iranian is already in operation; construction of a railroad line between Teheran and Zahedan, the Pakistani terminus, is well on the way.

Economically as well as strategically significant projects were under-

---

[34] It has been reported that an appointment of a joint commander of CENTO forces was prevented by the refusal of the Shah of Iran, Commander-in-Chief of Iranian armed forces, for reasons of protocol; *Neue Zürcher Zeitung*, August 16, 1962.

[35] Pakistanis are mostly Sunni Muslims, the Iranians Shiites, and Turkey is officially a "secular" state; see J. C. Hurewitz, "Regional and International Politics in the Middle East," in Georgiana G. Stevens (ed.), *The United States and the Middle East* (Englewood Cliffs, N.J., 1964), p. 105.

[36] On April 26–27, 1962, Turkish members of the military committee of CENTO, meeting in London, asked for the appointment of an American general to head the military staff of the organization, a suggestion which was opposed by other members; *Turkish Yearbook of International Relations, 1962*, p. 155.

taken with CENTO financing. Air navigational facilities have been improved and various kinds of technical assistance rendered. In the Turkish harbors of Trabzon and Iskenderun, installations have been modernized for the additional purpose of diverting Iranian trade with Europe through these outlets. A Research Institute for Nuclear and Applied Science was established at Teheran.

In February 1965, CENTO (including its first reincarnation, the Baghdad Pact) was ten years old, and it was believed that considerable progress had been made to enhance cooperation and mutual understanding among the members.[37] In the meantime, the original goal of the organization to meet, directly or indirectly, Soviet–Communist threats, seemed to have been superseded or, in the judgment of Pakistan, had become irrelevant. Nevertheless, the contacts established among the three regional governments offered so many potential advantages, especially in the areas of economics, culture, and technological development, that these were considered sufficiently worthy in themselves "to keep the candle burning."

The three Middle Eastern governments, with the blessing of the nonregional members of CENTO, set up in 1964 the Regional Cooperation for Development (RCD), a flexible program for the promotion of joint economic projects. Although a by-product of CENTO, the RCD soon outdid the mother organization in the variety and success of its achievements. Politically, the RCD cannot be accused of serving the interests of the United States or of Britain because only regional countries are its members. Thus, the latter organization is at times emphasized and CENTO de-emphasized.[38] The council meetings of the RCD are regularly attended by the foreign ministers of the three countries.

That CENTO is outdated and should be left "dormant," like the Balkan Defense Pact, has been suggested by press reports and supposedly discussed at its ministerial meetings.[39] On the other hand, it has been offi-

[37] See the message of Turkish Prime Minister Ürgüplü to Abbas Ali Khalatbary, the Iranian secretary-general of CENTO, on the occasion of this anniversary; *Turkish Yearbook of International Relations, 1965,* p. 226.

[38] The communiqué issued at the end of Turkish President Sunay's visit to Teheran in 1966 hardly mentioned CENTO but expatiated at length upon the success of the RCD; *Neue Zürcher Zeitung,* November 5, 1966. For the RCD see chapter VIII, pp. 339–43 below.

[39] *New York Times,* February 11, 1967; Ahmet Şükrü Esmer in *Ulus,* August 3, 1967, suggested that CENTO should be "put to sleep," but the RCD be enhanced. After the war with India over Kashmir in 1965, Pakistani President Ayub Khan in referring to CENTO stated: "These pacts have lost relevance" and are now "more an irritant than a help." C. L. Sulzberger in *New York Times,* March 14, 1969.

cially and repeatedly announced that there is no intention of discontinu-ing it, although its military role would be, however, de-emphasized.[40] It appears that Turkey was most emphatic in insisting on the continued importance of the organization. When the Iranian press office disclosed in Ankara the Shah of Iran's statement in New Delhi that CENTO was nothing more than a club for the discussion of economic and technical matters, the Turkish Ministry for Foreign Affairs issued a communiqué which stated that "the Turkish Government's stand on this topic is ob-vious: CENTO is a useful defense pact. It was useful in the past and it still is a source of stability in the region."[41] Foreign Minister Çağlayangil, on another occasion, defined CENTO as a "shield of defense in the region."[42]

Thus, not only is CENTO to continue but its role might again become significant, perhaps even more significant than in the past.[43] It should not be forgotten that CENTO has yet to live through a major crisis that would require military intervention. The region it encompasses has been in the past ten years immune to the kind of danger CENTO was founded to meet. The crises which occurred affected only individual members.

Pakistan, remote from the real Middle East, became a member of the Baghdad Pact and CENTO only by coincidence. The northern tier, as originally conceived, consisted only of Turkey, Iran, and Afghanistan, which (with Iraq) had concluded the Saadabad Pact in 1937. Pakistan has no direct border with the Soviet Union, and her participation in an essen-tially anti-Soviet defense treaty was rather artificial from the very outset.[44]

[40] Iranian Foreign Minister Ardeshir Zahedi reaffirmed Iran's loyalty to CENTO, denying rumors of its disbandment; *Milliyet,* October 18, 1967. Pakistan decided against leaving CENTO, the Turkish Ministry of Foreign Affairs announced; *Yeni Gazete,* September 26, 1967. The importance of the organization was underlined when the Turkish ambassador to Washington, Turgut Menemencioğlu, was elected secretary-general to succeeed Abbas Ali Khalatbary in January, 1968; *Ulus,* September 15, 1967.

[41] *Akşam,* January 16, 1969.

[42] *Dünya,* February 24, 1969.

[43] In May 1969, the Ministerial Council of CENTO met in Teheran (Secretary of State William P. Rogers attended) and focused more on problems of the Middle East than on the menace from Moscow. The Arab–Israeli war, the Shatt al Arab river border problem between Iran and Iraq, the withdrawal of Britain from East of Suez in 1971, and the Cyprus conflict figured prominently as topics of discussion. Çağlayangil ex-pressed a pessimistic tone when admitting that all these problems are "unfortunately not of a character which inspire confidence in the strengthening of hopes for a just and durable peace in the world." *New York Times,* May 27, 1969.

[44] "CENTO was misconceived because, by including Pakistan instead of Afghan-istan, the real Northern Tier nation, we injected ourselves into the Pakistan-India quarrel." C. L. Sulzberger in *New York Times,* January 28, 1966.

India was infuriated because Pakistan had departed from neutralism; she rightly attributed this move to the Pakistani desire to strengthen her armed forces—not so much to defend herself against the Soviet Union but to regain all of Kashmir.

Because Afghanistan's quarrel with Pakistan and friendly and neutral attitude toward Moscow[45] made her unavailable for membership, Pakistan was chosen by John Foster Dulles as a country whose eastern portion stretched out toward Southeast Asia. Thus, Pakistan became the connecting link between SEATO and CENTO, although, in fact, she was even less apprehensive about China than the Soviet Union.

Apart from CENTO, Pakistan was eager to maintain "special" ties with Turkey. It would be an exaggeration to maintain that Pakistan remained in CENTO because of Turkey; however, the desire not to offend Turkey certainly played a role. The foreign minister of Pakistan, Ali Zülfikar Bhutto, a convinced neutralist and an advocate of stronger ties with China and the Soviet Union, worked for a complete disengagement of his country from CENTO. Upon Bhutto's removal from office, however, Ayub Khan reverted to limited cooperation with the alliance.[46] Pakistan has not participated in CENTO military exercises since her war with India in 1965. On the other hand, she has received military help from Turkey, which tried to support Pakistan logistically during the Kashmir War.[47]

The Turco–Pakistani relationship was thus clarified in an official Turkish communiqué issued during the visit of Pakistan's Foreign Minister Arshad Hussein to Ankara:

The basic principles and objectives of the Turkish foreign policy are revealed in the Government programs. Turkey is motivated by the principle of maintaining good relations with her neighbors and all the countries of the world by remaining loyal to her treaty ties. She has no intention of establishing any mortgages on any country's foreign policy through these friendships and recognizes no mortgage on her own policy other than *her own national interests*.

Turkey's ties and heartfelt friendship with Pakistan *do not derive* from the CENTO alliance and Turkey finds no obligation to remain in this alliance at any cost in order that this friendship be continued and fortified. She believes in the existence of *much stronger ties* between the two countries. The decisions to

[45] Afghanistan was traditionally friendly toward Turkey. In the interwar period Afghan officers were trained in Turkey and at present high-ranking military leadership feels sympathetic toward Turkey.

[46] *Frankfurter Allgemeine Zeitung*, December 20, 1967.

[47] *Tercüman*, December 27, 1968.

be taken by Pakistan for her own national interests will always be received with respect and understanding by Turkey.[48]

In return, Pakistan pointed out that her friendship with Turkey is no mere "political slogan" but "a faith deriving its roots from history."[49] Pakistan supported the Turkish stand on Cyprus in the United Nations.

Because Pakistan and Turkey are not direct neighbors, friction between them can only arise from differing policies and not because of territorial contacts. With Iran, on the other hand, Turkey possesses a long and difficult frontier; relations between these two countries, though generally good or even excellent, are by no means immune to complications and conflicts.

Prior to 1732 Turkey and Iran engaged in a series of long and costly wars. Large slices of Western Iran, including the Turkish-inhabited province of Azerbaijan, with Tabriz, its capital, had been under Ottoman rule for some time. Although the border was drawn after the last war generally along the present line, a number of minor conflicts have arisen because the terrain made demarcation difficult.[50]

The real frontier problems are not those of demarcation, however; the population on both sides of the border is tribal and Kurdish. Although policing on the Turkish side of the frontier, where tribes had been officially disbanded, has greatly improved, tribal organizations continue on the Iranian side, and the authority of the central government is less complete than in the interior of the country. It was in this frontier region that the Soviet-sponsored Kurdish Mahabad government was set up in 1945. Further east from the Kurdish frontier belt, Iranian Azerbaijan is mostly inhabited by Azeri-Turks, an irritant which occasionally strains relations.

---

[48] *Milliyet*, July 6, 1968. (Italics added.) Previously, Pakistani Foreign Minister Arshad Hussein told Turkish journalists in Rawalpindi that Pakistan was staying in CENTO solely to please Turkey. He also said that CENTO had denied itself when it had remained indifferent to the Indian aggression against Pakistan in 1965; *Tercüman*, June 20, 1968.

[49] Statement by Iftikar Ali, Pakistani Ambassador in Ankara; *Tercüman*, June 29, 1968.

[50] A frontier rectification was required at the foot of Mount Ararat (near the point where Turkish–Soviet–Iranian borders meet), the area where Kurdish rebels resisted the Turkish Army in 1936. Both Turkey and Iran referred to strategical needs. Atatürk, with a generous gesture, invited Riza Shah to arbitrate the issue: of course, the result was favorable for Turkey. The Shah reportedly said: "There is only one thing I am interested in. That is friendly relations with Turkey." Kinross, *Atatürk*, p. 524.

Although the Turkish government has refused to foment irredenta feelings, press reports occasionally raise and try to exploit propagandistically real or exaggerated issues.[51] Besides the Azeri-Turks, there are Turkish or Turkic tribes in Iran; Turkomans in the northeast, the important Quashquai tribe in the south, and others. However, these tribal groups harbor no Turkish national sentiment, and in addition to giving allegiance to their tribal chiefs, they recognize Iranian overlordship.[52]

Iran has no reason to fear Turkish designs on her considerable Turkish population. On the other hand, Turks are occasionally apprehensive because they take a dim view of potential collaboration between Iranian and Kurdish elements. Although nontribal Turkish citizens of Iran live under administrative pressures (apart from the religious-medrese schools where the Koran is taught in Arabic, schooling is invariably in Persian), the treatment of Kurds in Iran remains benevolent, as long as there is no danger of secession. Tolerated by the authorities, Kurds and Iranians occasionally invoke their linguistic affinity and alleged common cultural heritage; it has been claimed that some Pan-Iranian agitation has been carried out among Kurds in Turkey.[53]

Despite these relatively small frictions, the Turco–Iranian relationship, as it was often officially emphasized, has remained basically good and undisturbed. One high Iranian official has declared that there is "no cloud over our relations."[54] The fundamental reason for this friendship and cooperation is rational and not emotional. "The enemy of Russia is the natural ally of Persia" was the maxim which in the past had thrown

[51] Thus, *Yeni Gazete* (September 12, 1968) complained that the Iranian government put restrictions on the movement of the Turkish cultural attaché to regions where Turks live. The Iranians have particularly objected to the introduction of the Turkish (Latin) alphabet among Iranian Turks. The number of Turks in Iran—according to the paper—is 11 million (the entire population of Iran is estimated to be 24–25 million).

[52] British agencies operating in the Persian Gulf region have in the past used their tribal contacts to put pressure on the government in Teheran. In 1945 the overthrow of the Tudeh (Communist) Party-controlled government was due to tribal uprising fomented by the British. The Quashquai tribe had maintained contacts with the British except at the beginning of World War II (and also during World War I) when it received support from the Germans.

[53] The Pan-Iranian Kurdish Party was said to be under the leadership of Ihsan Nuri, leader of the 1927–30 fight against the Turks. The party condemns "Semitic and Turkic influences" and stresses the community of Iran and Kurdistan as against alien Arabs and Turks; Kinnane, *Kurds and Kurdistan*, p. 58.

[54] See statement by Iranian Prime Minister Esadullah Alam when visiting Ankara in December 1963; *Turkish Yearbook of International Relations, 1963*, p. 330.

Persia into the otherwise unwelcome arms of the British.[55] Support was then offered by the United States and CENTO, the alliance sponsored by it. More so than Turkey, Iran would have been likely to continue her age-long neutralist stance between the north and south had it not been for Stalinist attempts to dislodge her. Iran joined the Western camp reluctantly and cautiously; Turkey enthusiastically welcomed her acceptance as another "European."

The parallel foreign policy interests of both countries are clear. Still, differences in political style and temperament and a different evaluation of their national interests has led them to follow slightly diverging paths. For her part, Turkey has felt the need to be linked with the West in every possible manner; Iran has harbored no such ambitions. She is more self-centered and has found fulfillment in her own cultural heritage. Iran has sought technological modernization and economic development and has advanced far, although her point of departure is lower than Turkey's.

Iran's evaluation of the Soviet danger is not as peremptory as Turkey's; Teheran has no equivalent to the straits problem. "Colonialist" dangers have threatened her from the south, from the British and other Western powers, in the past 50 years; during the same period, Turkey successfully disposed of capitulations and similar foreign exploitations. The leading circles in Teheran were always prepared to perform a balancing act between Moscow and its Cold War opponents. The economic assistance Iran received from the Soviet Union, although exiguous when compared to what she received from the United States and Western Europe, was relatively more important for her than similar Soviet aid received by Turkey.

Nevertheless, Iran was ready to continue participation in CENTO, primarily for the economic and financial benefits she could derive. An alliance with her western neighbor, Turkey, and with her eastern neighbor, Pakistan, was invaluable in itself. Lately, Iran has felt insecure because of the precariousness of the use of the Suez Canal, her maritime contact with Europe. The free flow of oil to European markets, the mainstay of Iran's economic existence, is so important for her that she has sought alternate ways of transportation should the Suez be permanently blocked. The pipeline from the Iranian oil fields to the Turkish port of

[55] See George Lenczowski, *Russia and the West in Iran, 1918–1948: A Study in Big Power Rivalry* (Ithaca, N.Y., 1949), p. 3.

Iskenderun could be a most significant project—both politically and economically. It would be developed bilaterally with Turkey and possibly financed under the aegis of the RCD.[56]

Occasional clouds still darken the horizon of Turkish and Iranian relations. Turkey, for instance, has complained that Iran was undercutting the export price of raisins, an important export of Turkey.[57] A main opium producer, Iran prohibited by law in 1955 the production and sale of the narcotic to fight addiction. On the other hand, Turkey has refused to prohibit the production of optium, and Iranians believe that much of it is being clandestinely introduced into Iran. In 1969 the Iranian government decided again to permit production and export of opium for medicinal purposes at less than half the world price in order to force Turkey to discontinue her production of the drug. The quarrel was submitted to the United Nations Commission on Narcotic Drugs and gave rise to heated polemics in the Turkish and Iranian press.[58]

In the politics of the Middle East, Iran has slightly different interests and displays attitudes different from those of Turkey. Iran's position concerning the Arab–Israeli conflict was that of a neutral, although with a certain bias toward Israel. She continued to maintain *de facto* relations with Israel even after the Arab–Israeli war of 1967 and remained her principal oil supplier. Strained relations ensued between Iran and the United Arab Republic as well as other Arab states.

In 1969 Iraq, Iran's only direct Arab neighbor, became involved in a serious conflict with Teheran over navigation rights in the Shatt-al-Arab, the river formed by the junction of the Tigris and Euphrates, which then flows into the Persian Gulf. Iran refused to abide by the terms of an earlier treaty which provided that, instead of the median line of the navigation channel, the Iranian shore of the Shatt-al-Arab should form the border between Iraq and Iran. According to Arab sources, taken up by the Turkish press, Iran's reason for putting pressure on Iraq was to divert the latter's attention from Israel and to weaken the anti-Israeli Arab front.[59]

[56] The pipeline project has been studied since 1967, and the necessary survey was completed in 1968; *Vatan,* July 28, 1967; *Cumhuriyet,* June 10, 1969.

[57] *Milliyet,* November 4, 1968. Turkey, Greece, and Australia have established minimal exportation prices for raisins; Iran started to sell at lower prices.

[58] About the "opium war" between Turkey and Iran, see *New York Times,* January 17, 1969. Afghanistan discontinued legal production of opium, but clandestine production continued.

[59] *Cumhuriyet,* April 23, 1969.

Iraq was reported to have asked Turkey to mediate her conflict with Iran which threatened to escalate into an armed clash. The spokesman of the Turkish Ministry of Foreign Affairs explained his government's view in the following terms: "It is Turkey's sincerest wish that the conflict between her friend and ally Iran and her neighbor Iraq with whom we have close relations be solved with understanding of the matter, before it grows into dangerous proportions."[60] It was hardly Turkey's intention to get deeply involved in this confrontation, the source of which was located some distance from her borders and in which she had no direct interest.

In all likelihood, the problems of the Persian Gulf, with the impending withdrawal of the British from that area, will attract the attention of the powers of the Middle East, including Turkey. Certainly, Turkey is interested in the future of the sheikdoms of the gulf, but she must recognize that her interests are little affected by it. She is, however, directly involved, and her direct interests may be at stake, in the relations between the two Arab states on her southeastern borders: Syria and Iraq.

SYRIA, IRAQ, AND THE KURDS

Syria was an Ottoman possession from 1516 to the end of World War I. It has been noted earlier[61] how the northwest corner of French-mandated Syria—the Sanjak of Alexandretta, now Hatay—was returned to Turkey in 1939. Syria was given independence in 1944, and her diplomatic relations with Turkey date from that time. Relations between the two countries were marked by unpleasant incidents, border clashes, and other friction, often the reflection of the internal political instability of the Syrian regimes. Most of these governments were mouthpieces for more-or-less militant Pan-Arab groups. Some ruling or opposition groups favored close collaboration or union with Egypt; others wished to promote either the federation of the Fertile Crescent (Syria, Iraq, and Jordan) or the formation of Greater Syria (with Lebanon, Jordan, and—as hoped for—the rest of Palestine). The Syrians participated in the war against Israel in 1948 and again in 1967. From February 1958 to September 1961, Syria was part of the United Arab Republic.

[60] *Ibid.* The visit of Amir Abbas Howeida, the Iranian prime minister, to Ankara in June 1969, was, according to press reports, connected with this question; *Yeni Gazete,* May 30, 1969; *Cumhuriyet,* June 11, 1969.
[61] See chapter I, pp. 26–27.

In the years 1954–55, Turkey vainly attempted to induce Syria to join the Baghdad Pact. Damascus retaliated with a pronounced anti-Turkish policy, joining Egypt in denouncing the "Middle Eastern agent" of Western imperialists. Syria has never been unmindful of the loss of Hatay; her aspirations to recover this territory have also animated her Turcophobia.

When Syria regained her independence in 1961, Ankara, in order to establish friendly relations with the new regime, hastened to recognize it. This move led to the rupture of diplomatic relations with Cairo. Diplomatic ties with the United Arab Republic (Egypt) were fully resumed only in 1965. Turkey's hopes that the Syrian governments would renounce militant Pan-Arab nationalism after their inauspicious experiment with Egypt remained unfulfilled. Even if no really serious conflicts existed between the two countries, a general malaise loomed over their mutual relations which can be explained only by the general historically motivated ethnic incompatibilities between Turks and Arabs.

Syria shares an extended frontier of 835 miles with Turkey; east of Hatay, the border has been artifically established along the railroad line known previously as the Baghdad Railway. Until after World War II, the Syrian border intersected the line, so that Turkish transports had to enter Syrian territory in the direction of Aleppo (Halep) and re-enter Turkey when moving toward the east.[62] Since 1945 a connecting railroad line which bypasses the Syrian sector of the Baghdad Railway has made entry into Syrian territory unnecessary. This long frontier on a steppe-like plain, intersected by a few settlements and some cultivated land, has not been easy to control, especially because ethnic affinities exist between the population on both of its sides. The main bone of contention with Syria, however, continues to be Hatay.

At the time of the cession of this administrative subdivision of the Ottoman state, Turks formed a plurality, though not quite a majority, of its population. Since Turkey acquired the area, the town and harbor of Iskenderun have been greatly improved. The region has become a center for tourism, and its agricultural and industrial resources have been de-

---

[62] France, acting on behalf of Syria, in her agreement with Turkey, dated October 20, 1921, allowed the latter to transport troops by railway across the Syrian section of the Baghdad Line. In return, Syria was given the right to use the railroad from north of Aleppo to its reentry into Syria for her military transports. See Váli, *Servitudes of International Law*, pp. 118–20.

veloped. Hatay's population is now largely Turkish. Nevertheless, Syrian–Arab irredentist tendencies have remained a permanent disturbing factor in Turco–Syrian relations. Syrian maps show Hatay as part of Syria,[63] and in the Syrian soldier's handbook Hatay is characterized as "usurped" territory.[64] The claim to it has also been stressed in other public announcements. Answering a question by a deputy relative to Syrian claims, the Turkish Ministry of Foreign Affairs once replied:

Hatay occupies an important place in Turkish-Syrian relations. . . . Syrian administrators and politicians launch this matter, which is easily exploited for political purposes, and endorse in their governmental programs a point according to which Iskenderun, "the usurped land," will be recovered by force along with Palestine. Our Government is vigilant in this matter that concerns our territorial integrity.[65]

In view of her vastly superior power potential, Turkey has little reason to fear Syrian irredentist ploys, even if other Arab states lined up against her.[66] Only if Turkey should succumb to more powerful pressures, such as those brought to bear by Russia, could Syria hope for the recovery of her irredenta.

Other irritants in the Turkish–Syrian relationship are various types of border incidents: illegal crossings, smuggling, and the question of border passes. Parts of the frontier lines had, until 1969, been mined by Turks to prevent such incidents.[67] Another question which has vexed relations between the two countries concerns reciprocal compensation for expropriated land.[68]

Turkey had no wish to interfere in the labyrinth of Syrian domestic politics. Of course, the apprehension that one day Syria might completely fall under the spell of Communist domination caused Turkey to watch

[63] Jäschke, *Die Türkei in den Jahren 1952–1961*, p. 37.

[64] Such handbooks were captured by Israelis in the 1967 war and promptly shown to Turks; *Cumhuriyet*, August 5, 1967.

[65] *Cumhuriyet*, February 11, 1968.

[66] President Cemal Gürsel, when handing flags to troops destined for Cyprus, said in his speech: "Hatay is Turkish and cannot be severed from us!" Jäschke, *Die Türkei in den Jahren 1952–1961*, p. 110.

[67] The Turkish press reports numerous cases of illegal entry by Syrian Turks who applied in vain for exit visas from Syria; *Hürriyet*, August 31, 1967. Demands are submitted to abrogate the border pass (*passavant*) agreement to prevent smuggling; *Cumhuriyet*, July 10, 1967; *Yeni Istanbul*, April 3, 1969.

[68] *Tercüman*, December 21, 1967; *Yeni Gazete*, February 26, 1968, which reported agreement on the principle of compensation. *Zafer*, January 2, 1969, reported no agreement on the amount of compensation.

developments in this neighboring land closely. Arab unity, as the Syrian precedent has demonstrated, appears to be utopian under present conditions. The changes which have taken place within Iraq, Turkey's other Arab neighbor, also corroborated the thesis that Pan-Arabism is practiced only against non-Arabs.

Unlike Syria whose population is ethnically and religiously fairly homogeneous, only 75 percent of Iraq's population are Arabs—and even they are divided between Sunnites and Shiites. The biggest ethnic minority is Kurdish and is located in the northeastern part of the country along the Turkish and Iranian border. This area, which Turkey had claimed in Lausanne, was eventually allotted to Iraq by the Council of the League of Nations.[69]

After the revolution of 1958, the relations between the new republican regime of General Abdul Karim Kassem and Turkey fluctuated between cordiality and animosity. Shortly after the take-over, Kassem expressed sympathies toward Turkey and deplored the necessity of his country's withdrawal from the Baghdad Pact. In July 1959, a Turkish delegation attended the anniversary of the revolution in Baghdad.[70]

In 1961 Iraqi planes began bombing Turkish border villages in their fight against the Kurdish insurgents. Kassem accused Turkey of supporting the Kurds and invited the "Turkish nation" to put pressure on their government to end the "hostile attitude" against Iraq. Ankara characterized the Iraqi accusations as mere provocations, in view of the well-known fact that Turkey could not have any interest in fomenting Kurdish unrest.[71] Baghdad expressed regret because of the bombing of Turkish territory.

In 1962, however, bombings took place again. In August Turkish fighter-planes shot down two Iraqi bombers,[72] and Baghdad accused Turkey of shooting down the Iraqi planes forty miles inside Iraqi territory. The Turkish government, while protesting these accusations, announced that it would withdraw jet fighter patrols from the Iraqi frontier regions "in the interest of good neighborly relations."[73] Seven villages on the Turkish side of the frontier were also evacuated in order to facili-

---

[69] See chapter I, pp. 20–21.
[70] Jäschke, *Die Türkei in den Jahren 1951–1961*, pp. 87 and 96.
[71] *Ibid.*, pp. 124–25.
[72] *Neue Zürcher Zeitung*, August 19, 21, 22, 1962.
[73] *Turkish Yearbook of International Relations*, 1962, p. 162.

tate border control.[74] In protest against continued hostile publications in the government-controlled press, the Turkish ambassador was recalled from Baghdad "to complete his unfinished leave."[75]

Turkey had good reason to seek friendly ties with the Kassem regime. The new revolutionary leader, much to Nasser's disappointment, refused to join the Egyptian–Syrian union. Both Kassem and Ankara were happy when this union was dissolved in 1961. Kassem's overthrow and execution in February 1963 did not improve Turco–Iraqi relations. When in May 1963 Abdel Salam Mohammed Arif established his dictatorship, he paid lip-service to a forthcoming union with the United Arab Republic. Under Arif, and his brother Abdel Rahman Arif, who succeeded the former after his death, relations with Turkey slowly improved. This was especially evident during the administration of Abdel Rahman al-Bazzaz, a civilian prime minister. Iraqi leaders began to understand the common interest of Ankara and Baghdad in the Kurdish uprising. When the Arif regime was overthrown in July 1968, the new government of Iraq was swiftly recognized by Turkey.[76] Subsequently, however, the new regime under Ahmed Hassan al-Bakr proved to be more extremist and more anti-Western than its predecessor. It even refused to consider itself fully nonaligned between "world imperialism" and the Communist countries by siding with the latter.[77] Such an attitude was, naturally, incompatible with genuine Turkish friendship.

Baghdad, under President al-Bakr, found itself entangled in two conflicts: one with Iran over the Shatt-al-Arab question, the other with the continued Kurdish insurrection.

Whereas the Turkish–Syrian relationship was constantly overshadowed by the memory of Hatay, no such hurdle was in the way of a Turco–Iraqi rapprochement. In fact, the only serious cause for hostile attitudes—namely, the Kurdish uprising in Iraq—was due to Baghdad's misunderstanding of Ankara's intentions. As soon as this was recognized, relations not only improved but even became cordial. It must have been evident to the rulers in Baghdad that Turkey no longer had any territorial demands on the Mosul area. Consequently, the Kurdish problem was not

[74] *Neue Zürcher Zeitung,* August 24, 1962.
[75] *Turkish Yearbook of International Relations, 1962,* p. 162.
[76] *Milliyet,* July 20, 1968. The new Iraqi president, Ahmed Hassan al-Bakr, welcomed recognition by saying: "Iraq needs close cooperation with Iran and with Turkey."
[77] *New York Times,* July 22, 1969. The regime arrested former Premier al-Bazzaz on the charge of spying for the C.I.A.

allowed to develop into an object of discord. Naturally, how far the interests of Ankara and Baghdad run parallel in this respect depends on how Iraq is able to handle this thorny problem.

Soon after his revolutionary take-over, President Kassem allowed the return to Iraq of those Kurdish leaders who had taken refuge in the Soviet Union during the post-World War II years. The most prominent among them was Mulla Mustafa Barzani, who had led several insurrections against the Iraqi government in the past. He had participated in the establishment of the ephemeral Kurdish government of Mahabad in Iran and after its collapse retreated into the Soviet Union. In 1961 he led another "war" against Iraqi forces and was able to hold his ground against the efforts of Baghdad.

Shortly before his overthrow, Kassem was compelled to open negotiations with the rebel Kurds. Although the Arif regime promised autonomy, eventually the Kurdish demands were considered nonnegotiable and the war was renewed in early 1963. In September 1965, a twelve-point settlement offered by Iraqi Prime Minister Bazzaz was accepted by Barzani, but fighting did not end.[78] Although the twelve points were never implemented, a *de facto* Kurdish revolutionary council continued to control large sections of Iraqi Kurdistan.[79] In March 1970 the Iraqi government officially recognized the autonomy of the Kurdish area. Kurds will receive the right to proportional representation in all governmental bodies and the Kurdish language will be, along with the Arabic, an official language in the autonomous territory.[80]

The status of Kurds in Iraq significantly differs from their status in Turkey. The League of Nations' commission that in 1924 recommended the inclusion of the Mosul district in Iraq also stressed the Kurdish ethnic character of the majority of its inhabitants and suggested that local autonomy be granted to them. Under the British mandate of Iraq, and even later, the local administration in the Kurdish area was in the hands of officials of Kurdish descent. Unlike in Turkey, the Kurdish element

[78] *New York Times,* March 30, 1969; *Yeni Gazete,* May 29, 1969.
[79] New negotiations for a settlement were being conducted during the spring of 1969; *New York Times,* May 24, 1969.
[80] *New York Times,* March 12, 1970. This news created considerable anxiety in Ankara because of the Turkish minority living in and around the town of Kirkuk. Questions were asked by the press about whether Turks in the Kurdish autonomous area will now be forced to use the Kurdish language or receive Kurdish instruction in schools; *Milliyet,* April 11, 1970.

played an officially significant and conspicuous role in the public life of Iraq. At times, even before 1961, Kurdish tribes lived in a state of revolt or semi-revolt against the central authorities of Baghdad.[81]

The Kurdish revolt created unpleasant problems for the Turkish authorities in the Hakkâri vilayet (province) adjacent to Iraq where the population was overwhelmingly Kurdish. The rugged mountain terrain proved difficult to control, and the border could not be sealed off completely. Refugees arrived from Iraq, not only because of Iraqi bombing or persecution but at times because of internecine warfare between the various tribes.

Kurdish sympathizers in Turkey helped to provide arms to the insurgents. According to newspaper reports, some of these weapons passed through the Black Sea port of Trabzon and were smuggled across the Turkish border to Iraq. Evidently, Turkish authorities attempted to intercept these shipments but were not always successful.[82]

Iraq never ceased to emphasize that her trouble with the Kurds was an internal Iraqi affair. Although Moscow sympathized with Kurdish aspirations for independence, Soviet representatives were reluctant to support Kurdish claims in the United Nations. As long as the Kurdish movement fails to obtain sponsorship from one of the major powers, the Iraqi Kurds may rely ultimately only on their fighting strength. Only the Soviet Union might choose to assume that task, but it would thereby incur the enmity of both the Arabs and Turkey. While it is doubtful that according autonomous status to the Kurds (similarly to earlier concessions made to them by Baghdad) will create a stable situation, it is also believed in Turkey that such a settlement would not satisfy Kurdish ambitions. The following analysis by a Turkish commentator is representative of reactions concerning developments in Kurdistan:

The autonomy for the Kurds in Iraq is the first step towards an independent Kurdish State in the Middle East, a development more important than the Israeli question in the region. So far the Barzani question was a domestic affair of Iraq. But now it also concerns Iraq's neighbors, Turkey, Iran, and Syria, because it is obvious that Barzani will not be content with what he has obtained

---

[81] For literature on the Kurdish question, see chapter II, pp. 49–50.

[82] Arms were arriving at Of and Trabzon from Eastern bloc countries via the Black Sea to be shipped to the Barzani forces—reports *Cumhuriyet*, October 9, 1967. Four hundred pistols were found in a Mercedes car arriving from Germany at Edirne customs; *Yeni Gazete*, December 12, 1967. Three hundred rifles were discovered in Kastamonu destined for Iraqi Kurds; *Cumhuriyet*, October 22, 1968.

and will try to unite Kurds in these countries. What are Turkey's plans about this development? If Barzani only calls to his new land those in Turkey who consider themselves Kurds there will be no problem. We can bid them farewell as we agreed to send Jews to the new Israeli State. But what will happen if Barzani puts forward some claims on Turkish territory on the grounds that these people are here? Certainly, a powerful Turkey of 34 million is not Iraq and can say: "Come and take it if you can." But have we preplanned everything so that things need not come to this point and at least so that another Cyprus is not created? Have we, for instance, thought of raising the question of the "Kirkuk Turks" and "Mosul"? The Kurdish problem which was until yesterday a domestic affair of Iraq is now about to knock at our door.[83]

Rallying Turkey, Iran, and Iraq to a common policy may doom the Kurdish independence movement. For this reason, the Kurds opposed the Saadabad Pact and the Baghdad Pact. On the other hand, they greeted the Kassem coup enthusiastically because it meant the end of anti-Kurdish cooperation among the three countries in which most of the Kurdish people reside. In the long run, even if Kurdish autonomy in Iraq should become sanctioned by her constitution, the relations between Turkey and Iraq would be largely influenced by their common or differing attitudes toward the Kurdish question.

Turkey and Iraq also share some common economic problems. The two main rivers of Iraq, the Euphrates and the Tigris, originate in Turkish territory; the economic uses of their waters must be a common problem for these two countries. Iranian oil, when carried through pipelines to Turkish Mediterranean ports, must conveniently pass through Iraqi territory.[84] As is usual with young and highly nationalistic nations, however, economic considerations are secondary to emotional and national issues. As with other Arab countries, Iraq was also deeply involved in the Arab–Israeli conflict. Her attitude toward Turkey, like Syria's, was also influenced by the Turkish approach to this issue. As Hasan Mureyvet, the foreign minister of Syria, has said about Turkish demands on Cyprus: "Our attitude is related to Turkey's relations with Israel. If Turkey insists on not giving a sincere form of these relations, it would be difficult to establish the desired relations between Turkey and Syria."[85]

These rather ambiguous remarks, even though made before the Arab–Israeli war of 1967, express Arab sentiment and sensitivity about this issue

---

[83] Hikmet Bil in *Yeni Gazete*, May 29, 1969.
[84] *Ulus*, October 24, 1967; *Cumhuriyet*, February 21, 1969.
[85] *Turkish Yearbook of International Relations, 1965*, p. 246. The above extract is from a speech made in Algiers on June 28, 1965.

which is so central to the Arab political mind. Turkey cannot escape it when dealing with the countries of the Arab World.

THE ARAB–ISRAELI CONFLICT

Turkey was one of the first countries, after the great powers, to recognize the state of Israel. In 1952 full diplomatic missions headed by ambassadors were exchanged between Ankara and Tel Aviv. Turkish–Israeli relations developed normally until the Suez crisis of 1956. When Israeli forces invaded the Sinai Peninsula, Turkey—in the wake of American disapproval of this action—recalled her ambassador, without, however, severing diplomatic relations.[86] Subsequently, the Turkish representative returned to his post.

At first, Turkey appeared unconcerned about Arab reactions to her increased trade and friendly contacts with Israel. After the collapse of the Baghdad Pact scheme, she was even less determined to heed Arab opinions. Cairo's enmity was aroused against Ankara, partly because of its role as exponent of American policy, but also because of the complete lack of solidarity shown by "Muslim" Turkey with the plight of her co-religionaries in Palestine. Egypt was fearful that Turkey would compete with her for the leadership in the Middle East—a sentiment inconsistent with the charge that Turkey was not interested in the Arab–Israeli struggle. As noted earlier, Cairo even disrupted diplomatic relations for nearly three years, during which time Ankara continued its pleasant relationship with Israel. Only after 1964, when support was needed in the United Nations, was a change of Turkish policy toward Arabs and Israelis discernible.

The exchange of ambassadors with Cairo heralded the new phase of Turkish–Arab relations. Although Turkey's contacts with her two Arab neighbors were intensive, though not always friendly, Nasser's government showed considerable reluctance to forgive Ankara for her lack of concern with Arab interests. Alexandria, with the consent of the United Arab Republic, served as a port of transshipment for weapons passed on to Makarios in Cyprus. Turkish recriminations against Nasser's anti-Muslim attitude were hardly conducive to an improvement of relations. Turkish "goodwill missions" dispatched in 1964 to various Arab govern-

[86] See Ülman, "Ikinci Dünya Savaşında," pp. 248–50.

ments avoided Cairo. Nasser must have realized, however, that this lack of understanding between his government and Turkey might boomerang in the long run: Cairo might one day need Turkish support in its struggle with Israel, and Ankara could mediate Nasser's quarrels with various governments, such as with Iran (the United Arab Republic was unable to resume full diplomatic relations with Teheran, broken off at the same time Nasser broke with Turkey).

When Turkish–Egyptian conversations concerning Cyprus were finally opened, Cairo indicated that it disapproved of Turkish claims to armed intervention in the island; Turkey was also asked to oppose the maintenance of British bases. In fact, Nasser suggested the withdrawal of *all* foreign troops from Cyprus, including the Turkish contingent.[87]

The events of 1967 were necessary to change Nasser's narrow-minded vision of neutralism. It must have occurred to him at last that, although he saw zionism was the greatest danger and evil (followed immediately by colonialism), Turkey could never be converted to such an attitude. On the other hand, it must have become obvious to the Turkish leadership that communism, compared to the above-mentioned sources of apprehension, carried no immediate sense of peril for the Arabs, especially for those who wished to promote Arab socialism, in either its Baath'ist or Nasserite form.

Even before the unleashing of hostilities, Turkey displayed understanding toward Egyptian viewpoints. She did not join the group of "Maritime powers" demanding the opening of the Gulf of Akaba to Israeli shipping, and her attitude toward the Arab cause during and after the Seven Days' War reflected benevolent neutrality. She voted in the United Nations for all moderate resolutions which invited Israel to withdraw her forces from the occupied Arab territories; she sponsored the Jerusalem Resolution of May 21, 1968, which opposed incorporating the whole city into Israel. She also advised Arab states not to resort to force because the preservation of peace appeared to her as the supreme requirement, although she also emphasized that the continued existence of Israel should not be questioned.[88]

[87] *Yeni Gazete,* March 18, 1968.
[88] Foreign Minister Çağlayangil declared in New York (after the United Nations General Assembly meeting on the Middle Eastern crisis): "We want conflicts to be settled peacefully. We are against territorial gain by force. We do not accept *faits accomplis." Cumhuriyet,* July 7, 1967. In an interview, Prime Minister Demirel said

The cautious attitude Ankara displayed during and after the 1967 conflagration was, in fact, diplomacy at its best, for Turkey was able to express sympathies toward the Arab states involved in the war without offending Israel.[89] United States officials were told that Turkey had no other option but to please the Arabs while simultaneously expressing understanding for the Israeli cause. Educated Turkish public opinion manifested admiration for the military achievements of Israel and some contempt for the incompetence of Arab military leadership. The opinion of the Turkish press remained divided: leftists blamed Turkey for having been a "guardian" of Western interests against Arabs and, therefore, approved Egypt's support for Makarios;[90] others expressed unhappiness because Soviet support to the Arabs would inevitably lead to Turkish involvement in case of a renewed Arab–Israeli war.[91]

Mahmud Riyad, the foreign minister of the United Arab Republic, visited Ankara in March 1968, thus inaugurating a new era of Turkish–Egyptian relations. The Israeli question as well as other long outstanding differences between Ankara and Cairo were discussed, among them the vexing question of compensation for Turkish property expropriated by Cairo.[92]

In March 1969, Foreign Minister Çağlayangil, in answer to a question on Turkey's position in the Middle Eastern crisis, said that since June 1967 Turkey had defended the thesis that it was impossible to restore peace in the region unless certain principles were observed:

One of these principles is that force cannot be used for obtaining territorial gains nor for the purpose of increasing one's bargaining power. Another principle is that conflicts cannot be solved by accomplished facts. These principles are today embraced by a great majority of the States. Turkey supports a political solution which safeguards the legitimate rights of the Arab countries. We believe that the Security Council Resolution of November 22, 1967, contains all the elements necessary for such a solution.[93]

---

that the existence of Israel cannot be denied. "Israel is there. This is a fact." He also mentioned that Turkey was the only Islamic country which had diplomatic relations with Israel. But he criticized Israel for not having withdrawn from Arab territory occupied in the 1967 war. "We do not approve of land-gain by force. If the men of Israel or of any other country are carried away by the desire to gain territory at gunpoint, there will be no end to it." (Announced by the Turkish Radio, June 3, 1969).

[89] *Yeni Gazete,* September 6, 1967.
[90] *Cumhuriyet,* March 14, 1968.
[91] *Yeni Gazete,* December 10, 1968.
[92] *Milliyet,* January 4, 1969.
[93] *Ankara Bayram,* March 1, 1969.

It is interesting that Turkish attitudes toward the Arab–Israel conflict during and after its "hot" phase in 1967 resembled a similar position taken by Greece. It almost seemed that the two rival Aegean powers were competing for Arab good will in their protracted quarrel over Cyprus.

Turkey's contacts with Jordan, another of Israel's Arab neighbors, were always characterized by cordiality and sincerity. Turkey encountered no difficulties in diplomatic and personal rapport with King Hussein's government or with the king himself, who during the past years had been a frequent visitor in the Turkish capital. Less than two months after the conclusion of the 1967 war with Israel, King Hussein again visited Ankara to exchange views on the situation with the Turkish leaders. Known as a pro-Western and moderate ruler, he received, as always, an excellent welcome. Unlike press reports on Nasser which tended to be ironic, King Hussein was greeted as a tragic but heroic figure. The well-known journalist Metin Toker wrote:

Jordan had been hit the worst by the Middle East war and lost territory. King Hussein's bad luck was his entering this adventure while being aware of its outcome. The King told me last November in Amman that Nasser's stand would result in such an outbreak in the Middle East though the Arabs needed time and more force to achieve victory. King Hussein's forecast came true. He had wanted to conclude a gentleman's agreement with Israel and recognize the existing status. But when the war broke out he did not wish to appear as a King who betrayed the Arab cause. . . . If he had acted otherwise he would have lost his throne. Now the young King is exerting himself to compensate his loss, and his visit to Turkey is important in this respect. . . . It is our duty to assist, as much as possible, in securing this outcome.[94]

Even though they would hate Turkish interference in their politics, the Jordanians and other Arabs would welcome a Turkish alignment against Israel which would surpass mere gestures of sympathy. Abdel Munen al-Refai, prime minister of Jordan, reproached Turkey for her passivity: "Jordan and other Arab countries are surprised by the Turkish Government's attitude because Israel is not just threatening Arab countries, she constitutes a danger for all Islamic countries and especially for Turkey."[95]

Recruiting membership in the Arab guerilla organizations has not

---

[94] *Milliyet,* September 5, 1967. When the Jordanian army and the Palestinian guerillas clashed in September 1970, Turkish circles sympathized with the former; *Tercüman,* September 20, 1970.

[95] *Hürriyet,* April 19, 1969.

halted at the borders of Turkey. Leaflets in Turkish and Arabic were distributed on behalf of *Al Fatah* Palestinian figthers in Diyarbakır calling on all Muslims to join in the *Jihad* (Holy War) against Istrael.[96]

On the other hand, some Turkish leaders feel that Turkey's present benevolent attitude toward the Arabs might entangle her in the Arab imbroglio and in the great power rivalry surrounding the conflict. Metin Toker's father-in-law, the octogenarian Ismet Inönü, raised his warning voice against taking up a position in favor of or against the various peace plans submitted by the Soviet Union or the United States.[97] Evidently, Inönü would favor a return to the Kemalist attitude of aloofness from Arab politics. It must be admitted, however, that this over-cautious and timid posture would no longer be in harmony with present-day Turkey's more complicated and flexible foreign policy and policy goals.

TURKEY'S NEW MIDDLE EASTERN POLICY

Kemalist Turkey, obliged to eliminate the Islamic and theocratic foundations of the Ottoman state to modernize her political and social structure, turned her back on the Middle East and especially on the Arab World, which in any case had deserted the Turkish cause during World War I. Only the need to achieve a modicum of security along her eastern borders persuaded Turkey in the late 1930's to conclude the rather harmless Saadabad Pact with Iran, Iraq, and Afghanistan.

As we have seen, in the 1950's Turkey directed her interest again toward the lands of the Middle East and particularly those Arab regions where she had ruled for centuries and where the Arabs had been her vassals. The failure to rally Arab states to the side of an alliance inspired by the West induced Ankara once more to show indifference toward the Arab world, an attitude shared by one of her regional CENTO partners, Iran.

The new flexible foreign policy initiated around 1964 was applied also to the non-CENTO Middle Eastern countries. This new policy raised certain points of principle, especially in regard to the Arab states, which may be summarized under the following six points.

1. Turkey wished to be on friendly terms with all nations of the Mid-

---

[96] Report by *Cumhuriyet,* April 29, 1969.
[97] *Milliyet,* January 13, February 3, 1969.

dle East. The measure of cordiality to be displayed would not depend on Turkey's attitude but rather on the readiness of the other states to develop more or less intimate relations with Turkey. In other words, Ankara did not wish to differentiate between the various countries of the area but offered friendship with equal sincerity to all, irrespective of their constitutional structure or domestic politics. Thus, there was to be no distinction between conservative royal states like Saudi Arabia, and an Arab Socialist country like the United Arab Republic. Prejudice against "neutralist" policies, as practiced before, was to be abandoned. Naturally, Turkey expected its Middle Eastern partners to drop, in turn, their prejudices against her policy of alliances.

2. Turkey did not wish to intervene in the conflicts between Middle Eastern countries. Refusing to take advantage, for instance, of inter-Arab rivalries, she intended to serve the cause of peace in the Middle East but would be a mediator only when invited by all the parties concerned.[98]

3. Turkey's determination not to interfere in the domestic or rival politics of these countries should not be interpreted as indifference; Turkey was and should be interested in the developments of an area crucially important for her both strategically and culturally. It was her ambition to have diplomatic and consular representations in those regions in order to establish a permanent Turkish presence there and also to act as a vigilant observer of trends and events.

4. Ankara wanted not only to foster trade with the countries of the Middle East and Africa but also to contribute, as far as it might be feasible, to their modernization and economic-industrial development. As one of those countries which had begun developing earlier than almost all the nations of Asia and Africa, Turkey believed that she could offer her experience to those who wished to move along the same path.

5. Turkey also sought to maintain close cultural contacts with the countries of Asia and Africa, in particular with those of the Muslim Middle East which were bound to her by ties of a common intellectual heritage. She also felt that, because of her past, she would be in a better position to become an interpreter of Western culture among these countries than the Western nations themselves.

[98] See Hamit Batu, "La politique étrangère de la Turquie," *Turkish Yearbook of International Relations, 1964,* pp. 1–12.

6. It was recognized that the strengthening of mutual relations based on the common Islamic faith offered some special difficulties for Turkey. Her secularist state system proved occasionally to be an obstacle to close relations with Muslim countries governed, more or less, by Islamic-theocratic principles. Personal contacts and official visits could create unpleasant incidents in Turkey or in the more strict Muslim lands.[99] Since the present Turkish government no longer finds it necessary to be as dogmatic about secularism as was thought indispensable in the time of Atatürk, tactful behavior and an understanding of the observances considered sacred by the others could now prevent any possible friction.[100]

It is no longer impossible for the Turkish government to harmonize its secular stance with the "Muslim" character of Turkey. The flexibility thus attained has provided Turkey with the advantage of participating in Islamic conferences; thus, the accusations by Middle East countries that Turkey was abandoning Islam have been countered.[101] The Turkish leaders have been particularly anxious to improve the image and prestige of the Turkish state among the peoples of the Middle East; they wish to dispel propaganda which at times has pictured them as agents of the West or, at other times, as atheists.[102]

The dual character of Turkey—both secular state and Muslim nation —may facilitate Turkish contacts both in the West and in the East. The flexibility and adaptability of the Turkish attitude in foreign relations was already demonstrated when Ankara, while officially emphasizing Turkey's "European" character, did not consider it incompatible to participate in the conference of independent Asian and African nations at Bandung, Indonesia, in April 1955. Turkey was represented by Minister of State Fatin Rüştü Zorlu, as chief delegate. Other members of the Western alliances clashed there with the noncommitted nations led by Nehru

[99] "The visits of the statesmen of some theocratic states began to give way to manifestations against our secularism principles, such as official receptions without women and official Friday prayers." Mehmet Barlas in *Cumhuriyet,* August 2, 1968.

[100] In the past, Saudi Arabian state visitors refused to be shown the Atatürk mausoleum in Ankara (or to lay a wreath before it) because human statues conflicted with their religious beliefs.

[101] Turkey was officially represented at the Fourth Islamic Research Conference in Cairo, a gesture found to be useful in her relations with Arab countries; *Tercüman,* October 25, 1968.

[102] Foreign Minister Çağlayangil, attending the General Assembly of the United Nations in New York, complained of the difficulties in making Turkey better known in the world; *Hürriyet,* October 11, 1968.

of India.[103] Despite her membership in the Council of Europe and other European organizations, Turkey attended the conference of Afro-Asian countries in Algiers in October, 1965.[104] Thus, Turkey is "European" and "Asian" not only because she straddles the two continents but also because her diplomacy has so skillfully managed to allow her recognition in both camps.

Since 1964 Turkey has attempted to be represented by resident diplomatic missions in as many Asian and African countries as was financially possible. Even if she had no permanent mission in many of the African capitals, she was able to open diplomatic contacts with them through nonresident ambassadors. In divided countries, Ankara generally maintained diplomatic relations with the pro-Western or anti-Communist part of the country: with South Korea (where Turkey enjoys great popularity because of the bravery of her troops in the war of 1950–54), South Vietnam, and the Republic of China (Taiwan).[105]

Relations between Turkey and India became "icy" after Pakistan joined the Baghdad Pact (CENTO). Nehru's India, more intransigent and intolerant in her doctrinaire neutralism than Egypt, displayed hostility. This was especially true when Turkey sided with Pakistan in the Kashmir conflict. In 1962 Communist China invaded Indian territory and compelled New Delhi to request arms from both the United States and Moscow. In the aftermath, India's rigid neutralism collapsed and only then did the stagnation of Turco-Indian relations give way to normalcy.[106]

Afghanistan's leaning on the Soviet Union for economic aid did not disturb the cordial relations of this kingdom with Turkey. Afghanistan supported Turkey on Cyprus in the United Nations.[107]

Turkey's alliance with Pakistan and Iran has been described earlier. CENTO appeared to be of more value to Iran than to Pakistan. The Regional Cooperation for Development organization was valuable to both. Pakistan was far more pro-Arab than either Iran or Turkey. Iran main-

---

[103] For the speeches made at Bandung, see *Documents on International Affairs, 1955*, pp. 397–438; Siyasal Bilgiler Fakültesi Dış Münasebetler Enstitüsü, *Olaylarla Türk Dış Politikası*, pp. 240–43.

[104] *Turkish Yearbook of International Relations, 1965*, p. 258.

[105] In June 1969, the Turkish government decided to establish diplomatic relations with the Mongolian People's Republic at an ambassadorial level. Ulan Bator is an excellent listening post for Sino-Soviet affairs. See *Milliyet*, June 24, 1969.

[106] See the press conference by the new Indian Ambassador Godburdhun in Istanbul; *Milliyet*, September 26, 1967.

[107] *Daily News* (Ankara), May 3, 1968.

tained *de facto* relations with Israel and supplied the latter with oil. Turkey maintained full diplomatic relations with Israel but displayed a pro-Arab neutralism in the Arab–Israeli conflict.

As noted above, Turkey's contacts with Syria were correct but lacked friendliness. The Syrian claim to Hatay was the only serious controversy between Turkey and an Arab country.[108] With Iraq, relations were generally good, although the Kurdish unrest was a headache to both countries.

While Turkey remained determined to keep out of inter-Arab feuds, she could not dissociate herself from the Arab conflict with Israel. While refraining from any hostile move against Israel, Ankara declared itself sympathetic with the Arab position, which required Israeli withdrawal to the pre-1967 armistice line. Turkish benevolence toward the Arab cause did not go so far as to condemn Israel for having committed an aggression. It had been explained to both Cairo and Tel Aviv that preservation of Middle Eastern peace was the goal of Turkish diplomatic endeavors. Turkey wished to maintain diplomatic contacts with Israel and also to continue her prosperous trade with that country.[109] Foreign Minister Hasan Işık thus defined the Turkish attitude even before the 1967 war: "Turkey's relations with Israel would not develop in the direction which would be against the interests of the Arab countries."[110]

Ankara hoped that the Turkish position was now well understood by the United Arab Republic. Whether Cairo will be satisfied with this limited pro-Arab support or whether it will continue to brand Ankara as a deserter from the Muslim cause will determine the future relations between the two countries.

Turkey's rapport with Lebanon was exceedingly good. Both Beirut and Amman shared Ankara's full confidence. With Kuwait, Turkey maintained important commercial ties. Forty percent of Turkey's oil imports were provided by Arab countries, among them Kuwait.

The government of Süleyman Demirel found it easier to pursue cordial relations with the conservative Islamic monarchy of Saudi Arabia because his government was supported by much of rural Turkey—that is, Muslim

---

[108] Batu, "La politique étrangère," p. 6.

[109] The diplomatic relations between Turkey and Israel were reduced after 1956 to the legation level. The two countries were reciprocally represented by diplomats carrying the unusual title of "Minister–Chargé d'Affaires." This title indicated that the relation may, at any time, be raised by the appointment of ambassadors. See *New York Times*, August 31, 1969.

[110] *Turkish Yearbook of International Relations, 1965,* p. 232.

Turkey *par excellence*. President Sunay was the first Turkish president to visit the Saudi Arabian capital in this capacity and, on this occasion, paid the ritual homage to the Holy Places of Mecca and Medina, a gesture hardly conceivable in Atatürk's time.[111]

The future of the Persian Gulf sheikdoms, left unprotected after the British withdrawal East of Suez, did not fail to occupy the attention of the Turkish press.[112] When Turkey refused to become involved in the developments of the Persian Gulf, it was only in conformity with her general Middle Eastern policy. The Turkish foreign minister evidently believed that this was a matter for discussion between Iran and Saudi Arabia, the two major powers along the gulf. Suggestion about an "Islamic Pact" between these two states for the protection of the Persian Gulf area, which should have included Turkey, among others, left Ankara rather cool. Such an alliance appeared to be directed against Nasser, and it would have been inconsistent for Turkey to take sides on such an issue. Turkey participated in the Islamic summit conference assembled in Rabat, Morocco, which was called to consider the fire at Al Aksa Mosque in Israeli-occupied Jerusalem but refused there to be involved in the Palestinian war, an agenda topic which went far beyond the subject that Turkey had been invited to discuss.[113]

Turkey was also represented by the secretary general of her foreign ministry, Ambassador Orhan Eralp, at the foreign ministers conference of Islamic countries in Jidda (Saudi Arabia) in March 1970. When the Libyan and Sudanese foreign ministers invited Ankara to sever diplomatic relations with Israel, the Turkish delegate rejected this demand, which he considered interference in Turkey's domestic affairs. Turkey also declined to support the idea of a permanent secretariat for Islamic nations.[114]

Turkey had not taken up diplomatic relations either with republican or with royalist Yemen during the Yemeni civil war, thus demonstrating her neutral attitude in this eminently inter-Arab dispute.

Turkey wished to develop her relations with African countries in all fields. She was one of the first states to sign the United Nations declaration for the independence of colonies.[115] For geographical and cultural-his-

[111] *Cumhuriyet*, January 23, 1968.

[112] *Yeni Gazete,* January 22, 1968; *Ulus,* January 23, 1968.

[113] *New York Times,* September 25, 1969.

[114] *Ibid.,* March 27, 1970; *Cumhuriyet,* March 24, 26, 1970.

[115] "To develop Turkey's relations in all fields with African countries was one of the unchanging principles of Turkey's foreign policy," said Zeki Kuneralp, secretary-

torical reasons, Ankara hoped to maintain close relations with the Arab states of North Africa, the Maghreb of the Arab world: Libya, Tunisia, Algeria, and Morocco. With Libya relations were the best; similarly, Tunisian and Turkish leaders could easily see eye-to-eye, even on such difficult issues as the conflict with Israel.[116] Friendship with Morocco was once more sealed when King Hassan visited Ankara in March 1969.[117] Relations with Algeria did not progress favorably because of the latter's pro-Soviet leanings and anti-Western bellicosity; there was, however, a notable improvement when Turkish Foreign Minister Çağlayangil included Algeria in his itinerary during a North African tour and received a warm welcome.[118]

The North African Arab states border the Mediterranean and, therefore, cannot help being affected by the transformation of the naval balance in that sea. This former *mare nostrum* of the West now has to be shared with the Soviet fleet. Simultaneously, Soviet influence has made deep inroads into areas of the Arab Middle East which had previously lived under Western influence and later attempted to maintain an uncommitted posture. Cairo, Damascus, and, to a lesser degree, Amman have become dependent on Soviet economic and logistic support; this support, with added Soviet advisory personnel, enabled these capitals to restore their armed strength after the disaster of the Seven Days' War of 1967. Soviet influence is also strong in Iraq, in the Sudan, and in Algeria; in Yemen in 1966 Soviet airmen personally intervened for the first time, if only for two days, to save Sana, the capital, from a royalist attack.

This Soviet build-up has taken place behind the line of the Northern tier states which were to protect the Middle East from Soviet invasion and establish a chain of defense between NATO and Southeast Asia. So far, Soviet penetration into Arab lands has not altered but rather strengthened Turkish determination to seek Arab friendship. In fact, Moscow has been anxious to avoid any sign which could indicate that its moves may possess

---

general of the Turkish Ministry of Foreign Affairs, to thirteen African ambassadors or heads of mission accredited to the United Arab Republic who officially visited Ankara; *Milliyet*, August 14, 1968.

[116] Shortly after the Arab-Israeli war of 1967, Tunisian Foreign Minister Habib Bourghiba, Jr. (the son of the president) came to Ankara, where he had talks with the Turkish leaders; *Cumhuriyet*, July 8, 1967.

[117] See statement by Çağlayangil after his visit to Morocco in March 1969; *Vatan*, March 4, 1969.

[118] See joint communiqué: *Cumhuriyet*, April 8, 1969. The Turkish press reminded their readers that Algeria used to be an Ottoman province.

an anti-Turkish edge. Nevertheless, both Ankara and Teheran are bound to observe this activity with total suspicion even if they are unable to object to it.[119] No doubt, the very presence of the Soviet navy in the Mediterranean, as well as the authority Moscow acquired in the area, enabled it to bring pressure to bear on Turkey from yet another direction.[120] The complexity of the Middle Eastern situation, the intermingling of Western and Soviet areas of influence, and the continued precarious situation between the Arabs and the Israelis have greatly increased the possibilities of not only a local but also a global conflict, from which Turkey could not remain immune.

All this explains the almost excessive concern of Turkish diplomacy for the maintenance of peace in the Middle East. Turkey's long-range foreign policy goals may only be realized, in fact, when peaceful conditions prevail around her and between the superpowers. Turkey has undertaken to emerge from the status of an industrially undeveloped country and to advance toward modernization and economic development. This endeavor is not only aimed at raising the standard of living of her people; it also will enhance the strength and secure the further survival of the Turkish state.

[119] See Walter Laqueur, "Russia Enters the Middle East," *Foreign Affairs* (January 1969): 296–308.
[120] See Bernard Lewis, "The Great Powers, the Arabs, and the Israelis," *Foreign Affairs* (July 1969): 642–52.

VIII
Development: A Foreign Policy Goal

Resistance to the flood-tide of Civilization is in vain; she is pitiless towards those who ignore or disobey her. . . . Nations which try to function with medieval minds, with primitive superstition, are—in the presence of her might and her sublime majesty—doomed to annihilation or, at best, to servitude or ignominy.—ATATÜRK.

Az veren candan verir, çok veren maldan. (He who gives little gives from the heart, he who gives much gives from wealth.)—Turkish proverb.

T HE LEADERS OF THE NEW REPUB-
lican Turkey were resolved to convert their country into a Western-type community: politically, socially, culturally, and economically. They clearly realized that Westernization could not be separated from economic and technological development.[1] Atatürk and his disciples were attracted by Western social and political patterns not only because they regarded them as the only acceptable forms of the contemporary civilization but because they believed that only by adopting this way of life would Turkey become a viable and sturdy nation.

The original reason for Ottoman modernization was the need for military machinery equal to the modern European forces the empire had to fight.[2] The military aspect of development was never overlooked even in Atatürk's time. The Turkish leaders of the first republic, however, understood what the Ottomans did not: that military technology could not be advanced without an overall economic and industrial development. In the 1920's, social and humanitarian considerations were hardly

---

[1] Because this study considers development an important element of Turkey's foreign policy, the inclusion of this necessarily sketchy chapter was thought indispensable. It should, therefore, be emphasized that its purpose is not to provide a basic exposition of a topic that would require both an economic expert and a separate book-size volume. This is only a brief summation of relevant facts and opinions.

[2] See chapter I, pp. 21–24.

prominent; the purpose of economic and technological progress was to strengthen the Turkish state as a political and military entity.

For more than two decades Turkish leaders smarted under the memories of Ottoman economic and financial dependence, perhaps best illustrated by the hated institutions of capitulations, the administration of Ottoman debt, and other paraphernalia of foreign interference. They vowed not to let themselves be drawn into a similar economic bondage and to rid themselves of the burden of remaining obligations. This suspicion of foreign interference, which made them rely solely on their own scanty domestic resources, hindered effective development. They hoped, however, to achieve economic progress as they had achieved political independence—by their own devices.

The first results of autarkic progress were most unsatisfactory. The devastations of the war of independence; the emigration of the Greeks, Armenians, and Jews, who contributed a major share of the entrepreneurial and technically skilled manpower; and the lack of experience of Turks in business—all were initial hindrances to any meaningful economic advancement. Legislation was introduced in the mid-1920's to encourage private investment; the autochthonous *Iş Bankası* (Business Bank) was created to further this end, but the expected development failed to materialize.

The world-wide depression of the early 1930's further slowed economic development. Turkish exports dipped still lower, while the already meager results of capital-accumulation came to a near standstill. While experiencing these difficulties, the Turks came to be impressed by the spectacular success of Soviet industrialization, which appeared unaffected by the malaise of the capitalist world. The Turkish emphasis, therefore, shifted to establishing government-owned industrial enterprises, a program known as *étatisme* (from the French)—that is, statism.[3]

The relative advantages of private and public enterprise have not ceased to plague Turkish political and economic leaders. The dichotomy between the two systems, in those early years as well as at present, pos-

---

[3] The chief agency for managing industrial plants for the government was the Sümer Bank; another bank, the Eti Bank, was established in 1935 to finance and operate state-owned mines. See Max Weston Thornburg, Graham Spry, and George Soule, *Turkey: An Economic Appraisal* (New York, 1949), pp. 28–31; Peter F. Sugar, "The Nature of Traditional Society: Turkey," in *Political Modernization in Japan and Turkey*, eds. Robert E. Ward and Dankwart A. Rustow (Princeton, N.J., 1964), pp. 167–69.

sesses political and foreign policy implications. To advertise its own system, the Soviet government extended financial and technical assistance in 1934 by setting up textile factories which then were run by the Turkish state.[4]

Indeed, the most significant development project in the pre-World War II period was financed by the government: the purchase of existing railroads from foreign owners and the further extension of the rail network deep into Anatolia. By 1923 Turkey had only one trunk line: the Balkan Railway, which crossed the European triangle of Turkey to Istanbul and continued from the Asian shore of the Bosporus along southern Anatolia to the Syrian–Iraqi border (the line known previously as the Baghdad Railway). Among its few branch lines, one branched off at Eski Şehir and led to, but went no farther than, Ankara.[5]

Since the late 1920's, the Turkish government had constructed new railroads, mostly for strategic reasons. From Ankara eastward another trunk line was laid which pushed via Kayseri and Sivas to the Soviet–Caucasian frontier beyond Kars. East of Ankara, this line also connected with the Baghdad line. The construction of railroads leading into eastern Anatolia continued throughout the life of the first republic, even during World War II.

By the end of the war and in the wake of Soviet threats, the military and economic weakness of Turkey and her dependence on friendly foreign assistance became all too obvious. A new effort was required to move that country nearer to its cherished goal of modernization, Westernization, and economic independence.

DEVELOPMENT GOALS AND PROBLEMS

According to the old Ottoman state philosophy, there could be no power without an army, no army without adequate sources of revenue, no revenue without the prosperity of the subjects, and no prosperity without justice.[6] This train of thought—rephrased and adapted to suit con-

[4] See Leo Tansky, *U.S. and U.S.S.R. Aid to Developing Countries* (New York, 1967), p. 38.
[5] The Ankara railhead was probably the reason for the choice of that city as the provisional and, later, permanent seat of the Turkish government. More centrally located towns, such as Kayseri, had no railroad connections at that time; the southern (Baghdad) line was too much exposed during the war of independence.
[6] See Halil Inalcık, "The Nature of Traditional Society: Turkey," in *Political Modernization*, eds. Ward and Rustow, p. 49.

temporary requirements—has remained the basic philosophy of Turkey's program of economic and industrial-technological development. It appeared to Turkish leaders that the satisfactory answer to the question of their country's independent survival—a question ominously raised by the Soviet threat—lay in speedy development of their resources. Industrialization, higher agricultural yields, increased trade, better education, and higher living standards were needed to strengthen national power and to raise the Turkish nation to the level of modern occidental European powers.

Turkey needed Western economic assistance—as she needed military aid—and the West, in the interest of its own safety, needed Turkey's collaboration and strengthening for the protection of that part of the world against potential Soviet aggression. Thus, Turkey benefited from the Marshall Plan from 1948 to 1951, and from successive foreign aid programs sponsored by the United States. Since 1955 she has also received loans from Germany, Britain, and other European countries.

By the late 1940's, it appeared that *étatisme* was on the way out. The emerging Democratic Party was dedicated to private enterprise and attempted, with little success, to sell some state-owned plants to private firms. Private capital was less available in the 1950–60 period than the government had expected. In fact, government investment in industrialization continued, but most of the aid money was used to improve agriculture, the transportation system, and, generally, the infrastructure of the country's economy.

Railroad construction continued, although at a slower tempo. In 1923, when the republic was proclaimed, Turkey possessed a railroad network of 2,100 miles; by 1945 the country had a network of 4,638 in operation.[7] Since then, another 1,400 miles have been added and the connection with the Iranian railroads established.

Although the extended rail-network certainly helped to improve lagging transportation, it was still inadequate to meet the economic and strategical needs of Turkey. The construction of roads had been neglected during the interwar period in favor of railroads. It was thought that Turkey had to imitate, step-by-step, the stages of Western development, which started with railroads; highway construction began only with the wide use of the automobile.

[7] Thornburg, *Turkey,* p. 298.

Road building, on a country-wide scale, started in 1947, when $5 million in United States military assistance was allocated for this purpose. Again, the emphasis was first on strategy and priority was given to those roads connecting Aegean and Mediterranean harbors with the interior and leading to the Black Sea or the Soviet border. In 1950 Turkey had not much more than 1,000 miles of hard-surfaced roads; by 1967 9,000 miles of such roads were in use; the mileage of macadam roads increased in the same period from 14,000 to 20,300 miles.[8] The significance of highway construction cannot be measured in terms of transportation only; highways established a previously nonexistent network of communication between rural areas and the towns and cities.[9]

During the first three years of the Menderes period, there was rapid expansion, especially in agriculture, electric power production, and transportation. In 1954 a catastrophic harvest produced a sharp setback; thereafter, until 1960, the rate of growth was steady but less rapid. Although the balance sheet of the Menderes period is not unimpressive, the uneven growth, lack of planning, inflation, and economic dislocations indicated that steady development can be successful only when planned and implemented in a more scientific manner and when the outlay is not influenced by day-to-day political motivations. The results also demonstrated that, despite the evident deficiencies and mistakes of the methods used, Turkey's basic assets—human and natural resources, a relatively favorable climate, ample land for expansion, and a central trade location —had been an important part in the advancement.

The land and people of Turkey have been previously assessed from the geopolitical point of view.[10] Here another short evaluation of their impact on development and technical modernization is called for. The average increase in Turkey's population at the rate of 2.5 percent during the past five years (between 1955 and 1960 the increase was 2.9 percent) suggests that, except for unforeseeable disasters, this population will double within the next 30 years.[11] The natural increase stands now at

[8] U.S. Agency for International Development, *Economic and Social Indicators— Turkey* (Ankara, July, 1969), p. 32.

[9] See A. Halûk Ülman and Frank Tachau, "Turkish Politics: The Attempt to Reconcile Rapid Modernization with Democracy," *Middle East Journal* (Spring, 1965): 154–55.

[10] See chapter II, pp. 43–49.

[11] From 1935 to 1965 the population of Turkey doubled. The average population increase between 1935 and 1945 was uneven; because of wartime mobilization, it was only 1.1 percent between 1940 and 1945.

about 800,000 per year. The Turks are a "young" people, in the sense that in 1965 51 percent of the population was below the age of twenty. In 1974 Turkey's population will have in all likelihood surpassed the 40 million mark.[12] In order to guarantee the growth of the economy and of the per capita income, an annual development rate of 6 to 7 percent must be maintained. The ratio of population to developmental increases appears to be highly promising in Turkey, more so than in many developing countries, such as India.

The greatest social impediment to Turkey's modernization has been the cleavage in Turkish society. Ziya Gökalp complained that there were three layers of people in his time: the peasants, living almost in the shadow of central Asian civilization; those educated in the Koran schools and living in the Islamic civilization; and those who had been educated in modern (secular) schools and had embraced Western civilization.[13] In our time, we may still speak of a twofold division: the rural peasant masses and the educated people of the towns and cities—although there are, of course, elements in an intermediary or transitory stage. A social merger can only be effected by the integration of the rural masses into the civilizational fold of the Western-educated element. This problem can only be solved by schooling and mobility.

The literary rate, a clear indicator of educational progress, increased from 10.6 percent of the population six years old and over in 1927 to 48.7 percent in 1965, mostly as a consequence of the introduction of the Latin alphabet and of general schooling. The proportion of the male population among the literate is naturally higher: 64 percent, as against 32.3 percent of the female population. The impact of military enrollment on the average male citizen must not be overlooked; in addition to literacy, military instruction provides for a wide range of technical skills and general life experience by removing the soldiers from their own region and bringing them together with those of other areas.

The agricultural situation is far from optimistic. Erosion threatens a considerable portion of the cultivated areas and limits the number of new tracts of land that can be brought under cultivation.[14] Use of ferti-

---

[12] Although birth control is being studied by governmental agencies, it is frowned upon by many for traditional, military, or nationalistic reasons. A birth control lecture given with the participation of American experts was disrupted in Ankara by angry demonstrators shouting: "Kennedy has eleven children!" *Akşam,* June 27, 1969.

[13] Gökalp, *Turkish Nationalism,* p. 278.

[14] See Eren, *Turkey Today,* p. 110.

lizers, irrigation, drainage, and mechanization would effect higher yields, but progress in this respect has been unsatisfactory in terms of Turkey's rising population and rising living standards.

The progress of industrial production since 1950 has been phenomenal. Mining production has also significantly increased. The least satisfactory development took place in Turkey's foreign trade balance, which has consistently shown an annual deficit since 1951 of from $100 to $250 million. The balance of payments deficit has been, naturally, even larger. Another weakness of Turkey's economy has been the slow growth of domestic accumulation: on the average, the domestic investment has remained at the level of 12 percent of the Gross National Product (which in Greece was 15.6 in 1957, in France 19.7, and in the United States 17.3). The dependence on foreign financial and economic assistance for the achievement of development goals is the single greatest problem of the Turkish economy. The procurement of this transitional assistance, coupled with the ultimate liquidation of the natural dependency which follows such assistance, are the principal objectives of Turkey's economic policy—an endeavor closely linked to other foreign policy objectives of the Turkish state.

The attainment of self-sufficiency through development, to ensure further self-engendered development, was to be achieved through three Five Year Plans.

THE FIVE YEAR PLANS

After the revolution of 1960, partly in protest against the desultory management of the economy under Menderes, a new era of systematically planned development commenced. Three consecutive development plans, each of them to last five years, were to achieve self-sufficiency and raise Turkey's economy from the level of a "progressive" developing country to that of an "industrialized" community.[15] The first Five Year Plan cov-

[15] Prime Minister Demirel classified states from the point of view of per capita Gross National Product as: primitive economies (between $50–$200); developing economies, like Turkey ($200–$600); fully industrial communities ($600–$2000); and progressive industrialized economies (above $2000). He said that Turkey is the "most progressed" of the $200–$600 group, and it is Turkey "to which the world looks with the highest hopes." Demirel then said that Turkey has a vast potential and a great past of which the Turkish nation should take pride. "The nations which are devoid of this national pride are demoralized in their efforts to develop. This grandeur which we have inherited from our ancestors is our greatest hope." *Tercüman,* October 7, 1968.

ered the period 1963–67, and the second Five Year Plan was slated to run from 1968 to 1972. Both plans foresaw a 7 percent growth rate under conditions of stable prices; continued democratic political order and the principle of social justice were listed as concomitants of economic development.

The actual growth rate for the first Five Year Plan period was 6.6 percent. The Gross National Product reached $10.5 billion and per capita income rose to $318. Thus, the Gross National Product increased from 1948 to 1967 by 160 percent, whereas the per capita rise was only 55 percent, due to the population increases. The share of GNP going into investment increased from 13.2 to 18.1 percent in 1967. Despite the real growth, the price index rose only 4.4 percent annually. Domestic saving (less the net foreign balance) increased from 9.7 percent of consumption to 16.5 percent of consumption.

The industrialization of a developing country is regarded as the hallmark of modernization. Turks are particularly proud of their progress in this field and greater sufficiency in industry is considered more important than it is in agriculture. But Turkish industrial production is generally expensive and can be maintained or developed only when protected against foreign competition by tariffs and quotas.

From 1962 to 1967, Turkey's annual imports ranged between $537 and $718 million, and her exports between $368 and $522 million. Deficits of the trade balance thus varied yearly between $310 and $108 million. In addition to this foreign exchange liability, Turkey was obligated to make amortization and interest payments of her debts amounting to over $100 million per annum. The balance of payments deficit was only partially met by "invisible" exports, such as Turkish workers' remittances from Western Europe. The bulk of the deficit was met by foreign loans and grants made by the United States (about 40 percent) and by the consortium of 14 countries organized in 1962 and administered by the Organization of Economic Cooperation and Development (OECD), the successor to the Marshall Plan Administration. Foreign private investment, compared to the magnitude of public economic aid, remained relatively small. The United States economic assistance was handled by the Agency for International Development (AID).

More than 85 percent of Turkey's exports were agricultural products; cotton, tobacco, nuts, dried fruit, livestock, and mohair were the principal items during the first Five Year Plan period. Among nonagricultural goods, copper, chrome, borates, and processed food were the most important.

Only 10 percent of the articles imported into Turkey were consumer goods. The remaining 90 percent were almost equally divided among capital goods (machinery and equipment), raw materials (metals, rubber, chemicals, etc.), and spare parts.

The countries of the European Economic Community were Turkey's chief trading partners. West Germany, France, Italy, Belgium–Luxembourg, and the Netherlands together imported about one-third of Turkey's entire volume. The European Free Trade Area countries (Austria, Denmark, Britain, Sweden, Switzerland, Norway, and Portugal) accounted for less than 20 percent and the United States accounted for the same amount, while the countries of the Eastern bloc (including the Soviet Union) handled about 10 percent.[16]

In 1968 the second Five Year Plan went into operation. It is also based on an overall 7 percent growth rate by the continued rapid development of industry with emphasis on intermediate goods (distinguished from final, consumer goods) and on industries which can rely on Turkish natural resources. The new plan was devised on the basis of a mixed economy—that is, it prescribed imperative instructions for the public sector and indications for the private sector. The government was to concentrate on infrastructural investments (transportation, irrigation, power, social welfare investments, etc.), while the development of manufacture was to be essentially left to the private sector.[17]

According to the AID evaluation of the second plan, the amount of foreign aid likely to be forthcoming would be considerably less than assumed in the plan. There is also a bureaucratic reluctance to assist the private sector and the possible lack of experienced staff in both public and private sectors. Among the favorable factors, the relative success of the first Five Year Plan was cited, along with the zeal for advancing development of the high officials in the government and in the State Planning Organization.[18]

---

[16] The results of the first Five Year Plan are listed in U.S. Agency for International Development, *Briefing Papers on the Turkish Economy* (Ankara, January 3, 1968), mimeograph; and in USAID, *Economic and Social Indicators—Turkey*.

[17] See Republic of Turkey, Prime Ministry, State Planning Organization, *Second Five-Year Development Plan, 1968–1972* (Ankara, 1969).

[18] USAID, *Briefing Papers,* p. 7.

Agricultural growth was very much dependent on the weather and, therefore, impossible to estimate. In the past, agriculture has increased by 3 percent per year on the average—that is, an increase which was in pace with the population expansion. The second plan envisaged a growth of 12 percent per annum in the industrial sector. It intended to lay the foundation for the production of capital goods in the third Five Year Plan projected for 1973–77.

The second Five Year Plan calls for a 50 percent increase in imports and a 40 percent increase in exports. The resulting greater foreign trade deficit is to be met by a projected rise in tourist receipts and workers' remittances. During the five-year period of the plan, the overall gap of 1.6 billion dollars is to be filled by foreign aid and the influx of private capital. Short-term credits by the European Monetary Agency and the International Monetary Fund are also to be extended.

Turkish President Cevdet Sunay, addressing the National Press Club in Washington, expressed his expectations for the second Five Year Plan in the following words: "We firmly hope that by the mid-1970's, after the completion of the Second Five Year Plan, the Turkish economy will have reached a stage enabling it to continue self-sustaining growth without foreign aid on special terms."[19]

It was also clear, however, that the success of the plan itself depended largely on the availability of foreign assistance. In the words of the plan: "Realization of investment and development targets foreseen in the Second Plan depends to a large extent on availability of foreign credits. The character of credits to be borrowed is closely linked with reducing the economy's dependence on foreign sources."[20]

The procurement of foreign credits remains a task of Turkish diplomacy and depends on the evolution of Turkey's relations with foreign countries. Although, as in the past, the lion's share of foreign aid is expected from the West, the Turkish government is not unwilling to accept some modest assistance from the Soviet Union as well. To depend so much on foreign powers for her economic development—as Turkey was forced to do for military equipment—is regarded as a necessary evil. To get rid of this dependence as soon as possible is an aspiration; in the meantime, realism must be the present course.

[19] *New York Times,* April 5, 1967.
[20] See *Development Plan of Turkey: Second Five-Year Plan (1968–1972),* Summary (Ankara, 1967), p. 40.

AID FROM THE WEST AND FROM THE EAST

Public criticism of foreign policy has been made possible by the evolving democratization of the political process and the multiparty system. Although it is badly needed for the fulfillment of the country's development program, critics have not exempted foreign economic assistance from their purview. Since Western—primarily, American—aid has been pouring into Turkey since the early 1950's, this Western assistance has been scrutinized most closely by political leaders and the press and often has been subjected to scathing criticism. That a proud nation has had to rely on and ask for financial help seems humiliating to many and has become one of the sources of anti-Americanism.[21]

While it may seem odd that the donors of assistance or the vital assistance itself were being assailed, it must be understood that spokesmen of the leftist or extreme leftist opposition do not agree that such aid is needed nor do they approve of the manner in which it has been proffered. Apart from unsophisticated opinions which propose that Turkey rely solely on her own resources for her development,[22] more informed critics argue against the way aid has been spent and against "strings" said to be attached to Western assistance.[23] Others have deplored the "niggardliness" of the assistance and explain that assistance is not an act of generosity but a duty.[24] In intellectual circles, it is widely held that although the assistance is needed it is "too expensive" and that Turkey is being exploited by the West, especially by the United States.[25] On the other hand, the government and its experts, as well as leaders of most of the political parties, are fully aware of the usefulness and necessity of Western

[21] See chapter IV, pp. 145–46.

[22] The proponents of such views were either extreme leftists who thought in terms of the "Soviet example" or xenophobic nationalists.

[23] For instance, the agreement concerning the Black Sea copper complex was said to contain "capitulatory provisions" and the right to interfere in domestic affairs (referring to the clauses according to which American material must be purchased, AID was to be supplied with information on how the loan was spent, that AID representatives should be on the board of the company, etc.); *Cumhuriyet*, February 4, 1969.

[24] Some intellectuals also submit that American assistance is aimed at strengthening the security of the United States (not primarily that of Turkey); therefore, such aid should be regarded as an "investment" and not economic assistance to Turkey; *Milliyet*, June 13, 1969.

[25] This was especially maintained in connection with investment by private foreign capital. Profit transfers often exceeded the invested capital within a few years. *Yeni Gazete*, June 24, 1969; *Milliyet*, July 4, 1969.

assistance, although they have been often critical of some details.[26]

The Marxist-influenced or étatist critics, in addition to their opposition to the existence or development of the private sector, have deprecated the American tendency to favor the latter type of industries.[27] Other extreme leftists who have clamored for a "change of the order" would like to see a social transformation combined with a massive development program, similar to that accomplished by Russia in the early 1930's. For them, and also for protagonists of moderate views, speedy industrialization is the essence of the matter, and they are inclined to jettison democracy to build an industrial base quickly.

Thus, the various questions arising in connection with the economic development problem raise basic foreign policy issues: they even place in doubt the principle of Westernization. Mehmet Turgut, the Minister of Industry, responded to such "heretical" views in the following manner:

Arguments by some quarters on whether Turkey should be in the Eastern or Western Bloc . . . have still not ended. Our answer to them is: *Turkey is in the Western World and an integral part of it.* This is not just a requirement of political or commercial agreements, as some may think. It is a natural outcome of a 600-year historic development and a 150-year cultural evolution. An overwhelming majority of our people believe in *development in democracy.* The method is planned development with western measures. Those who think otherwise are not the friends of the nation, to say the least.[28]

It has never been asserted that Western economic aid, more specifically American development aid, was given for humanitarian and exclusively altruistic motivations. Since the end of World War II, the United States has programmed a great variety of assistance plans: the UNRRA (United

---

[26] Prime Minister Demirel gave the following explanations in a press conference: "It should be clearly understood that the extremist views against the foreign capital have today been abandoned even in the countries governed by a Communist regime and it is an outdated view. The reality is that foreign capital naturally aims at making a profit. Certainly it does not come with an altruistic aim, without aiming at a profit. But it is wrong to describe foreign capital as a device of international exploitation harmful to national interests." *Cumhuriyet,* July 7, 1969.

[27] Associate Professor of the Istanbul University, Vural F. Savaş, came to the conclusion that private foreign capital had nothing to do with Turkey's industrialization. "On the contrary," he wrote, "it hampers industrialization." In his view, the influx of foreign capital did not help the balance of payments but gave the foreign investors a "monopoly domination" and prevented the use of national capital. *Milliyet,* Nov. 25, 1968.

[28] *Son Havadis,* November 21, 1968. (Italics added.)

Nations Relief and Rehabilitation Administration), to rebuild the economies of war-ravaged countries; the Marshall Plan, to stabilize the economies of European countries; and the Technical Assistance Program, to provide expert advice. The United States has been instrumental in setting up international agencies to assist in development, such as the International Bank for Reconstruction and Development, the International Monetary Fund, and the Organization for European Cooperation and Development (OECD). It was realized soon after the beginning of the Cold War that communism should not be opposed only by military measures; economic and social conditions should be created that would immunize peoples to the allure of revolutionary change. It may, therefore, rightly be said that development aid is, indirectly, in the interest of the United States; but, directly, it has helped the recipient countries raise their living standards and establish a greater measure of social justice. Its effects are thus humanitarian as well.

Soviet economic assistance was also basically politically motivated: it wished to advertise Socialist-type institutions (including the Soviet Union itself) and to compete with, and eventually to disrupt, economic relations between the West and the developing countries. Its practical effects on the recipient countries may also be, like American aid, humanitarian and social.[29]

The United States gave Turkey economic aid totaling $2,531.2 million to December 31, 1968; this amount was in addition to military assistance. Some of the military aid, such as the road-building program, also aided Turkey's general economy. The development aid was provided in three forms: outright grants ($951 million) or loans; Public Law 480 shipments (surplus agricultural goods sold under the Agricultural Development Act of 1954 for local Turkish currency); and technical assistance. Turkey ranked sixth among other countries receiving United States aid.[30]

The American assistance was handled by the Agency for International Development (AID) and channeled by it to the recipients, which were mostly Turkish governmental agencies or private firms. Individual agreements had to precede the release of the amounts. The terms for production loans were generally as follows: a 10-year grace period followed by 30-year amortization, with interest rates of $\frac{3}{4}$ to 1 percent during the grace period and 2 to $2\frac{1}{2}$ percent thereafter.

[29] See Tansky, *Aid to Developing Countries,* pp. 4–12.
[30] After India, Korea, Pakistan, Brazil, and Vietnam; *ibid.,* p. 15.

It is only understandable that the United States government (and the Congress) was anxious that its taxpayers' money should be put to proper use. This concern made it necessary for the AID to investigate those receiving assistance and to inquire into the employment of the amounts released. Similarly, private investors wishing to protect their interests restricted the freedom of action of the beneficiaries. The strings so frequently criticized were necessary concomitants of the Turkish dependency on aid and not a result of a United States policy to control the Turkish economy. Washington was by no means enthusiastic about having to provide assistance and would have been happy to see the end of it. Because the intention was to put Turkey (and other recipients of aid) on its own feet, it nonetheless appeared necessary to control the use of assistance to produce the optimum results.

In fact, the United States assistance has been annually reduced by Congress (and against proposals of the president); Turkey experienced a constant decrease of aid in what was perhaps the most critical period of her development program. Thus, American economic assistance, which was $135 million in 1968, was reduced to $60 million in 1969 and to $43.5 million in 1970.[31]

In recent years the loans provided under the United States aid program have been divided between industrial development loans and loans to assist Turkey in her import requirements. Among the 35 project loans (industrial loans for specific targets), those given for the construction of the Ereğli Iron and Steel Plant, the Keban Dam,[32] the Black Sea Copper Plant, and Ambarlı Power Plant, and two loans to construct the rail line between Muş and the Iranian border and the Gökçekaya Dam and transmission lines were particularly significant; smaller loans were given to, among others, the Middle East Technical University, to the Hacettepe University, the Waterworks Department of Ankara, the Atatürk University of Erzerum, and the Goodyear Tire Plant.[33]

The development plans, intended to achieve a continuous growth in industry, mining, and agriculture, were geared to a constant rise in imports. To balance the importation of machinery and raw material, exports

[31] *New York Times,* January 13, 1969, March 20, 1970.
[32] The United States is only one of the contributors. Others are the European Industrial Bank, the West German Government, France, Italy, and the World Bank. The total costs were estimated at $125 million; the American contribution was $40 million.
[33] See *Daily News* (Ankara), July 11, 1968.

have to grow. In view of the steadily declining American aid, the Turkish government was anxious to find alternative sources of assistance, primarily to control the balance of payments during the first and second Five Year Plans.

On July 31, 1962, an aid consortium within the OECD was established by fourteen countries (Austria, Belgium, Canada, Denmark, the Federal Republic of Germany, France, Italy, Luxembourg, the Netherlands, Norway, Sweden, Switzerland, the United Kingdom, and the United States), and the International Bank for Reconstruction and Development (World Bank) to provide program aid and help to balance the payments deficit. Between 1963 and 1965, the consortium disbursed $705 million.[34] In 1967 the annual aid was $269.15 million; in 1968 it dropped to $165 million.[35] Turkey also obtained aid from the International Monetary Fund and the European Monetary Agency.

During the past five years, the development aid (in addition to the defense aid) given by West Germany has gradually increased; Bonn was able to grant financial assistance even outside the consortium commitments. This led some Turkish press organs to announce that "Uncle Hans is to replace Uncle Sam."[36] Indeed, economic relations between Turkey and West Germany have been gaining momentum; in 1968 the Federal Republic headed the list of Turkey's trade partners (accounting for 20.4 percent of Turkey's imports and 17.4 percent of her exports), overtaking the United States (accounting for 15.8 percent of Turkey's exports and 14.6 percent of her imports). Britain was third, Italy fourth, and the Soviet Union fifth.[37]

It can easily be imagined how Turkish diplomacy (including the activities of the representatives of her economic ministries and of the State Planning Organization) has to exert itself to maintain contact with the various assisting governments and aid organizations, as well as with their delegations in Ankara. Much of the approval of grants and loans is made only after scrupulous investigation, criticism of past practices, and ex-

[34] Z. Y. Hershlag, *Turkey: The Challenge of Growth* (2d ed.; Leiden, 1968), pp. 261–63; Duygu Sezer, "Türkiyenin Ekonomik İlişkileri," (Economic Relations in Turkey), in *Olaylarla Türk Dış Politikası,* ed. Siyasal Bilgiler Fakültesi Dış Münasebetler Enstitüsü, p. 403.
[35] *Milliyet,* September 4, 1967; *Yeni Gazete,* July 7, 1968; *Cumhuriyet,* July 29, 1968.
[36] *Milliyet,* September 6 and 11, 1968; *Hürriyet,* September 6, 1968.
[37] *Yeni Gazete,* June 4, 1969.

hortations for the future—a combination of procedures often distasteful and humiliating to the Turkish partner. In its proposals, the consortium has not stood behind the American reservations and conditions when asking for guarantees regarding the uses of the amounts it was ready to release. It is not suggested here that the reasons for accepting Soviet aid were due to a sense of frustration or the wish to oppose competition to Western aid. A certain amount of satisfaction was derived, however, from the fact that at least a modicum of aid was to come from the other side of the Iron Curtain.

In March 1967, an agreement was signed between Turkey and the Soviet Union providing for a loan in the amount of $200 million in the form of equipment, technical assistance, and material deliveries for the establishment of certain industrial plants. The plants envisaged were a petroleum refinery at Izmir, an aluminum complex near Konya, a sulphuric acid factory at Bandirma, and a fiberboard factory with an undetermined location. Negotiations for a third Turkish steel plant to be constructed with Soviet assistance near Iskenderun were also pursued, although by early 1969 it had become evident that the amount of $200 million would be insufficient to cover all of these projects. A glass factory project and the project for a vodka factory were reportedly dropped, the latter because Moscow insisted on obtaining a permanent license fee.[38]

A particular feature of these agreements is the repayment clause: redemption of the loans will be effected by export deliveries within 15 years. The goods to be supplied include tobacco (15 percent), nuts, olive oil, citrus fruits, and raisins (45 percent), and manufactured goods (40 percent). The loans carry an interest of 2.5 percent per annum.[39]

Neither the amounts involved nor other features of the aid agreement with Russia were spectacular. Nevertheless, the event attracted much attention both in Turkey and abroad. The Turkish government pointed to this agreement as a demonstration of its independence from the West and of the fact that the development aid received was not unilateral. Western capitals were interested but less excited than some press organs. The Soviet assistance, compared with the Western aid efforts, appeared insignificant: in fact, it represented less than 4 percent of the total military and economic assistance obtained by Turkey since 1950. Western circles were

[38] *Cumhuriyet,* March 15, 1969.
[39] *Daily News* (Ankara), July 11, 1968; *Cumhuriyet,* July 8, 1968.

also convinced that Moscow's fulfillment of its commitments would compare unfavorably with Western achievements and might have a disenchanting effect on Turkish officials and the public.[40]

In addition to the advantage of having another source of assistance, the Turkish government did not wish to stand behind other governments of the Middle East, whether committed to the West or not. Iran, for example, received some Soviet aid as well as assistance from the West.[41]

In the wake of the Turco–Soviet political rapprochement, trade relations between the two countries, and between Turkey and other Eastern bloc countries, intensified. Russia now ranks fifth in volume among Ankara's trading partners; Hungary, East Germany, Czechoslovakia, Poland, Rumania, and Bulgaria (in that order) have also increased their commercial exchanges with Ankara. They have also discussed with Turkey individual industrial development projects.[42]

Although it is consistent that with the improvement of her political relations with the Soviet Union and other bloc countries Turkey also strengthened economic ties, the character of these ties and the way in which agreements have been negotiated reaffirm that Turkey has no intention of loosening her economic contacts with the West. On the contrary, during the past ten years she has sought to intensify them. Most significant in this respect are Ankara's endeavors to join the Common Market (European Economic Community or EEC).

TURKEY AND THE EUROPEAN ECONOMIC COMMUNITY

On July 31, 1959, the Menderes government addressed an application to the Commission of the European Economic Community in Brussels for association with the community under Article 238 of the Treaty of Rome. A similar application had been submitted by Greece on June 8, 1959. In December 1959, exploratory talks were held between the Commission and the Turkish government; however, these talks were interrupted by the revolutionary events in Turkey. Only in April 1962 were the negotiations resumed which led to the community's second association agree-

[40] Difficulties in Soviet cement deliveries gave rise to some angry exchanges between Turkish authorities and the Soviet embassy in Ankara in 1968.

[41] When asking for Ankara's reasons, this writer was told by a high official of the Ministry of Foreign Affairs: "They offered us the loan and we had no reason to refuse it."

[42] Daily News (Ankara), April 11, 1968.

ment with Turkey, signed in Ankara on September 12, 1963.[43] The agreement, signed on behalf of Turkey by Feridun Cemal Erkin, Minister of Foreign Affairs, and by the president of the Council of Ministers of the community, as well as representatives of the six member states (Belgium, the Federal Republic of Germany, France, Italy, Luxembourg, and the Netherlands), entered into force on December 1, 1964.

On the occasion of the signature of the association agreement with Turkey, Professor Walter Hallstein, then president of the commission, made the following remarks in his speech:

Turkey is part of Europe. That is really the ultimate meaning of what we are doing today. It confirms in incomparably topical form a truth which is more than the summary expression of a geographical concept or of a historical fact that holds good for several centuries. Turkey is part of Europe: and here we think first and foremost of the stupendous personality of Atatürk whose work meets us at every turn in this country, and of the radical way in which he recast every aspect of life in Turkey along European lines. . . .

Turkey is part of Europe: today this means that *Turkey is establishing a constitutional relationship with the European Community.* Like the Community itself, that relationship is imbued with the concept of evolution.[44]

The negotiations between the community and Turkey were marked by several difficulties. Interestingly, however, the question whether Turkey was "European" (the Treaty of Rome speaks of "European" nations becoming members of the community) hardly came up during these talks. Turkey, by her membership in various European organizations, was already recognized as being "European" politically, if not geographically.

It is difficult to ascertain how far the Greek application for association influenced the Turkish decision to follow suit. The Turkish action may, however, be cited as yet another example of the *complexe de mimétisme* (imitation complex) that characterizes the relationship of Turkey and Greece.

During the long negotiations, the parties concentrated on the economic aspects of the Turkish plea for association. Both the Greek and the Turkish association agreements declared in their Preambles that the assistance to be provided to the applicant countries by the community aimed at preparing them for their subsequent entry into the Common

[43] The association agreement with Greece was signed on October 9, 1961, and came into force on November 1, 1962.

[44] Information Memo No. 8667/X/63–E issued by the official spokesman of the EEC, Ankara, September 12, 1963. (Italics added.)

Market. Article 238 of the Treaty of Rome was intentionally vague; the concept of "association" had to be determined individually for each applying state.

Whereas the agreement with Greece was based on a formula of a customs union and envisaged full membership after the transition period of 12 years (possibly extended to 22 years), when Greece will adopt the community's external tariff (by gradually abolishing tariffs and quota restrictions between her and the other six), the agreement with Turkey foresaw economic union only after three stages: a five-year preparatory stage (which could be extended to nine years), a twelve-year transition period in which a customs union could be established; and a final period when the customs union would develop toward full economic union. It was expected that by that time Turkey would be economically strong enough to comply with the requirements of full membership.

Turkey entered the preparatory stage on the day her association agreement came into force. During that period, she was reaping only benefits from the agreement: the community was assisting her economy by granting duty-free import quotas to four of Turkey's staple exports, tobacco, raisins, figs, and nuts and hazelnuts.[45] Furthermore, the community was, through the European Investment Bank, granting Turkey a loan in the amount of $175 million for the five-year period.[46]

Under Article 6 of the agreement, an Association Council was established which was comprised of representatives of the six governments, of Turkey, and of the EEC commission. The council was to examine the results of the association arrangement and decide on concerted action on issues which might arise. Decisions were to be made unanimously. During the preparatory stage, relations were established between the European Parliament and the Turkish Grand National Assembly: an association assembly with 15 delegates from each body was to meet in regular intervals.

Article 1 of the agreement provided that four years after its entry into force the Association Council was to propose, if it thought fit, the terms, conditions, and timing of the transition stage; this proposal required

---

[45] Upon Turkey's request this list was extended by the Association Council in December 1967, to include quotas of following articles: fish and shellfish, grapes, oranges, wines, and some textiles. *Vatan*, December 6, 1967.

[46] For the text of the agreement, see Information Memo No. P–35/63 of the official spokesman of the EEC, Brussels, November 7, 1963.

ratification by the legislatures of the seven contracting states. These negotiations were opened on December 1, 1968, and had not been completed at the time of this writing. In July 1970, however, a draft agreement provided for the commencement of the transition stage, following ratification by the signatories. Within 12 years, a customs union was to be established between Turkey and her partners; internal tariffs were gradually to be reduced and eventually eliminated. Within 22 years, Turkey was to become a full member of the EEC.

It is the general view in Turkey and by the leaders of the European Community that Turkey applied for participation in the Common Market for political rather than economic reasons.[47] At the time the application was filed, although this was not so true later, it appeared that the community could develop into the nucleus of not only an integrated European economy but also of a political federation of European states. Turkey certainly wished to join a politically united Europe, and it seemed that such a united Europe was to be achieved through the economic back door rather than through a direct political fusion. Turkey, indeed, wished to obtain a much more extensive treaty than the one she was able to negotiate.

Among the economic leaders and experts in Turkey, there was no unanimity about the advisability of Turkey's accession to the Common Market; even the transition period was viewed skeptically by many. It was realized that "transition" meant transition into the customs union which would require Turkey gradually to reduce and eventually to abolish tariffs and quotas vis-à-vis the other members of the community.[48] Fear was expressed that even a gradual lowering of protective tariffs would be detrimental or even ruinous to Turkey's fledgling industry. Similarly, the "harmonizing" of Turkey's agricultural policy with the joint principles accepted by the Common Market could not be

[47] See Besim Üstünel, "Turkey's Attitude Towards Common Markets," *Turkish Yearbook of International Relations, 1964,* pp. 13–18. When Jean Rey, president of the commission of the EEC, visited Ankara, he said in connection with the negotiations on the transition stage: "Turkey's participation in the European Economic Community was entirely for political reasons. There is no need to change these motives now." *Cumhuriyet,* June 6, 1968.

[48] According to newspaper reports, Turkey is expected to apply a 60 percent general tariff reduction during the transition period. The remaining 40 percent is to be eliminated within two years after the completion of the transition phase; *Milliyet,* March 5, 1969.

achieved quickly. The differences in the wage and productivity levels between Turkey and the Common Market countries presented additional reasons for caution.[49]

It is understandable that the Turkish government does not want to jeopardize the success of the three Five Year Plans by any precipitate move, even if such a move would expedite their country's entry into the community.[50] The negotiations of an agreement relative to the transition stage were bound to be cautious and slow. During the preparatory phase, Turkey had to make no sacrifices; she only benefited from the association. In the second stage, Turkey will have to meet the demands of the community.[51] Hard bargaining is certainly to be expected; financial aid will have to be continued even during the initial years of the transition period. Since this period is to run for at least 22 years, later adjustments will have to be made as Turkey advances toward self-sufficiency.

There was no doubt that a new "model" of a transition program had to be established which would suit both the interests of Turkey and comply with the requirements of the community. Clearly, even the gradual exposure of the secluded Turkish market to the large economy of the Common Market area will have a somewhat traumatic effect on the former. The air of the bristling economy of Western Europe will, it is hoped, exercise an electrifying influence on Turkey's development, both economic and social. While it may kill some nonviable industrial enterprises, it will enliven others. The effect of such a merger on Turkish agriculture is difficult to foresee; competition with Italy and Greece in the

[49] According to a press report, an inquiry made by Common Market experts found that wages in the community were three times higher than in Turkey, while workers' productivity was 2.5 times lower in Turkey. Turkish workers' productivity while working in Germany, Belgium, or France compared favorably with that of local workers. Therefore, the study concluded, low productivity in Turkey was due to organizational, administrative, and local factors which could be overcome when stimulated by foreign competition; a speedier entry would not be harmful but would shorten the "breaking in" period, such as happened with the Italian industry, which was also thought to be endangered. *Son Havadis,* September 26, 1968.

[50] The Turkish Planning Organization suggested two conditions to be applied during the transition stage: (1) Turkey's development growth rate must be maintained; (2) an increase of Turkish exports into the community area should be secured. *Cumhuriyet,* February 25, 1969.

[51] Aydın Yalçın, an economist and member of the Turkish parliamentary delegation to the Association Assembly, suggested that the preparatory stage should not be extended because the transition stage would not slow down Turkey's industrialization and economic development. Turkish industry, he wrote, was developing in complete disregard of international competition. "We have to bring rapidly the competitive discipline of international markets to the Turkish economy." *Milliyet,* October 3, 1968.

field of citrus and other fruit products will be difficult. It is likely, how-ever, that the present-day export problems could be solved; the Common Market countries already offer Turkey the widest market for her exports. This trend will increase many times over.

As with other Turkish foreign policy goals, the aspiration to move into the European Economic Community is characterized by a measure of ambivalence. Turkey is a country keenly interested in her independence and the preservation of her sovereign rights. Even the ties with NATO are resented by many, and Ankara has been anxious to follow a policy of the "free hand," as far as is compatible with the alliance. On the other hand, accession to the European Economic Community would greatly reduce her freedom in matters of economic policy; she would become bound in an almost indissoluble customs and economic union where, in many respects, she will have to bow before the will of the majority of member states. Should a European political federation evolve as a result of this cautious beginning, her national independence will be restricted even more, if not entirely curtailed, in favor of the federal agencies to be established. It appears that the present Turkish government, however, wishes to go ahead with the policy of penetrating into the "heart of Europe" and to avoid being "left out" of anything European. There seems to be no dissent in this respect between the government and the main opposition party.

Turkey has sought to promote the movement for a united Europe be-cause she also wishes to be a part of it. Integration, however, is not only a European phenomenon. Economic cooperation is particularly an answer to poverty and retardation; in cooperation there is strength. Another aspect of Turkey's ambivalence is that while she is looking primarily toward the West she does not wish to overlook the East. While seeking to enter the most advanced economic union of our times, she took care to participate in a cooperative venture with her two Eastern allies.

REGIONAL COOPERATION FOR DEVELOPMENT

As described in chapter VII, the political-military alliance created to extend the containment zone against Soviet aggression east of Turkey and, at the same time, to protect Turkey's eastern flank, suffered a relative depreciation in the eyes of its participants. CENTO was the alliance sys-tem salvaged from the Baghdad Pact and, thus, in the estimation of Middle

Eastern political leaders, was somewhat tainted by this birth defect. The participation of Britain, the former principal colonial power in the area, and in an unofficial manner by the United States (which many view as the chief "imperialist" power) also affected the reputation of the Central Treaty Organization. Its strict military significance suffered because of Pakistan's abstention from planning and maneuvers. On the other hand, there was agreement about the potentials of this association in the field of mutual economic assistance and cooperation. The leaders of the three regional powers (Turkey, Iran, and Pakistan) agreed that it was useful to separate their reciprocal economic activities from CENTO and thought it prudent to create a purely economic organization among themselves, excluding the nonregional participants in CENTO.

In April 1964, when the three foreign ministers met at the CENTO Ministerial Council at Washington, the establishment of the tripartite organization was agreed upon in principle. In July of the same year, when Pakistan's President Ayub Khan and the shah of Iran visited Turkey, their ministers prepared the texts of an agreement which the heads of state of Turkey (President Cemal Gürsel), Iran, and Pakistan approved on July 22, 1964, in Istanbul.[52]

The agreement provided for the creation of a Ministerial Council composed of the three foreign ministers and ministers in charge of other portfolios, a Regional Planning Committee composed of the heads of the planning organizations in the three countries, and a Secretariat to serve the above institutions.

The signatories further agreed in principle to promote a freer movement of goods, closer collaboration between their chambers of commerce, formulation and implementation of joint purpose projects, reduction of postal rates among their three countries, and improvement of air, sea, road, and rail transportation. They also wished to promote tourism, to abolish visa formalities, and to provide technical assistance to one another. They agreed to expand cultural cooperation,

particularly oriented towards creating mass consciousness of the common cultural heritage, disseminating information about history, civilization, and culture of the peoples of the region, *inter alia*, through establishment of chairs in universities, the exchange of students, the granting of scholarships, the establishment of cultural centers and the joint sponsorship of an institute for initiating studies and research on their common cultural heritage.

[52] For the text of the agreement, see *Turkish Yearbook of International Relations, 1964*, pp. 172–74.

The activities thus planned and implemented were to bear the name of Regional Cooperation for Development (RCD).

References to the common cultural heritage of Turks, Iranians, and Pakistanis, while historically accurate, might have been politically undesirable in an international instrument during Atatürk's time. They certainly reflect an abandonment of ideological rigidity but are coupled with the flexibility and ambivalence characteristic of Turkish foreign policy since the mid-sixties.

Ayub Khan of Pakistan, at the ceremony of the signing of the agreement, made the following remarks, which seemed to ignore the alliance ties of the three countries:

In the condition of the world and in view of the confrontation of great state-communities, the preservation of the identity of small nations remains difficult. Today four Great Powers divide the world. These are: America, Russia, China, and India. From their point of view, small nations are like pawns in a chess game unless the latter will mutually add to one another's strength. For this reason, Turkey, Iran, Pakistan, and even Afghanistan, should unite in friendship. We should begin this collaboration in the fields of culture and economics if not in that of politics.[53]

By September 1964, the Regional Planning Committee met and submitted plans to the Ministerial Council meeting in Teheran in October 1964. It was decided to form committees to deal with the following tasks: trade, tourism, shipping, and cooperative project enterprises (to be chaired by Turkish chairmen); cultural cooperation, road and rail transportation, oil, and technical cooperation (to be headed by Iranian chairmen); mail-telegraph-telephone, insurance, and air transportation (to be headed by Pakistani chairmen).[54]

The Ministerial Council of the RCD met every six months in the capitals of the three member countries. In November 1967, the number of committees was reduced to six: industrial, commercial, communications, technical cooperation, social affairs, and petroleum and petrochemical committees.[55] In some areas, such as mail-telegraph-telephone communications, where rates were lowered, progress could speedily be made. In many other fields, however, much detailed work was required before

[53] Siyasal Bilgiler Fakültesi Dış Münasebetler Enstitüsü, *Olaylarla Türk Dış Politikası*, pp. 425–28.
[54] *Ibid.*
[55] *Cumhuriyet*, November 7, 1967.

realistic plans could be prepared. Transportation facilities among the three countries were notoriously poor; exchange of goods was hampered because their products were competitive rather than complementary. Furthermore, capital for investment was insufficient, and foreign, nonregional sources had to be tapped.[56] Nevertheless, some progress was made, at least in the preparation of blueprints for joint enterprises.[57] Most promising, however, were the plans to promote transportation between the three countries, an area in which CENTO was also pushing with its nonmilitary program.[58]

Even more ambitious schemes have been voiced in connection with the RCD, especially by its non-Turkish members. The establishment of a "Common Market," in which tariffs between Turkey, Iran, and Pakistan would be abolished, has been suggested.[59] However, the Turkish side has pointed out that such a move would be incompatible with Turkey's future membership in the European Economic Community.[60]

It may rightly be said, perhaps even with greater justification than in the case of Turkey's association with the Common Market, that her participation in the Regional Cooperation for Development was motivated by political rather than economic reasons.[61] Turkey could no doubt gain by intensifying her trade with Iran and Pakistan, although this relationship has hardly any significance compared with Turkey's export-import relations with European countries and the United States. It may be presumed that the original protagonist of the RCD was Pakistan, a disgruntled member of CENTO. While maintaining cordial relations with Turkey and Iran, Pakistan preferred to place that relationship on a

[56] *Vatan*, September 5, 1968.
[57] In June 1968, it was reported that 14 "memoranda of agreement" regarding joint ventures would be signed; oil-refinery, ball-bearing, jute, and aluminum plants were planned. *Milliyet*, June 18, 1969.
[58] The railway link between Turkey and Iran having been completed, through trains could be run from the Bulgarian–Turkish border to the Iranian border of Turkey (passenger and freight cars have to be ferried across the Bosporus at Istanbul). Papers reported that Turkey thus had become the transit center between Europe and the Middle East. See *Vatan*, September 13, 1968; *Zafer*, October 17, 1968.
[59] The shah of Iran suggested setting up a Common Market of the RCD states in an interview with a reporter of *Cumhuriyet*; see May 27, 1968. A similar suggestion was made by the Pakistani representative at the meeting of the Regional Planning Council of RCD at Ankara; *Cumhuriyet*, December 3, 1968.
[60] See *Tercüman*, January 2, 1969.
[61] Üstünel, "Common Markets," in *Turkish Yearbook of International Relations, 1964*, p. 18.

strictly regional level without political alignments of any kind. She also hoped, as suggested by Ayub Khan, that nonaligned Afghanistan and perhaps other uncommitted countries of the Middle East would join this nonpolitical economic and cultural organization. For Turkey, as for Iran, it appeared important to maintain close contacts with Pakistan in view of the latter's neutralistic proclivities and flirtations with China. The RCD may indeed be presented as no offshoot of CENTO and unconnected with the superpowers of West and East. It may preserve collaboration between the powers of the northern tier, even if one or two of them decided to choose the road of official nonalignment. Although the RCD was called into being to pursue economic and cultural goals, these cannot fully be separated from politics. The regular meeting of their foreign ministers, the increasing contacts between their other high officials, and frequent visits of their experts cannot fail to affect political relations among the three countries.

It was particularly important for Turkey to project an image before the peoples of the Middle East that differed from that attributed to her by Nasser and his vehemently anticolonialist supporters. As a member of the RCD, Turkey was no longer an exponent of the imperialist West but an independent Middle Eastern power, one that wished to promote co-operation among the Islamic countries of the area.[62]

Thus, through the medium of economics and cultural relations, Turkey displayed her non-European face. Yet the face she shows to the West remains her more genuine appearance, both politically and economically. Turkey expects the West to help her achieve industrialized Western-type nationhood. Compared to this ambitious goal, the Eastern economic-cultural relations are bound to be considered secondary.

THE OUTLOOK

Turkey's sustained development cannot be doubted: her GNP is soaring with the expected annual growth of around 7 percent, and annual per capita production is rising despite the population expansion. By 1969 the estimated GNP exceeded $10 billion and its per capita value rose above

[62] When Turkish President Sunay visited Baghdad, his conversations with Iraqi President Aref included the idea of an "Islamic Common Market," which would include Turkey, Iraq, Iran, Pakistan, Afghanistan, Kuwait, and Saudi Arabia. There was, however, no sequel to this conversation, which was probably the result of some "mutual good feeling" rather than serious consideration; *Milliyet*, May 1, 1968.

the $300 mark.[63] It is therefore expected without undue optimism that this increase will continue throughout the second and during the third Five Year Plan periods, unless unforeseen domestic or international events intervene.

Turkey's goal is not just the achievement of a constant increase of the GNP by systematically expanding her industry, agriculture, mining, and services. All of this is regarded as a stepping-stone to surpass what is known as the take-off stage of economic development—that is, the level of stabilized growth at which massive economic assistance is no longer needed.[64] Since World War II, many developing nations have received massive assistance but few, if any, have been able to pass beyond this dependence.[65] The doubters or critics of Turkey's economic success do not deny the evidence of growth, but they are skeptical that the level of assured self-sustaining growth can be attained through the three Five Year Plans.

Estimates of the date when Turkey will no longer need massive aid from abroad have varied from 1972 to 1977, the end of the third Five Year Plan.[66] Others, in Turkey and abroad, doubt whether any of these predictions can be considered realistic.[67] The opposition parties have often criticized the government for its unfounded optimism about the economic status of the country and the success of the development plans. Some of this criticism is directed toward the slow speed of development;

[63] In 1955 the per capita production was $192; in 1967 it was already $279. Iran, starting from a lower level ($156 in 1955), achieved a similar rise to $249 by 1967.

[64] See W. W. Rostow, *The Stages of Economic Growth* (New York, 1960), pp. 274–306.

[65] Only Nationalist China (Taiwan) was credited with having reached that stage; American development assistance was consequently discontinued there.

[66] "It is considered possible that after the implementation of the Second Plan, the Turkish economy will continue to develop at a fast rate without feeling the need for foreign aid in the form of development credit as a result of bridging the deficit on the balance of payments and rapid increases in domestic savings." *Development Plan of Turkey: Second Five-Year Plan,* Summary, p. 18. The prediction that foreign aid will not be needed by the end of the second plan (1972) was later modified and the year 1975 indicated as the end of foreign aid. More cautious estimates spoke of the end of the third plan (1977); see statement by Turgut Ozal, under secretary for planning, in *Yeni Gazete,* September 12, 1967.

[67] Professor Besim Üstünel denied that it will be possible to dispense with foreign aid in 1975; *Milliyet,* October 17, 1967. Alparslan Türkeş said that Turkey would, with a 7 percent annual growth rate, catch up with the developed nations only in 249 years. *Yeni Gazete,* February 3, 1969.

some claim the necessity of "structural changes" before genuine development can take place. Still others proclaim that the economy of Turkey is
bankrupt and at an impasse.[68]

In reply, government spokesmen do not deny that Turkey has "a big
gap to close."[69] Turgut Özal, Under Secretary in charge of the State
Planning Organization, declared:

The balancing of the balance of payments which has been a dream for years,
now appears to be a thing of the near future.
Turkey is not in a narrow pass as certain quarters claim. But development
has certain problems. Planned development does not mean development with
no problems.[70]

Foreign experts make no secret of the fact that Turkey will need important amounts of foreign aid during the entire second Five Year Plan
and thereafter. A report drawn up by the World Bank team and given
wide circulation in the Turkish press suggested that "important changes
in the basic economic policy" have to be made in order "to prevent a drop
in investment and growth rate due to the reduction of foreign aid." The
report also noted that the foreign exchange rate policy should not only
be a device to prevent a foreign trade crisis but also "a factor encouraging
economic development."[71]

No doubt the years ahead will be critical in determining whether
Turkey's economy can stand on its own feet. Eventually, new capital for
continued development will have to come primarily from domestic savings. If the national community is unable to accumulate reserves spontaneously, the new capital needed will have to be obtained by denying
commodities and services to the very people producing them. Because the
Turkish leaders believe—and this belief is shared by foreign observers—

[68] Besim Üstünel (professor of economics and also deputy secretary-general of the
People's Republican Party) said: "It is obvious that Demirel's development philosophy
would lead Turkey into an impasse soon. They have not taken the necessary measures
in accordance with the development plan and have worked in the reverse direction."
Cumhuriyet, July 10, 1969.

[69] Prime Minister Demirel on July 2, 1969, when opening the petrochemical works
at Yarimca; *Milliyet,* July 3, 1969. Against the pessimistic appraisals of Turkey's economy, Falih Rıfkı Atay wrote: "Demirel is right: no one gives loans to the sinking one.
We are sinking only in the eyes of the opposition and leftist press. In no other period
has Turkey dreamed of so much investment, let alone realized it." *Dünya,* July 9, 1969.

[70] *Zafer,* July 8, 1969.

[71] See *Milliyet,* April 19, 1969.

that their country cannot wait indefinitely, "when" becomes the important question; whether basic self-sufficiency can be attained is not doubted.

The dilemma which faced European countries—namely, whether a measure of austerity should speed up the attainment of subsequent prosperity—is constantly hanging above the head of Turkey like a sword of Damocles. Thus far, the government has hoped that sustained development and, eventually, self-sufficiency in capital accumulation might be reached without rigid controls of consumption or a halt in the rise of the standard of living.[72] On the other hand, both the political left and the extreme right have clamored for stringent measures in order to hasten development. Some of the protagonists of such a policy are ready "to pay with freedom" for the success of industrialization and modernization.[73] It is generally deemed questionable that the authoritarian tools required for a "structural change" speeding development would be compatible with the democratic type of government. A certain polarization exists between the various age groups of the political elite: the younger generations generally favor a "fast but disciplined," the older ones a "slow but democratic," way of development.[74]

The government of the Justice Party, however, solidly clung to the policy which supported continuous growth and a simultaneous rise in living standards in the hope that the democratic form of government could be maintained.[75] It may be that the prime minister viewed the situation, as the opposition alleged, "with rose-tinted glasses" when it made such declarations as: "In ten years Turkey will have a population of fifty

[72] Nadir Nadi, a well-known publicist, wrote: "Be it a capitalist or a socialist country, a community which wants to develop should first of all curtail consumption, economize on everything it can spare and allot it to investments, thus raising the production level." *Cumhuriyet*, July 4, 1969.

[73] The "left-of-center," as represented by the secretary-general of the People's Republican Party, Bülent Ecevit, as well as the Marxist opposition, clearly advocated "structural changes," the meaning of which was left in doubt. Extreme rightists as Alparslan Türkeş, suggested that the aim (development) justified the means (authoritarian government); *Yeni Gazete*, February 3, 1969.

[74] See Nermin Abadan, "Some Aspects of Political Behavior in Turkey," in *Turkish Yearbook of International Relations, 1965*, pp. 163–69.

[75] "The freedom order is the best. Nothing can be solved by an exploitation of poverty. . . . Turkey has prestige so that our friends accord us loans. Those who want to deny freedom to the Turkish nation are committing treason against democracy, the Republic, and Atatürk." From a speech by Demirel, *Cumhuriyet*, July 3, 1969.

million. It will be a happy and prosperous Turkey." But even he found it necessary to add a warning about possible alternatives: "We are a peace-loving nation. But our nation is more fond of honor and dignity than bread. The Turkish nation can live without bread, but not without honor."[76]

The Turkish public, long unwilling or unable to grasp the significance of trade, industry, or finance, has overnight become conscious of the urgency of economic development. This economic-mindedness is of the utmost importance if Turkey is to overcome psychological inhibitions and other obstacles during the critical years of the take-off stage of development. Prominent among such inhibitions is the animosity toward "foreign dependency" which has been politically exploited by the enemies of the regime.[77]

In the process of industrialization, Turkey has had to go through all the birth pains of an emerging modern industrial state. She felt that she had to maintain a relatively powerful army (the "guns versus butter" dilemma); NATO assistance thus helped her to achieve economic development, a fact overlooked by many adversaries of the Western military alliance.[78] So far, unlike other emerging nations, Turkey has also been able to avoid a permanent military or oligarchic dictatorship.

If Turkey is to continue to live under a democratic type of government, the advantages of the development process must become evident and palpable to everyone.[79] The success of development should not be measured only in terms of material well-being or prosperity. More and better education is another gain that should result from development;

[76] *Istanbul Bayram,* January 2, 1968.

[77] Minister of Industry Mehmet Turgut asked during the budget debate in the National Assembly for a definition of "dependent on abroad." He said that all economies, including that of the Soviets, are dependent on abroad; *Milliyet,* January 14, 1969. It has been submitted that after the achievement of a higher level of economic growth, emerging nations lose their fear of foreign investment, which they previously considered a threat to their sovereignty; Max F. Millikan and Donald L. M. Blackmer (eds.), *The Emerging Nations: Their Growth and United States Policy* (Boston, 1961), p. 67.

[78] Millikan and Blackmer, *Emerging Nations,* pp. 33–34.

[79] "If development is to depend on popular participation, then there must be a system of popular rewards. There can be no effective advance if the masses of the people do not participate; man is not so constituted that he will bend his best energies for the enrichment of someone else. As literacy is economically efficient, so is social justice." John Kenneth Galbraith, *Economic Development in Perspective* (Cambridge, Mass., 1962), p. 13.

education in turn contributes to further development. Indeed, the success of development depends on a complex of factors, among which material considerations are by no means primary. Technical and scientific skills, initiative, imagination, and the energy and determination to achieve the goals set, are often of equal or greater importance.

Some waste or inappropriate application of funds, some measure of disorganization and confusion, are inevitable during development and modernization. In this respect, Turkey does not stand alone. All of these maladies, if not as harmful as in the Menderes period, may be overcome by effective progress and prudent allocation of resources. Among resources, manpower and its proper use are of eminent importance. Turkey has trained and qualified manpower which, when given opportunity to gain more practical experience, may be mobilized for the purposes of development.

Turkey, like other developing countries, has a problem of uneven growth in various parts of the country. As Italy has the problem of her south, the less-developed Mezzogiorno, so Turkey has had to struggle with the retarded eastern part of Anatolia, which is, as we have seen, an economic, social, and, last but not least, a national problem.

The social forces in Turkey striving for better living standards and more public participation in national affairs are still quiescent, except for some urban centers where intellectuals and students appear to be sources of ferment. The transition from a traditionalist to a modern society is bound to affect increasing numbers of industrial workers and the peasantry. It is in this transitional stage that revolutionary change, which in most cases is identical with communism, presents its greatest appeal. Despite the experience of Stalinist terrorism, the Soviet example does not fail to impress certain segments of the population by its simplistic answers to complex questions. What most impresses some non-Communist intellectuals in Turkey is the brutal efficiency of the Communist system— the peculiar technique of mobilizing all human and material forces to produce industrial growth.[80] This alternative to the methods employed by the present regime appear enticing. Generally, these persons would prefer more Soviet economic aid and an elimination, or at least a reduction, of Western assistance. For these members of the intelligentsia, the

[80] Millikan and Blackmer, *Emerging Nations,* pp. 86–87.

Soviet method of asking for repayment in the form of local products, instead of monetary amortization, appears more logical, equitable, and, therefore, preferable.[81]

Still, the magnitude of Western aid, compared to the aid now or in the future available from Moscow; the technician's distaste for dealing with two types of machinery or methods of operation; and the general adaptation of the Turkish economic leaders to dealing with their Western counterparts (which also includes the knowledge of Western languages) —all seem to predestine Turkey to follow the Western forms of development and modernization. Unless there is a complete reversal of political goals and national ideals—which is very unlikely—Turkey is bound to her charted course toward the West.

Even the movement of travellers to and from Turkey is primarily flowing in the west-east, and east-west directions. For Turkey, there would be little advantage to be gained from tourists from the Soviet Union and Communist East Europe, even if they were allowed to visit Turkey in great numbers. On the other hand, Western tourists bring badly needed convertible currency to fill Turkey's balance of payments gap. Yugoslavia and Greece have developed their "tourist industry" to the extent that it is an important source of foreign currency revenue. Even if Turkey is more distant from West and Central Europe, she is a "virgin touristic paradise."[82]

Turkey is also on the main arterial road from Europe into the Middle East and into India and Southeast Asia. It has been noted earlier that railroad connections across Turkey to Iran have been established; however, the transit route is intersected by the Turkish straits. These waterways, especially the Bosporus at the nodal center of Istanbul, not only divide European from Asian Turkey (and the city of Istanbul from its hinterland in Anatolia) but also constitute an obstacle to the flow of surface traffic in the west-east direction. The ferry from the Rumelian to the Anatolian side of the Bosporus is often delayed for hours or even days when cars and trucks have to line up for embarkation. In order to elimi-

---

[81] Because the United States loans ask mainly for repayment in local (Turkish) currency, they are a lesser burden on the economy; furthermore, Soviets hardly ever offered outright grants. See Tansky, *Aid to Developing Countries*, pp. 173–74.

[82] Prime Minister Demirel, speaking in Erdek (the ancient Greek Kyzikos); *Hürriyet*, July 10, 1969.

nate this bottleneck, which is so costly for transportation and so disturb-ing to tourist traffic, the Turkish government decided in 1968 to construct a bridge over the Bosporus just north of Istanbul.

This ambitious project, to bridge Europe and Asia, attracted financiers and technicians of many countries, among them Japan, which has ex-perience in bridging sealanes between her islands.[83] A Bosporus-bridge consortium was formed in 1969, with the participation of Japan ($30 million), the European Investment Bank ($20 million), West Germany ($10 million), Britain ($8 million), France ($5 million), and Italy ($2.5 million). Turkey herself contributes the equivalent of $20 to $30 million.[84] On January 26, 1970, an agreement for the construction of the bridge was signed between the Turkish government and the British–German con-tracting group Hochtief–Cleveland. Prime Minister Demirel announced on this occasion: "This project is not for Istanbul alone, it is for the whole of Turkey and for all humanity wishing to pass from Europe to Asia."[85]

As expected, this magnificent scheme was opposed by some political leaders and left-wing papers because it was considered a luxury for a "poverty-stricken" country and because the money should be used for other, "more urgent" purposes.[86] For Turks with a visionary outlook, however, the Bosporus bridge has a significance broader than its economic objectives would indicate. Bridging two parts of Turkey and, thereby, two continents, would demonstrate the solid determination of their nation to join Europe. As noted earlier, the waterlanes of the straits constitute a geographical partition but are meaningless from historical, ethnological, and sociological points of view. When one crosses the Bosporus in either direction, one does not feel more in Asia or in Europe. A change of ecology is only experienced when moving further from western into eastern Turkey or in the reverse direction. The Bosporus bridge would, therefore, connect not two different ethnicities or political entities but would technically link an area that is already united by all factors except that of geology.

---

[83] The Japanese consul general of Istanbul said: "It will be an honor for us to build the Bosporus bridge. Japan is more interested in the moral aspect of the matter than its material aspect. Just think, is it not nice that the Japanese should unite Europe to Asia with a bridge?" *Cumhuriyet,* October 10, 1968.

[84] *Milliyet,* June 15, 1969; *Cumhuriyet,* July 2, 1969.

[85] *Cumhuriyet,* January 27, 1970.

[86] Ilhan Selçuk in *Cumhuriyet,* September 3, 1968.

Symbolically, a bridge uniting their European and Asian possessions would be more meaningful for the Turks than, for instance, the Aswan Dam is for the Egyptians. Such a bridge would be the material representation of their major domestic and foreign policy goal: Europeanization. The ambition of Turkey to become part of Europe will thus be given "concrete" realization.

IX

Ambitions and Realities of Turkish Foreign Policy

To mingle along, as one in the midst,
To seem a part, yet hold apart,
To build a shield, with bewildering art,
To outwit, and persist.

—MELVILLE CANE, *Strategy*

Sabreden derviş muradına ermiş. (The persistent dervish attains his aim.)—Turkish proverb.

TURKEY IS ONE OF THE FEW COUNtries which, during the past half century, has pursued a continuous national policy. Although led by different governments and torn by a revolution, the primary political goal has not changed. This national purpose, the raising of Turkey to "the level of contemporary civilization,"[1] has been a program to be implemented by domestic reforms and a prudent foreign policy.

Domestic transformation requires time and, most of all, peaceful conditions, so that all energies might be focused on internal development. Turkey's peace and security, however, were not to be bought by territorial or economic concessions, "appeasement," or humiliating surrender of national sovereignty (as had been the case during the 200 years of Ottoman decay), but by integrally maintaining the nation's independence and freedom of action. Internationally, it was a status quo policy for the sake of a change in the internal status quo.

This overall policy was pursued throughout the first and second Turkish republics. During these 50 years, Turkey passed through different regimes: the authoritarian period of Atatürk, the one-party regime of the People's Republican Party, two periods of multiparty government, and a

---

[1] As Prime Minister Demirel expressed it: "Turkey's objective is to attain the contemporary level of civilization in a world where peace prevails." *Cumhuriyet,* March 17, 1969.

military dictatorship. But the course of the essential national policy line which was guided by expediency not ideology—was not altered because of domestic oscillations.

After the disintegration of the Ottoman Empire, the Turkish nation-state was established at the price of a ferocious war. Previously, the empire had been involved for centuries in a rarely interrupted series of armed conflicts. The nearly five decades of peace following the conclusion of the Lausanne Peace Treaty were a new experience for the war-weary people of Anatolia. Even if nothing else had been achieved by the foreign policy of the new Turkey, peace was preserved without the sacrifice of the national status quo, although this success was by no means easy. There were dangers other than the risk of war, but Turkey was able to avoid pitfalls which had trapped other countries in comparable geographical centers. In order to appreciate the present international position of the Turkish republic, it is pertinent to survey its past experience.

THE BALANCE SHEET

The abortive Peace Treaty of Sèvres was to accomplish the following purposes: first, to sever territories from the Ottoman Empire which were inhabited by non-Turks; and second, to amputate even Turkish areas of the empire and to make a Western dependency of the remaining trunk. Aware of this attack on her national existence, Turkey was anxious to prevent future encroachments on her sovereignty and was firmly resolved to attain a status equal to that of other independent states of Europe.

Between the two world wars, Turkey achieved two outstanding diplomatic successes, both of which were of prime importance for later developments. First, the Lausanne-established regime of the straits was eliminated. This regime had subjected these internationally prominent waterways and their surrounding territory to the control of an international commission and had prohibited military installations along this vitally important portion of Turkey. Second, Turkey succeeded in reincorporating the topographically significant area of Hatay, which enhanced Turkey's geostrategical position in the eastern Mediterranean.

Turkey firmly and successfully followed her intended policy course in the critical wartime years: of entering the fighting only when attacked or in the face of mortal danger. She formed her alliance ties with the flexibility which least restricted her decision-making freedom and remained steadfast against Soviet blandishments and threats and against British and American pressures to join the hostilities without due preparatives and guarantees. She also remained immune to temptations to seize immediate advantages that were ephemeral and incompatible with her obligations.

If one compares the policy pursued by sultanic Turkey (which plunged her into the war in 1914) with Turkish diplomacy during World War II, the superiority of the latter over the former becomes strikingly evident. Whereas the earlier policy was hesitating, haphazard, and even irrational, the later diplomacy was characterized by singleness of purpose, cold calculation, and farsightedness.

Even after the pact with Germany had been concluded in 1914, a divided Turkish leadership offered simultaneous alliances to Great Britain, Russia, and France. The governing clique allowed themselves to be overly impressed by an emotional issue: the sequestration of their two warships by Britain and the arrival of the two German warships, the *Goeben* and the *Breslau*, which took refuge in Turkish waters and were then presented as a "gift" to the sultan. The Turks entered the war on the side of the Germans only after the latter had lost the Battle of the Marne—at a moment when the chance for a victory, or victory at all, was already gone.[2]

In contrast to Turkey's imprudent and shortsighted attitude in 1914, the Turkey of 1939 carefully weighed her steps before departing from neutrality, as advised by Atatürk. She entered into an alliance with Britain and France only when she had no other choice. At that time Germany and Italy threatened to upset the peace of the Balkans and of the eastern Mediterranean area, while Russia, the greatest danger of all, was turning away from Turkey and returning to the tsarist policy of expansionism. Even so, the treaty with Britain and France contained loopholes, permitting Turkey to apply its provisions according to the demands of her national interest. Thus, she managed to wade through World War II without openly breaking her treaty commitments and without provoking the belligerents—while at the same time adjusting to the realities of the military and political situation.

Turkey foresaw the fate of the small nations of East and Central Europe in the event of a Soviet victory over the Germans. She thereby proved—and would prove again and again—that she was able to evaluate

---

[2] Erkin, *Relations Turco-Soviétiques,* pp. 51–52; this author calls this decision one of "national suicide."

Soviet intentions more accurately than the highly sophisticated statesmen of the West. She refused to incur the risk of being "liberated by the Russians" and becoming their satellite. With her exposed location between the Black Sea and the Mediterranean, she sensed that any Soviet occupation of the straits was bound to become permanent and would presage the end of Turkish national independence.

Ankara met the Soviet threats of 1945–46 with an apparent sang-froid; Russian claims were bluntly rejected, though at that time she could not have been fully certain of American assistance. For the leaders of Turkey, this was a point at which negotiations were considered even more risky than a principled refusal. How right they were! Washington and London were ready to compromise on the issue of the straits, as is evident from the minutes of the Potsdam Conference. Had the Turks shown the slightest inclination to enter into bilateral talks with the Russians on the matter, full American and British support for the Turkish case would not have been available. Even so, only the clumsily menacing posture of Moscow and its exaggerated territorial claims saved Turkey from the necessity of accepting a revision of the Montreux convention that would have increased Russian influence over the vitally important waterways. In this instance, Turkey's stubborn determination rather than the assistance of the West saved her from sharing the fate of nations like Poland, Rumania, Bulgaria, or Hungary; she even escaped the dependency to which Finland was subjected by the USSR.

Because of her self-centered wartime policy, it was unavoidable that Turkey should be somewhat isolated from the powers that had waged war against Nazi Germany. Yet, the only permanent disadvantage that resulted from her postwar diplomatic handicap was the necessity of acquiescing without overt protest to the cession of Rhodes and the Dodecanese Islands to Greece. Her last-minute declaration of war on the Germans nonetheless secured her founding membership in the United Nations.

According to Turkey's analysis of her postwar predicament, it was fully within her national interest to seek integral alignment with the Western powers; this was even more true of Ankara's eagerness to gain the favor of the strongest Western power, the United States.

It has been noted earlier how everything—national preservation, security, economic advancement, and national purpose—predestined Turkey to want to be fully accepted in the political and military organizations of the West. Her Korean gambit was an act of astute diplomacy which contributed much to the opening of the gateways of the West to her.

Having been admitted to NATO and other European and Atlantic organizations, Ankara appeared to have relaxed her erstwhile watchfulness; she avoided examining foreign policy issues only in the light of Turkish national interest. She seemed to feel that what was good for NATO was good for Turkey—or rather what the United States wanted should not be questioned. Subsequent critics compared this attitude with the servility with which the Ottoman Empire reacted to the demands of European powers in some periods of its history.

Thus, the Turkish government failed to respond immediately to intimations that the Soviets would favor more relaxed relations—which might have been used to Ankara's advantage in dealing with neutralist powers. Turkey's Arab policy in the 1950's was pursued under the guidance of Britain and the United States and without sufficient consideration for the state of mind prevailing in the Arab world. Turkey also plunged into the Cypriote quagmire without adequate diplomatic preparation and without the backing of interested powers.

None of these omissions or inadequacies, however, put Turkey at a permanent disadvantage. Belatedly, but still successfully, she was able to normalize her relations with the Soviet Union and establish a modicum of cordial contacts without departing from her Western course. The transformation of the Baghdad alliance into a lower-keyed CENTO initiated a slow improvement in her relations with most of the Arab countries. Since the mid-sixties, the policy toward the Middle East has given proof of a subtle diplomacy. After the defeat of the Arabs in 1967, Ankara could easily afford to be pro-Arab while dealing in friendship with Israel "under the counter."

Concerning Cyprus, it should be asked whether Turkey's policy realistically stood as high in her hierarchy of interests as she proclaimed and her actions appeared to indicate. Were Atatürk alive, of course, one could question whether he would have considered his country's attitude on Cyprus compatible with the status quo policy he had advocated. On the other hand, it can be justly maintained that the exchange of Greek sovereignty for British rule over the island signified such a change in Turkey's geostrategical status quo that it demanded her opposition.

Assuming that Cyprus is a question vitally affecting Turkey's national interest, it should be asked whether she has been skillful in protecting these interests since the late 1950's. Originally, Turkey's political and legal positions were weak; had the British not supported Turkey diplomatically, her political moves would have been abortive. Her legal position was even more tenuous; Cyprus was a British possession, formally ceded to London under the Lausanne Peace Treaty, and Ankara had no right to oppose a transfer of sovereignty over the island to Greece. In light of this situation, the Zurich–London agreement must be evaluated as a clear success for Turkish diplomacy, for that agreement granted Turkey an international legal *jus standi*—a right to participate in decisions concerning the affairs of Cyprus. The Cyprus policy, however, inevitably estranged Ankara from Greece, whose future is geopolitically intertwined with Turkey's. *Enosis* was prevented at a price. As long as the Cyprus problem is not solved to the satisfaction of Ankara and Athens, as well as the Greek and Turkish communities of the island, no final judgment can be passed on the correctness of Turkish foreign policy on this issue.

In the post-World War II period, and particularly after 1960, Turkey's foreign policy was aimed at obtaining the maximum possible assistance for economic development and modernization. The simultaneous progress of industrialization, the rise in the standard of living, and the modernization of her army would not have been feasible without the aid she received. It also should be noted that these changes are being implemented in an open society under a democratic form of government.

Ankara's improved relationship with Moscow contributed little to the easing of the global East–West tension. For the time being at least, it simply removed Turkey from the center of continued rivalries and confrontations. American–Soviet crises, when they occur, would not necessarily extend automatically into the area of Turkish–Soviet contacts. The seismic effects of this rapprochement have been felt in Turkey's relations with the Communist states of the Balkans and East and Central Europe. Even the traditional enmities with Turkey's immediate Balkan neighbor, Bulgaria, have given way to a restrained cordiality.

The leadership of Turkey can hardly feel totally assured by the expressions of Soviet sympathy. The extension of Moscow's long arm across the Turkish straits into the Mediterranean Sea has created forebodings in Ankara, for this move raises related problems of profound importance: (1) whether Turkey is thereby in danger of being encircled; and (2) whether she can counter deterioration of her strategical status that would accompany such an encirclement. The solutions depend on the intensity and stability of Soviet influence in the Arab Middle East. Soviet boasts that the USSR is a Mediterranean power seem to forecast a new wave of Russian unhappiness about the straits and to place Turkey before a new era of jeopardy.

This possible new phase of Turkey's struggle to defend her territorial patrimony would demonstrate, as the history of the Turkish nation-state has demonstrated, that her interests, especially those stemming from her geopolitical location, are constant and that only the means and methods used to protect them might change. The continuity of Turkey's foreign policy and the strategic requirements needed to bolster it also tend to discount the theory that a country's foreign relations are only a by-product of its domestic policies.[3] Nevertheless, in a multiparty political system, criticism of a government's foreign policy is part of the all-out struggle for political control, and this criticism necessarily affects decision-making in the foreign policy field as well. The tastes of the electorate may bring about a change of government, and a new government might introduce a change in methods and style without changing the general direction of policy.[4]

Accordingly, Turkish foreign policy cannot remain immune to the influences of party politics, and the domestic political climate is bound to have an impact on the conduct of international affairs.

THE WEIGHT OF DOMESTIC POLITICS

For most of the Turkish leaders, the national policy objective appears so obvious that any deviation from this salutary course is out of the question. Except for the Turkish Labor Party, the essentials of this objective —membership in the Atlantic community—support and promote this policy. Save for the extreme leftists, the political elite views the pursuit of this national policy as the only "national" policy; to oppose it is tantamount to being "unnational." Of course, for those who oppose Western

---

[3] See Roy C. Macridis (ed.), *Foreign Policy in World Politics* (3d ed.; Englewood Cliffs, N.J., 1967), pp. 1–4.

[4] The impact of internal political changes on foreign policy is frowned upon by Turkish leaders. "I do not believe that the domestic policy of Turkey has weight enough to affect her foreign policy," said Foreign Minister Çağlayangil; *Yeni Istanbul,* June 30, 1969.

ties and the Western ways of development, this policy is "unnational," and theirs is the truly "national" policy.[5]

It should be remembered, however, that the foreign policy elite which supports Western ties and the democratic form of government does not support the manner in which Turkey is going along with the West without serious reservations and objections. While the "unnational" left, vociferous as it may be, has little or no impact on the conduct of foreign relations, the critical pro-Westerners are to be found in all political parties, including the Justice Party.

This criticism is directed against the loyalty, admiration, or trust displayed toward *any* foreign nation. Any such attachment is considered harmful and something that could result in the neglect of genuine Turkish interests. This attitude, a strain of special Turkish xenophobia, stems from historical experience and is a reaction to the characteristic Turkish inclination to cherish idols. No "foreign nation idols" should henceforth stand in the way of the pursuance of strictly Turkish national objectives.[6]

In the view of these governmental critics—who are by no means anti-Western—the Demirel government was pro-American to an excessive degree. This could harm Turkish national interests or, at best, lead to a disregard for them. Naturally, such warnings coming from circles near or inside the ruling "establishment" could not be cast aside. They have acted as a brake on governmental decision-making when Ankara has dealt with the Americans and, second, as an incentive to exhibit attitudes "independent" of American influences.

A corollary to infatuation with one foreign country is the obsessive feeling of hatred toward another. Clearly, those who display such an attitude against Russia rank among the admirers of the United States. In

[5] "Today there are two fronts in Turkey, the national front and the 'unnational' front. The latter is the front of those who want to continue with the present imperialistic exploitation order. . . . The national front is running against domestic and external exploiters." Ilhan Selçuk in *Cumhuriyet*, April 29, 1968.

[6] "For a long time the Turkish people were admirers of the French. This was followed by attachments to the Germans. Admiration for the British appeared and died a few times. During the Second World War we tried to keep pace with Hitler's goose steps, with American and British boots called the 'Roosevelts' and the 'Churchills' on our feet. Finally, an unparalleled admiration for the Americans appeared here to such an extent that we changed 'Russian salad' into 'American salad.' Now we see more self-respect, the revival of national feelings in the youth's demonstrations in Istanbul." *Yeni Gazete*, February 13, 1969.

this and many other respects, Turkish public opinion tends to be polarized. Fortunately, the foreign policy leadership is generally aloof from such extremist attitudes.

Respect for the opinions of other nations has been exploited for domestic political purposes in the past. The Menderes government often sought to impress its followers and the electorate by hinting that the Americans were giving an ear to its suggestions or wishes. The Turkish public, however, is extremely sensitive to what it might consider foreign "interferences" in domestic affairs. As interpreted in Turkey, such interference has a much broader meaning than in most other countries. Views expressed by foreigners in Turkey—not only by foreign diplomats—concerning the internal conditions or political problems may be condemned as undue interferences in domestic affairs which infringe upon the precepts of decent conduct and constitute an abuse of the hospitality offered by Turkey.

Simultaneously, whispering campaigns or press opinions, especially at election times, may give hints as to which political party is the favorite of the United States. Whether such intimations may or may not be useful to the party thus named remains to be seen. Before the general elections of 1969, some press organs reported that the Justice Party was no longer favored by the Americans and that Washington had concluded a "secret deal" with the moderates of the People's Republican Party, whose victory it would welcome. But there were also suggestions that this innuendo originated in the Justice Party, which in this way wished to split its main opponent.[7]

Fortunately, the masses of the electorate seem little influenced by the pro- or anti-Americanism of political parties and their leaders. They vote for individuals whom they trust and whom they consider the repositories of honesty, prosperity, patriotism, and religion. In the rural areas, local interests play important roles in determining voting behavior. As long as Turkey continues to be ruled democratically, the chance of any major deviation from accepted foreign policy lines is minimal.

---

[7] Kemal Bisalman wrote that the People's Republican Party was spreading the news that the USA had turned its back on Süleyman Demirel, the Justice Party prime minister. He asked how, at the same time, the former party could accuse Demirel of being pro-American and the USA of "Süleymanism!" *Milliyet*, April 9, 1969. Ismet Inönü, leader of the People's Party, expressed his disapproval over such machinations by saying: "To use relations with any foreign country in domestic politics is against the security, interests, and dignity of an independent Turkey." *Ulus*, April 11, 1969.

The concept of national sovereignty introduced by Atatürk has never been repudiated by any political group; however, the question of how national sovereignty is exercised still haunts many. As Prime Minister Demirel lately expressed it:

Today not even the basic concept of national sovereignty, which is the common denominator of the 1924 and 1961 constitutions, has obtained a common understanding among political organizations and organs and jurists outside their ranks.[8]

Thus, this great question has yet to receive a final answer: is popular democracy the agency for establishing national sovereignty, or are there certain segments of the population which, because of their status and education, are better equipped to represent and interpret the "national will"? In this respect, the role and meaning of the 1960 revolution remains a question of intense discussion. Former President Celâl Bayar, himself deposed by this revolution, sentenced to death, and then pardoned, has staged a limited political comeback. He has also provided a new explanation of the concept of "national sovereignty" and of the dramatic events of 1960.[9]

The aged Bayar (born in 1884) considered the Ottoman state to have been ruled by a triad: the palace (the sultan and his advisers), the Medrese (the School—that is, the community of Koranic scholars), and the military (who succeeded the corps of Janissaries). Atatürk's constitution of 1924, however, declared that national sovereignty "belonged unconditionally to the nation." He thus wished to eliminate "middlemen"—that is, intermediaries for the expression of the national will.[10] Although the partnership of the army and of the Medrese (now the universities and other intellectuals) in the affairs of state was ended, the tradition of a "thousand years" enabled these two institutions to survive latently. In 1960 it was the Army-Medrese cooperation which established their de facto authority by the revolution. While maintaining the principle of national sovereignty, the constitution of 1961 provided that the nation shall exercise its sov-

---

[8] From a statement at a press conference; see *Milliyet*, July 6, 1969.

[9] Bayar wrote a series of articles under the title, "My Prime Minister Adnan Menderes," published by *Hürriyet* in June–July, 1969.

[10] The former president omitted mentioning that under Atatürk (and Inönü) the People's Republican Party acted as the "middleman" between the people and the Grand National Assembly.

ereignty "through the authorized agencies" as laid down in the constitution itself. The new constitution gave a role to the army by setting up the National Security Council, and to the intellectuals through such constitutional organs as the Constitutional Court, the State Planning Organization, and the nonelected members of the Senate. The constitution itself was drafted by a group of university professors and invested the president of the republic with powers "which call to mind the powers of the Sultan."[11]

If Bayar's interpretation of developments should prove correct, national sovereignty may be again exercised at some future time by certain decision-makers who may pretend a better knowledge of what the national will is or what is good for the nation. This would end the democratic order in Turkey but would not necessarily alter the present foreign policy course. It has been noted that among those intellectuals who favor the liquidation of the democratic form of government as it exists at the time of this writing, four groups should be distinguished: those who sincerely believe that democracy and reform are incompatible; those who believe that Turkey can only develop under a left-wing military administration; those who believe that they can obtain power only outside a democratic order; and, finally, the Turkish Communists, who hope that a military coup would be the first stage for a Marxist–Leninist dictatorship.[12]

In the wake of student unrest in the universities of the United States and of Western Europe, student riots erupted during 1968 and 1969 in Istanbul and Ankara, many of them with anti-American overtones and Marxist–Leninist orientations. Concern was felt among Turkish and foreign observers that, as in 1960, these disorders might tempt the army to intervene once again in politics.[13] While, on the one hand, these demonstrations differed from those which prompted the military coup in 1960, it should be remembered, on the other, that the military take-over did not result in a change in foreign policy.

It is difficult to assess realistically the chances for future military intervention. The top leadership of the armed forces has stated that "the Turkish Armed Forces personnel are in the service of national defense,

[11] Cited in *Hürriyet,* June 29, 1969.
[12] Metin Toker in *Milliyet,* May 30, 1969.
[13] See *New York Times,* June 15, 1969.

outside all political trends."[14] Nevertheless, both leftist and rightist extremists occasionally appeal to officers for assistance against the opposite type of extremism.[15] How far the army may exercise pressure on the government in matters of domestic politics will depend on such contingencies as whether the government is to rule constitutionally; whether the attitudes or actions of government leaders will not endanger what the army leadership may consider national security; and, finally, whether the peril of extremism will jeopardize internal stability.[16] Even if another military intervention were to take place, a drastic change in the foreign policy of Turkey can hardly be expected. The only—although improbable —exception to this forecast would be a leftist military coup which placed in power an extreme political party seeking to establish a strictly neutralist or pro-Soviet policy.[17]

A radical volte-face in Turkey's relations with the outside world and in her pro-Western political orientation may be realistically discounted. However, the influence of the political parties and segments of the intelligentsia should not be underrated on particular issues and on the pattern of the government's foreign policy style and methods. In certain eventualities, the so-called 3 percent (that is, those who voted for the Turkish Labor Party) could be augmented by an unknown number of intellectuals expressing solidarity with the position held by the extremist group on a certain issue without sharing their other opinions. The government may not only be influenced in its particular decision, but the extremist left and its opportunist fellow-travelers may also create an exaggerated impression about their size and power.[18]

[14] Instruction issued by General Tural, chief of the general staff; *Adalet,* May 7, 1968.

[15] "If the leftists get out of hand, the gallant Turkish Army will intervene and make short work of the Communists as was done in Greece," said Selahattin Arikan, president of the Nationalist Teachers' Federation; *Tercüman,* October 9, 1967. On the other hand, a declaration issued by the officers of the Naval War School spoke up against rightist tendencies; *Cumhuriyet,* November 3, 1968.

[16] In the spring of 1969 a draft law providing for political rehabilitation to former Democratic Party deputies was dropped because of alleged opposition by the Armed Forces.

[17] Metin Toker wrote that the extreme leftists hoped for a victory of the Justice Party in the 1969 elections which, in their view, will make a military coup inevitable. Next will come the "real revolution" staged by Marxist–Leninists. *Milliyet,* August 27, 1969.

[18] Such an impression was given in April 1969, when the Nixon Administration recalled Robert W. Komer, American ambassador to Turkey. Soon after his arrival to his post, Komer became a target of left-wing student demonstrations and also attacks by

External events have far greater effect on foreign policy decisions in Turkey than the oscillations of domestic politics. The ideological cleavage which separates the masses of Turks may have a pervasive influence on the manner of handling public affairs, including external relations. Although Atatürk's and Inönü's strict secularism, and the cautious return to Islam under Menderes, affected the conduct of foreign policy little, if at all, the ideological affiliation of political leaders may still determine priorities or influence the methods or style of foreign policy. Options such as *étatisme*, free enterprise, rapprochement with Moscow, relations with the United States, attitudes on Cyprus, or the evaluation of the Arab–Israeli conflict cannot escape the impact of ideologies.

THE WEIGHT OF IDEOLOGY

In addition to political and economic unheavals, the Turkish people have experienced a series of ideological revolutions during the past 50 years. The concept of the Turkish nation-state was a revolt against the idea of Ottoman universalism; the concept of a secular state and society militated against the accepted Islamic way of life; political democracy was the antithesis of previously practiced authoritarian rule.

Turkism itself became accepted after the refusal to follow the tenets of another universalist idea—namely, Turanism. How far the Turks have been alienated from a consciousness of their own ethnicity by Islamic ideology is strikingly demonstrated by the fact that it was a non-Turk who first developed the idea of Turanism.[19] After 1920, however, the vague and utopian pan-Turanism gave way to the more realistic Turkism that meant the formation of a national identity based on Turks living within the confines of the Turkish republic. Nevertheless, the idea of the

---

the leftist press. The moderate Turkish press sadly registered that this was a "victory for the 3 percent." In fact, Komer's replacement was actually due to the reshuffling of diplomatic posts following the change in the American presidency. However, it is suggested that under the existing circumstances it was unwise to withdraw Ambassador Komer, thus giving satisfaction to the left extremists and disavowing critics of the campaign against Komer. See *New York Times*, April 10, 1969.

[19] Léon Cahun of France is regarded as the first to propound the idea of the great Turanian race which inhabited Europe before the arrival of Celts, Germans, and Latins. However, he may have been preceded by Mustafa Celaleddin (Konstanty Borzecki), a Polish convert to Islam, who wrote of the Touro–Aryenne race which originally populated Europe; he considered the Westernization of the Turks as their turning away from Semitic (Islamic) civilization to join their racial relatives. See Berkes, *Development of Secularism*, pp. 314–18; Luke, *The Old Turkey and the New*, p. 153.

nation-state encountered numerous and considerable obstacles which had to be overcome: the allegiance to religion, the loyalty to tribe, and the resistance of tradition had to be surmounted and absorbed into the all-pervasive concept of Turkish nationalism. In fact, by the late 1920's nationalism had become the official ideology of the Turkish state.[20] "Atatürkism"—the six principles of the Turkish republic—were all anchored in the concept of nationalism.[21] Even *étatisme*, as the method of economic development, had its ideological source in the supreme will of the nation-state.

By the late 1940's, large segments of Turkey's population were imbued with Turkish national sentiment and the concept of a Turkish nation-state no longer needed to be vindicated. Within the general fabric of a nationalist Weltanschauung, other ideologies emerged which partly corresponded to the pluralistic division of Turkey's social structure. Among intellectuals the concept of a new secular and social republic gained acceptance at the same time conservative-traditionalists wished to promote a return to Islam.[22]

The principal ideological positions are those held by the protagonists of socialist-reformist ideas and the adherents of a democratic-constitutional evolution, and by strict secularists and the supporters of various types of Islamic revivalism. Followers of these differing schools of thought are often, though not exclusively, partisans of different foreign policy lines.

Moderate Socialist, not necessarily Marxist and reformist, ideas were closely associated with the left-of-center program of the People's Republican Party. The "new order" which this party sought to establish, though not quite clear in its content, may be considered a renewed emphasis on *étatisme* and on the raising of living standards (particularly for the rural population), coupled with radical modernization of the administration and the elimination of bureaucracy. The future of this program largely depended on the electoral success of Inönü's party. Its foreign policy implications were somewhat obscure: they were likely to show less determination to go along with NATO and with the United States but were to continue the trend toward Westernization. It was, however, doubtful whether they would wish to enter the European Eco-

[20] See Karpat, *Political and Social Thought,* pp. 297–99.
[21] See chapter II, pp. 55–60.
[22] Karpat, *Political and Social Thought,* pp. 304–5.

nomic Community with its clear commitment to the free market system.

Followers of a Marxist–Leninist ideology are anti-NATO and vehemently anti-American. As noted earlier, their chances of gaining governmental power are extremely slim. Communism remains and will continue to remain anathema to the overwhelming masses of Turks, if only because of its association with the Soviet–Russian peril.

The government controlled by the Justice Party stands for parliamentary democracy and for evolutionary development toward social justice. It has gambled its future on the achievement of economic self-sufficiency by the mid-1970's. It believes that current social problems will be solved with the mounting success of economic development. As Prime Minister Demirel put it:

Sure, we have lots of problems, social problems—education, health. We have unemployment problems. We have poverty. But without economic expansion, how are you going to solve them?

Some say, solve these other problems first, then the expansion will come. But it's not possible. It is possible to go from Ankara to Istanbul on your feet. Go ahead and do it. It will take you 15 days. But if you have money, it will take one hour by plane.[23]

In this question of priorities, the parliamentary democrats have preferred to follow the example of the West rather than to accept the priorities of the East: prosperity will solve social problems, not socialist egalitarianism.

Unless policies of extremism are followed, there exists the possibility of reconciling these two ideologies. Undoubtedly, extreme statism and social revolution would estrange the West from Turkey and reduce its willingness to help. Such a state of affairs would unquestionably have a far-reaching foreign policy impact and slam the door on Turkey's endeavors to become part of Europe. On the other hand, a continued effort to achieve development and modernization through a liberal economic policy and political democracy would secure Turkey, as they have in the past, the sympathies and assistance of Western Europe and of the United States.

Most adherents of moderate social reform and all supporters of extreme leftist ideas are secularists. On the other hand, followers of

[23] *New York Times,* September 3, 1969.

liberal-democratic ideas may be either moderate secularists or prudent disciples of Islam. Except for those who are militant secularists or fanatical Muslims, the majority of the educated stratum of the society approaches religion as is customary in the West. Religion is not an affair of state but the concern of the private individual or family and of the community voluntarily formed by religious persons. The difficulty of such an approach, however, is that it deviates from the traditional role and purpose of historic Islam. For the strongly devoted traditional Muslim, a religious allegiance without temporal corollaries appears absurd or heretical.

Secularists often identify religious practices and those who participate in them with the fanatic Islamists. Because of the nature of Islam, it is difficult to draw a strict distinction between those who seek to depoliticize and spiritualize their loyalty toward the faith of their ancestors and those who wish to adhere strictly to the traditional public role of Islam. As Demirel declared:

I should state that the use of the constitutional right of religion and conscience, as provided by the Turkish Constitution and laws, can never be considered as "extreme rightist." There are some who regard as reactionary even the exercise of the right to religion and freedom of conscience. . . .

The aim of the extreme right is to set up a state on theocratical principles. There may be supporters of this as there are for any movement. They are not more than a handful and they can do no harm to Turkey. Our nation is not faced with a choice today. It has made its choice. The Turkish State is a democratic, secular, social state.[24]

The foreign policy impact of the secularist religious conflict is by no means less significant than the socialist–democratic-liberal controversy. The complexity of these ideological confrontations is increased by the doubts of some Islamic rigorists who believe that even democracy is incompatible with the principles of their religion.[25]

The educated Turkish masses yearn for an ideology to satisfy their intellectual and emotional needs. Turkish nationalism alone is no substitute for religious belief; the search for a substitute has led many to find

[24] *Tercüman,* May 12, 1968.
[25] Nadir Nadi referred to Toynbee's views when raising the issue. He expressed hope that Toynbee will be wrong as far as Turkey is concerned; *Cumhuriyet,* March 28, 1969.

idols in "social justice," socialism, the democratic ideal, or the basic or austere Islam. This is why an observer may be struck by what could be called "cultural confusion" in Turkey.[26]

So far Turks have not found a way "to reconcile a revival of Islamic faith with the social, political, and cultural reforms accomplished in the last century."[27] At the moment, it appears that culturally they are on the road to Europe but have not yet reached their destination. Yet, they are no longer Orientals. If one would try to define them for what they are, the only correct answer would be that they are something "special," in a transitional stage, like the Franks, Goths, and other Germanic peoples must have been before they were finally assimilated into the Graeco–Roman-Christian world, or like the Magyars, an Oriental people, in their century of transition from a nomadic steppe-folk to European–Hungarians.

Any such analogy misses one important point: the Turkish transition faces a special difficulty. Unlike the heathen Germans or Hungarians, who were barbarians from the Graeco–Roman point of view, the Turks were for nearly a millennium part of a highly developed and refined Islamic civilization. In view of this, the question arises whether an abandonment of Islam would be required for them to become really "Europeanized." This involves a step which hardly anybody in Turkey would dare advise. To give up Islam for what? In the Middle Ages European meant Christian; is this qualification still true today? Since the Renaissance, European nations have become "secularized" and, while Christianity is still a part, it is questionable whether it is an essential part, of their civilizational and cultural substance.

Suat Sinanoğlu, professor at the University of Ankara, has attempted to find a solution to the ideological yearning of his countrymen.[28] He noted a grave intellectual crisis in Turkey, one which—in his view—the West overcame 400 to 600 years ago. Following Atatürk's teachings, he considers Western civilization superior to all other civilizations and the one which Turks should embrace.

According to Sinanoğlu, European civilization is a secular civilization which has its basis in Graeco–Roman humanism. The mediating role of

[26] Anthony Lewis in *New York Times,* February 16, 1969.
[27] Bernard Lewis, "Turkey: Westernization," in *Unity and Variety in Muslim Civilization,* von Grunebaum, p. 327.
[28] See his remarkable book, *L'Humanisme à venir* (Ankara, 1960), *passim.*

Christianity was once important but has ceased to be so since the end of the Middle Ages. It is this humanism which should be absorbed by all mankind so as to end the "famous antinomy between East and West."[29]

Sinanoğlu did not suggest a servile imitation of Western ideology by the Turks; he suggested, however, the adoption of the value-and-belief system of European Graeco–Roman civilization (such as political-legal equality, freedom of expression) creating thus what he calls "Turkish humanism."

Sinanoğlu's views demonstrate the importance that Turkish thinkers attribute to the intellectual problem of their nation. He did not suggest an abandonment of Islam; rather, he seemed to suggest that Islam might be made compatible with the classical humanism described as a secular belief-system and not a substitute for faith.

Indeed, Turkey's permanent and final alignment with the West— culturally and in the sphere of internal and external politics—would appear to depend on the reconciliation of the Islamic philosophy of life with the European system of values.[30] The Turks, because of their advance toward Westernization and their disestablishment of Islam, are more likely than other Islamic nations to achieve a synthesis of modernism with the Muslim faith. It should not be forgotten that like Islam the Christianity of the Middle Ages was not only a religion but a way of life. Of course, it was easier to separate the secular and spiritual in Europe than it would be in the Islamic Orient because of the Graeco–Roman past of Europe and its impact on the Christian Church itself. A Turkish "reformation" of Islam is unlikely, but, as Professor Lewis suggested, a realistic Turkish genius might one day produce a Muslim Turkish "equivalent to the Anglican Church."[31]

The Turkish determination to be part of Europe and of European civilization—and its corollary, the Western-oriented foreign policy of Turkey—cannot be a one-sided exercise. To be successful, it must find understanding and acceptance primarily by the Western world but also

---

[29] *Ibid.*, p. 126.

[30] See H. A. R. Gibb, *Modern Trends in Islam* (Chicago, 1950), especially pp. 64–65.

[31] Lewis, "Turkey: Westernization," p. 327. In 1928 Atatürk appointed a committee under the chairmanship of Professor Fuat Köprülü (foreign minister from 1950 to 1956) for reforming religion. The committee made a number of recommendations concerning a modernized religious service and the use of the Turkish instead of the Arabic language. See Eren, *Turkey Today,* p. 91.

by other members of the family of nations. In other words, it must be harmonized with the international environment in which this great transformation is being performed.

THE WEIGHT OF INTERNATIONAL FACTORS

Although Turkey wants to be accepted as a European nation, she often feels rejected by the community to which she professes to belong. It can hardly be doubted that there still is an invisible partition or wall between Turkey and the Western–Christian world; however, the wall appears to be maintained or reinforced by the attitudes on both sides. There is an Arab-Islamic saying that "all those who deny Islam are one nation," which has two meanings: it may signify that for true Muslims all non-Muslims are equally condemnable; it may also signify that all non-Muslims always will oppose the true believers. Accordingly, when the Western nations are reluctant to recognize unequivocally the European-ness of Turks, this adds to the self-doubts of a naturally introverted and reserved nation.

The influence of these mutual inhibitions on the relations between nations of the West and the Turks is well substantiated, although their impact is often exaggerated. No doubt, the image of Turkey in the West, and particularly in the United States, as well as the image of the West in Turkey, often suffer major distortions. If each side could readjust its evaluation of the other, the mental boundary which divides them may be overcome. Furthermore, in view of the enormous intellectual and physical impediments which face the Turks in their effort to achieve their dearly cherished objective, it is suggested that the West might meet them more than halfway.

Because American–Turkish relations symbolize in large measure the contact which Turkey maintains with the West, this relationship offers the best standard for judging the difficulties encountered by both sides.

It can hardly be charged that American foreign policy is in any way biased against Turkey. On the contrary, the value of Turkish friendship is properly assessed in the Department of State and by all American experts. This may not be equally true as far as the American public at large is concerned. Although outspoken hostility or latent prejudice may still linger in the memories of those who have not forgotten Ottoman misrule or the fate of the Greeks and Armenians, the greatest stumbling block is American indifference toward or sheer ignorance of the essential aspects of Turkish life.[32]

Communication with Turkey in matters of military or economic assistance or in political business is not easy. Indeed, it would be well-nigh impossible if the Western negotiators did not realize that Turkey has never been a colony or administered from a European capital and that she is accustomed to administer her affairs according to her own concepts. She will consider "advice" but would never accept it as an implied instruction. Turkey rightly regards herself as an equal member of the Western alliance; yet, at the same time, she is a developing nation in need of foreign assistance on, as she is told, "concessionary terms." This ambivalence is compounded by the Western attitude which expects Turkey to be a fully cooperating partner in NATO as well as in other Atlantic or European organizations, but simultaneously wishes to subject her to all the inquisitory scrutiny and mortifying censures due to an underdeveloped country dependent on charitable donations from abroad. At one moment she is the bulwark of NATO's southeast corner, the next she is pauper sustained by assistance.[33]

Even those Americans and West Europeans who generally have a better comprehension of matters Turkish have difficulty realizing how complex and intricate the political, social, and psychological fabric of modern Turkey really is. She is in a state of transformation—politically, economically, and socially—and, therefore, she has many faces and contradictory habits and reactions. The paradox of Turkey has to be taken into account by all those in the West who wish her a safe berth within the confines of the European family of nations.

---

[32] "The danger is that if the complacent detachment of the West—this isolation from profound Turkish things while professing friendship for the Turks all the while— might in some near or distant time contribute to wholly estranging Turk from the humanism of the West; that the West's failure to comprehend as well as just help might frustrate the still unspoiled idealism of millions of modern, especially young, Turks." Charles E. Adelsen in the *Christian Science Monitor,* January 14, 1969.

[33] See John White, *Pledged to Development* (London, 1967), pp. 91–97. The author thus describes one aspect of the difficulties dealing with Turkey: "The difference in Turkey's case—and this where the backlog of history really begins to wreak havoc— is that the aid-giving countries, through long association, have acquired sensitivities and blind spots which coincide with those of the Turks. The result is that the representatives of Turkey's creditors insist on discussing Turkey's performance, the representatives of Turkey insist on discussing Turkey's aid requirements, and both sides assume, wrongly but with fierce conviction, that they are talking about two quite different things" (p. 95).

Just as Turkey cannot seek fulfillment of her dreams without the helpful cooperation of the West, so the West would lose its entire political and military posture in the Middle East without the collaboration of Turkey.[34] The importance and usefulness of the Turkish alliance cannot be overemphasized; even her guardianship of the straits may have consequences more far-reaching than the military control of these waterways.[35]

The Truman Doctrine, which officially extended United States involvement into Greece and Turkey and thus into the Middle East, must remain a basic premise of American foreign policy, unless Washington is willing to sacrifice the areas east of Italy. Turkey's geopolitical location makes her a cornerstone of the Atlantic alliance, the overlapping link in the NATO–CENTO chain, and the bastion of the eastern Mediterranean. Her cooperation may be considered of equal, if not greater, importance than that of the nations of the central region of Europe. In defending Turkey, the United States would not be acting as "global policeman" but as a nation whose own interests are global and would be seriously endangered if Turkey faltered.[36]

To seek to protect Turkey with the consent of Turkey herself cannot be construed as interference in Turkey's internal affairs.[37] To assure the best possible defense has required joint arrangements and joint installations. Thus a "special relationship" has evolved. Because the United States is the more powerful partner and because it provides military hardware and logistic knowledge, this relationship must resemble a "rabbit pie" composed of an American horse and a Turkish rabbit.[38] Despite the disproportionate power-status, however, there is no need for a relationship of subordination and superordination.[39]

[34] "It is Turkey more than any other nation, which is needed for Middle East defense, both military and political. And it is Turkey which stands firmest against all threats and blandishments from the North. Whatever the efforts that may be necessary elsewhere in the Middle East, they should not divert us from recognition of this political fact, or from the measures required to assure its performance." Campbell, *Defense of the Middle East,* p. 349.

[35] For instance, Soviet missiles destined for Cuba in 1962 were first sighted in the straits; *The Times* (London), April 27, 1966.

[36] See *New York Times,* March 12, 1967.

[37] "The claims that we interfere in Turkey's internal affairs are untrue. The United States attaches great importance to Turkey's friendship and relations with the USA on sound ground." From an interview with Ambassador Parker Hart before his departure from Turkey; *Milliyet,* October 3, 1968.

[38] The simile was used by C. L. Sulzberger; *New York Times,* January 29, 1969.

[39] "We want partners and not clients. I think that these are the directions in which

Servility and obsequiousness, on either side, do not promote a real partnership. Turkish leaders should not be expected to be "more pro-American than Americans," and Americans should not try to appease demonstrating Turkish students or leftist press critics by unnecessary permissiveness. Attempts at appeasing anti-Americans are tantamount to exposing and betraying Turkish promoters of American friendship.

Doubtless, many Turks resent the presence of American forces and American bases in Turkey, but only a relative few really believe that Turkey's security could dispense with them. Naturally, it would be more pleasing to Turkey's self-esteem if she could be safe without NATO bases, or even without being a member of that alliance. But she has had to weigh carefully the pros and cons of disengagement and, undisputedly, has come to the conclusion that her essential interests demand not only continued membership in the Atlantic alliance but also the presence of American forces. Naturally, she is apprehensive, as European members of the alliance are, that Washington will use its nuclear arsenal only if American territory or American military dispositions are attacked. There-fore—so Turks believe—the American military presence serves as an incentive for American participation in case of an armed conflict.[40] There is also a widespread belief in Turkey that Washington regards American bases as indispensable in six countries throughout the world, including Turkey.[41]

The question whether Turkey needs America more than whether the United States needs Turkey certainly troubles Turkish foreign policy-makers. Only a partial return to isolationism would be felt disastrous by Turkey. President Nixon's new Asian policy is one under which the United States would not render military assistance unless the attacked country made a good initial stand alone. Such an interpretation of Amer-ica's pledge of military assistance would not be welcome in Ankara. Not that Turkey could not resist an aggression; she would do so better than many another ally of the United States. That Washington might not im-mediately and automatically proffer help would upset all of Turkey's strategical and political expectations.

---

we ought to persist." From an interview with Walt W. Rostow, special assistant to President Johnson on national security affairs; New York Times, January 5, 1969.

[40] See C. L. Sulzberger in New York Times, July 30, 1969.

[41] The other countries are Spain, West Germany, the Philippines, South Korea, and Japan; Yeni Gazete, April 15, 1969.

There are few, if any, Turks who advocate U.S. withdrawal from Europe and the establishment of an integrated European defense force in lieu of the present NATO arrangements, which created a *de facto* United States leadership.[42] Nor is Turkey enthusiastic about a European security conference, as proposed by Moscow. Turkey's nightmare, and that of other European powers, is a deal between Moscow and Washington that would supersede NATO.[43] Spheres of influence, if formally drawn up and agreed upon by the superpowers, would not be to Turkey's liking, even were she "assigned" to the American sphere, as one expects she would be. If the present Turkish leadership had a choice, it would prefer continued membership in NATO with flexible commitments toward the United States and American commitments to defend Turkey. The liberty of action she already enjoys in her contacts with the Soviet Union or the Arab states has conferred upon her practically all the advantages of an uncommitted nation, while she also enjoys the advantages of being protected by the nuclear umbrella of a superpower.

The key to Turkey's approach toward a neutralist status is held by Moscow. The dismantling of American bases could be proposed by Turkey only if "all the clouds in these relations" have been dispelled.[44] Despite the recent improvements in the Turkish–Soviet relationship, the confidence which existed during the interwar period has not been restored. A nonaggression pact, reserving NATO commitments, might be a practical step toward better understanding but would provide no realistic guarantee in view of Moscow's poor record on such pacts. On the other hand, one has the feeling in Ankara that unfounded fears or suspicions might do more harm than good.

Turkey's power status is critical: she is too important to play no role in international politics, but she is not strong enough to keep other powers in balance. She must therefore seek protection from that group of powers which does not constitute a threat to her security and independence.

Moscow clearly wants Ankara to move toward the status of an uncommitted nation. An open demand to Turkey to give up membership in

---

[42] Mehmet Barlas, however, believes that the defense of Europe, without NATO, is possible; *Cumhuriyet,* February 25, 1969.

[43] C. L. Sulzberger in *New York Times,* April 16, 1967.

[44] *Milliyet* (July 10, 1968) quoted *Pravda* after Çağlayangil's meeting with Soviet Foreign Minister Gromyko that, despite this contact, "the clouds have still not been dispelled."

NATO, as submitted by Khrushchev in return for improved relations, has not been repeated recently. Instead, Soviet leadership wishes to use persuasion and indirect coercion. The anti-American campaign of indigenous Turkish origin, but discreetly encouraged by Moscow, is a windfall that could be exploited at a moment's notice. Of course, anticommunism is so strong in Turkey that the relatively tiny segment of those who are genuinely anti-American can do very little. Events such as the invasion of Czechoslovakia act as counter-stimulants to any hostility against the United States. Nothing could have better strengthened Turkey's determination to stick with NATO than the proclamation of the Brezhnev Doctrine; for the Turks this meant that a "Socialist state" must needs be a Russian satellite.

Although the effects of the Czechoslovak crisis might fade away (although in Turkey the memories of the Hungarian tragedy of 1956 are more keenly felt than anywhere else in the free world), the Soviet naval penetration into the eastern Mediterranean will remain a permanent reminder of a potential threat to Turkey's security. The official Moscow announcement that the Soviet Union is a "Mediterranean power" was perceived by some leaders in Ankara as a claim that Turkey's territory is a Soviet "security zone." The various wartime and postwar calls by the Soviets for such a zone along their western and southern borders are well remembered by the Turks. If the eastern Mediterranean, as declared by Moscow, is an area over which the Soviet state wishes to exercise authority, the regions between that sea and Soviet territory proper—that is, all of Turkey—will also be seen by the Russians as a zone of influence. The danger that such claims for the control of the Turkish straits might be pressed, as they have been in the past, seems to Turkish leaders and other observers less remote than the present silence would indicate.

After the experiences with Moscow during and after World War II, bilateral negotiations with the Soviet Union over basic security questions, and the status of the straits in particular, are considered distasteful and dangerous by the realistic and clear-sighted leadership in Ankara. Thus, U.S. and Western European participation in Turkey's future negotiations with Russia over such questions is just as essential for her as the contractual guarantee by these powers to resist outright aggression.

Turkey realizes that she cannot enjoy the benefits of the Western alliance and, at the same time, profit from the unfettered freedom that uncommitted nations enjoy in their relations with Moscow and with other neutralist countries. The protection of the United States and other NATO members increases Turkey's defensive status. Being essentially a status quo power, the defense of her existing real estate and power status must be her primary concern. Such a position is not suitable for self-assertive actions. Thus, Turkey's campaign for control over all or part of Cyprus was more impeded than assisted by her system of alliances. Arab and other uncommitted governments are inhibited in their relations with Ankara as long as Turkey is "tainted" by her exclusive ties with "imperialist" or "ex-colonial" powers.

Because of her central position in the confrontation between East and West, Turkey fears that she may be directly involved in any acute conflict between the two superpowers, even if the immediate topic of the controversy is outside her range of interest. The precedent of the Cuban missile crisis, when American missile sites on her territory became an object of bargaining and when she felt exposed to Soviet nuclear attack, is well remembered. Little, however, could be done in such a matter. Commitment to common defense is accompanied by the danger of being drawn into relatively distant conflicts. Because of Turkey's forward position, she may actually be hit first. All she can do is avoid provoking the potential aggressor while contributing to peaceful developments—without, however, weakening her defense posture.

Politically, Turkey's vital interests and long-term foreign policy objectives demand that she belong to the West. To belong to the East would be tantamount to losing her independence; moreover, she would be cut off from the West, where ideologically she feels she belongs. Economically, however, Turkey is part of the Third World of developing nations.[45] As a modern and industrialized nation she is still in *statu nascendi,* much more vulnerable physically and psychically than other nations that have reached that level of development. At her present stage, she wants external peace and tranquility in order to accomplish the transition she desires. The primary criterion, then, for Turkish foreign-policy decision-makers is the prime goal of Westernization. The leaders of Turkey cannot approach this coveted goal without taking account of the realities of their country's domestic situation and international posture.

[45] See Irving Louis Horowitz, *Three Worlds of Development: The Theory and Practice of International Stratification* (New York, 1966), *passim.*

REALITIES VERSUS AMBITIONS

After the end of the war of independence, Atatürk was able to carry out his reforms in an atmosphere of relative international calm and security. The Turkey of our day, however, seems to be condemned to continue and, it is hoped, complete her transformation process in an era of domestic turbulence and international controversy. The course which the Turkish ship of state has to follow leads through a narrow, dangerous channel. The task which she is determined to fulfill requires both unselfish idealism and an acute sense of the realities of life.

Among her domestic difficulties, the commotion created by the small but noisy exponents of red and black fanaticism are the most conspicuous. The first group would wish to regiment the country into a new order of "social equality" and then strait-jacket it into economic development; the second wishes to turn back the course of history by re-establishing the political power of Islam and swaying Turkey away from Europe. While these are the two extremist trends, compromisers seeking unprincipled solutions might also easily steer the vessel aground.

The unhealthy stratification of Turkish society, the gap between the urban and rural populations, the paternalistic attitudes of the bureaucratic elite toward the governed, and the contrasts between the Turkish east and west—to mention only some of the outstanding issues—are all potential time bombs which the government will have to defuse before they explode. Any such explosion would irreparably damage Turkish national advancement and jeopardize Turkey's international stature.

Turkey's east-west problem is also complicated by the Kurdish issue, a domestic problem laden with definite international overtones. An improvement in the economic and social status of some 18 eastern provinces which have lagged behind the rest of the country and the integration of their inhabitants, including the Kurds, into national life, should be given first priority.

The country had been roused by the promise that it should look forward to greatness and prosperity. Impatience at the delay in achieving this goal is at the root of such discontent, including that displayed by the students. The urgency of specific demands makes the choice of priorities exceedingly difficult. It is only natural that the rulers seek first to appease the largest part of the electorate—namely, the peasantry, which,

377

according to Demirel, should be "saved from medieval conditions."[46]

It would be a great mistake if Turkey succeeded in Westernizing only the urban superstructure and left the rural masses in their backward way of life. Peter the Great, the Russian reformist, and his successors created such a cleavage by depriving the Russian peasantry of civilizational advance, a task which only Communist rule strove to surmount.[47] Until the Turkish case, Muslim reformists had all stopped short of extending their reforms into the villages or to the people at large. The Ottomans had concentrated mostly on modernizing their armed forces; in Egypt, Mehmed Ali and his successors restricted their reforms to the urban elite; other present-day reformists have limited themselves to economic development rather than the all-out Westernization which is the ambition of Turkey.

The Turkish government faces some of the gravest roadblocks in the field of development. The developmental process is so much the focus of interest that it distracts attention even from some crucial questions of world politics. The success of governmental policy, by its own declaration and in the vision of the public, is closely linked to economic development. Expectations and pressures of urgency are the greatest in this respect. The Turkish people, patiently enduring suffering and deprivation, are utterly impatient in their expectation of success and triumph. One of the principal arguments of those who advocate strict *étatisme* and methods of regimentation for the sake of development *à la Soviet* refer to the short time Turkey has for the fulfillment of this task. But the Justice Party government wishes to abide by "the determination . . . to attain the level of contemporary civilization within a democratic system marked by freedom and justice."[48]

It is realized by foreign and Turkish experts that the period of the second Five Year Plan, ending in 1972, constitutes "the most critical years for the Turkish nation in its efforts to attain economic self-sufficiency."[49]

---

[46] He also said on this occasion: "It is impossible to lay the foundations of a great and powerful Turkey when you forget or neglect the Turkish peasant. Villages which house twenty-four million, stretch from one end of the country to the other. Conditions are not modern, yet the Turkish peasant has not been defeated by hardships and difficulties. It is a must to take amenities of civilization to the Turkish peasant." *Son Havadis*, March 18, 1968.

[47] See Toynbee, *A Study of History*, vols. VII–X, pp. 169–70.

[48] From the Foreword to the *Second Five-Year Development Plan* (Ankara, 1969), p. v.

[49] *Ibid.*, p. 5.

Turkish and foreign sources already have issued warnings that the hoped-for self-sufficiency may be reached only in, or even after, 1975. Of course, even if independence from foreign aid could be attained, it is still no panacea for social and economic hardships. The success of the development plan appears to depend on so many contributive factors, the unforeseeable and the imponderable, that one can only hope "kismet" favors this grandiose venture.

Among the impediments which could thwart the fulfillment of the plan, one should list the uncertainties of the measure of foreign aid (a foreign policy problem *par excellence*), the question of economic growth and its proportion to the increase of population, the availability and magnitude of domestic sources of foreign exchange, the uncompetitive nature of Turkish industry, and the backlog of agricultural production (dependent also on weather conditions).

The "success story" of Turkey's economic development could have a broad impact on international developmental policies in general. It could prove, in this instance, that the non-Communist model for development is superior to that offered by communism.[50] It seems, therefore, very much in the interest of the United States to further as best it can the auspicious completion of Turkey's national development project. It is desirable that American economic assistance be used to promote foreign policy goals and be allotted in amounts proportionate to the purpose for which it is assigned, taking into account the relative importance of the countries thus benefited.[51]

The high rate of population growth has consumed a considerable amount of the resources needed for investment; also, humanitarian concern for the welfare of children induced the government to encourage voluntary family planning. However, such a policy is counterproductive to any expectations that there will be 50 million Turks in the 1980's, as predicted by Prime Minister Demirel,[52] nor does such a program assuage the fears of the general staff that the age groups eligible for military service

---

[50] See the interview with Walt W. Rostow, who considered Turkey among the "success stories" of non-Communist development methods; *New York Times,* January 5, 1969.

[51] "While the United States fiddles with the idea of cutting overseas commitments, the Soviet Union gives every sign of doing precisely the reverse." C. L. Sulzberger in *New York Times,* July 4, 1969.

[52] *Milliyet,* September 30, 1968. The *Second Five-Year Plan* estimated Turkey's population at a high fertility rate increase to be 47,402 in 1980 (p. 60).

will be depleted.[53] It is highly questionable whether in these times the power of a nation is calculated in manpower rather than in terms of economic production.[54]

The most ambitious Turkish venture is no doubt her intent to be, after a transitional phrase, admitted to full membership in the European Economic Community. At present it seems highly questionable whether Turkey would be able to survive economically a customs and economic union with the highly industrialized countries of Western Europe at any time during the next two or three decades. The uncompetitiveness of Turkish industrial articles will be the greatest hurdle to be overcome; in any case, economic union will entail sacrifices and risks for the Turkish economy. Turkey's decision to join the Common Market was political, and the political advantages of belonging to this "inner circle" of the European family were considered worth the risk.

According to a recent classification,[55] Turkey is no longer regarded as a "traditional" but as a "transitional" society. This writer would add that she is the most advanced among transitional societies, one which not only has contact with Western civilization but is well on the road to embracing the civilizational values and methods of the West.

Notwithstanding Turkey's desire to be European, her people have not completely broken their ties with the traditional Islamic culture and are not expected to disavow their ancestral faith. Turkey's divesting herself of the nonreligious aspects of Mohammed's all-embracing ideological tenets is unique in history. So far no Islamic people has voluntarily given up devotion to the teachings of the Prophet. In Spain, the Muslims who remained after the reconquest were forcibly Christianized by the Spanish; many Muslims in Russia were converted to Christian Orthodoxy under duress. Turkey, however, embarked upon a road which distinguishes between the faith which is prescribed by the Koran and its political, social, and legal principles. While discarding the latter, Turks are free to believe in the former and to practice religion accordingly.

---

[53] General Cemal Tural, chief of the general staff, declared himself against family planning. He said that neighboring countries were constantly increasing their population and Turkey should put an end to birth control. *Milliyet*, March 1, 1968.

[54] The same General Tural said on another occasion: "We are not a nation that can be expressed in calculations and statistics." Andrew Mango, *Turkey* (London, 1968), p. 169.

[55] Norman J. Padelford and George A. Lincoln, *The Dynamics of International Politics* (2d ed.; New York, 1967), pp. 65–66.

History has not yet had the last word about this unmatched experiment. It is still premature to forecast either the success or failure of a venture which could revolutionize the entire *Daru'l Islam*. Realities in the lives of millions are juxtaposed with the aspirations of those who want to weave Western philosophy and Western ways into the social fabric of all Turks while leaving their faith in Allah unimpaired. The intangibles of this transformation, if successful, are bound to influence all tangible aspects of Turkey's social and political development.

Among the realities of Turkey's political status, her geopolitical location requires the closest consideration. It has been noted earlier that this geostrategical phenomenon is obviously double-edged: it raises Turkey's value as a confederate and attracts potential aggressors. Turkey, as an independent state, cannot subsist without her straits; but with the straits under her control she lives a perilous life.[56]

Germany sought an alliance with Turkey in World War I because she held the keys to the Black Sea and could prevent the supplying of Russia; for the same reason a breakthrough across the Dardanelles was attempted by the Entente. In World War II, Turkey managed, though with considerable risk, to avoid active belligerency because her neutrality happened to be in the interests of the Western powers, Russia, and Germany during the critical period of the war.

In a possible future military confrontation between the superpowers, Turkey could hardly hope to remain aloof, even should she assume the posture of an uncommitted country. Regardless of whether the conflagration will be restricted to conventional weapons, or Turkey has nuclear missiles on her territory, geography has placed her in the area between the Soviet Union and the Mediterranean, and neither belligerent can avoid passing over her territory by air, by sea, or by land. Nor could Moscow tolerate that her Mediterranean navy or the Arab states, which these forces undertake to protect, be physically cut off by the closure of the straits. Turkey can only hope that she will be spared nuclear devastation

---

[56] According to *Yeni Istanbul* (April 17, 1969), Turkey is indispensable to the United States because of her geopolitical location; inasmuch as Turkey is useful to the United States, she becomes, to the same degree, a source of danger to the Soviet Union. Consequently, a cold or hot war between the United States and the Soviet Union without Turkey's involvement is unimaginable. Turkey would become one of Moscow's first targets in a conventional as well as in a nuclear war. The Soviets would attack Turkey without any warning for reasons of self-defense and to prevent Turkish territory from being used to destroy their own land.

and that her territory will be protected from enemy invasion. These two expectations may be better realized if Turkey remains attached to the Atlantic alliance. A wish to return to a status of neutrality in the present troubled conditions of the world, even if this status were regarded as ideally best suited to Turkey, would be highly unrealistic. Although he advocated Turkey's neutralism during the first fifteen years of the republic, even Atatürk sought alliances for his country when another world war seemed to approach.[57]

To a greater extent than that of most medium powers, Turkey's independence depends on the global balance of power that has been struck between the United States and the Soviet Union. Turkey can do very little to ensure that this global power balance is maintained. Like the rest of humanity, Turkey has to rely on the wisdom, foresight, and moderation of the principal nuclear powers so that the relative stability between them will not be overturned by some irrational behavior or unjustified grievance. There is no absolute security for any state in our time; a country with Turkey's exposed geographical location is particularly vulnerable.

Turkey's safety may also be threatened by other factors. She is surrounded by a number of countries that confront her or confront one another. A local balance of power exists between Turkey and Greece; a local balance system is operative in the Balkans, in which Turkey participates; a particular state of equilibrium governs the military confrontation between Israel and her Arab neighbors; another balance has to be maintained among the Arab states themselves, as well as between Turkey and her Arab neighbors. In respect to these regional balancing situations, Turkey, as a leading power in the Near and Middle East, has increased responsibilities and an important task to fulfill. In dealing with these historical and sensitive relationships, much depends on her wisdom and vision, on her moderation and firmness. She must be conscious of the realities she has to face and must restrain her aspirations in the face of these realities. She will never obtain all she wants, but with cautious and

[57] "Turkey has been in alliances to protect her independence in every period of her history. This is a requirement of her *geopolitical situation*. This *reality* was also valid during Atatürk's time. Atatürk himself made the Balkan Pact and the Saadabad Pact which he described as a joint work for the ideal of peace. He himself prepared the Turkish–British–French tripartite alliance shortly before World War II." Foreign Minister Çağlayangil in answering questions by journalists; *Ankara Bayram,* March 1, 1969. (Italics added.)

skillful diplomacy, she might avoid losing what she already possesses and yet make gradual gains.

No one wants Turkey to sacrifice herself for NATO or to defend Europe or the United States. She can only be expected to defend her interests as long as they are in harmony with the interests of the alliance. Of course, one has to distinguish between immediate and more distant interests. The latter may also be called questions of principle. If Turkey refused to act if Berlin or Norway were threatened or attacked, she could not count on the help of her allies should she suffer invasion. To decide what to do at the critical moment and not to be overly impressed by ephemeral advantages is the test of genuine statesmanship.

In the Turkish–American relationship, an artificially heated atmosphere has been created by a vocal minority which fails to assess the realities of this relationship. Turkey is right in insisting on equal partnership. There is no reason to believe that Washington has or ever had any intention of treating her differently. If inequalities have arisen, they are partly the result of international power realities for which neither Turkey nor America can be made responsible, partly the outcome of permissiveness on behalf of Turkish negotiators, or a lack of restraint or understanding on the American side. All of these problems can be easily remedied. For the rest, the anti-American campaign is either directed by ulterior political motives, prompted by an ultra-nationalist need to find a target to hate, or is the result of an incompatibility of national temperaments. Turks should know, and their responsible leaders do know, that America cannot be taken for granted either.

Despite the artificially labored anti-Americanism of a few, it is well understood that today's Turkey stands closer than ever before to the United States and Western Europe. Demonstrating youth are allowed to indulge in such exploits only because Western liberalism, the political ideal of the West, and the idea of freedom of expression have finally been adopted in Turkey. Nowhere in the Middle East or Eastern Europe, including the empire of the Soviets, would such an exhibition of discontent be tolerated. No progressive Turk can feel genuine affinity with systems repressive to human freedom. Anti-Americanism is a fashion—and Turks like to appear fashionable; such fashions die out when there is no fuel to keep the fires burning.

It would be a fatal mistake if the Turkish leadership allowed themselves to be guided by emotional motives instead of cool reason. Unlike the Ottoman Empire at the time of its final collapse, the Turkish republic has committed no major mistake in its foreign policy. On the contrary, it set out a course for the Turkish nation that promises to turn it, in the words of Süleyman Demirel, into "a powerful member of the Western community."[58]

Contemporary Turkey is like a huge human laboratory. While the processes of industrialization, modernization, advances in education, and acculturation to the Western ideal carry their own momentum, experiments are being conducted to find the methods most conducive to these ends. For the promotion of internal transformation, the foreign policy has set into motion initiatives to cement friendships and preserve peace. It is an ambitious and a dynamic policy—one might even say overly ambitious—but it is certainly not adventurous.[59] In almost every respect, modern Turkey has turned completely away from the policies of the declining Ottoman Empire. If the latter was forced to use inadequate resources in its last stand against total collapse, present-day Turkey's dynamism is directed toward progress and the generation of a new nation. Only the future will tell whether her resources are adequate to attain this lofty goal.

Ottoman Turkey fought for time to survive; Atatürk's Turkey also needs time, another generation or more, to become a modern European power. Will she succeed? So far she has achieved what few would have foreseen half a century ago. In 1914, at the outset of the World War I, Winston Churchill asked himself: "What was to happen to scandalous, crumbling, decrepit, and penniless Turkey in this earthquake?"[60]

Some 50 years ago, the Treaty of Sèvres, expressing the judgment of the victorious powers over the prostrate body of the defunct empire, sentenced it to death. A few years later, phoenix-like, a new Turkey emerged. Nobody in the West would now repeat Lord Salisbury's remark recalling the Anglo–Turkish alliance during the Crimean War: "We have put our money on the wrong horse." In the present critical period, when Turkey has a good chance of gaining economic self-sufficiency, it would be ill-advised to consider her a "wrong horse."

[58] New York Times, September 3, 1969.
[59] Quoted after Çağlayangil who said: "Turkey's foreign policy had taken on a dynamic nature. . . . But this dynamism was never adventurous." Son Havadis, July 31, 1969.
[60] Churchill, The Aftermath, p. 374.

Inside and outside Turkey, there are voices of skepticism concerning the ultimate success of her economic, ideological, and foreign policy exploits. Others, both within Turkey and abroad, express optimism. The rise of Turkey from the ruins of empire seems to inspire confidence; however, the enormous task of transforming and readapting an entire nation, as well as economically revitalizing it, appear to be gigantic in the face of the realities Turkey still must encounter. It is customary to speak of "economic miracles" when a country unexpectedly recovers its economic strength. Should Turkey achieve its national purpose, one could characterize this feat with greater justification as the "Turkish miracle."

Chronology of Foreign Policy Leadership (1923-1970)

Year	President of the Republic	Prime Minister	Minister of Foreign Affairs
1923–24	Mustafa Kemal (Atatürk*)	Ismet (Inönü*)	Tevfik Rüştü (Aras*)
1924	" "	Ali Fethi (Okyar*)	" "
1925	" "	Ismet (Inönü*)	" "
1937	" "	Celâl Bayar	" "
1938–39	Ismet Inönü	Refik Saydam	Şükrü Saracoğlu
1943	" "	Şükrü Saracoğlu	Numan Menemencioğlu
1944	" "	" "	Hasan Saka
1946	" "	Recep Peker	" "
1947	" "	Hasan Saka	Necmettin Sadak
1949	" "	Semseddin Günaltay	" "
1950	Celâl Bayar	Adnan Menderes	Fuat Köprülü
1955	" "	" "	Adnan Menderes
1956	" "	" "	Fuat Köprülü
1957	" "	" "	Ethem Menderes
1958	" "	" "	Fatin Rüştü Zorlu
1960–61	Cemal Gürsel	Cemal Gürsel (Head of State)	Selim Sarper
1962	" "	Ismet Inönü	Feridun Cemal Erkin
1965	" "	Suat Hayrı Ürgüplü	Hasan Işık
1965	" "	Süleyman Demirel	Ihsan Sabrı Çağlayangil
1966	Cevdet Sunay	" "	" "

* Family name adopted in 1934.

Bibliography

An all-encompassing bibliography of the questions discussed in this book would have grown into elephantine proportions. The following list of publications is, therefore, strictly selective. Limitations of space forbade the listing of all printed material consulted. Furthermore, many of the observations in this work rely on views expressed to this writer by persons in and outside Turkey whose anonymity had to be safeguarded. In this respect, too, the source material hereafter submitted is necessarily incomplete.

The division of published material into primary and secondary sources, as well as the separation of historical and background works from books and articles closely related to the central topic of this volume, though often arbitrary, has been adopted for reasons of expediency.

PRIMARY SOURCES

Documents and Official Publications

Actes de la Conférence de Montreux concernant le régime des Détroits. 22 juin–20 juillet 1936. Compte-rendu des séances plénières et de procès-verbal des débats du comité technique. Liège, Belgium, 1936.

Bilsel, Cemil. *Türk Boğazları* (The Turkish Straits). Istanbul: Ismail Akgün, 1948. (Documents and texts of Soviet and Turkish diplomatic notes relative to the straits.)

Bishop, Donald G. (ed.). *Soviet Foreign Relations. Documents and Readings.* Syracuse, N.Y.: Syracuse University Press, 1952.

British Government. *Cyprus (Constitution)* Cmnd. 1093. London: Her Majesty's Stationery Office, 1960.

Cyprus. A Handbook of the Island's Past and Present. Nicosia: Publication Department, Greek Communal Chamber, 1964.

Devlet Istatistik Enstitüsu (State Statistics Institute). *1963 Turkiye Istatistik Yıllığı* (Turkish Statistical Yearbook, 1963). Ankara, 1963.

Documents on International Affairs, 1930. London: Oxford University Press, 1931.

Documents on International Affairs, 1933. London: Oxford University Press, 1934.

Documents on International Affairs, 1936. London: Oxford University Press, 1937. [The Montreux Straits Convention, July 20, 1936, pp. 643–67.]

Documents on International Affairs, 1951. London: Oxford University Press, 1954.

Documents on International Affairs, 1953. London: Oxford University Press, 1956.

Documents on International Affairs, 1954. London: Oxford University Press, 1957.

Documents on International Affairs, 1955. London: Oxford University Press, 1958.

Great Britain. Foreign Office. *Treaty of Peace with Turkey, and Other Instruments Signed at Lausanne on July 24, 1923, together with Agreements between Greece and Turkey signed January 30, 1923, and Subsidiary Documents forming part of the Turkish Peace Settlement*. Foreign Office Treaty Series No. 16 (1923), Cmnd. 1929.

Great Britain. Foreign Office. *Convention Regarding the Regime of the Straits, with correspondence relating thereto*. Montreux, July 20, 1936. Cmnd. 5249.

Hurewitz, J. C. *Diplomacy in the Near and Middle East: A Documentary Record*. 1535–1914, Vol. I. 1914–1956, Vol. II. Princeton, N.J.: D. Van Nostrand, 1956.

Millet Meclisi. *Tutanak Dergisi* (The Official Records of the Turkish National Assembly). Ankara.

Millet Partisi. *Kıbrıs Meselesi ve Adalet Partisi Hükûmeti Programı Hakkındaki Görüşü, 1965–1966* (Nation Party, Views Concerning the Cyprus Problem and the Program of the Justice Party Government). Ankara: San Matbaası, 1966.

———. *Osman Bölükbaşının Radyo Konuşmaları* (Radio Speeches by Osman Bölükbaşı). Ankara: San Matbaası, 1966.

———. *Genel Başkanı Osman Bölükbaşı'nın Avrupadaki Türk Işçileri ve Kıbrıs Konulararında Sayin Başbakana Sundukları Muhtiralar* (Nation Party, Memorandum Submitted by the General President Osman Bölükbası to the Honorable Prime Minister on the Subject of Turkish Workers in Europe and of Cyprus). Ankara: Atli Matbaası, 1967.

Noradounghian, Gabriel (ed.). *Receuil d'actes internationaux de l'Empire Ottoman; traités, conventions, arrangements, déclarations, protocoles, procès-verbaux, firmans, berats, lettres patentes relative au droit public extérieur de la Turquie*. Paris: F. Pichon, 1897–1903 (Vols. I–II, 1900.) 1300–1789, Vol. I; 1789–1856, Vol. II; 1856–1878, Vol. III; 1878–1902, Vol. IV.

Turkish Embassy. Office of the Information Counselor. *The Turkish Constitution*. Washington, D.C.: n.d.

Turkish Ministry of Foreign Affairs. Department of Information. "The Question of Cyprus." *Turkish Yearbook of International Relations, 1963*. Ankara.

Turkey, Republic of. Prime Ministry. State Planning Organization. *Second Five-Year Development Plan, 1968–1972*. Ankara: Central Bank of Turkey, 1969.

Türkiye Işçi Partisi Programı (Program of the Turkish Labor Party). Istanbul: 1964.

U.S. Department of State. *The Problem of the Turkish Straits*. Written and compiled by Harry N. Howard. Washington, D.C.: Government Printing Office, 1947.

———. *The Conferences of Malta and Yalta, 1945*. Washington, D.C.: Government Printing Office, 1955.

————. *The Conference of Berlin (The Potsdam Conference), 1945.* Washington, D.C.: Government Printing Office, 1960. Vols. I and II.

————. *Conferences at Cairo and Tehran, 1943.* Washington, D.C.: Government Printing Office, 1961.

World Peace Foundation. *Documents on American Foreign Relations, 1947.* Vol. IX. Princeton, N.J.: Princeton University Press, 1949.

Yeni Türkiye Partisi. *Seçim Beyannamesi* (New Turkey Party, Election Manifesto). Ankara: Kars Matbaası, 1961.

————. *Seçim Beyannamesi* (New Turkey Party, Election Manifesto). Ankara: 1965.

————. *Tüzüğü ve Programı* (New Turkey Party, Statutes and Program). Ankara: 1967.

Memoirs, Speeches, and Reference Books

Atatürk, Kemal. *A Speech Delivered by Ghazi Mustapha Kemal, President of the Turkish Republic, October 1927.* Leipzig: K. F. Koehler, 1929.

Atatürk, Mustafa Kemal. *Söylev ve Demeçler* (Speeches and Pronouncements). Speeches in the Grand National Assembly and in the People's Republican Party Congresses (1919–1928), Vol. I. Istanbul: Maarif Matbaası, 1945. Other Speeches (1906–1938), Vol. II. Ankara: Türk Tarih Kurumu Basimevi, 1952. Statements (1918–1937), Vol. III. Ankara: Türk Tarih Basimevi, 1954.

Churchill, Winston S. *The World Crisis: The Aftermath.* Vol. IV. New York: Charles Scribner's Sons, 1929.

————. *The Second World War.* 6 vols. Boston: Houghton Mifflin, 1950, 1951, and 1953.

C.K.M.P. (Cumhuriyetçi Köylü Millet Partisi). *Radyo Konuşmaları* (Republican Peasants Nation Party, Radio Speeches). Ankara: Arı Matbaası, 1966.

Eden, Anthony (Earl of Avon). *Full Circle.* Boston: Houghton Mifflin, 1960.

Hopper, Jerry R., and Richard I. Levin. *The Turkish Administrator: A Cultural Survey.* Ankara: USAID, Public Administration Division, 1967. (Mimeographed.)

Institute of Public Administration for Turkey and the Middle East. *Organization and Functions of the Central Government of Turkey.* Report of the Managing Board of the Central Government Organization Research Project. Ankara: 1965.

————. *Turkish Government Organization Manual.* Prepared under the direction of the Managing Board of the Central Government Organization Project. Ankara: 1966.

Jäschke, Gotthard. *Die Türkei in den Jahren 1942–1951.* Wiesbaden: Otto Harrassowitz, 1955.

————. *Die Türkei in den Jahren 1952–1961.* Wiesbaden: Otto Harrassowitz, 1965.

Kennedy, Robert F. *Thirteen Days: A Memoir of the Cuban Missile Crisis*. New York: W. W. Norton & Company, 1969.

Knatchbull-Hugessen, Sir Hughe. *Diplomat in Peace and War*. London: John Murray, 1949.

Papen, Franz von. *Memoirs*. London: André Deutsch, 1952.

NATO. *Facts About the North Atlantic Treaty Organization*. Paris: NATO Information Service, 1965.

Survey of International Affairs, 1925. The Islamic World Since the Peace Settlement, Vol. I. London: Oxford University Press (for the Royal Institute of International Affairs), 1927.

Survey of International Affairs, 1936. With a contribution by D. A. Routh, "The Montreux Convention Regarding the Regime of the Black Sea Straits." London: Oxford University Press, 1937.

Survey of International Affairs, 1951. London: Oxford University Press, 1954.

Survey of International Affairs, 1953. London: Oxford University Press, 1956.

Survey of International Affairs, 1954. London: Oxford University Press, 1957.

Survey of International Affairs, 1956–1958. London: Oxford University Press, 1962.

Survey of International Affairs, 1959–1960. London: Oxford University Press, 1964.

Survey of International Affairs, 1961. London: Oxford University Press, 1965.

Siyasal Bilgiler Fakültesi Dış Münasebetler Enstitüsü (Institute of Foreign Relations of the Political Science Faculty). *Olaylarla Türk Dış Politikası, 1919–1965* (Events of Turkish Foreign Policy, 1919–1965). Ankara: Dışişleri Bakanlığı Matbaası, 1968.

U.S. Agency for International Development. *Briefing Papers on the Turkish Economy*. Ankara: January 3, 1968. (Mimeographed.)

———. *Three Papers on Turkey's External Economic Relations (1966–1968)*. Ankara: October, 1968. (Mimeographed.)

———. *Economic and Social Indicators—Turkey*. Ankara: July, 1969. (Mimeographed.)

TURKISH POLITICAL PERIODICALS AND NEWSPAPERS

Periodicals

Akis (Istanbul) Discontinued.

Ankara Üniversitesi Siyasal Bilgiler Fakültesi Dergisi (Review of the Political Science Faculty, University of Ankara)

Ant (Istanbul)

Devrim (Ankara)

Forum (Ankara)

Hayat (Istanbul)

Outlook (Ankara). English language weekly.

Turkish Yearbook of International Relations. Published by the Institute of International Relations, University of Ankara.
Yol (Ankara)
Yön (Ankara)

Newspapers

Adalet (Ankara)
Akşam (Istanbul)
Cumhuriyet (Istanbul)
Daily News (Ankara)
Dünya (Istanbul)
Hürriyet (Istanbul)
Istanbul Bayram—Ankara Bayram (Istanbul and Ankara) Holiday paper.
Milliyet (Istanbul)
Pulse (Ankara) English review of the Turkish press.
Son Baskı (Ankara) Discontinued.
Son Havadis (Istanbul)
Tercüman (Istanbul)
Ulus (Ankara)
Vatan (Ankara)
Yeni Gazete (Istanbul)
Yeni Sabah (Istanbul) Discontinued.
Yeni Tanın (Ankara)
Zafer (Ankara)

SECONDARY SOURCES

Historical and Background Works

Almond, Gabriel A., and James S. Coleman (eds.). *The Politics of the Developing Areas.* Princeton, N.J.: Princeton University Press, 1960.
Berkes, Niyazi. *The Development of Secularism in Turkey.* Montreal: McGill University Press, 1964.
Brüel, Erik. *International Straits: A Treatise of International Law.* Vols. I–II. Copenhagen: Nyt Nordisk Forlag, 1947.
Cahun, Leon. *Introduction à l'histoire de l'Asie: Turcs et Mongols, des origines à 1405.* Paris: A. Colin, 1896.
Cohen, Saul B. *Geography and Politics in a World Divided.* New York: Random House, 1963.
Evans, Laurence. *United States Policy and the Partition of Turkey, 1914–1924.* Baltimore: The Johns Hopkins Press, 1965.
Fairgrieve, James. *Geography and World Power.* London: University of London Press, 1915.

Frye, R. N. (ed.). *Islam and the West*. Den Haaag: Mouton, 1957. With a contribution by Dankwart A. Rustow, "Politics and Islam in Turkey, 1920–1955."

Gibb, H. A. R. *Modern Trends in Islam*. Chicago: University of Chicago Press, 1950.

Goriainov, Serge M. *Le Bosphore et les Dardanelles: Étude historique sur la question des Détroits, d'après la correspondance diplomatique déposée aux Archives centrales de Saint-Petersbourg et à celles de l'Empire*. Paris: Plan–Nourrit, 1910.

Graves, Philip Perceval. *The Question of the Straits*. London: E. Benn, 1931.

Hammer-Purgstall, Freiherr Joseph von. *Geschichte des Osmanischen Reiches*. 10 vols. Pest: C. A. Hartleben's Verlag, 1827–1835.

Howard, Harry N. *The Partition of Turkey: A Diplomatic History, 1913–1923*. New York: Howard Ferig, 1966.

Karpat, Kemal H. (ed.). *Political and Social Thought in the Contemporary Middle East*. London: Pall Mall Press, 1968.

Khadduri, Majid. *Independent Iraq, 1932–1958: A Study in Iraqi Politics*. 2d ed. London: Oxford University Press, 1960.

Kili, Suna. *Kemalism*. Istanbul: Robert College, 1970.

Kirk, George E. *A Short History of the Middle East: From the Rise of Islam to Modern Times*. 6th ed. New York: Praeger, 1960.

Köprülü, Mehmet Fuad. *Les Origines de l'Empire Ottoman*. Paris: Institut Français d'Archéologie de Stamboul, 1935.

Köprülüzade Mehmet Fuat (Fuad Köprülü). "Bizans Müesseselerin Osmanli Müesseselerine Tesiri hakkında bazı Mülahazalar" (Some Considerations Concerning the Influence of Byzantine Institutions on Ottoman Institutions). *Türk Hukuk ve Iktisat Tarihi Mecmuası* (Turkish Review of Legal and Economic History). Vol. I. (1931), pp. 165–313.

Lamouche, Léon (Colonel). *Histoire de la Turquie depuis les origines jusqu'à nos jours*. Paris: Payot, 1953.

Lenczowski, George. *United States Interests in the Middle East*. Washington, D.C.: American Enterprise Institute, 1968.

Mehmed Pasha, Sari, the Defterdar. *Ottoman Statecraft: The Book of Counsel for Vezirs and Governors*. Translated by Walter Livingston Wright, Jr. Princeton: Princeton University Press, 1935.

Mischef, P. H. *La Mer Noire et les Détroits de Constantinople*. Paris: Arthur Rousseau, 1899.

Mosely, Philip E. *Russian Diplomacy and the Opening of the Eastern Question in 1838 and 1839*. Cambridge, Mass.: Harvard University Press, 1934.

Papoulia, Basilike D. *Ursprung und Wesen der "Knabenlese" im Osmanischen Reich*. Munich: Oldenbourg, 1963.

Puryear, Vernon J. *Napoleon and the Dardanelles*. Berkeley and Los Angeles: University of California Press, 1951.

Ramazani, Rouhollah K. *The Northern Tier: Afghanistan, Iran, and Turkey.* Princeton, N.J.: D. Van Nostrand, 1966.

Sousa, Nasim. *The Capitulatory Régime of Turkey: Its History, Origin, and Nature.* Baltimore: Johns Hopkins Press, 1933.

Sumner, B. H. *Peter the Great and the Ottoman Empire.* Oxford: Basil Blackwell, 1949.

Toynbee, Arnold J. *The Western Question in Greece and Turkey: A Study in the Contact of Civilizations.* London: Constable & Co., 1922.

—— and Kenneth P. Kirkwood. *Turkey.* New York: Charles Scribner's Sons, 1927.

Trumpener, Ulrich. *Germany and the Ottoman Empire, 1914–1918.* Princeton, N.J.: Princeton University Press, 1969.

Tukin, Cemal. *Osmanlı Imperatorluğu devrinde boğazlar meselesi* (The Problem of the Straits in the Epoch of the Ottoman Empire). Istanbul: Üniversite Matbaacılık Kommandit Şirketi, 1947.

Wittek, Paul. *The Rise of the Ottoman Empire.* Royal Asiatic Society Monographs. Vol. XXIII. London: Luzac & Co., 1958.

Zenkovsky, Serge A. *Pan-Turkism and Islam in Russia.* Cambridge, Mass.: Harvard University Press, 1960.

Books

Arfa, Hassan. *The Kurds: An Historical and Political Study.* London: Oxford University Press, 1966.

Ataöv, Türkkaya. *Turkish Foreign Policy, 1939–1945.* Ankara: Publication of the Faculty of Political Sciences of the University of Ankara, 1965.

Aydemir, Şevket Süreyya. *Tek Adam* (The Unique Man). 3 vols. Istanbul: Yükselen Matbaası, 1966–67.

Bahrampour, Firouz. *Turkey: Political and Social Transformation.* Brooklyn, N.Y.: Theo. Gaus' Sons, 1967.

Başgil, Ali Fuad. *Din ve Lâiklik* (Religion and Secularism). 2d ed. Istanbul: Yağmur Yayinevi, 1962.

——. *La révolution militaire de 1960 en Turquie* (Ses origines). Contribution à l'étude de l'histoire politique intérieure de la Turquie contemporaine. Geneva: Perret–Gentil, 1963.

Black, Joseph E., and Kenneth W. Thompson (eds.). *Foreign Policies in a World of Change.* New York: Harper & Row, 1963. With a contribution by Nuri Eren, "The Foreign Policy of Turkey."

Bois, Thomas. *The Kurds.* Beirut: Khayats, 1966.

Broekmeijer, M. W. J. M. *Developing Countries and N.A.T.O.* Leyden: A. W. Sijthoff, 1963.

Campbell, John C. *Defense of the Middle East: Problems of American Policy.* New York: Harper, 1958.

————. *The Middle East in the Muted Cold War*. Denver, Colo.: The Social Science Foundation and Department of International Relations Monograph Series in World Affairs, University of Denver, 1964–65.

The Cyprus Question. Chicago: Institute of Greek–American Historical Studies, 1965.

Davison, Roderic H. *Turkey*. Englewood Cliffs, N.J.: Prentice–Hall, 1968.

Dodd, C. H. *Politics and Government in Turkey*. Berkeley: University of California Press, 1969.

Dranov, B. *Chernomorskie Prolivy—Mezhdunarodno-pravovoi rezhim* (The Black Sea Straits—International-legal regime). Moscow: Yurid, izd-vo, 1948.

Dzelepy, E.-N. *Le Complot de Chypre*. Brussels: Les Éditions Politiques, 1965.

Eagleton, William. *The Kurdish Republic of 1946*. London: Oxford University Press, 1963.

Eren, Nuri. *Turkey Today—and Tomorrow: An Experiment in Westernization*. New York: Praeger, 1963.

Erkin, Feridun Cemal. *Les Relations Turco-Soviétiques et la Question des Détroits*. Ankara: Başnur Matbaası, 1968.

Falk, André. *Turkey*. New York: Viking Press, 1963.

Frey, Frederick W. *The Turkish Political Elite*. Cambridge, Mass.: The M.I.T. Press, 1965.

Gallman, Waldemar J. *Iraq Under General Nuri*. Baltimore, Md.: The Johns Hopkins Press, 1964.

Geshkoff, Theodore J. *Balkan Union: A Road to Peace in Southeastern Europe*. New York: Columbia University Press, 1940.

Ghassemlou, Abdul Rahman. *Kurdistan and the Kurds*. Prague: Publishing House of the Czechoslovak Academy of Sciences, 1965.

Giritli, Ismet. *Kommünizm, Sosyalizm ve Anayasamız* (Communism, Socialism, and Our Constitution). Istanbul: Baha Matbaası, 1967.

Gökalp, Ziya. *Turkish Nationalism and Western Civilization*. Selected Essays of Ziya Gökalp. Edited by Niyazi Berkes. New York: Columbia University Press, 1959.

Harris, George S. *The Origins of Communism in Turkey*. Stanford, Calif.: Stanford University Press, 1967.

Harrison, Richard. *Meet the Turks*. London: Jarrolds, 1961.

Hartmann, Hans Walter. *Die auswärtige Politik der Türkei, 1923–1940*. Zurich: Leemann & Co., 1941.

Hershlag, Y. Y. *Turkey. The Challenge of Growth*, 2d ed. Leiden: E. J. Brill, 1968.

Heyd, Uriel. *Foundations of Turkish Nationalism: The Life and Teachings of Ziya Gökalp*. London: Luzac & Co., 1950.

Hostler, Charles Warren. *Turkism and the Soviets: The Turks of the World and Their Political Objectives*. London: George Allen & Unwin, 1957.

Hurewitz, J. C. *The Background of Russia's Claims to the Turkish Straits*. Ankara: Türk Tarih Kurumu Basimevi, 1964.

Iatrides, John O. *Balkan Triangle: Birth and Decline of an Alliance Across Ideological Boundaries*. The Hague: Mouton, 1968.

Ilkin, S., and E. Inanç (eds.). *Planning in Turkey (Selected Papers)*. Ankara: Faculty of Administrative Sciences, Middle East Technical University, 1967.

Imhoff, Christoph von. *Duell in Mittelmeer: Moskau greift nach dem Nahen und Mittleren Osten*. Freiburg i. Br.: Rombach, 1968.

Jackh, Ernest. *The Rising Crescent: Turkey Yesterday, Today, and Tomorrow*. New York: Farrar and Rinehart, 1944.

Karpat, Kemal H. *Turkey's Politics. The Transition to a Multi-Party System*. Princeton, N.J.: Princeton University Press, 1959.

Kiliç, Altemur. *Turkey and the World*. Washington, D.C.: Public Affairs Press, 1959.

Kinnane, Derk. *The Kurds and Kurdistan*. London: Oxford University Press, 1964.

Kyriakides, Stanley. *Cyprus: Constitutionalism and Crisis Government*. Philadelphia, Pa.: University of Philadelphia Press, 1968.

Ladas, Stephen P. *The Exchange of Minorities: Bulgaria, Greece and Turkey*. New York: Macmillan, 1936.

Lewis, Bernard. *The Emergence of Modern Turkey*. London: Oxford University Press, 1961.

——. *Turkey Today*. London: Hutchinson & Co., 1940.

Lewis, Geoffrey L. *Turkey*. 3d ed. London: Ernest Benn, Ltd., 1965.

Luke, Sir Harry. *The Old Turkey and the New: From Byzantium to Ankara*. London: Geoffrey Bles, 1955.

——. *Cyprus*. 2d ed. London: George R. Harrap, 1965.

Mango, Andrew. *Turkey*. London: Thames and Hudson, 1968.

Masar, Ilhami. *Das wahre Gesicht der Türkei*. Istanbul: Kulen, 1967.

Mauriès, René. *Le Kurdistan ou la mort*. Paris: Robert Laffont, 1967.

Miller, Linda B. *Cyprus. The Law and Politics of Civil Strife*. Cambridge, Mass.: Harvard University, Center for International Affairs, June 1968.

Nollau, Günther, and Hans Jürgen Wiehe. *Russia's South Flank. Soviet Operations in Iran, Turkey, and Afghanistan*. New York: Frederick A. Praeger, 1963.

Orga, Irfan. *Phoenix Ascendant: The Rise of Modern Turkey*. London: Robert Hale, Ltd., 1958.

—— and Margaret Orga. *Atatürk*. London: Michael Joseph, 1962.

Özbudun, Ergun. *The Role of the Military in Recent Turkish Politics*. Cambridge, Mass.: Harvard University, Center for International Affairs, 1961.

Price, M. Philips. *A History of Turkey: From Empire to Republic*. London: George Allen & Unwin, 1956.

Psomiades, Harry J. *The Eastern Question: The Last Phase. A Study in Greek-Turkish Diplomacy*. Salonika (Greece): Institute for Balkan Studies, 1968.

Purcell, H. D. *Cyprus*. New York: Frederick A. Praeger, 1969.

Reuther, Helmut (ed.). *Deutschlands Aussenpolitik seit 1955.* With a contribution by Franz von Cancig, "Die Türkei, Griechenland und die deutsche Aussenpolitik." Stuttgart–Degerloch: Seewald Verlag, 1965.

Robinson, Richard D. *The First Turkish Republic: A Case Study in National Development.* Cambridge, Mass.: Harvard University Press, 1963.

Roux, Jean-Paul. *La Turquie.* Paris: Payot, 1953.

Shorter, Frederic C. (ed.) *et al. Four Studies on the Economic Development of Turkey.* New York: Augustus M. Kelley, 1967.

Shotwell, James T., and Francis Deák. *Turkey at the Straits: A Short History.* New York: Macmillan, 1940.

Sinanoğlu, Suat. *L'Humanisme à venir.* Ankara: Dil ve Tarih-Coğrafya Fakültesi (Faculty of Languages, History, and Geography), 1960.

Smith, Elaine Diana. *Turkey: Origins of the Kemalist Movement and the Government of the Grand National Assembly (1919–1923).* Washington, D.C.: Judd & Detweiler, 1959.

Sokolnicki, Michael. *The Turkish Straits.* Beirut: American Press, 1950.

Spyridakis, C. *A Brief History of Cyprus.* Chicago: Argonaut, Inc., 1964.

Tansky, Leo. *U.S. and U.S.S.R. Aid to Developing Countries: A Comparative Study of India, Turkey, and the U.A.R.* New York: Praeger, 1967.

Thomas, Lewis V., and Richard N. Fry. *The United States and Turkey and Iran.* Cambridge, Mass.: Harvard University Press, 1951.

Thornburg, Max Weston, Graham Spry, and George Soule. *Turkey: An Economic Appraisal.* New York: Twentieth Century Fund, 1949.

Tunaya, Tarik Zafer. *Türkiyede Siyasi Partiler* (Political Parties in Turkey). Istanbul: Doğan Kardeş, 1952.

Türkeş, Alpaslan. *Dış Politikamız ve Kıbrıs* (Our Foreign Policy and Cyprus). Istanbul: Publication of the Istanbul Cypriote–Turkish Society, 1966.

Üstünel, Besim. *Milletlerarası iktisadi birleşmeler teorisi: Avrupa Müşterek Pazarı ve Türkiye* (The Theory of International Economic Unions: The European Common Market and Turkey). Publications of the Political Science Faculty, No. 107–89. Ankara: Siyasal Bilgiler Fakültesi yayınları, No. 107–89, 1960.

Vere-Hodge, Edward Reginald. *Turkish Foreign Policy, 1918–1948.* Ambilly-Annemasse: Imprimerie Franco-Suisse, 1950.

Von Grunebaum, Gustave E. (ed.). *Unity and Variety in Muslim Civilization.* With a contribution by Bernard Lewis, "Turkey: Westernization." Chicago: University of Chicago Press, 1955.

Ward, Robert E., and Dankwart A. Rustow (eds.). *Political Modernization in Japan and Turkey.* Princeton, N.J.: Princeton University Press, 1964.

Webster, Donald E. *The Turkey of Atatürk.* Philadelphia, Pa.: American Academy of Political and Social Science, 1939.

Weiker, Walter F. *The Turkish Revolution, 1960–1961.* Washington, D.C.: The Brookings Institution, 1963.

White, John. *Pledged to Development: A Study of International Consortia and the Strategy of Aid.* London: The Overseas Development Institute, 1967.

Xydis, Stephen G. *Cyprus: Conflict and Conciliation, 1954–58.* Columbus: Ohio State University Press, 1967.

Yalman, Ahmed Emin. *Turkey in My Time.* Norman, Okla.: University of Oklahoma Press, 1956.

Articles

Abadan, Nermin. "Some Aspects of Political Behavior in Turkey." *Turkish Yearbook of International Relations, 1965,* pp. 161–69.

Armaoğlu, Fahir H. "Turkey and the United States: A New Alliance." *The Turkish Yearbook of International Relations, 1965,* pp. 1–15.

Ataöv, Türkkaya. "Turkish Foreign Policy: 1923–1938." *Turkish Yearbook of International Relations, 1961,* pp. 103–42.

Batu, Hâmit. "La politique étrangère de la Turquie." *Turkish Yearbook of International Relations, 1964,* pp. 1–12.

Bayülken, Ümit Halûk. "Turkish Minorities in Greece." *Turkish Yearbook of International Relations, 1963,* pp. 145–64.

Bilsel, Cemil. "International Law in Turkey." *American Journal of International Law,* October 1944, pp. 546–56.

————. "The Turkish Straits in the Light of Recent Turkish-Soviet Russian Correspondence." *American Journal of International Law,* October 1947, pp. 727–47.

Cohn, Edwin J. "The Climate for Research in the Social Sciences in Turkey." *Middle East Journal,* Spring 1968, pp. 203–12.

Deshocquets, Claude. "La Turquie de 1960 et la stratégie globale." *Revue de Défense Nationale,* 17 (1961), 222–36.

Edmonds, Martin, and John Skitt. "Current Soviet Maritime Strategy and NATO." *International Affairs,* January 1969, pp. 28–43.

Ellis, Ellen D. "Turkish Nationalism in the Postwar World." *Current History,* February 1959, pp. 86–91.

Eren, Nuri. "Die türkisch-sowjetischen Beziehungen." *Europa-Archiv,* September 1965, pp. 337–48.

Esmer, Ahmed Şükrü. "The Straits: Crux of World Politics." *Foreign Affairs,* January 1947, pp. 290–302.

————. "Cyprus, Past and Present." *Turkish Yearbook of International Relations, 1962,* pp. 35–36.

Fairfield, Roy P. "Cyprus: Revolution or Resolution." *The Middle East Journal,* Summer 1959, pp. 235–48.

Fernau, Friedrich-Wilhelm. "Nachbarschaft am Schwarzen Meer. Wendepunkte in den türkisch-sowjetischen Beziehungen." *Europa-Archiv,* September 1967, pp. 613–20.

Harris, George S. "The Role of the Military in Turkish Politics." *Middle East Journal,* 1 (Winter 1965), pp. 54–66; (Spring 1965), pp. 169–76.

Heinze, Christian. "The Cyprus Conflict: The Western Peace System Is Put to Test." *Turkish Yearbook of International Relations, 1963,* pp. 44–62.

————. "Der Zypern-Konflikt, eine Bewährungsprobe westlicher Friedensordnung." *Europa-Archiv,* 1964, pp. 713–26.

Howard, Harry N. "The United States and the Question of the Turkish Straits." *Middle East Journal,* January 1947, pp. 59–72.

————. "Changes in Turkey." *Current History,* May 1965, pp. 296–300.

Hurewitz, J. C. "Russia and the Turkish Straits." *World Politics,* July 1962, pp. 605–32.

Karpat, Kemal H. "Recent Political Developments in Turkey and Their Social Background." *International Affairs,* July 1962, pp. 304–23.

————. "Ideology in Turkey After the Revolution of 1960." *Turkish Yearbook of International Relations, 1965,* pp. 68–118.

Kohn, Hans. "Ten Years of the Turkish Republic." *Foreign Affairs,* October 1933, pp. 141–55.

Kostanick, Huey Louis. "Turkish Resettlement of Refugees from Bulgaria, 1950–1953." *Middle East Journal,* Winter 1955, pp. 41–52.

Lawson, Ruth C. "New Regime in Turkey." *Current History,* February 1967, pp. 105–28.

Lewis, Bernard. "History-Writing and National Revival in Turkey." *Middle Eastern Affairs,* April 1955, pp. 101–8.

McGhee, George C. "Turkey Joins the West." *Foreign Affairs,* July 1954, pp. 617–30.

Pipes, Richard E. "Muslims of Soviet Central Asia." *The Middle East Journal,* Spring and Summer 1955, pp. 147–62, 295–308.

Pipinelis, Panayotis. "The Greco-Turkish Feud Revived." *Foreign Affairs,* January 1959, pp. 306–16.

Rohn, Peter H. "Turkish Treaties in Global Perspective." *Turkish Yearbook of International Relations, 1965,* pp. 119–60.

Routh, D. A. "The Montreux Convention Regarding the Regime of the Black Sea Straits." *Survey of International Affairs, 1936.* London: Oxford University Press, 1937.

Sadak, Necmeddin. "Turkey Faces the Soviets." *Foreign Affairs,* April 1949, pp. 449–61.

Sar, Cem. "L'association entre la Communauté Économique Européenne et la Turquie." *Turkish Yearbook of International Relations, 1962,* pp. 89–114.

Szyliowicz, Joseph S. "Political Participation and Modernization in Turkey." *Western Political Quarterly,* June 1966, pp. 226–84.

Tachau, Frank. "The Face of Turkish Nationalism as Reflected in the Cyprus Dispute." *Middle East Journal,* Summer 1959, pp. 262–72.

———— and A. Halûk Ülman. "Dilemmas of Turkish Politics." *Turkish Yearbook of International Relations, 1962,* pp. 1–34.

Ülman, Halûk. "Türk ulusal savunmasi üzerine düşünceler" (Thoughts Concerning Turkish National Defense). *Siyasal Bilgiler Fakültesi Dergisi,* 21 (1967).

————. "Türk Dış Politikasına Yön Veren Etkenler (1923–1968)" (Controlling Factors of Turkish Foreign Policy, 1923–1968). *Siyasal Bilgiler Fakültesi Dergisi* (Review of the Political Science Faculty), 23 (1968).

———— and Frank Tachau. "Turkish Politics: The Attempt to Reconcile Rapid Modernization with Democracy." *Middle East Journal,* Spring 1965, pp. 153–68.

Wright, Walter Livingston, Jr. "Truths about Turkey." *Foreign Affairs,* January 1948, pp. 349–59.

Yalçın, Aydın. "Turkey: Emerging Democracy." *Foreign Affairs,* July 1967, pp. 706–14.

Index

Turks—*Continued*
ganization of, 1–4; relations with Kurds, 51–52; their views of Arabs and Persians, 273–75
Turner, U.S. destroyer, 195

Ukraine, 6
Ulay, Sıtkı, 92
Ülman, Halûk, 158–59
Ümmet, 59n
Union of Soviet Socialist Republics. *See* Soviet Union
United Arab Republic, 195, 285, 306–7, 314. *See also* Egypt
United Kingdom. *See* Britain
United Nations: Cyprus question before, 73, 236–37, 253, 256; forces in Cyprus, 254, 263, 265; Jerusalem resolution (1968) of, 307; Turkey's membership in, 33, 64
United States of America: in alliance with Turkey, 35, 38, 125–46, 359–60, 372–74, 381n; American views of Turkey, 127–28, 370–71; economic aid to Turkey, 325–27, 330–31, 349n; interest in the Middle East, 42–43, 116, 285–86; landing in Lebanon (1958), 127, 176, 285; Sixth Fleet, 143, 173, 195–96, 214, 258; Turkish views of, 134–46; U.S. forces in Turkey, 124–25, 137–41, 163, 268–87, 371–73; USIS (United States Information Service), 137, 142; U–2 incident, 176
Unity Party, 92–93
UNRRA (United Nations Relief and Rehabilitation Administration), 329–30
Uralo-Altaic language family, 48n, 53
Ürgüplü, Suat Hayrı, 66, 71, 74, 178, 291n
USSR. *See* Soviet Union
Üstünel, Besim, 344n, 345n

Van, 16, 50
Vance, Cyrus R., 132, 258
Varlık Vergisi, 223
Venice, Republic of, 6–7, 150, 229
Venizelos, Eleutherios, 225, 270
Victoria, Queen, 230
Vienna, siege of, 6
Vietnam War, 142, 145, 195

Wallachia. *See* Danubian Principalities
Warsaw Treaty Organization, 157
Western Ideal, 58
William II, Emperor, 153–54
William V. Pratt, U.S. destroyer, 196n
Wilson, President Woodrow, 45n
Wolseley, Sir Garnet, 233n
World Bank, 332

Yalçın, Aydın, 81, 92, 338n
Yalta Summit Conference (1945), 34, 190
Yassiada trials, 54n
Yavuz, Battleship, 225
Yemeni civil war, 315
Yenişehir, 1
Yıldız, Saban, 99
Young Turks, 13, 18, 33
Yugoslavia: joins Balkan Defense Pact (1954), 174n, 199–201, 206; joins Balkan Entente, 26; relations with Turkey, 206–7; Turks in, 26. *See also* Serbia

Zagros Mountains, 120, 281
Zahedan, 290
Zahedi, Ardeshir, 292n
Zaza dialect, 50, 52
Zeno, Emperor, 230
Zhivkov, Todor, 203
Zhukov, Marshal G., 175
Zorlu, Fatin Rüştü, 236n, 237n, 312
Zurich-London Agreement. *See* Cyprus

THE JOHNS HOPKINS PRESS

Designed by Arlene J. Sheer

Composed in Sabon-Antiqua text with Palatino display
by Typoservice Corporation

Printed on 55 lb. Lockhaven
by Universal Lithographers, Inc.

Bound in Interlaken Arco Vellum
by L. H. Jenkins, Inc.

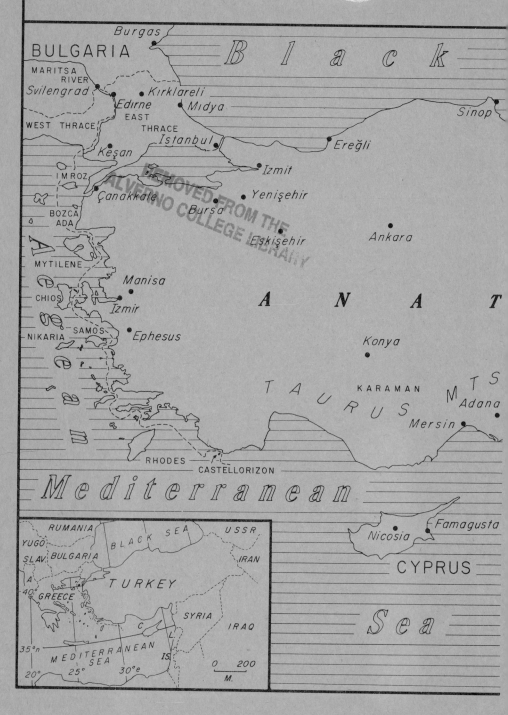

BULGARIA

MARITSA
RIVER
Svilengrad
WEST THRACE

Burgas

Kırklareli
Edirne
EAST
THRACE
Keşan
İstanbul

Mıdya

İzmit

İMROZ
Çanakkale
BOZCA
ADA

Yenişehir
Bursa

Black

Sinop

Ereğli

Ankara

MYTILENE

Manisa

CHIOS
İzmir

NIKARIA
SAMOS
Ephesus

Eskişehir

A N A T

Konya

KARAMAN
TAURUS
Mersin

M T S
Adana

RHODES
CASTELLORIZON

Mediterranean

Nicosia

Famagusta

CYPRUS

Sea

RUMANIA
YUGO
SLAV.
BULGARIA
A
40°
GREECE
35°n
20°
MEDITERRANEAN
SEA
25°

BLACK SEA
USSR
TURKEY
IRAN
SYRIA
IRAQ
C
L
IS.
30°e

0   200
M.